IN & AROUND
⸤THE⸥CAPITAL
REGIN

Albany, Troy, Schenectady & Saratoga

IN & AROUND
THE CAPITAL
REGIN

Albany, Troy, Schenectady & Saratoga

4th Edition
Ann Morrow & Anne Older

Washington Park Press Ltd.

IN & AROUND THE CAPITAL REGION

Washington Park Press Ltd.
7 Englewood Place
Albany, NY 12203
(518) 465-0169
www.washingtonparkpress.com

Reader response is welcome. Please send comments to the above address.

Book and Cover Design: Media Logic, Inc.
Printing: Thomson-Shore, Inc.

We are again indebted to:

The community groups, colleagues, and individuals who generously responded to our requests for information and supplied photographs.

Family and friends who provided enthusiasm and encouragement.

Jo Dziuban and Marianne Quinn for initiating the work on this edition.

And especially, to Bill Dumbleton, who contributed his time and expertise to the editing.

BOOKS PUBLISHED AND AVAILABLE FROM
WASHINGTON PARK PRESS LTD.

The Astor Orphans: A Pride of Lions
By Lately Thomas 1999

Mayor Corning: Albany Icon, Albany Enigma
By Paul Grondahl 1997

An Albany Girlhood
By Huybertie Pruyn Hamlin, edited by Alice P. Kenney 1990

PREVIOUSLY PUBLISHED BY WASHINGTON PARK PRESS LTD.

Style Follows Function: Architecture of Marcus T. Reynolds
By Eugene J. Johnson 1993 (co-published by Mount Ida Press)

In & Around Albany, Schenectady and Troy
By Anne Older, Peggy DiConza and Susanne Dumbleton 1992

Saving Union Station: An Inside Look at Historic Preservation
By Thomas Finegan 1988

Provisions: 109 Great Places to Shop for Food in the Capital District
By Peter Zaas, Sue Jones, Gary Jones, Lindy Guttman 1987

Flashback: A Fresh Look at Albany's Past
By C.R. Roseberry 1986

In & Around Albany, Schenectady and Troy
By Susanne Dumbleton and Anne Older 1985

O' Albany! Improbable City of Political Wizards, Fearless Ethnics, Spectacular Aristocrats, Splendid Nobodies, and Underrated Scoundrels
By William Kennedy 1983 (co-published by Viking Press)

In & Around Albany: A Guide for Residents, Students and Visitors
By Susanne Dumbleton and Anne Older 1980

ABOUT THE AUTHOR & EDITOR

Ann Morrow is a feature writer and arts critic based in the Capital Region. Her work appears regularly in Hudson Valley Magazine and Metroland newsweekly. A native of Albany, she is an avid history buff, an environmentalist and a walking tour marathoner.

Anne Older is the President of Washington Park Press Ltd., a regional press founded in Albany in 1980. She has been a community leader serving on several arts and educational Boards, and is Chairman Emeritus of the Preservation League of New York State.

TABLE OF CONTENTS

INTRODUCTION

New York State's Capital Region is conveniently located at the crossroads of the northeastern United States, almost equidistant from New York City, Boston and Montreal. Discovered in 1609, it is one of the oldest and most fascinating areas in the nation, and a place of spectacular natural beauty. With the capital city of Albany at its center, the region ranges from the endlessly recreational Hudson and Mohawk Rivers to the world-famous Saratoga Race Track. This diverse metropolitan setting is an exciting place to visit year-round, as well as an enriching place to live. From sophisticated art galleries to huge arenas attracting international talent, from superlative urban architecture to a dazzling array of eateries, there is truly something for everyone within its borders.

In fact, the Capital Region has more to offer than most areas of comparable size and population density. Add to the list of attractions the monolithic Empire State Plaza, which draws a million visitors a year to its events and celebrations; the exceptionally scenic Saratoga Performing Arts Center, host to the New York City Ballet and the Philadelphia Orchestra every summer; and the State Capitol Building, a marvel of 19th-century architecture unanimously regarded as the most magnificent capital building in America. Troy, a birthplace of the American Industrial Revolution, boasts whole streets of Gilded-Age buildings and a famed abundance of Tiffany stained-glass windows. The historic downtowns of the region are so evocative, they've been used as settings for several major motion pictures, earning the area the not-entirely-in-jest moniker of "Hollywood on the Hudson." These films include the 1989 Oscar-winner *Ironweed*, adapted from the Pulitzer Prize-winning novel by Albany author William Kennedy. The arts, especially, thrive in this moderately paced and moderately priced environment.

In addition, less than an hour's drive will bring travelers to a wide variety of destinations such as picturesque Columbia County, bustling Lake George, all-American Cooperstown, and the beautiful Berkshires – home of Tanglewood and the Williamstown Theater Festival.

But perhaps more importantly for the 21st century is the region's legacy of education and innovation. Rensselaer Polytechnic Institute, founded in 1824, is one of the largest and most esteemed technological universities in the world, and is helping to lead the area to a second revolution: the technological. Tech Valley is the region's newest nickname, and it is rapidly being recognized as one of the country's leading areas for the development and marketing of cutting-edge, high-tech firms.

It is not always easy, however, to discover the assets of the Capital Region. No resource explores the advantages of the area as a whole. Although specialized works describe the architecture or survey the restaurants or narrate the history, none portray the wide spectrum of opportunity open to visitors and residents alike. Since 1980, Washington Park Press Ltd. has published three editions of *In & Around*, starting first with the focus on Albany and the capital area. The second and third editions were expanded to include Troy and Schenectady.

This book – the fourth edition – is expanded to include Saratoga and updated with a greater regional emphasis. It is a composite depiction of the area's history and people; a compendium of information about schools, health care, and transportation; and a selective reference for hotels, restaurants, and shopping. New to the guide is a chapter on activities for children and their parents. In a single volume, this book aims to provide a valuable and useful source of information that everyone in the area – whether for a few hours, a few weeks, or a lifetime – might look for.

Nelson A. Rockefeller Empire State Plaza, Albany   *Photography by: Gary Gold*

POINTS OF INTEREST

Sightseeing in the downtowns of Albany, Troy, Schenectady and Saratoga is an especially rewarding activity. The region's great prosperity and acts of philanthropy in the 19th century left a rich inheritance of superlative residential and public architecture, while the area's colonial past is still evident – especially in the walkable street patterns. Community preservation efforts have made these venerable old cities even more appealing. Modern and historic aesthetics cohabitate, sometimes uneasily but always strikingly, and the Hudson and Mohawk rivers provide scenic views from many vantage points. Walking tours for each city follow. At the end of the chapter is information on other local areas of interest.

Historic Churches

Many of the churches of the Capital Region have fascinating stories attached to them. St. Peter's on State Street in Albany, for example, is the burial place of colonial hero Viscount George Augustus Howe, the only English lord buried in North America. Some churches were erected as splendid houses of worship for the affluent families who shaped the industrial era. Others were for the laborers who came to construct the great buildings and work in the factories. Because many of the laborers were immigrants, these churches often assumed an ethnic identity that influenced their design. Almost all of the region's churches are adorned by beautiful works of art, including significant stained-glass windows.

ALBANY

Downtown

Albany Heritage Area Visitor Center, 25 Quackenbush Square (corner of Clinton Ave. and Broadway next to I-87 overpass) is the ideal place to start a tour of Albany. The staffed information booth offers an abundance of brochures, including a parking and free-shuttle guide, and a walking-tour pamphlet for lower downtown. The center's Albany history gallery is highly recommended: It covers 400 years beginning with Native American culture and continues through the industrial era on to 20th-century politics. The center also displays architectural and archeological exhibits, including the USS Albany Heritage Navy Gallery. It houses the Henry Hudson Planetarium (see Parents and Children, pg. 207), which presents introductory multi-media programs, including *Albany: A Cultural Crossroads*. Gift shop. Open Mon-Fri., 9am-4pm, Sat-Sun., 10am-4pm. Group tours by appointment. Free parking. 434-0405 (1-800-258-3582). www.albany.org

1

MAJOR DOWNTOWN ALBANY STREETS

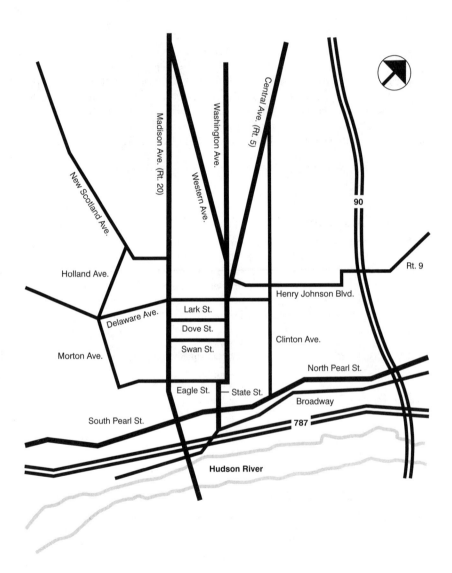

Quackenbush Square was restored in 1976. The distinctively Dutch Quackenbush House, built in 1736, is the oldest structure in Albany. It's currently occupied by Nicole's Bistro (see Restaurants, pg. 80), which has a Colonial-style herb garden on view during summer.

Albany City Trolley operates out of Quackenbush Square. This recreated, open-air trolley offers three different narrated tours. The Downtown Tour departs at 11am on Fri., and 10:30am on Sat. Adults $10, seniors $9, children 14 and under $5. Also regularly scheduled are the Historic Homes Tour (Schuyler Mansion, Cherry Hill and Ten Broeck Mansion) and the Historic Cathedrals Tour (All Saints and Immaculate Conception). The trolley, which seats 25, rides higher than traffic, offering unobstructed views along the way. Adults $12, seniors $10, children 14 and under $6. 434-0405. www.albany.org

Palace Theater, corner of North Pearl St. and Clinton Ave., was once a glittering movie palace, built in 1931 as a jewel in the RKO theater chain. The gilded, baroque interior – including a stage for live performances and balcony seating – has been wonderfully refurbished. Of particular note are the ceiling murals, decorative plasterwork, and magnificent, 3,000-pound chandelier. Replaced in the 1950's, the marquee is currently undergoing reconstruction. The theater is in active use as a performance venue. 465-4663.

St. Joseph's Church, First St. and Ten Broeck St., was designed in 1856 by Irish Catholic architect Patrick Keeley. This beautiful, blue-sandstone Gothic Revival was built to serve Albany's growing Irish population following the construction of the Erie Canal. The exquisite spires are an integral part of the Albany skyline; the grounds once held a graveyard but now host a community garden. St. Joseph's was closed by the diocese in the 1980s and is currently undergoing renovation.

Ten Broeck Mansion, 9 Ten Broeck St., was built in the late 1790s for Revolutionary War General Abraham Ten Broeck. It houses the Albany County Historical Association (see Museums and Historic Sites, pg. 43).

First Church in Albany, 110 North Pearl St. (at the corner of Orange St.), is the fourth church to be erected for the Dutch Reformed parish in Albany. Established in 1642 by the region's founding patroon, it is the oldest parish in upstate New York. The graceful, late-Georgian building that stands there now was designed by noted Albany architect Philip Hooker in 1798. It was partially remodeled in the mid-1800s, but the distinctive acorn finials atop the two towers are original. The wood-carved pulpit (complete with hourglass for timing sermons) is the oldest in America, purchased from Holland for 26 beaver pelts. The fabled brass weathercock from the first First Church resides in a glass case on the second floor, along with other historic artifacts. The balconied interior was redecorated by the Tiffany Studios in 1910 and is lined with geometric stained-glass windows.

ALBANY POINTS OF INTEREST

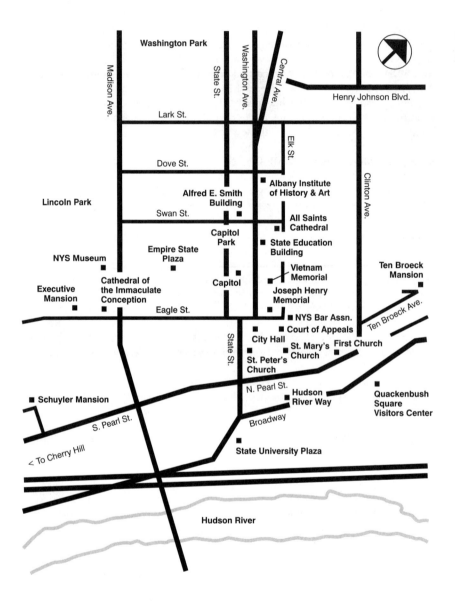

In the lobby at the back of the church is the Sarah Fay Sumner "waterfall" window, one of Louis Comfort Tiffany's greatest masterpieces. Self-guide tour cards and pamphlets on the church's history can be found on a nearby table. Open 8:30am-3pm. 463-4449.

State University of New York Plaza, at the foot of State St. and Broadway, is a spectacular, Flemish-Gothic palazzo built 1914-18 to glorify the city's waterfront. Designed by prominent Albany architect Marcus T. Reynolds in the style of a medieval Belgian guildhall, its 660-foot-length is rhythmically punctuated by intricate dormers, with a complex facing of granite, cast stone, and terra cotta. Atop the central tower reigns a 9-foot replica of the Half Moon, the ship in which Henry Hudson sailed the great river in 1609. It is the largest weathervane in America.

Formerly the offices of the Delaware and Hudson Railroad (hence its nickname among long-time residents: "The D and H") and the Albany Evening Journal, the plaza was renovated in the 1970s for the central offices of the State University of New York. More recently, an extensive preservation effort has restored the facade, which is richly decorated with enchanting carved-stone sculptures: The colonial seals of Holland, England and France can be seen above the three grand arches of the central tower. The arcade, which runs the length of the building, is open to the public. Placed along the wall are displays describing the building's construction, as well as historical events such as the landing of the Half Moon and the launch of the first steamboat, the Clermont, which occurred nearby.

Hudson River Way, Broadway and Maiden Lane, is the pedestrian bridge that connects downtown Albany with the Corning Riverfront Park. Opened in summer of 2002, this architecturally evocative structure is embellished with trompe l'oeil paintings that appear as "windows" into Albany history, placed on each of the bridge's 30 lamppost obelisks. Mise-en-scene murals of the 17th-century Dutch era are painted on the two landings of the Grand Walkway, which is paved with inscribed bricks purchased by residents. On the river side of the bridge is an open amphitheater used for summer concerts.

Albany City Savings Institution, 100 State St., is the first of Marcus T. Reynolds' many acclaimed bank designs. Completed in 1902, it represents the culmination of the city's unprecedented economic expansion. A single, round-arch entranceway takes up almost the entire width of the base, with six imposing stories above topped by a rich display of Second-Empire exuberance. The gilded interior now serves as a copy shop. This part of State Street (between Broadway and Lodge St.) was once known as "Banker's Row" and contains several historic bank buildings.

St. Peter's Episcopal Church, 107 State St. (by Lodge St.), was founded in 1712, soon after the English took over the settlement from the Dutch. St. Peter's was rebuilt in 1860, but many relics of the church's earlier incarnation remain, and the bell, struck in 1751, is still in use. This French-Gothic Revival – the impressive tower is decorated with gargoyles – was designed by the acclaimed architect Richard Upjohn. The interior has many notable features, including a Tiffany rose window, mosaic pavements rich in artistic Christian symbolism, and the silver communion set given by Queen Anne of England to Reverend Thomas Barclay, founder of St. Peter's parish. Colonial hero Lord Howe is buried under the front vestibule. The church serves an active congregation, and its peal of Meneely chimes can be heard every Sunday morning. Interesting booklets on the church's art and history are available in the entranceway. 434-3502. www.stpeterschurchalbany.org

Capital Hill

Albany City Hall, Eagle St. (between Pine St. and Lodge St.), erected in 1882, is a fine example of the influential architecture of Henry Hobson Richardson. Of particular interest are the common council room and the murals that line the corridors, and the 60-bell carillon that rings each weekday at noon. On summer Sunday afternoons, international carilloneurs perform from the bell tower. A statue of Revolutionary War General Philip Schuyler stands guard out front. 434-5090.

St. Mary's Church, corner of Lodge St. and Pine St., was built in 1869, the third church to occupy the site on which Father Isaac Jogues knelt in prayer before his Iroquois captors executed him. This charming, Romanesque church with white-marble trim features a bell tower topped by a trumpeting angel – a departure from the cross traditional to Roman Catholic churches. Inside are Italian frescoes and Austrian stained glass, and the original cornerstone from 1797 can still be seen in the church sacristy. St. Mary's serves an active congregation. 462-4254.

New York State Court of Appeals, Eagle St. and Pine St., is the oldest state office building in the region, and the only surviving work of important Albany architect Henry Rector. Extensively remodeled, this Greek Revival remains an imposing structure inside and out. Visitors are welcome to sit in on the hearings of the highest court in the state (the oak-carved courtroom was designed by H. H. Richardson), and to view the impressive rotunda, the State Seal on the inside of the dome, and the portrait-lined hallways.

New York State Bar Center, 1 Elk St., stands opposite Academy Park. In the late 1960's, the Bar Association purchased the three 19th-century townhouses on the corner of Elk opposite the Court of Appeals. The association's plan to demolish the buildings and construct an office complex roused the local citizenry

New York State Capitol, Albany   *Photography by: Gary Gold*

to furious protest. The two groups reached a compromise, incorporating the fronts of the three houses into a modern office complex. The project attracted national attention and won an architectural honor award. In 1988, 5 and 6 Elk St. were also incorporated. The facades are individually noteworthy, and the bar center is open to the public by appointment. 463-3200.

Joseph Henry Memorial, opposite City Hall in Academy Park, was designed by Philip Hooker in 1815 as the Albany Academy, a private school for boys (Herman Melville was among its graduates). When the academy outgrew the building, it was renamed the Joseph Henry Memorial in honor of Joseph Henry, who in 1830 discovered the properties of magnetic induction within its walls. A statue of Henry stands at the walkway. The building now houses the offices of the Board of Education and is not open to the public.

Lafayette Park, between Washington Ave. and Elk St., was created in the 1920s, almost a century after Academy Park. The two parks are joined by a charming greenery containing dwarf shrubs from around the world, unusual trees and ferns, and native wildflowers. Stone benches encourage a respite from the bustle of downtown.

Vietnam Veterans Memorial, in the middle of Lafayette Park, was designed by Merlin Szosz. Made from 60 tons of pink granite mined in Brazil and cut in Portugal, it has two six-foot bronze tablets: One tablet lists the names of the 66 killed and the four missing-in-action from Albany County in the Vietnam War, the other depicts a soldier assisting a wounded comrade under a jungle canopy. A joint project of the Tri-County Council of Vietnam-Era Veterans and the city of Albany, the memorial was dedicated in 1992.

East Capitol Park, Washington Ave. across from City Hall, surrounds the Capitol's great stone staircase of 77 steps. Completed in 1898, the park was designed by the Olmsted brothers. An equestrian statue of Civil War hero General Philip H. Sheridan stands at the center of the formal gardens. Dedicated in 1916, the statue's design was begun by "the Dean of American Sculptors," John Quincy Adams Ward, and completed by the great Daniel Chester French after Ward's death in 1910.

New York State Capitol, Washington Ave., is a spectacular example of civic architecture, conceived along the lines of an Italian Renaissance chateau but composed of many different styles. It was completed in 1899 after 30 turbulent years of construction and design changes. Built by hand out of solid masonry, for the (at the time) staggering sum of $25 million, the Capitol is a National Historic Landmark and is especially admired for its stone sculpturing and other decorative arts.

The opulent Senate Chamber, once host to Theodore and Franklin D. Roosevelt, is considered to be one of the most beautiful public rooms in America. Designed by H. H. Richardson, it features exceptional furniture, ornate wall sconces and chandeliers, gothic-style masonry, and stained-glass windows, including a replica of the State Seal. The central courtyard is an evocative reminder that the building was planned in the days before electricity; in 2002, the skylight was restored, filling the area with natural light for the first time since before World War II. The truly magnificent "Million-Dollar Staircase," decorated with portraits both venerable and amusing; and the "Evolution Staircase" (named for its depictions of creatures that increase in complexity from bottom to top), were carved by master stonemasons from Europe. Also not to be missed is the Governor's Reception Room (formerly the "War Room"): The ceiling is painted with glorious military murals by William deLeftwich Dodge from the 1920s. A floor above, the Flag Room showcases flags flown by New York military units in every war in which the United States fought.

The history, ongoing restoration, and current functions of the Capitol are detailed in a photo-filled visitor's guide. Also recommended is the lavishly illustrated pamphlet describing the murals and Dodge's career. Both brochures are available at the Albany Visitors Center. Free guided tours of the Capitol are available daily at 10am, 12pm, 2pm and 3pm. Group tours available by appointment. 474-2418.

West Capitol Park, behind the Capitol (across the street from the Alfred E. Smith building), was created in the 1920s and is a favorite spot to this day for people who work downtown. During lunch hours, street vendors sell food and musicians perform while workers and visitors enjoy the open air.

Nelson A. Rockefeller Empire State Plaza, between State St. and Madison Ave. (just below South Swan St.), is the vast marble-and-granite plateau that dominates southeastern downtown Albany. This monolithic government complex encompasses state office buildings, the Empire Center at the Egg, the Cultural Education Center, and 11,000 state employees. The design is by Wallace K. Harrison, the architect for Lincoln Center. The idea for a modernist superstructure adorned by major works of contemporary art was conceived by Gov. Nelson A. Rockefeller in 1962, and was to be completed in the late 1960's at an estimated cost of $350 million. Construction was mired in labor disputes, and the Plaza wasn't completed until 1978 – at a cost of $2 billion. Forty city blocks were demolished to make way for its 98-acre site.

Cultural Education Center is the huge marble structure at the Madison Ave. end of the plaza promenade, across from the State Capitol. It houses the State Museum (see pg. 37), the State Library, and the State Archives (see pg. 301).

The Platform is a great public square with a reflecting pool, flower beds, fountains, a brick promenade, two memorials (for state crime victims and state police officers), and monumental modernist sculpture (see pg. 62). It is beautifully lit at night, and a popular free concert series is staged across from the Cultural Center during summer (see pg. 191). The platform is actually the roof of a structure that descends six floors below ground, with a square footage of nearly twice the floor space of the Empire State Building. Four of the floors provide for parking, service areas, and the concourse.

The Concourse is a quarter-mile walkway just below the platform, accessible by elevators and stairways. A network of hallways connect all 11 buildings in the Plaza with the State Capitol on the other side of State St. The concourse is lined with shops, services, and restaurants, as well as pieces from the Plaza Art Collection. This assemblage of New York School art from the 1960s and '70s can be seen throughout the Empire State Plaza (see Arts and Venues, pg.62). The width of the concourse allows for public events such as boat and auto shows, craft fairs, farmer's markets, music performances, food festivals and more. The Convention Center on the same level holds larger events.

The Corning Tower is a 42-story marble structure dedicated to Mayor Erastus Corning 2nd, the country's longest tenured mayor (1941-1983). It is the tallest building in the state outside of New York City. The top-floor observation deck is open daily (10am-2:30pm) and provides spectacular views of the city and the Hudson Valley. On weekends visitors must enter the tower from the concourse. The lobby gallery contains several important artworks including pieces by David Smith and Louise Nevelson, and the concourse level is considered to contain the best works of the Plaza collection.

The Empire Center at the Egg is the performing arts center that hovers over the plaza like a flying saucer. The Egg contains the Kitty Carlisle Hart Theatre, the Lewis A. Swyer Theatre (see pg. 46), and a spacious wrap-around lounge.

The Vietnam Memorial on the first floor of the Justice Building is dedicated to New York's fallen and living Vietnam War veterans. It consists of bronze tablets bearing the names of the state's 4,194 dead and missing in the war, as well as a garden courtyard, a resource center, and a memorial gallery displaying changing exhibits of artwork by Vietnam War veterans.

The Korean War Memorial is located in the park on the west side of the Cultural Education Center. The memorial consists of a polished granite wall with four plaques commemorating New York State veterans and fallen, and a reflecting pool and fountain with plaques representing the combat nations that participated in the conflict. Also in the park is the bas-relief sculpture of the Women Veterans War Memorial.

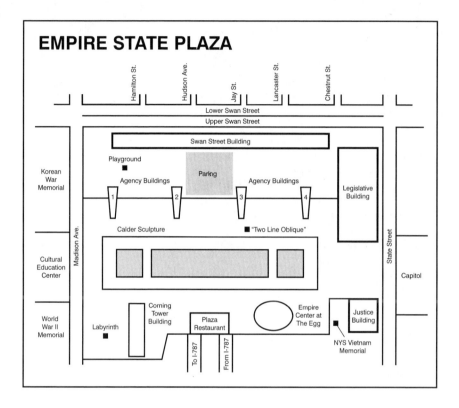

Parking: There is one underground parking lot, the "V" lot, available to visitors with a photo ID. Other convenient lots can be found on Madison Ave. and Eagle St.

The Empire State Plaza is open to the public free of charge, 6am-11pm. For information, brochures on its artworks and memorials, or a special-events calendar, stop by the Office of General Services, Rm. 130 in the concourse, or call 473-0559 (toll free 1-877-659-4377). For guided tours, call 473-7521. www.ogs.state.ny.us/plaza

State Education Building, Washington Ave. (across the street and just north of the Capitol), was built 1908-12, and was the largest state construction project after the Erie Canal. This Greco-Roman colossus – a full city-block long – with Doric columns was modeled on the Parthenon. The massive colonnade repays close study, for many works of sculpture (such as the groups of children on the electroliers at the entry) are there to be discovered. The vast interior was the original location of the New York State Library, and features a sky-lit, neo-Roman rotunda, allegorical murals, and vaulted, 50-feet ceilings. 474-3852.

Cathedral of All Saints, 62 South Swan St. (behind the State Education Building), is the seat of the Episcopal diocese of Albany and one of the symbols of the city's wealth and prestige in the 19th century. Although its 1880s construction was never completed, and the Swan Street entranceway is covered with a modern facade, the rest of the exterior impresses with its Early Gothic lineaments. The soaring interior of vaulted arches and hand-carved stone (by the master stonemason of the Capital building) resembles the great cathedrals of England it was modeled after. Of particular interest are the English Arts & Crafts stained-glass windows, the Renaissance choir pews from Belgium, and the seraphim mosaics in the Lady Chapel. All Saints serves an active congregation and contributes to the city's cultural life by sponsoring concerts and festivities throughout the year. A self-guide pamphlet is available in the vestibule, and the web site contains information on its art and history. 465-1346. www.cathedralofallsaints.org

Alfred E. Smith Building, Swan St. between State St. and Washington Ave., was built to house state-agency offices and symbolized the rise of state government in the 1920s. This Art Deco "skyscraper" is named after the man who served as governor of New York until his fateful run for the presidency in 1928. The facade is inscribed with the names of the counties of New York State, and the vaulted lobby has portraits of governors on the ceiling, stone-carved emblems, and bronze fixtures.

Mansion Hill

Executive Mansion, 138 Eagle St., is the official residence of the Governor of New York. The Italianate mansion is situated on five acres of gardens and imported trees. It was built in 1850 for the son of banker Theodore Olcott (who owned the Ten Broeck Mansion), and wasn't purchased by the state until 1877. In the 1860s, Gov. Samuel Tilden added the mansard roof, towers and side porches. In 1961 the mansion was severely damaged by fire, and was subsequently restored and fireproofed. Its furnishings and art works have been collected over many eras, and reflect the mansion's history as both a monument and a private home. A more recent addition is the Governors Memorabilia Room. Free one-hour guided tours require a group of ten or more, and two-week advance reservations. Thurs. afternoons only at 12pm, 1pm and 2pm. 473-7521.

Cathedral of the Immaculate Conception, Eagle St. at Madison Ave., is the seat of the Roman Catholic diocese of Albany, and the third oldest active cathedral in the country. Inspired by the Cologne Cathedral, this Gothic Revival was designed in the mid-1800s by Irish-Catholic architect Patrick Keeley (who later designed St. Joseph's). The red-sandstone exterior is currently undergoing a large-scale restoration. Once the most imposing structure in the region, the cathedral now reigns in subdued splendor just below the Empire State Plaza.

World War II Memorial, Madison Ave. (between the cathedral and the Cultural Center), was created in 2002 as the region's first tribute to New York State's World War II military personnel. The bold design is dramatized by an outsized steel eagle descending upon a monument inscribed with Franklin Roosevelt's "Four Freedoms" on the north side, and quotes from General Eisenhower and General MacArthur on the south side. Two fountain pools echo the eagle's upraised wings. The memorial is enclosed by granite retaining walls embossed with a timeline and the place-names of conflict. Behind the laurel-wreath-shaped hedge fly seven flags of honor.

Center Square

Lark Street in Center Square runs north from Madison Ave. (several blocks up the hill from the Cathedral of the Immaculate Conception) to Central Ave., and is lined with 19th-century rowhouses. This eclectic shopping and dining route is the city's bohemian mecca and a lively hangout for college students and artists, as well as the residents of this restored area. In September, it hosts an enormously popular street festival, Lark Fest (see Seasonal, pg. 199)

State Street between Lark St. and Western Ave. was built primarily in the second half of the 19th century by lawyers, bankers, lumber barons, and affluent merchants. It is one of the most architecturally impressive streets in Center Square, the 22-block residential historic district that runs (roughly) from the Capitol Building to Willett Street at the east end of Washington Park. The block across from the park contains many exceptional examples of ornamental ironwork. Perpendicular to State is Willett Street, a close rival in stylistic grandeur. Both streets are best viewed during a leisurely stroll around the park.

Washington Park, between Willett St. and South Lake St., and State St. and Madison Ave., is an 81-acre park of considerable historic significance and beauty. Created in the 1880s, its centerpiece is a picturesque lake with a Spanish-Revival lakehouse and a Victorian footbridge. The grounds are graced by several impressive statues and monuments, as well as tennis courts and a playground.

The winding bridle paths, wooded glades and open meadows are hallmarks of its planner, the great landscape architect Frederick Law Olmsted, best known for Central Park in New York City. Olmsted's vision was implemented by two proteges from Albany, who added the formal gardens and statuary. The most beloved attraction is "Moses Smiting the Rock" (Madison Ave. side), featuring a monumental bronze Moses raising his staff atop a rock-formation fountain. In springtime, the graceful hills turn into a sea of flowers, with thousands of tulips reflecting Albany's Dutch heritage giving the park an air of festivity timed to coincide with the Tulip Festival (see Seasonal, pg. 189).

Other points of interest in Albany

Albany Rural Cemetery, Cemetery Ave. (off of Broadway), Menands, was established in 1844. This important American landscape holds the graves of soldiers from every war fought by America, as well as some noteworthy individual graves – President Chester A. Arthur, Gen. Philip Schuyler, and Mayor Erastus Corning among them. Also of interest are the sublime monuments, some of them by esteemed sculptor Erastus Dow Palmer, and some by renowned architect Marcus T. Reynolds. Both men are buried here. Albany Rural also contains original stones relocated from the 18th-century cemetery off of State St. that became Washington Park. The Gothic lodge and chapel were designed by Robert Gibson, the English architect of All Saints Cathedral. Maps are available in the mailbox on the office porch. Open dawn to dusk.

TROY

Downtown

Riverspark Visitors Center, 251 River St. (one door north of City Hall), is ideally located across from Monument Square in the heart of historic Troy. The center offers multi-media displays to introduce visitors to the rich social and industrial history of the seven communities of the area, as well as a variety of exhibits illustrating its preeminence in manufacturing. Information on local attractions and special events is available, as are several self-guide tour pamphlets, including a Tiffany-windows walking tour. Open Tues-Sat., 11am-5pm. 270-8667.

Monument Square, intersection of Broadway, Second St. and River St., has always been a public commons looking much as it does today. The gracefully towering Sailors and Soldiers Monument was erected in 1891 to commemorate the citizens of Rensselaer County who served in America's wars.

Troy Savings Bank (Top), Troy Savings Bank Music Hall (Bottom)   *Photography by: Gary Gold*

TROY POINTS OF INTEREST

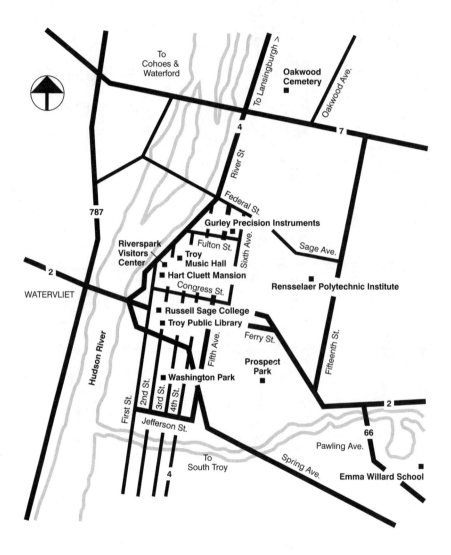

Riverfront Park is a public park overlooking the river, with a scenic riverside walking path. The entrance (River St. and Front St.) is marked by a statue of Uncle Sam, a Troy native. Free festivals and concerts are held year-round. For a schedule of events, contact the Riverspark Visitor Center. 270-8667.

Rensselaer County Vietnam Veterans Memorial, Riverfront Park, lists the names of 42 county soldiers and one civilian photographer killed or missing in the war. A statue in the center depicts three Vietnam veterans facing the memorial wall. Funds for the memorial were raised from contributions throughout Rensselaer County.

Second Street
Second Street is one of the finest streetscapes of 19th-century architecture in the United States. Featuring a variety of period styles, it serves as a standing illustration of the area's Gilded Age, and has been filmed as a setting for several major Hollywood movies; the John Paine Mansion at 49 Second St. was prominently featured in the Oscar-winning film, *The Age of Innocence*. 153 Second St. was an important stop on the Underground Railroad. Many of these stately residences have been restored and converted to law offices.

The Troy Savings Bank Music Hall, 32 Second St. (corner of State St.) is an imposing structure of Beaux Arts and French Renaissance design, built in the early 1870s to be both a bank and a premier concert center (see Arts and Venues, pg. 47). The Music Hall is nationally renowned for its superb acoustics, along with its 1882 Odell concert organ, "a distinguished example of Romantic organ design." Most of the original frescoes are still visible. A brochure on the hall's colorful history is available. 273-0038. www.troymusichall.org

Hart-Cluett Mansion, 59 Second St., is nicknamed "the Marble House" in honor of its elegant, white-marble facade. Built in 1827 by financier William Howard for his daughter, Betsey, and her husband, Richard Hart (a founder of the Troy Savings Bank), the late-Federal-style building is the exemplar of an upper-class townhouse-very few of which still exist. Its innovative design elements were widely influential, especially in New York City. Of particular interest are the urn-style iron newels on either side of the front steps, and the double-portico entranceway adorned with Tuscan columns and leaded-glass fanlights. Tours of the Hart-Cluett are available through the Rensselaer County Historical Society, which is housed in the Gen. Joseph B. Carr Building next door (see Museums and Historic Sites, pg. 38). 272-7232. www.rchsonline.org

Troy Public Library, corner of South Ferry St. and Second St., is a beautiful structure of white marble in the American Renaissance style, built in 1897 as a memorial gift to the city by the widow of Troy entrepreneur William Howard Hart. The exterior is decorated with carved arched windows and a full balustrade. The interior retains much of its Gilded-Age adornment, with marble walls, gold-leaf highlights, coffered ceilings, decorative iron railings, marble sculptures, and many fine old oil paintings. Behind the desk is a Tiffany window designed by Frederick Wilson and portraying Venetian scholar and printer Aldus Manutius. Upstairs in the reading room are six swivel windows by the Tiffany Studios. 274-7071.

Russell Sage College Campus, between First St. and Second St., is marked by an iron-and-brick arch, constructed to harmonize with its many historic buildings. The college was founded in 1916 by Mrs. Russell Sage, wife of the famous financier. Distinctive Gurley Hall and Russell Sage Hall, with mustard-brick accents, and the gabled Plum Memorial Building, were originally the foundation of Emma Willard School, which moved to Pawling Ave. in 1910. An 1895 life-size, bronze sculpture of Emma Willard, a pioneer in the education of women, remains on campus in her honor. The Bush Memorial, now in use as a 400-seat performance space, was formerly the First Presbyterian Church; the Doric-temple facade is nationally recognized as one of the earliest and most accurate examples of Greek Revival. The interior contains two Tiffany windows and a dramatic domed ceiling. Over the last century, the college acquired many of the Victorian brownstones around picturesque Sage Square, a public common donated to the people of Troy in 1796 by Jacob Vanderhyden. 244-2248. www.sage.edu

Washington Park, beginning at 189 Second St., is an ornamental green surrounded by beautiful row houses dating to the 19th century. It is one of the last private parks in the country with access still limited to residents of the adjoining streets.

Other Downtown Buildings

Hall-Rice Building, River St. and First St., is the dramatically triangular, High-Victorian Gothic structure that serves as a focal point for the River Street area. The 1871 office building was designed by acclaimed architects Calvert Vaux and Frederick Withers. After decades of vacancy, it is once again the home base for prestigious, newly emerging companies, with nanotechnology replacing the telegraph as the catalyst for commercial growth. The building was filmed as an exterior for *The Age of Innocence*.

St. John's Episcopal Church, 146 First St. (corner of Liberty St.), contains many beautiful English-medieval-style and American-opalescent stained-glass windows. At the west end is the landmark, five-lancet "St. John's Vision of the Holy City," an acknowledged Tiffany masterpiece. 274-5884.

St. Paul's Episcopal Church, Third St. and State St., is a turreted Gothic Revival built in 1826. Gloriously redecorated by the Tiffany Company in the mid-1890s and containing several important stained-glass windows, the church is one of the finest examples of an intact Tiffany interior in existence. Highlights of the beautifully integrated Byzantine decor are the dramatic altar window and mosaic altar walls, the lime-and-tangerine chancel lamp, the jewel-glass choir railing, the brass lectern and pulpit; and the wood-carved baptistery in back, which is lined with mosaics and murals by A. J. Holtzer. 273-7351.

Ilium Building, 400 Fulton St. (at Fourth St.), was designed by local architect Frederick M. Cummings in 1904 and has an impressive masonry exterior. The five-story structure – and its beautiful counterpart nearby at 297 River St. – were Troy's first "skyscrapers," and have always contained shops on the ground floor and offices above.

W. & L.E. Gurley Co., corner of Fifth Ave. and Fulton St., was founded in 1845. The company's 1865 brick office building is a National Historic Landmark and a superior example of the Norman style, distinguished by its arched windows and ornate cornices. The building contains a one-of-a-kind exhibit room of surveying instruments and engineering tools, made by Gurley and other local firms in the 19th century. Now known as Gurley Precision Instruments, the company is an internationally prominent business to this day. Call ahead for a tour (group tours require one-week advance notice). 272-6300.

Up the Hill

Emma Willard School, 285 Pawling Ave., occupies a 55-acre campus on the east side of Troy called Mount Ida. The oldest secondary school for girls in the country, Emma Willard was founded in 1814, incorporating the radical idea that young women should be educated in the same disciplines as men. Built at exorbitant cost, the architectural grandeur of the college's construction is not likely to be seen again. The original collegiate Tudor-Gothic buildings of 1910 were commissioned by Mrs. Russell Sage, an Emma Willard graduate. Slocum Hall, Sage Hall, and the Alumnae Chapel (formerly the gymnasium) feature elaborate exterior stone sculpturing designed by Abraham Mosely of England, who considered the campus to be his finest work. The campus was filmed as the setting for the 2002 film, *The Emperor's Club*.

Of particular interest are the hand-carved stone gargoyles, busts, and whimsical animals, over 100 of which peer down from the buildings with highly individual expressions (one droll example is the medieval frogman clinging to the underside of the chapel archway). Most unusual is that many of these historical and imaginary stone figures are female. The campus also includes two mansions built around the same time: one is Tudor Style, the other is Georgian Style and was designed by Marcus Reynolds. Both mansions were owned and donated by members of the Cluett family, the prominent shirt manufacturers. The modernist library-arts-music complex was built in 1970, and echoes the architecture of the original buildings. 273-8135. www.emma.troy.ny.us

Rensselaer Polytechnic Institute Campus, 110 8th St., is a 260-acre area built into the hillside overlooking the Hudson River. Founded in 1824 by Stephen Van Rensselaer, RPI is the first degree-granting technological university in the United States, and a globally recognized leader in education in modern science. The campus is easy to identify from a distance by its many fine old brick buildings with copper roofs. A blend of modern, post-modern, and historical styles, the campus contains several architecturally noteworthy buildings, including West Hall, originally a Civil War hospital; and the Voorhees Computing Center, a striking example of adaptive reuse located within a 1933 Gothic chapel. The Approach, just south of Eighth Street, is a stepped granite walkway (look for the gray columns) offering panoramic views of the city. It was commissioned by the city in 1907 as a monument after the Great Fire of 1904 destroyed the main building. Renovated in the early 1990s, the walkway physically and symbolically connects the campus to Troy's downtown. 276-6000. www.rpi.edu

South Troy

St. Joseph's Church, 416 Third St., contains over 40 Tiffany windows, more than any other structure in the country. Notable among its flocks of stained-glass angels (circa 1902) are the pair of exquisite cherub-face rondelles at the west end, and the regal archangels in the chapel. Also not to be missed are the church's beautiful baptistery and staggeringly ornate, Italian-marble altarpiece. 274-6720.

Burden Iron Works Museum, at the foot of Polk St. in South Troy, is located in the crenelated-brick office building of the Burden Iron Company – the last significant structure left of a manufacturing complex that stretched for more than a mile, and that turned out a million horseshoes a week during the Civil War. The museum contains important artifacts of Troy's industrial era, including a Meneely bell and an iron plate from the warship Monitor. The building also houses the Hudson Mohawk Industrial Gateway, which spearheaded its restoration. The Gateway sponsors several excellent tours interpreting the industrial and architectural heritage of Rensselaer County. Open by appointment. 274-5267. www.troyvisitorcenter.org

Other points of interest in Troy

Oakwood Cemetery, 50 101st St., North Troy, is the third largest cemetery in the United States, and a historic site of endless interest – not the least reason being its many famous gravesites, including those of education pioneer Emma Willard; financier Russell Sage and his wife, Olivia Slocum; Civil War soldier and memoirist Rice Bull; and "Uncle Sam" Wilson, the Troy meatpacker who became a patriotic icon for his efforts during the War of 1812. This Victorian-Romantic landscape is also renowned for its many impressive mausoleums, towering obelisks, and notable sculptures. The grounds range from grassy knolls surrounded by shale cliffs (with panoramic views of the Hudson-Mohawk region) to atmospheric stands of oak-hickory and beech-maple trees. The grounds also contain more than 600 botanical species, including several rare specimens.

The rustic, English-Gothic Warren Chapel alone is worth a lengthy amble, but the cemetery's stunning centerpiece is the Earl Chapel and Crematory. Designed in the grandly Romanesque style known as "Richardsonian" (look for the gargoyle high atop the gatehouse tower), the structure was built at staggering cost by "cuffs and collars" manufacturer William Spencer Earl and his wife as a memorial to their only child. The spectacular interior is open by guided tour. Open dawn to dusk. The Oakwood Association offers a variety of fascinating tours from spring through fall. A newsletter and schedule is available by request. 272-7520.

Melville House, 2 114th St., Lansingburgh in North Troy, was the home of the young Herman Melville and his family from 1838 to 1847 (see Museums and Historic Sites, pg. 41).

Lansingburgh Village Cemetery, Third Ave. and 107th St., holds the graves of many early colonial and Revolutionary War soldiers (northeast corner). Open dawn to dusk.

SCHENECTADY

Schenectady Heritage Area Visitors Center, located at the Schenectady Museum, Nott Terrace Heights, is marked by a locally built American Locomotive Company train car at the entrance. It contains exhibits displaying 300 years of Schenectady history, and several displays on the theme of workers and their labor movements. The center offers brochures, self-tour pamphlets, and an introductory multi-media presentation, *Labor and Industry*. The Schenectady Museum and Planetarium is described in Museums and Historic Sites (pg. 38). Open Mon.-Fri., 10am-4:30pm, Sat-Sun., noon-4:30pm. 382-5128.

Union College, Schenectady   *Photography by: Gary Gold*

Downtown

Proctor's Theatre, 432 State St., is a former 1920s vaudeville hall designed by famed theater architect Thomas Lamb and built at extravagant cost: the palatial interior is graced by gilt-and-crystal chandeliers and marble drinking fountains, and decoratively painted with gold leaf. A premier attraction from the Jazz Age to the big band era to the Golden Age of Hollywood, the theater's fortunes declined in the 1960s. A decade later, it was saved from the wrecking ball by concerned residents, and gradually restored to its former opulence. This 2,750-seat theater is now a National Historic Landmark and an acclaimed non-profit performing arts venue (see Arts and Venues, pg. 46). The charming arcade – a precursor to the modern shopping mall – is lined with interesting little shops, movie memorabilia, and window displays from local museums. For information on guided tours, call the box office at 346-6204. www.proctors.org.

City Hall, 105 Jay St., is a superb example of Georgian-Revival style, lavishly constructed in the early 1930s and designed by world-famous architects McKim, Mead and White. This colossal edifice is distinguished by its tower and gold-leaf dome, a visible landmark throughout the downtown area.

The Stockade

Stockade District, Front St. and Union St., is a residential area of several hundred houses, built on the site of an early-colonial Dutch trade settlement. It was home to most of Schenectady's important 17th-, 18th- and 19th-century figures. Although the original houses were all destroyed by the French and Indian massacre of 1690, and many of their replacements were demolished by a catastrophic fire in 1819, over 100 historic structures from 1690 to 1930 remain intact, displaying almost every architectural style and era of religious and residential building. All of the houses function today as private homes in a high-density but old-fashioned urban neighborhood.

There are three historic churches within the district. The English St. George's, North Ferry St., was founded in 1735, and Scottish First Presbyterian Church, Union St., was founded in 1809. These two churches are right beside each other, and both have old cemeteries in their churchyards. Dutch First Reformed Church, at the corner of Union St. and Church St., was founded before 1674, and was the first church in the Mohawk Valley. From its Church Academy of 1785 evolved Union College. In 1962, the Stockade was designated New York State's first historic district. A tour brochure is available at the Schenectady Visitors Center. An interesting "walkabout" is held every September. www.historicstockade.com

Lawrence the Indian in Circular Park (Front St. and Green St.), marks the spot of a British fort built in 1704. Lawrence was a Mohawk who helped rebuild the Stockade after the 1690 French and Indian attack.

SCHENECTADY POINTS OF INTEREST

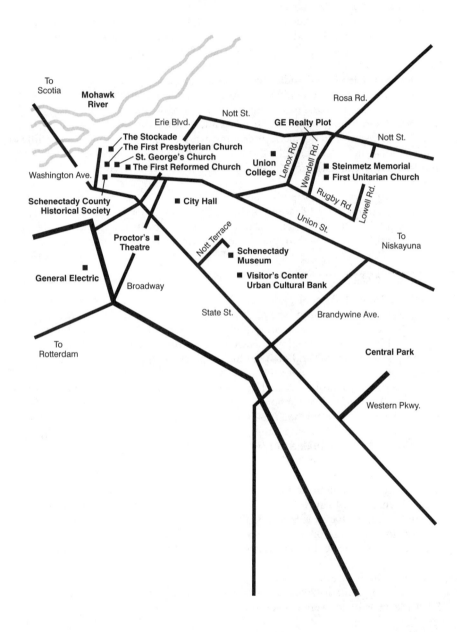

To
Scotia

**Mohawk
River**

Rosa Rd.

Nott St.

Erie Blvd.

GE Realty Plot

Nott St.

The Stockade
The First Presbyterian Church
St. George's Church
The First Reformed Church

**Union
College**

Lenox Rd.

Wendell Rd.

■ **Steinmetz Memorial**
■ **First Unitarian Church**

Washington Ave.

**Schenectady County
Historical Society**

Rugby Rd.

Lowell Rd.

■ **City Hall**

Union St.

To
Niskayuna

**Proctor's
Theatre** ■

Nott Terrace

■ **Schenectady
Museum**

■ **Visitor's Center
Urban Cultural Bank**

■
General Electric

Broadway

State St.

Brandywine Ave.

To
Rotterdam

Central Park

Western Pkwy.

Dora Jackson House, 32 Washington Ave. in the Stockade District, houses the Schenectady County Historical Society (see Museums and Historic Sites, pg. 42)

Realty Plot

General Electric Realty Plot, bounded by Lowell Rd., Nott St., Lenox Rd., and Rugby Rd., was begun in 1899 by the General Electric Company as a park-like enclave for the company's top-level scientists and executives, among them Charles Steinmetz, the eminent electrical inventor; Ernest Alexanderson, the television pioneer; and Irving Langmuir, a Nobel Prize-winner. The plot contains a wonderful variety of turn-of-the-century architecture, and is noted for its wealth of decorative detailing. One unusual home is the 1905 Harry Hillman House (1155 Avon Rd.), the world-famous prototype of an "electric house" full of newly invented modern conveniences. A tour brochure of the plot is available at the nearby Schenectady Visitors Center. www.realtyplot.org

Steinmetz Memorial Park, Wendell Ave., marks the site of the former home and laboratory (1903 to 1923) of "the electrical wizard" Charles Proteus Steinmetz, who worked for General Electric and served as Professor of Engineering at Union College. In the early 1890s, Steinmetz developed the theory of alternating current.

The First Unitarian Society, 1221 Wendell Ave., built in 1961, was the first church to be designed by Edward Durrell Stone, the architect for the State University at Albany. The modernist exterior is constructed of cement blocks that form interlocking circles. Inside the Great Hall is an amphitheater with a 60-foot-wide dome and 300 seats on circular benches. The hall serves as a religious center, performance stage, and recital hall, and houses the Oakroom Artists Gallery. Also of interest are the gardens and sculptures, and the reflecting pools and fountains, which are lighted at night to dramatic effect. 374-4446.

Union Street Historic District

The Union Street Historic District follows the street from the Mohawk River to Phoenix Avenue, encompassing 650 acres of notable 19th-century and early 20th-century architecture. The area is most enjoyed for its plenitude of towers and turrets, as the predominant style is Queen Anne. The district includes Union College, the Schenectady Veterans Memorial, Ellis Mansion, and the Church of St. John the Evangelist. Tour brochures are available at the Schenectady Museum and Visitor Center, located a short walk away on Nott Terrace Heights.

Union College Campus, Union St. and Nott St., is the third home of the college, which dates to 1795. Sixteen years after the colonial victory over the British at Saratoga, several hundred northern New Yorkers realized their dream of the state's first non-denominational college – the name "Union" anticipated a new national identity. One of the many national figures to graduate from the college was President Chester A. Arthur. Called "the Grounds," the current campus was designed in 1813 by France's renowned classical architect, Joseph Ramée. His distinctive white arches and pilasters still dominate the wheel-like layout, although expansion of the facilities to accommodate a growing student body has noticeably altered the original plan. 388-6000. www.union.edu

Nott Memorial is the most unusual structure among the college's eclectic assemblage of buildings. Completed in 1879, this fantastically ornate, 16-sided "stone cylinder" is a National Historic Landmark and an unrivaled example of American High-Victorian architecture. Conceived in collaboration with Ramee by Eliphalet Nott, a Union president for 62 years, the Nott is dramatized by a cast-iron and steel-ribbed dome covered in three colors of Vermont slate, and sprinkled with over 700 colored-glass windows in the shape of stars. The tiered interior rises to 102 feet, with a colorfully patterned floor of encaustic English tile and cryptically symbolic ornamentation. The Nott is home to the Mandeville Gallery of Arts and Sciences, which holds changing exhibits on the second-floor balcony. On the first floor is a large-scale, 1839 oil portrait of Nott by Henry Innan. The building is open to the public noon-5pm daily; until 10pm, Sun-Fri., during the academic year. 388-6004.

Memorial Chapel, facing the Nott Memorial, was built in 1926 as a monument to the Union students killed in World War I. A marvel of acoustic architecture designed by McKim, Mead and White, it hosts the college's classical concerts and is home to the International Chamber Music Festival. 388-6427.

Jackson's Garden is eight acres of beautifully designed gardens and woodland. The plantings, begun in the 1830's by Captain Isaac Jackson of the mathematics department, have been continued since then by college gardeners. A brook winds through the area, which is open to the public.

Church of St. John the Evangelist, 816 Union St. (across the street from Union College), is a massive, red-sandstone structure with a central tower rising 230 feet. This strikingly geometric tower is capped by a conical dome of galvanized iron, topped by a cross of gilded iron 14 feet high. Four matching towers stand at each corner. Constructed between 1899 and 1904, St. John's is an "auditorium" church planned for acoustic excellence, and as such makes a unique contribution to American church architecture. The fan-shaped interior is surrounded by tiers of stained-glass windows (some of them from the Royal Bavarian Art Institute), and is distinguished by a soaring sanctuary filled by a monumental, white-marble statue of St. John and a flock of angels. Be sure to look up at the dome skylight, which is lined with sculpted-marble cherub heads peering down. The church serves an active congregation and holds mass daily. 393-5331.

Other Points of Interest in Schenectady

Central Park, Fehr Ave. (off State St.), is an extensive landscape of gentle hills and small lakes. The slopes are filled with tobagganers and skiers in winter; the rest of the year offers ball fields, tennis courts, and a swimming pool (see Recreation and Sports, pg. 155). The park features a picnic pavilion and an excellent outdoor stage (see Arts and Venues, pg. 55). Don't miss a visit to the rose garden (Wright Ave. entrance), where thousands of roses in 200 varieties bloom from early spring until first frost. This beautifully maintained floral oasis also has cedar arbors, weeping cherry trees, a rockery pool, and a footbridge. 382-5152.

SARATOGA SPRINGS

Saratoga Springs Visitors Center, 297 Broadway across from Congress Park, is the best place to begin a tour of the "Spa City." A former trolley station, this beautiful, 1915 beaux-arts building has Doric columns and bas-reliefs on the exterior. Trolley benches carved out of chestnut still line the walls, and in the gazebo an exhibit traces the evolution of the mineral springs. The center provides information, maps and "strolling" brochures, including a "tasting tour" of Saratoga's famous mineral springs. The city trolley runs a downtown loop during summer. Open 9am-4pm daily. 587-3241.

Adelphi Hotel, 365 Broadway, is a rare surviving High-Victorian hotel, built in 1877 during the height of the American rage for taking the waters – a pastime that made Saratoga "the Queen of Spas." The Italianate facade is graced by slender columns capped with Victorian fretwork, and the 90-foot-long piazza overlooks historic Broadway. The lobby is decorated with elaborate stencils, hand-painted by a master of the art. The parlor and 37 guestrooms feature original woodwork and lavish period decor. The hotel also serves as a fashionable rendezvous spot during the racing season. 587-4688.

Canfield Casino, Congress Park, is an 1870s gambling hall built in the High-Victorian Italianate style, with Tiffany windows and panels. It was once host to Diamond Jim Brady and actress Lillian Russell, who gambled $10,000 chips with other infamous personages. In 1941 the casino was converted into a "drink hall" for the mineral waters. It now houses the museum of the Saratoga Springs Historical Society, which has exhibits on the resort's glamorous 19th century. Open July-Aug., Mon-Sun., 10pm-4pm. Closed Mon-Tues. from Sept-June. Adults $3, seniors/students $2, children under 12 are free. 584-6920.

SARATOGA POINTS OF INTEREST

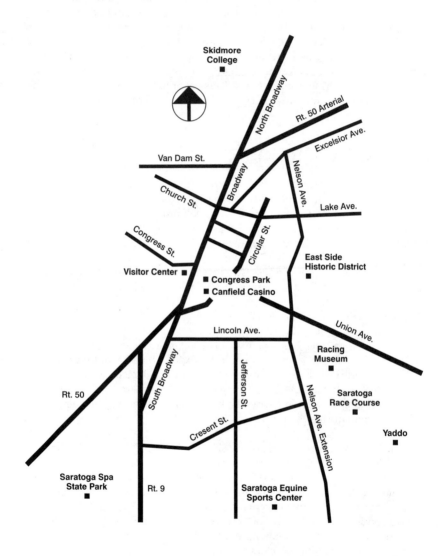

Skidmore College

North Broadway

Rt. 50 Arterial

Excelsior Ave.

Van Dam St.

Broadway

Nelson Ave.

Church St.

Lake Ave.

Congress St.

Circular St.

East Side Historic District

Visitor Center

Congress Park

Canfield Casino

Lincoln Ave.

Union Ave.

Racing Museum

Rt. 50

South Broadway

Jefferson St.

Saratoga Race Course

Nelson Ave. Extension

Cresent St.

Yaddo

Saratoga Spa State Park

Rt. 9

Saratoga Equine Sports Center

Congress Park, between Broadway and Circular St., is a genteel, 33-acre park featuring picturesque springs and the much loved "Spit and Spat" statuary fountain. There are many sights of artistic interest, among them the early-1800s cast-iron vases by Danish sculptor Albert Thorvaldsen (donated by Gideon Putnam); the Civil War Monument, placed on Broadway in 1875 and moved to the park in 1921 (due to traffic mishaps); the 1914 Spencer Trask Memorial bronze sculpture by Daniel Chester French; and the Italian Gardens by Spring Street. The gardens were added in 1902 to imitate European spas, and the beautiful statuary is made out of Carrara marble. A more recent addition to the park is a historic carousel pavilion, with a herd of 28 hand-carved horses and their chariots (rides are 50 cents). Open dawn to dusk.

East Side Historic District, adjacent to Congress Park, is an architecturally fascinating neighborhood, built in the late-1800s for the area's well-to-do business community. Almost 400 houses represent a wide variety of "fashionable" styles, from Colonial Revival to French Renaissance. A self-guide walking tour is available at the Saratoga Visitors Center. 587-3241.

Yaddo Rose Gardens, Union Ave., were restored from the 400-acre rose and rock gardens of Yaddo, the famous and influential artists' community (the remainder of the estate is private). This romantic landscape, a gift of love from Spencer Trask to his wife, Katrina, was designed in 1899 in the style of classical-Italian gardens. The garden features four beds of floribunda and hybrid tea roses centered by a fountain, and including a rose-covered bower. Terraces and a balcony overlook the grounds, which are also graced by Italian marble statutes and flowering perennials and annuals. Open 8am-dusk. Guided tours are conducted July-Labor Day, Sat-Sun. (plus Tuesdays during the August track season) at 11am. $3. 584-0746.

Other Points of Interest in Saratoga

Bacon Hill, in the heart of Saratoga County, is a bucolic hamlet of family farms and historic structures. Set amid verdant hills, these diverse and scenic farms encompass dairy herds and horse paddocks, apple orchards and berry patches, beehives and flowerbeds, and llamas, alpacas and other fiber-fur animals (see Parents and Children, pg. 213). Farm stands provide a cornucopia of fresh-produce shopping, from bedding plants to organic beef. The area also offers less tangible attractions, such as rural character and the exhilaration of living close to the land.

Saratoga Farms, an informational brochure available from the Cornell Cooperative Extension, contains a map, a directory of farm tours and farmer's markets, and a list of seasonal events. A 17-mile driving-tour brochure is also available. Free. 885-8995. www.saratogafarms.com

Saratoga Race Course, Saratoga

Photography by: Gary Gold

Saratoga Battlefield is described in the chapter Museums and Historic Sites, pg. 41.

Saratoga Race Course is the oldest and one of the most prestigious Thoroughbred racetracks in the United States (see Recreation and Sports, pg. 172). The course opened in 1865, with just as much effort expended on creating enjoyable surroundings as to providing outstanding sport. The famous steepled grandstand is augmented by salons and a clubhouse, and in the early 1900s, William Whitney (namesake of the Whitney Stakes) added ornamental iron railings and gates. There are several interesting aspects to this historic venue in addition to watching the equine athletes earn their oats. For many spectators, people watching is almost as exciting as wagering – the season is known for attracting celebrities from near and far. For others, the course is best enjoyed just after dawn, when the horses have their morning workout. At this time, the thundering of hooves is undiminished by cheering crowds, and these graceful animals can be observed for their beauty rather than their effect on the daily-double windows.

Breakfast at the track (7am-9:30am) is a tradition dating to the Civil War. Morning walking tours of the paddocks and tram tours of the backstretch are free. Visitors leaving before 10am receive a parking refund. Open late July to early Sept. Closed Tuesdays (no tours on Aug. 26). 584-6200. www.nyra.com

Other Points of Interest in the Capital Region
Cohoes and Waterford
Riverspark/Cohoes Visitors Center, 58 Remsen St. (inside the Cohoes Music Hall) promotes recreation, preservation and tourism within Cohoes, Green Island, Waterford, and Watervliet. The center has exhibits of local history, and a 20-minute audio-visual presentation, *A Day in the Life of Cohoes: 1882*. Remsen Street is the main street of Cohoes' tiny but eclectic downtown. Open Tues-Fri., noon-5pm. Group tours by appointment. 237-7999.

Cohoes Music Hall, 58 Remsen St., was built in 1874 to serve the mill workers of the mighty Harmony Manufacturing Company (an imposing structure still visible along the Mohawk River). This charming vaudeville hall was host to many legendary personalities, including George M. Cohan, Harry Houdini and Sarah Bernhardt – and is believed to be haunted by Ziegfeld Follies star Eva Tanguay, who grew up in Cohoes. One of the last pre-1900 vaudeville theaters in existence, the hall has been lovingly restored and serves as a performance space (see Arts and Venues, pg. 46). 434-1703. www.cohoescaretakers.com

Cohoes Falls Overlook, School St. off North Mohawk St., provides a breathtaking view of the falls, which are 120 feet high, approximately 1,000 feet across, and the most impressive natural wonder in the region. In spring, you can see rainbows rising above the falls and feel the mist from the churning waters as you look across the river at ancient shale rock beds. The falls are second only to Niagara Falls in power, and once drew just as many sight-seers. Contact Cohoes Visitor Center for information. 237-7999.

Waterford Canal Visitor Center, Tugboat Alley, provides an introduction to the area's historic barge canals, which now draw hundreds of recreational boaters. The two-story center contains small exhibits related to the Erie Canal, a boat launch and services for boaters, and a walking tour of the tow path. A schedule of canal events is available. Open April-October, 7am-7pm. Off-season by appointment. 233-9123.

Waterford Flight is the highest in the world. A series of five "lift locks" raises boats to a combined height of 170 feet, from the Hudson River to the Mohawk River above the Cohoes Falls. The river trail is well marked, and facilities are provided. There is a kiosk with information about the canal in the park beside Lock 2 on Fifth Street. For canal paddle expeditions and other information, contact the Waterford Visitor Center. 233-9123.

Waterford Village has many brick houses built during the shipping boom of the early 1800s. These houses are marked by their distinctive "Waterford gables." 237-7999.

Hoosick Falls

Grandma Moses Gravesite, Maple Grove Cemetery (off Main St.), is the resting place of America's most beloved folk artist. Moses (1861-1961), who began painting at 78 and died at the hearty old age of 101, was "discovered" by art collector Louis Caldor in a Hoosick Falls drugstore. Her paintings of winter scenes, village life, and rural celebrations are renowned for capturing the essence of the land and a simpler way of life, and many of them were inspired by the landscape of Rensselaer County. The largest public collection of Moses paintings and memorabilia can be seen at the Bennington Museum in Vermont (see Not Far Away, pg. 262).

Round Lake

Round Lake Village (Rte. 9), was founded in 1868 as a Methodist "camp" that hosted the largest tent meetings in the country. Due to the efforts of the Round Lake Historical Society, much of the village's charmingly eccentric camp-Victorian architecture remains, with large houses and "gem" cottages nestled within a tiny village of narrow streets and walkways. The houses are distinguished by fairy-tale colors and gingerbread trim, with prominent front porches that help to retain the community's sociable, meeting ground atmosphere. The village green hosts a large antiques festival every August.

Round Lake Auditorium, 2 Wesley Ave. (in the center of the village), was built in 1886 to hold religious lectures. Begun as an open-sided structure with canvas flaps, it was enclosed and enlarged to house a 1847 Ferris "tracker-pipe" organ, acquired from a Calvinist church in New York City. The timber-frame bell tower was added shortly after. The auditorium presents organ recitals – the Ferris is the oldest and largest organ in America still in its original form – and a four-month summer concert series of jazz, country and acoustic music. 899-7141. www.roundlakevillage.org

Albany Institute of History & Art   *Photography by: Gary Gold*

MUSEUMS & HISTORIC SITES

From the oldest pulpit in America to the first Shaker homestead to the Saratoga Battlefield, "turning point of the American Revolution," the Capital Region abounds with fascinating evidence of its illustrious history. Many area museums have recently undergone multi-million-dollar expansions, while new sites from a 400-year-old past have been unearthed and conserved – making the region an even more attractive destination for historical forays. (Additional museums and sites are described in Not Far Away.) Calling ahead is suggested, as fees and hours are subject to change or interruption by special events.

Albany Institute of History & Art, 125 Washington Ave., Albany, is the oldest museum in New York State, tracing its founding to 1791. In 2001, this venerable downtown institution underwent a large-scale, nearly $18 million expansion, joining the 1908 institute to the 1890s beaux-arts palazzo next door. The two buildings are connected by an "architecturally daring" three-story glass atrium that is both Victorian and 21st century in ambience – an appropriate addition for a museum that looks to the future as it celebrates the rich cultural heritage of the upper Hudson Valley region. State-of-the-art climate controls allow the museum to host major traveling exhibits, as well as changing exhibits from its own vast collections of furniture, portraits, sculpture, decorative arts, photographs, and societal objects.

AIHA is renowned for its collections of Hudson River School paintings and Albany-made silver, and other permanent assets include the colorful Egyptology Room (the mummies are a beloved attraction), the sunlit sculpture gallery in the atrium, the regional contemporary art, and the Museum Explorers Gallery for youngsters. A wide range of educational programs, lectures, and tours are offered regularly. Gift shop. Open Weds-Sat., 10am-5pm, Sun., 12-5pm. Research library is by appointment. Adults $5, seniors/students $4, youths (6-12) $2.50. Children under six are free. 463-4478. www.albanyinstitute.org

Brookside Saratoga County Historical Society, 6 Charlton St., Ballston Spa, is housed in a 1792 "society hotel" that once hosted Washington Irving, who etched his name on a window pane. The museum celebrates local history with changing exhibits, a history room, and community events. Painting and crafts classes. Gift shop. Open Tues-Fri., 10am-4pm; Sat. noon-4pm. Adults $3. 885-4000. www.brooksidemuseum.org

Grant Cottage, Mt. McGregor Rd. (Rte 9), Wilton, was the final home of President Ulysses S. Grant and his family, and the place where the disgraced former president wrote his memoirs – on the advice of Mark Twain. Grant died in the house in July of 1885; his military memoir broke sales records and made his family wealthy. The cottage has been preserved exactly as it was during the Grant's occupancy, with original furnishings and displays of the president's personal possessions, including clothing. Set high atop Mt. McGregor, the site has an outlook with lovely views of the Hudson Valley. Civil War events are held during summer, and there is an annual Victorian picnic in August. Open Memorial Day-Labor Day, Wed-Sun., 10am-4pm. Weekends only through Columbus Day. Adults $2.50, seniors $2, youths (6-16) $1, children under six are free. 587-8277.

Empire State Aerosciences Museum, 250 Rudy Chase Dr., Glenville, is located at the Schenectady County Airport, a former rocket-and-jet development site that was once the landing strip of Charles Lindberg's 1928 flight. The museum is an educational and entertaining facility that travels through the aviation history of New York State while exploring the scientific principles of flight. It features dozens of restored aircraft (including an F-14A Tomcat), scale and life-size models, dioramas, photos, interactive displays, and a Simulated Flight Reality Vehicle. New aircraft are added and exhibits are changed frequently. The museum offers a multitude of programs for all ages, and spectacular air shows every summer. Research library and gift shop. Open April-Oct: Tues-Sat., 10am-4pm, Sun. noon-4pm. Nov-March: Thurs-Sat., 10am-4pm. Group tours by appointment. Adults $5, children $2, Reality ride $2. 377-2191. www.esam@esam.org

Junior Museum, 105 8th St., Troy, is described in Parents and Children, pg. 211.

National Museum of Dance, 99 South Broadway, Saratoga State Park, is the only dance museum of its kind, focusing on all aspects of professional dance from classical ballet to ethnic-folk dance. The museum is housed in the former Washington Bath Pavilion, a National Historic Landmark. Displays of artifacts and memorabilia are augmented by seasonal changing exhibits. The facility includes research materials, films, books and recordings. Windows allow for viewing of the museum's dance studios. Gift shop. Open Tues-Sun., 10am-5pm. Adults $5, seniors/students $4, children under 12 are $2. 584-2225.

    Lewis A. Swyer School for the Performing Arts is located within the National Museum of Dance. A state-of-the-art facility with three studios (that open into one large studio) and three grand pianos, it offers master classes as well as dance programs in a variety of dance disciplines. For information, call 584-2225.

National Museum of Racing and Hall of Fame, 191 Union Ave., Saratoga Springs, interprets the history, celebrates the heroes, and conveys the excitement of Thoroughbred racing in America. Exhibits include fine paintings and sculptures of equine athletes, behind-the-scenes recreations, and changing displays such as "The Legend of Sea Biscuit." The Anatomy Room for youngsters has a horse skeleton. Gift shop. Open Mon-Sat., 10am-4:30pm, Sun 12-4:30pm. August (racing season): Mon-Sun., 9am-5pm. Adults $7, seniors and students $5, children under five are free. 584-0400. www.racingmuseum.org

New York State Museum, Empire State Plaza, Madison Ave., Albany, is the oldest, largest, and in many ways the most exciting state museum in the United States. The 11,000-year-old Cohoes Mastodon greets you in the lobby of this state-of-the-art research facility, which interprets the geology, biology, anthropology and cultural history of New York. Life-size recreations and dioramas are enhanced by video presentations and historic photographs, allowing the visitor to vividly experience whole centuries from the Ice Age to the Jazz Age. The redesigned fourth-floor Terrace Gallery has glass walls providing spectacular views of the Capital Region and contains the museum's signature "Windows on New York" exhibit.

Permanent exhibits include:

Adirondack Wilderness illustrates how this spectacular region was transformed through the interaction of humans and nature from a prehistoric wilderness 5,000 years ago to a major recreational area of today.

New York Metropolis traces the evolution of the city: A natural harbor is converted into a bustling port, open spaces into canyons of skyscrapers, and forest wilderness into a world center. Displays recreate memorable places such as Chinatown, Millionaires' Row, Harlem in the Roaring '20s, Ellis Island, and Sesame Street.

Native Peoples of New York depicts Ice Age Hunters, Forest Foragers and a Mohawk Iroquois Village that includes a life-size, fully appointed longhouse.

Windows on New York is a colorful, interactive introduction to the seven regions of the state, from the Adirondacks to Coney Island. Objects include Franklin D. Roosevelt's gleaming Packard, a hovering biplane, and an antique carousel that can be ridden. The memorial to the Sept. 11 World Trade Center bombings is the first of its kind.

Temporary exhibits change 10 times a year, and feature items from the museum's collection of five million artifacts, as well as displays from throughout the country. The museum also offers lectures, workshops and guided tours, and the Discovery Place for youngsters. Café and gift shop. Open 10am-5pm daily. Closed Thanksgiving, Christmas and New Year's Day. Free ($2 donation suggested.) 474-5877.

Rensselaer County Historical Society Museum, 57 and 59 Second St., Troy, occupies three historic buildings, offering a comprehensive as well as picturesque experience. Built in 1827, the Hart-Cluett Mansion is an architecturally innovative, Federal-style townhouse (see Points of Interest, pg. 17). Its 125-year occupancy by two of the city's most entrepreneurial families kept the residence in remarkably original condition, and the opulent interior reflects the industrial prosperity of the era. In 2001, the society completed its renovation of the 1836 Gen. Joseph B. Carr Building next door, connecting the two houses with a glass hallway. The Carr contains three galleries covering 300 years of regional history, with changing exhibits from the society's superb collections of furniture, paintings, decorative arts and domestic artifacts, as well as a staffed genealogical and research library. The adjoining Hart-Cluett carriage house hosts regularly scheduled events and workshops. Open Tues.-Sat., 10am-4pm; Thurs.,10am-8pm. (The library opens at 1pm.) Handicapped access. Closed in January. Adults $4, seniors and youths (12-18) $3, children under 12 are free. The first Saturday of every month is free. Guided tours of the mansion are an additional $2. 272-7232. www.rchsonline.org

Saratoga Automobile Museum, 110 Avenue of the Pines, Saratoga Spa State Park, preserves and interprets the automobile heritage of New York State with exhibits of automobiles, carriages, and other vehicles and artifacts. Displays celebrate design and engineering excellence, race cars and important racing venues, and the role New York State-built vehicles played in the automotive history of America. Among the permanent collection are a 1931 Pierce-Arrow (Buffalo), a 1915 Rolls Royce (Brewster), and 1936 Franklin (Syracuse). Located in a former bottling plant, this large, two-story museum holds more than 30 vehicles, and mounts two major exhibits yearly ("Ferrari Roadburners") in addition to numerous special-interest lawn events ("Citroen Weekend"). Built in 1934, the neo-Georgian building is also of interest, and is located adjacent to the Gideon Putnam Hotel. Open Tues.-Sun., 10am-5pm, Nov-April; daily May-Oct. Adults $7, seniors $5, students $3.50, children under 6 are free. 587-1935. www.saratogaautomobilemuseum.com

Saratoga Raceway Museum, 352 Jefferson St., Saratoga Springs, traces the history of Saratoga's harness track through photographs from its beginnings in 1941. There is also a blacksmith room, a sulky room, and a reference library. Open July-Oct., Tues.-Sat., 10am-4pm. Nov-June, Thurs.-Sat., 10am-4pm. Free. 587-4210.

Schenectady Museum and Planetarium, 15 Nott Terrace Heights (off State St.), is a discovery center specializing in science, technology, and cultural history. Founded in 1934 and dramatically remodeled in 2002, the museum celebrates the city's ethnic heritage, fine arts and crafts, and the Schenectady-built products (such as steam locomotives, refrigerators and fuel cells) that were symbols of power and industry around the world. The Hall of History is dedicated to the artifacts and heritage of the electrical industry, such as the first-ever television broadcasts. The museum also features an "object theater" and interactive kid's exhibits. The building also houses a multi-media planetarium and the Schenectady Visitor Center. In addition to the gift shop is a shop for juried arts and crafts by regional artists. The adjoining nature preserve has walking trails. Open Tues-Fri., 10am-4:30pm; Sat-Sun., noon-5pm. Planetarium shows are held Sat-Sun., 1pm, 2pm and 3pm, and during school vacations. Closed major holidays. Handicapped access. Adults $5, children $3. $1.50 more for the planetarium. 382-7890. www.schenectadymuseum.org

Throop Pharmacy Museum, Albany College of Pharmacy, 106 New Scotland Ave., Albany, is an authentic recreation of the complete Throop pharmacy. The Schoharie drugstore was established in 1800 by Jabez Throop, and operated by family members until 1930. Visitors can look through the window to see the original fixtures, including a stove, cuspidors, old-fashioned globe jars, and the porcelain-pull drawers where herbs and medicines were stored. Open by appointment only. Free. 445-7228.

U.S.S. Slater DE-766, Snowdock at Broadway and Quay (Exit 3B of 787 South), Albany, is the last Destroyer Escort warship still in World War II battle configuration. This unique floating museum offers a vivid experience in how the 216-man crew lived and carried out its missions of anti-submarine warfare. Guided tours (many guides are Navy veterans) go above and below deck; the armament, combat information and radio rooms, pilot house, officers' and crew's quarters, galley, and mess have all been authentically restored. Of particular interest are the rare "hedgehog" depth-charge weapon and the rotating radar antenna. Gift shop. Open April-Nov., Thurs-Sun., 11am-4pm. Adults $5, seniors/youths $3. 431-1943. www.ussslater.org

HISTORIC SITES

Cherry Hill, 523 South Pearl St., Albany (just off Interstate 787, Exit 2), is a gracious, Georgian-style mansion built in 1787 by Philip Van Rensselaer and lived in by his descendants until 1963. It offers a rare opportunity to see the continuum of life in Albany for more than 200 years. As each generation passed to the next, it handed down the possessions it had accumulated, bestowing the museum with a vast assemblage of furniture, portraits, china, documents, and personal artifacts. These collections possess a great deal of family interest as well as historic significance: visitors can learn about the long life of Catherine Putnam, spanning three wars; and her daughter, Emily Rankin, who died in 1963, bequeathing the house and its contents to Historic Cherry Hill. Open Tues-Fri., 12-3pm; Sat. 10am-3pm; Sun. 1pm-3pm. Closed January and major holidays. Tours run on the hour. Adults $3.50, seniors $3, students $2. 434-4791. www.historiccherryhill.org

Crailo State Historic Site, 9 1/2 Riverside Ave., Rensselaer, is a house museum of early Dutch history and culture in the upper Hudson Valley region. Located on a portion of what was once the immense manor of Rensselaerswyck, it's believed that the fortified house was built around 1705 by Hendirck Van Rensselaer, grandson of Kilaen, the first patroon. His son added the Georgian-style east wing. In 1924, a family descendant donated Crailo to the state. Exhibits are augmented by archeological finds from the 1970-71 excavation of Fort Orange (circa 1624) in Albany, and by special programs such as tile painting and open-hearth cooking. Open April 15-Oct. 31, Weds-Sat. 10am-5pm; Sun. 1pm-5pm. Closed major holidays. Tours are on the half-hour, the grounds are available dawn to dusk. Adults $3, seniors $2, youths 5-12 $1. Children under five are free. 463-8738.

Knickerbocker Mansion, Knickerbocker Rd. (off Rte. 67), Schaghticoke, was built by Johannes Knickerbocker during the Revolutionary War, replacing the house of his settler grandfather. The largest early-Dutch structure in the region, the mansion is currently undergoing a grass-roots restoration to its documented, 1860s Georgian-style design. The Knickerbocker name became a household word when Washington Irving, a family friend, wrote the popular *Knickerbockers' History of New York* in 1809. The property is also known for being the site of the 1676 Witenagemot Peace Treaty; remains of the "Witenagemot Oak Peace Tree" are on view in the attic. Of particular interest is the family cemetery, which has gravestones dating to the mid-1700s and its original retaining wall. Open July-August, Sun., 11am-3pm, or by appt. Free. Harvest and Halloween events are held every autumn (see Seasonal, pg. 199). 753-4175. www.knic.com

Mabee Farm, 1080 Main St., Rotterdam Junction (Rte 5S), is the oldest continuously habituated farm in the Mohawk Valley. Situated on rolling fields along the Mohawk River, the Stone House is the centerpiece of the site where for over 300 years the Mabee family helped to develop the valley and adapted to its changing fortunes. Three stone, brick, and frame buildings, dating from 1680-1735 and in remarkably original condition, remain on the 9-acre site, as does the family cemetery and a large collection of farming artifacts. Exhibits on Mohawk Valley history are contained in the 1760 Dutch barn and the 1800s English barn. Annual events include harvest festivals, art fairs, and militia reenactments. Open Memorial Day to Labor Day, Wed.-Sat., 10am-4pm; spring and fall by appointment. Adults $3, students/children $2. 887-5073. www.schist.org

Melville House, 2 114th St., Lansingburgh, is situated in one of the earliest river-oriented communities along the Hudson River. The house was once the home of the great American writer Herman Melville and his family, who lived there from 1838 to 1847 (Melville's grandfather was the Revolutionary War hero Gen. Peter Gansevoort of Albany). The small park across the street was a boat-building area, where Melville learned about sloop building and may have first heard the story of the great white whale that later became *Moby-Dick*. Home to the Lansingburgh Historical Society, the house includes small exhibits on local history and Melville memorabilia (for Melville's Arrowhead House, see Not Far Away, pg. 267). Open March-Nov. on the first and third Sun., 1-3, and Nov-April by appointment. Free. 235-3501.

Pruyn House Historic and Cultural Center, 207 Old Niskayuna Rd., Newtonville (Northway 87, Exit 5), features the summer house of Casparus Francis Pruyn, land agent to the last patroon, Stephen Van Rensselaer. Now home to the Colonie Historical Society, this 1830's Federal- and Greek-Revival country manor preserves the old Dutch ambience with a vast center hall, 10 fireplaces, a winding staircase, and a period-furniture collection. The grounds include the Buhrmaster Barn, with hand-hewn beams and a cupola; the one-room Verdoy Schoolhouse (with Meneely bell); herb and perennial gardens; a tool museum/privy, potting shed and carriage house. The buildings host events, including contra dances and Civil War reenactments, and are available for rental to community groups. Open year-round, Mon-Fri., 9am-4:30pm, or by arrangement. Free. 783-1435.

Saratoga National Historical Park, 648 Rte. 32, Stillwater, includes the preserved battlefield where American militiamen defeated the British in 1777. The Battle of Saratoga (actually, it was two battles) is justly famed as "the turning point of the Revolution," and the best time to visit is in September, when the battles are reenacted as authentically as possible by living-history groups wearing uniforms, carrying weaponry, and setting up camp. A 4.2-mile military road tour provides a soldier's-eye view as it leads to battle positions and defensive lines. The visitor center includes an orientation film, a small museum and a bookstore.

    Saratoga Battle Monument, in the nearby village of Victory, is a 155-foot memorial commemorating Gen. Burgoyne's surrender to Gen. Gates in 1777. Erected in 1883, it stands within Burgoyne's entrenchment during the last days of the campaign.

    Gen. Philip Schuyler House, Schuylerville (eight miles northeast of the battlefield), was the general's home both before and after the battles. The original house was burned by the British; the present house was built in 1777 and served as the center of Schuyler's farming and milling operations. Both sites are part of the Historical Park and information is available through the visitor center. Open daily 9am-5pm, April-mid-Nov. The park and house are free, the battlefield is $5 per vehicle, $3 per pedestrian/bicyclist. 664-9821. www.nps.gov/sara/

Schenectady County Historical Society, 32 Washington Ave., Schenectady, is located in the 1895 Dora Jackson House in the heart of the Stockade District. It is both a house museum, with several period rooms including a Shaker Spinning room; as well as a research library, including almost 3,000 books of local history and genealogy. On display are artifacts of early life in Schenectady including regional paintings (Ezra Ames, Thomas Wilkie), dolls, guns, clothing, and furniture – the pianoforte once resided in the Glen Sanders Mansion. Of particular interest are the dollhouse that belonged to the family of Gov. Joseph Yates (1823-1825), and the memorabilia of electrical inventor Charles Steinmetz. Open Mon-Fri. 1pm-5pm (the second Saturday of every month 9am-1pm). Adults $2, children $1, families $5. Grems-Doolittle Library $3 per day. Call ahead for group tours. 374-0263.

Schuyler Mansion, 32 Catherine St., Albany, is an elegant, 1762 English Georgian-style mansion built by Gen. Philip Schuyler, scion of one of Albany's most prominent families. This state historic site was once surrounded by acres of lawns and gardens, through which strolled heroes of the Revolutionary War and patricians of the era, including George Washington and Benjamin Franklin. Alexander Hamilton married Schuyler's daughter, Elizabeth, in a ceremony held in the drawing room – an oil portrait of the young Hamilton hangs there today. The mansion features furniture and decorative objects typical of the 18th-century aristocracy in Albany. Of particular interest are the authentically reproduced flock wallpapers and the family's Hepplewhite pianoforte. Out back, an herb garden duplicates the original. The carriage house next door has an orientation exhibit with interesting artifacts, including the rhinestone shoe buckles of Gen. John Burgoyne, who stayed at the house as Schuyler's "gentleman prisoner." The mansion hosts seasonal chamber-music concerts by The Musicians of Ma'alwyck. Open mid-April-Oct., Wed-Sun., by guided tour 10am-4pm. Tours start on the hour; group tours by appointment year-round. Closed holidays except Memorial Day, Independence Day, and Labor Day. Free parking is available behind the building. Adults, $3, seniors/children under 12, $2. 434-0834.

Shaker Heritage Society, 875 Watervliet-Shaker Rd. (across from Albany International Airport), is located on the grounds of the first Shaker settlement in the United States, founded 1775-76. Displays and exhibits illustrate the creativity and industry of the Shakers who lived there communally until 1924. There are eight buildings and an herb garden, including the 1848 Shaker Meeting House, which contains the museum; the 1822 Brethren's Workshop; and the restored 1916 Church Family Barn. The cemetery is a major Shaker burial ground (1785 to 1938) that includes the grave of Mother Ann Lee. The 770-acre historic site encompasses the Ann Lee Pond Nature Preserve. Self-guide tour pamphlets are available in the Meeting House. Gift shop. Open Mon-Sat., 9:30am-4pm, and by appointment. Closed first week of January. Guided tours are conducted Sat., June-Oct, 11:30am and 1:30pm. Adults $3, children under 12 are free. 456-7890. www.crisny.org/not-for-profit/shakerwv

Ten Broeck Mansion, 9 Ten Broeck Place, Albany, is a three-story, Federal-style mansion built in the 1790s for Gen. Abraham Ten Broeck and his wife, Elizabeth Van Rensselaer. In 1848, the house was purchased by Theodore Olcott; his descendants lived there for 100 years and donated the house to the Albany County Historical Association in 1948. This beautiful colonial residence is situated on three hilltop acres with gardens, and features period furniture, decorative art, and changing exhibits on local history. The mansion's wine cellar is the oldest to have been in continuous use in the country. Open Thurs-Sun., 1pm-4pm, May-Dec. Closed holidays. Adults $3, children $1. 436-9826. www.tenbroeck.org

Waterford Historical Museum, 2 Museum Lane (off Rte. 32), Waterford, is housed in the 1830 Hugh White Homestead, a splendid example of the transition from Federal Style to Greek Revival. In 1964, the mansion was scheduled for demolition but was saved by concerned citizens, who moved it from Saratoga Avenue to its present site overlooking the Mohawk River. It features the history of Waterford, "the oldest incorporated village in America," as well as small changing exhibits on local history, two Victorian Rooms, and a library. Open late April-early Nov., Sat-Sun., 2pm-4pm. Call for off-season hours and tours by appointment. Free. 238-0809.

Watervliet Arsenal Museum, Broadway (Rte. 32,), Watervliet, is housed in Major Mordecai's 1859 "cast-iron storehouse," a historic landmark. The Greek Revival museum features rare cannonry artifacts and displays on the history of the arsenal, the U.S. Army's oldest manufacturing arsenal. Founded to supply the War of 1812, the facility became "America's Cannon Factory" in 1887, and is still the sole manufacturer of large-caliber cannon in volume. The storehouse also serves as a memorial to all the wars the arsenal has supported. Nearby are several historic residences, including the home of poet Stephen Vincent Benet. Open Mon-Thurs., 10am-3pm. Free. 266-5805.

*Many of these museums and historic sites hold festive holiday events in early December.

Ellen Sinopoli Dance Company, Albany   *Photography by: Gary Gold*

ARTS AND VENUES

The Capital Region's music, art, theater, and dance resources have all experienced a surge of growth and diversification recently, with major expansions at established arts centers as well as the arrival of several innovative newcomers – making the arts one of the area's most vibrant attractions. Classes and other participatory experiences are abundant. And the region's many stages are a magnet for world-renowned performers, especially in summer when numerous outdoor venues burst into activity. For arts enthusiasts of every kind, it's seek and ye shall find.

    Albany-Schenectady League of Arts, 161 Washington Ave. (third floor), Albany, is the oldest arts council in the country. Since 1946, the League has provided technical, legal, promotional, and administrative services to artists and arts organizations throughout the Capital Region, with the aim of fostering a welcoming environment for artists of all disciplines to live and work in. The league's award-winning newsletter and events schedule is published bi-monthly. 449-5380. www.artsleague.org

ARTS CENTERS

Arts Center of the Capital Region, 265 River St., Troy, is both an exhibition space for innovative artworks and an arts-advocacy organization situated in the heart of the city. Established in 1962, the center moved in 2000 to a row of 19th-century retail buildings, which were beautifully restored in a $5.3 million conversion project. The center's sunlit, storefront gallery faces Monument Square; upstairs is a state-of-the-art "black box" theater. ACCR sponsors workshops and classes in visual, literary, folk, and fine arts, and in other artistic disciplines including acting and dance. The center also sponsors outreach programs for special-needs populations. A newsletter and catalog of classes is published bi-monthly. 273-0552. www.theartscenter.cc

Saratoga County Arts Council and Center, 320 Broadway, Saratoga Springs, is a non-profit council of artists that advocates for the arts. Begun as a grass-roots effort, it now has a 2,000-square-foot gallery and a gallery shop. The council stimulates students of all ages and skill levels with workshops and classes; assists artists in developing their work and audiences; and coordinates and helps to fund programs that bring the arts to all of Saratoga County. The performance space welcomes visitors with exhibits, films, concerts, theater stagings, lectures, and special events. A newsletter and calender is published monthly. 584-4132. www.saratoga-arts.org

Performing Arts Centers

Cohoes Music Hall, 58 Remsen St., Cohoes, is one of the few pre-1900 American theaters in operation today. This evocative, gilded hall hosts a variety of performances, from musicals to folk singers to magic acts. Seating capacity is 400. 434-1703.

Empire Center at the Egg, Empire State Plaza (between Madison Ave. and State St.), is shaped like a salad bowl, with curved walls and Swiss-pearwood veneers for the acoustic enhancement of its two theaters. The 450-seat Lewis A. Swyer Theatre is used for chamber-music concerts, cabaret, lectures, multimedia presentations, and solo performers. The 980-seat Kitty Carlisle Hart Theatre, which boasts a state-of-the-art sound system, is used for larger productions and a fabulously diverse array of concerts. The Egg is also home to the Ellen Sinopoli Dance Company (see pg. 59) Box office: 473-1845. www.theegg.org

Palace Theater, 19 Clinton Ave. (corner of North Pearl St.), Albany, is a gilded 1930s movie palace, built as the "crown jewel" of the RKO theater chain (look for the palatial, 3,000-pound chandelier). Beautifully refurbished in 2002, the 2,900-seat theater (with balconies) presents a variety of theatrical performances and concerts. Box office: 465-4663.

Pepsi Arena, 51 South Pearl St., Albany, is a large-scale circular arena that hosts a wide variety of concerts, including traveling musicals, circuses, and ice-skating shows, and the biggest pop, rock and classical acts in the world (from U2 to the Three Tenors). The arena's curtaining system allows it to change capacity from 17,500 to 6,000 seats, and it has 25 luxury "box" suites with private bathrooms and refrigerators. Box office: 487-2000. www.pepsiarena.com

Proctor's Theater, 432 State St., Schenectady, is an opulent, 2,750-seat (with balconies) 1920s vaudeville hall that presents Broadway and Off-Broadway shows, concerts, opera, dance, comedy, and film screenings. Proctor's is home to the Schenectady Orchestra, and has an old-fashioned arcade lined with boutiques and exhibit windows. Box office: 346-6204. www.proctors.org

Rensselaer Newman Chapel & Cultural Center, Burdett Ave. (two blocks northeast of the RPI Student Union), Troy, is located within an award-winning, multi-use structure. This exceptionally striking performance space hosts acoustic and avant-garde music concerts, drama and multi-media performances, and readings from local and national authors of literature, poetry, and inspirational nonfiction. The sacristy walls display changing exhibits of local art and photography, and the entire cultural center is adorned with modernist religious artworks. 274-7793. www.rpi.edu

Saratoga Performing Arts Center, (SPAC), open in the summer, is the center-piece of the lush Spa State Park in Saratoga Springs. Since 1966, this nationally acclaimed Amphitheatre has presented New York City Ballet in July and the Philadelphia Orchestra in August. SPAC hosts Jazz and Chamber Music festivals, Pre-Performance Talks, Saratoga Wine & Food Festival, and legendary and emerging pop and rock artists. Indoor, balcony and lawn seating available by reservation and at the gate. Special pricing for groups. Video screens enhance visibility for outdoor guests. Dining in SPAC's Hall of Springs restaurant and picnicking on the grounds are encouraged. New members welcome. Box Office: 587-3330. For schedules and information 584-9330. www.spac.org

Troy Savings Bank Music Hall, 32 Second St., presents stellar jazz, classical, folk, and world-music concerts. The hall is nationally acclaimed for its superlative acoustics (see Points of Interest, pg. 17) and distinguished Odell concert organ, built in 1882 during the "golden age" of organ crafting. Once graced by Paderweski, Rubenstein, and Horowitz, the hall has more recently been used for recordings by contemporary artists such as Isaac Stern, Yo-Yo Ma, and Emmanuel Ax. It also serves as a recording space for Dorian Recordings. Box office: 273-0038. www.troymusichall.org

Union College Memorial Chapel, Union St., Schenectady, is a High Victorian "shoebox" auditorium with sublime acoustics (see Points of Interest, pg. 26). It hosts the college's classical concerts and is home to the International Chamber Music Festival. 388-6427.

WAMC Performing Arts Studio, 399 Central Ave. (at the corner of Quail St.), formerly a 1926 bank building, was constructed in 2002 to host studio audiences for the station's live broadcasts and recording sessions of performers and concerts. The soaring, two-floor auditorium seats 200, and programming has expanded from classical, jazz and folk to include children's folk singing, small theatrical productions, poetry readings, art exhibitions, debates, and film screenings. The space alone is worth a look: the $1.3 million conversion project kept many of the bank's original features intact, including a two-feet-thick vault door (the vault is now a dressing room), arched floor-to-ceiling windows, and a marble sales counter. Box office: 465-5233.

Ticketmaster is a national computerized ticket service with numerous outlets in the area. For a fee, it provides reserved tickets to all major concerts and shows in the greater Capital Region. Charge-by-phone: 476-1000. www.ticketmaster.com

CLASSICAL MUSIC

Music at Noon, Troy Savings Bank Music Hall, is a free, weekday concert series held at lunchtime. Keep an eye on the schedule for the not-infrequent appearances of big-name talent. 273-0038.

Troy Chromatic Concerts, Troy Savings Bank Music Hall, is a 150-year-old, non-profit organization that presents four diverse classical-music concerts of the highest quality. Selections are frequently aired on National Public Radio, and the list of past Chromatic performers is a veritable Who's Who of classical talent (Rachmaninoff, Horowitz and Leontyne Price, for starters). For classical-music lovers, these concerts are not to be missed. Subscriptions available. Tickets: 273-0038. Information: 235-3000.

Chamber Music

Capitol Chamber Artists, 263 Manning Blvd., Albany, specializes in rare chamber-music transcriptions of classical masters. The group performs frequently and has appeared everywhere from the Governor's Mansion to Carnegie Hall. 458-9231. www.capitolchambers.qpg.com

Friends of Chamber Music, Kiggins Auditorium, Emma Willard School, 285 Pawling Ave., Troy, has presented a widely diverse roster since 1949. The repertoire concentrates on important works that are infrequently heard, from baroque to Bartok. High-quality chamber-ensemble concerts of string, piano, wind, and voice are held six times yearly at the intimate Kiggins hall, known for the excellence of its resident Steinway piano. 274-2098. www.friendsofchambermusic.org

International Festival of Chamber Music, Union College, Union St., Schenectady, presents acclaimed national and international chamber ensembles (regulars include the Emerson String Quartet and Boston Camerata). Matinee and evening performances are held in the acoustically superb Memorial Chapel. Subscriptions are available with discounts for students. Union students are free. Tickets: 388-6131. General information: 372-3651.

L'Ensemble, the Egg, Albany, performs all facets of chamber music, from Bach's unaccompanied sonatas to fully staged productions. The non-profit ensemble's mission is to joyously stretch the boundaries of chamber works with adventurous programming that includes jazz and cabaret. The group's core artists have prestigious resumes, and perform at a variety of Capital Region venues in addition to the Egg's intimate Swyer Theater. 475-9001.

Maverick Concerts, Maverick Rd., Woodstock, features quality chamber-ensemble concerts in a historic woodland setting (see Not Far Away, pg. 249) from late June to early September. Free children's concerts on Saturdays at 11am. (845) 679-8217. www.maverickconcerts.org

Musicians of Ma'alwyck, an ensemble in residence at both the Schuyler Mansion, and at the University at Albany specializes in programs that present music from America in the late 1700's and early 1800's. 393-4828.

Renaissance Musical Arts Ltd., Albany, presents concerts during the year with musicians from major orchestras and music schools, and hosts a lecture series on individual composers and their music. Money raised through these endeavors supports a scholarship program for area students to attend the Tanglewood Institute. 482-5334.

Choral Music

Albany Pro Musica is a semi-professional mixed chorus that performs both accompanied and a cappella, with an emphasis on less familiar compositions as well as choral masterpieces. The repertoire ranges from madrigals to oratorios, and from medieval to modern. In addition to a schedule of regional performances (often with acclaimed guest artists), the chorus presents a yearly three-concert series. APM is often heard on National Public Radio, and recordings are available. Tickets and information: 438-6548. www.albanypromusica.org

Capitaland Chorus, a member of Sweet Adelines International, is a non-profit, award-winning, 80-member chorus of women who sing four-part harmony, barbershop-style. The chorus performs at various community events. New members welcome. 237-4384.

Mendelssohn Club, Chancellor's Hall, Albany, is a male glee club composed of regional singers. Formed in 1909, the club presents concerts of light music throughout the year at various music halls. 395-8863.

Octavo Singers, Schenectady, was established in 1933 as a WPA community chorus. The 90-member vocal group presents four yearly concerts of sacred-classical music at Union College Memorial Chapel. Auditions available. 344-SING.

Orchestral

Albany Symphony Orchestra, 19 Clinton Ave., Albany, is one of the nation's most innovative orchestras, performing the works of established and emerging American composers while respecting and bringing new vision to time-honored classical music. Nine major concerts are held yearly; performances are held at the Palace Theater and the Troy Savings Bank Music Hall, with a three-concert series at the Canfield Casino in Saratoga. 465-4755. www.albanysymphony.com
   Dogs of Desire is the ASO's cutting edge, 18-member chamber ensemble. Since 1993, the Dogs have been premiering newly commissioned works by contemporary composers (from symphonist Kamran Ince to rock drummer Stewart Copeland) to explore and celebrate American popular culture. The ensemble plays one major concert in March. 465-4755.

Boston Symphony Orchestra, Rte. 183, Lenox, Mass., presents a summer performance series at Tanglewood, an outdoor amphitheater renowned for transcending the barriers between performers and audiences (see Not Far Away, pg. 269) Full orchestra concerts with all-star conductors (John Williams, Andre Previn) and soloists (Itzhak Perlman, Yo-Yo Ma) are conducted on weekends (Sat. morning rehearsals can be attended for reduced admission); during the week there are concerts by the Boston Symphony Chamber Players.

Tanglewood also presents three summer shows by the Boston Pops, and the Boston Early Music Festival in June. The BSO and Tanglewood schedule is released in February. Tickets and schedules: (617) 266-1492 or (886) 266-1200. www.bso.org.

Empire State Youth Orchestra, 432 State St., Schenectady, was founded in 1979 to provide high-quality training for talented school-age musicians from the Capital Region (graduates include Grammy nominee Stefon Harris). ESYO encompasses two full orchestras and six companion ensembles, and performs concerts at the Troy Music Hall, Proctor's Theater, and other local venues, as well as Tanglewood and Carnegie Hall. 382-7581.

Philadelphia Orchestra, Saratoga Performing Arts Center, is in residence for three weeks every August. Founded in 1900, the orchestra is esteemed as one of the best in the world, and is revered for its extraordinary discipline, unity, and world-class soloists and conductors. Schedules are released in February. SPAC box office: 587-3330. www.philorc.com

Schenectady Symphony Orchestra, 432 State St., Schenectady, is a community orchestra that presents four annual concerts and one children's concert at Proctor's Theater, in addition to performing in various ensembles with youth groups. 372-2500.

Opera

Berkshire Opera Company, 14 Castle St., Great Barrington, Mass., presents a summer series of classical and contemporary operas, performed by professionals and accompanied by the 50-piece Berkshire Opera Orchestra. The BOC performs at the historic Mahaiwe Theater, a 700-seat former vaudeville palace purchased by the company for restoration to its 1905 acoustic and architectural grandeur. Box office: (413) 644-9988. Information: (413) 644-9000. www.berkop.org

Glimmerglass Opera, Rte. 80, Cooperstown, is an internationally acclaimed company attracting audiences from around the globe (see Not Far Away, pg. 259). The opera's summer festival presents a mix of familiar favorites and neglected masterpieces, as well as contemporary American operas, some of them premieres. These innovative productions are often broadcast on PBS. Performances of four new works per season (43 showings in repertoire) are held at the festival's 900-seat Alice Busch Opera Theater, an intimate space with superlative acoustics. Schedules are released in January, and tickets sell out quickly. Box Office: (607) 547-2255. www.glimmerglass.org

Lake George Opera, Spa Little Theater, Saratoga State Park, presents two or three major productions, with renowned guests and accompanied by the LGOF orchestra, for eight performances during one week in July. The 40-year-old company also offers chamber-music recitals and master classes year-round at various venues. Opera on the Lake, a performance cruise on Lake George featuring selections from operas and musicals, is held every June, SPAC box office: 587-3330. LGO office: 584-6018.

Organ

Cathedral of All Saints, 63 Swan St. (corner of Elk St.), Albany, presents organ concerts as well as classical-music performances throughout the year. Free. 465-1346. www.cathedralofallsaints.org

First Methodist Church, 603 State St., Schenectady, sponsors free public concerts by virtuoso organists. Receptions with the musicians follow. 374-4403.

First Presbyterian Church, 400 Glen St., Glens Falls, features a large, 4-manual Reuter pipe organ, and a Casavant organ. For concert schedule call. 793-2521.

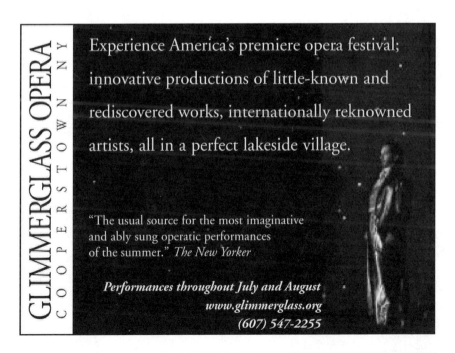

Round Lake Organ Concerts, Round Lake Auditorium, feature an extraordinary musical instrument: a rare 1847 Ferris Tracker pipe organ. The Round Lake Historical Society sponsors Sunday recitals during July and August, and theatrical and musical stagings throughout the year. 899-5726.

Proctor's Theater, 432 State St., Schenectady, presents noontime pipe-organ concerts on "Goldie the Mighty Wurlitzer Organ" every Tuesday. Free. 346-6204.

St. Peter's Episcopal Church, 107 State St., Albany, presents noontime organ concerts on Fridays from September to May. Free. 434-3502.

Westminster Presbyterian Church, 85 Chestnut St., Albany, is home to a noteworthy 4-manual E. M. Skinner pipe organ. First installed in 1929, the instrument has recently been restored and enlarged. Concerts of organ, choral, and chamber music are held regularly and feature local, national and international musicians. 436-8544.

JAZZ AND FOLK

A Place for Jazz, 1221 Wendell Ave., Schenectady, isn't really a place – it's an organization whose programs include information about jazz and support of jazz musicians in the greater Capital Region. A Place presents a fall concert series, held in the beautiful Whisperdome at the First Unitarian Society in Schenectady, and publishes a bi-monthly calendar of jazz concerts, venues, and organizations. Information and calendars: 465-1278.

Caffe Lena, 47 Phila St., Saratoga Springs, is a national landmark of acoustic music. This homey, non-profit coffeehouse was a stop on Bob Dylan's first tour, and the place where Don McLean first played "American Pie." Lena's reputation attracts the finest folk and traditional-music performers. Coffees, desserts, and, on occasion, dinners are available. Smoke- and alcohol-free. For reservations or a calendar of events: 583-0022. www.caffelena.com

Eighth Step is known as the longest running non-profit coffeehouse in the country, and attracts a loyal roster of acclaimed national folk acts (from Arlo Guthrie to Ani DiFranco), as well as blues, jazz, and world-music performers. The organization is in the process of procuring a permanent home; in the meantime, concerts are presented at a variety of local venues. Call for a schedule: 434-1703. www.eighthstep.com

Parting Glass, 40-42 Lake Ave., Saratoga Springs, is a lively Irish pub famed for its Celtic and bluegrass performances. 583-1916.

Revolution Hall, 421-425 River St., Troy, is a 500-person concert venue and theater, adapted in 2003 from a 19th-century collar factory. The hall, which has balcony seating and a state-of-the-art sound system, presents folk, jazz, rock, and world-music shows, and is home to the Masque Theatre. This stylish, two-story space is setup like a nightclub, and the bar serves award-winning, handcrafted beers tapped from the Troy Pub & Brewery next door. 273-2337. www.troypub.com

Second Wind Productions is a summer concert series held at the Agnes Macdonald Music Haven stage in Central Park in Schenectady, and at the Washington Park Lakehouse in Albany. The eclectic schedule includes the finest in avant-garde jazz, folk, and world music. July-Aug. (see Seasonal, pg. 191). Free. (800) 776-2992. www.swconcerts.org

Van Dyck Restaurant & Brewery, 237 Union Ave., Schenectady, is second only to the Troy Music Hall for presenting the most acclaimed jazz performances, as well as folk, blues, cabaret, and pop. Located in the historic Stockade, its atmospheric dining rooms (see Restaurants, pg. 74) are on the first floor; the intimate stage is on the second floor, and dinner is available at the surrounding tables. The room also has a handsome bar. Schedules and information: 381-1111. www.thevandyck.com

THEATER

Albany Civic Theater, 235 Second Ave., Albany, is a community troupe with its own playhouse: a converted 19th-century firehouse. In this cozy theater all seats are orchestra seats. The troupe offers four productions yearly; each production is presented every weekend for three weeks. Seats may be reserved by phone. 462-1297.

Capital Repertory Company, 111 North Pearl St., Albany, is a resident Equity theater that employs local and national talent to stage eclectic, challenging, and high-caliber productions. Whether tackling Oscar Wilde or Toni Morrison, this award-winning company is always willing to take risks. Shows are held in the company's 286-seat Market Theater; pre-theater dinner arrangements with downtown restaurants are available. Box Office: 462-4531. www.capitalrep.org

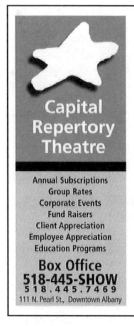
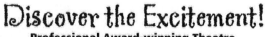

Home Made Theater, Spa Little Theater, Saratoga State Park, is Saratoga's resident theater, and is highly regarded as "a community theater with a professional edge," due to its unique mix of professionals and dedicated volunteers. HMT presents popular plays and musicals during a four-show season that runs from October to May, with a Theater for Families production every December. Dinner packages with area restaurants are available, and ticket prices are moderate. Box office: 587-4427. www.homemadetheater.org

New York State Theatre Institute, 37 First St., Troy, is a nationally acclaimed professional and educational state theatre producing quality entertainment for family audiences (so high quality, in fact, that NYSTI's smash hit, *A Tale of Cinderella*, was released on Warner Bros. Home Video and broadcast on PBS). Performances of theatrical classics, imaginative original productions, and world-premier musicals take place at the Schacht Fine Arts Center at Russell Sage College. Box office: 274-3256. www.nysti.org

Schenectady Civic Players Inc., 12 South Church St., Schenectady, has been an all-volunteer community theater for more than 75 years. The Players present five diverse productions annually, with eight performances of each play from October to May. Shows are held in the 261-seat Schenectady Civic Playhouse, a converted, Gothic-style Masonic Temple with stained-glass windows and excellent sight lines. Tryouts for all roles are open to the public. Tickets and information: 382-2081.

Schenectady Light Opera Company, 826 State St., Schenectady, is a non-profit theater organization dedicated to presenting quality amateur theatrical productions "by the community for the community." The company has operated out of its 250-seat opera house for over 75 years, and specializes in Broadway-style musicals. Tryouts for all productions are open to the public. Tickets and information: 393-5732. www.sloctheater.com

Steamer No.10, 500 Western Ave., Albany, was once a fire station and home to a horse-drawn, steam-powered fire engine. A century later, it was converted to a 120-seat theater powered by imagination. This award-winning theatre group – which writes and creates its own productions – presents theatrical entertainments for youngsters and families known as Kids Fare (see Parents and Children, pg. 210), and for adults as Live at Steamer No.10. The emphasis is on local history and madcap whimsy, and in summer there is a Shakespeare production. Tickets and information: 438-5503.

ZuZu's Wonderful Life, 299 Hamilton St., Albany, is a natural food café that doubles as a performance space, with two diverse resident performance groups: Pintimento Playback Theatre Players and the Wit and Will Improv Troupe. ZuZu's also presents original musicals, local film screenings, literary readings, and belly dancing. This cheerful space really does have "all the ingredients for a wonderful life," including the ambience of off-Broadway without the big-city pretensions. Schedules available. Free parking across the street in Robinson Square. 462-1269.

Summer Theater

Park Playhouse, Washington Park at the Lakehouse, Albany, presents wonderful, family-oriented plays and musicals in July and August. Show time is usually 8pm, Wed-Sun. It's free, but the tree-shaded hillside bleachers fill up early and reserved seating is $12. 434-2032.

Saratoga Shakespeare Company, Congress Park, Saratoga Springs, is Saratoga County's only professional theatre, founded in 1999 to provide "a Shakespeare for the enjoyment of everyone of every age." The company of local and national actors perform physically exuberant stagings of a comedy by the Bard every summer; ten shows are presented during the last week of July and the first week in August. Free. For more information, contact the Saratoga County Arts Council. 584-4132.

Not Far Away

Some of the finest summer theater in the country is within an hour's drive of the Capital Region. For more information on many of these theaters, see the chapter Not Far Away.

Berkshire Theatre Festival, East Main St., Stockbridge, stages professional productions of traditional theater from May through October. The third oldest theatre festival in the nation, BTF is known for attracting famous actors to its floorboards. The historic Playhouse is augmented by the Unicorn Theater, which presents more adventurous fare as well as the festival's youth theatre, BTF Plays! Box Office: (413) 298-5576. www.berkshiretheatre.org

Mac-Haydn Theatre Inc., 1925 Rte. 203, Chatham, presents lively renditions of popular Broadway musicals, produced "in the round" in a rustic, hillside theater from late May through September. In July and August, musical adaptations of popular children's stories are performed on weekend mornings. Ticket prices are moderate. 392-9292.

Shakespeare & Company, 70 Kemble St., Lenox, is one of the largest and most critically revered Shakespeare festivals in the country. Distinguished by director Tina Packard's scholarly yet innovative stagecraft, the company produces plays by Shakespeare and original adaptations of Edith Wharton, Henry James, and other Berkshire writers. In 2001, the company left its longtime home at the Mount for a new residence a block away, in Lenox Center. The $5 million, 63-acre complex houses three theaters. Look for an authentic recreation of Shakespeare's 1587 Rose Playhouse in the future. Box Office: (413) 637-3353. www.shakespeare.org

Williamstown Theater Festival, Williamstown, Mass., is considered to be the finest regional summer theater in the Northeast. The festival's productions often transfer to bigger stages, including Broadway, and celebrity participants from Ethan Hawke to Arthur Miller are a common sight. The intimate Nikos Stage augments the atmospheric Main Stage, and a popular free family theater is held in a nearby field. Box office: (413) 597-3400. www.wtfestival.org

DANCE

Albany Berkshire Ballet, 25 Monroe St., Albany, is nationally recognized for performing classical and contemporary dance with excellence. The ballet performs the works of resident and master choreographers at Jacob's Pillow in summer, and at other venues in the greater Capital Region year-round, including an annual holiday presentation of The Nutcracker at the Palace Theater in Albany. Tickets and schedules in Albany: 426-0660. In Pittsfield: (413) 442-1307.

Chinese Dance Troupe, Chinese Community Center of the Capital Region, performs a variety of traditional Asian dances (Mongolian, Sword, Fan), accompanied by authentic music and attired in stunning ethnic dress. Presented as a way to introduce audiences to the art and culture of the Chinese provinces, the troupe's colorful dances can be seen at community and arts events throughout the region. For a schedule, contact xinhualee@hotmail.com

eba Theater and Center for Dance and Movement, 351 Hudson Ave., Albany, is the home of Maude Baum and Company, a resident professional touring dance ensemble that performs adventurous, original works in its 200-seat theatre. The center also offers classes for adults and children in ballet, jazz, modern dance, and creative movement. 465-9916. www.eba-arts.org

Ellen Sinopoli Dance Company, the Egg, Madison Ave., Albany, is a premier resident modern-dance company, reflecting a unique synergy of provocative athleticism and daring musicality under the artistic direction of choreographer Ellen Sinopoli. The company is known for its technically gifted dancers, and performs at a variety of venues from local stages to Lincoln Center. 473-1845. www.sinopolidances.org

Emma Willard Dance Company, Emma Willard School, 285 Pawling Ave., Troy, is a touring ensemble of students, ages 14 to 18, who perform choreography by students, faculty and guest artists. Dedicated to stretching the versatility, expressiveness, and technical virtuosity of each dancer, the company holds performances of ballet, jazz, ethnic, and tap dance in Kiggins Auditorium during March, April and May. 833-1340.

Hudson-Mohawk Traditional Dances, Inc., 207 Old Niskayuna Rd., Colonie, is dedicated to the enjoyment, preservation and study of traditional dance and music. The non-profit organization holds contra dances (New England-style country dance) accompanied by live string bands at the historic Buhrmaster Barn (see Museums and Historic Sites, pg. 41) from mid May to late October. It hosts five other dance series in three counties, including swing and English-country dances. A three-day Dance Flurry is held annually (see Seasonal, pg. 204). 292-0133. www.danceflurry.org

Jacob's Pillow Dance Festival, Lee, Mass., is located in the pastoral Berkshires and features acclaimed dance companies from around the globe. Established over 70 years ago, the 10-week festival attracts the world's finest choreographers and dancers in every style (Twyla Tharp and Mark Morris are regulars), as well as presenting specially commissioned new works. Performances are held in the Ted Shawn Theatre – the first stage in America designed specifically for dance – and the smaller, more informal Doris Duke Theatre. The festival also offers free outdoor preview performances. Schedules are released in March. Tickets and information: (413) 637-1322. www.jacobspillow.org

Kaatsbaan International Dance Center, Tivoli, is the dream-in-progress of Gregory Cary, Bentley Roton, Kevin McKenzie and Martine Van Hammell. Kaatsbaan, which means "playing field" in Dutch, is located on a former horse farm in a picturesque Catskills village. The Studio Complex is a distinctive building with three studios, one of which serves as a 160-seat theater. Look for the opening of the historic Music Barn, which will house a visitor center and a 500-seat performance theater. In addition to its mission of promoting and preserving professional dance, the center holds seasonal gala performances featuring the best dance companies from around the world, from the Eifman Ballet of St. Petersburg to Flamenco Vivo Carlota Santana. (845) 757-5106.

New York City Ballet, Saratoga Performing Arts Center, is in residence for the month of July, and presents a varied program ranging from audience favorites to world premiers. Among the foremost modern dance companies in America, the ballet is famous for its discipline and spectacular principal dancers. Most of the repertoire is by the troupe's founder, the late George Balanchine, augmented by newer choreography by Peter Martins, Jerome Robbins and Christopher Wheeldon. Schedules are released in February. SPAC box office: 587-3330.

ART

Galleries

Albany Center Galleries, Albany Public Library (second floor), 161 Washington Ave., Albany, exhibits serious contemporary art in all media by artists of the greater Capital Region. Founded by Les Urbach in 1977, this exceptionally curated, non-profit gallery is also an epicenter for area artists and patrons. Memberships and exhibit schedule available. Open Tues-Thurs., noon-7pm, Fri-Sat., noon-5pm. Free. 462-4775. www.albanycentergalleries.org

Albany International Airport Gallery, (third floor), Albany-Shaker Rd., Albany, is a large, light-filled and glass-divided space that overlooks the airport's observation area. Innovative exhibits designed to "connect with the community" focus on regional contemporary art, in addition to co-displays with area museums, and traveling national exhibits of regional interest. Important large-scale sculptural works are displayed in various locations throughout the terminal, as are changing display cases. Departures, the museum shop, is located on the second floor and sells the work of regional artists and selections from local museums. Open daily 7am-7pm. Free. 242-2243.

Changing Spaces Gallery, 306 Hudson Ave., Albany, is a small but adventurous space, and a good site for viewing emerging local talent. It also presents regional independent films and poetry readings. Schedules available. Open Thurs-Sat. Free. 433-1537.

College of Saint Rose Art Gallery, 324 State St., Albany, exhibits 20th- and 21st-century art from local, regional, and national artists. Open Mon-Thurs. 10am-4:30pm, and 6pm-8pm; Fri. 10am-4:30pm, Sun. noon-4pm. Free. 485-3900.

Dietle Gallery at Emma Willard School, 285 Pawling Ave., Troy, hosts exhibits of visual art by regional artists from Sept. to June, and holds an annual invitational exhibit of senior-student artworks. Open daily 9am-5pm, closed school holidays. Free. 274-4440.

Empire State Plaza Art Collection, between State St. and Madison Ave., Albany, is the finest assemblage of American modern art in existence outside of a museum. The public collection includes 92 paintings and sculptures by some of the most important artists of the 20th century, strategically placed throughout the Plaza's state-agency buildings, underground concourse, and platform (see Points of Interest, pg. 10). Mostly 1960's and 70's work of the avant-garde New York School, each piece is annotated for both casual visitors and serious art lovers. Masterpieces by Jackson Pollock, Robert Motherwell, and Clyfford Still are showcased in the Corning Tower Gallery. Inside the concourse is artwork by Ellsworth Kelly, Al Held, and Isamu Noguchi. Outside on the platform are monumental sculptures by George Rickey, Claes Oldenburg, and Alexander Calder, whose popular stabile, "Triangles and Arches" rises out of a reflecting pool. The concourse and platform are open 6am-11pm. Corning Tower is open 10am-2:30pm. Free. A free pamphlet, "The Empire State Collection," with directions and parking information, is available at the Office of General Services, Rm. 130 in the concourse, and by calling 473-0559 or 1-877-659-4377. For guided tours, call 473-7521. www.ogs.state.ny.us/plaza

Gallery 100, 445 Broadway (2nd floor, Suite A), Saratoga Springs, opened in winter of 2001 in a former beauty salon. A spacious retail and fine-arts gallery dedicated to regional artists, it specializes in paintings, as well as prints, photography, sculpture, and ceramics. Open Weds-Sun. Free. 580-0818. www.gallery100.net.

New York Folklore Society Gallery, 133 Jay St., Schenectady, features folk art and other traditional handmade arts from around the state, including Amish and Iroquois crafts. The gallery presents unique artistry demonstrations on scheduled Saturdays. Open Mon-Fri., 9am-5pm. Free. 346-7008.

Print Club of Albany was founded in 1933 to promote appreciation for fine-art prints. The club sponsors changing print exhibits, along with guest lectures and demonstrations. A new gallery for displaying exhibits from its permanent collection of important 20th-century prints is in the planning stage; until then, prints can be viewed at the online gallery. 432-9514. www.pcaprint.com

Sage Colleges Opalka Gallery, 140 New Scotland Ave., Albany, constructed in 2002, is a 7,400-square-foot, $2.8 million gallery with high-tech capabilities. This structure encloses a surprisingly lofty space, which serves as a "gateway" to the campus. The Opalka exhibits national and international contemporary art, including installation and performance art, in addition to student and faculty shows. It also contains a 75-seat lecture center. Open daily except for school vacations. Free. 292-1778.

Tang Teaching Museum and Art Gallery, Skidmore College, 815 North Broadway, Saratoga, opened in October, 2000 – the first new museum in the Capital Region in over a century, and the first-ever art museum in Saratoga. The Tang is housed in a dynamic, conceptual building of split-face block, metal and concrete textures by architect Antoine Predock. Two dramatic gallery spaces exhibit contemporary, visual, and interdisciplinary art, including large-scale installations. Open Tues-Sun., 11am-5pm. Free. 580-8080. www.skidmore.edu/tang

Union College Mandeville Gallery, Nott Memorial, Schenectady, is dedicated to exploring the links between science and the arts. It exhibits contemporary and historical artworks, permanent treasures (including Audubon prints and Olivier models), changing displays from the Union collection, and traveling exhibits from the Smithsonian and other national museums. The gallery is located on the second floor of the fantastical Nott Memorial, a landmark work of architectural art. Open daily. Free. 388-6004. www.union.edu.links/gallery

University Museum Gallery, University at Albany Art Building, 1400 Washington Ave., is a soaring space exhibiting contemporary art in all media (including performance art) by national and international artists, as well as graduate and faculty shows. Open Weds-Fri., 10am-5pm, Sat-Sun., noon-4pm. Closed school vacations. Free. 442-4035. www.albany.edu/museum

The following venues provide exhibition space for artists

Congregation Beth Israel Center, 2195 Eastern Pkwy., Schenectady 377-3700
Justin's, 301 Lark St., Albany 436-7008
Nisk-Art Gallery, 1626 Balltown Rd., Niskayuna 382-2511
Rensselaer Newman Foundation Chapel
    and Cultural Center, RPI, Troy 274-7793
Saratoga Shoe Depot, 138 Broadway, Saratoga Springs 584-1142
Spectrum 8 Theatres, 290 Delaware Ave, Albany 449-8995
ZuZu's Wonderful Life, 299 Hamilton St., Albany 426-1269

Outdoor art events are a common occurrence during summer. These festival-like arts gatherings feature juried art shows and regional art exhibits and sales, as well as food booths, live entertainment, and kid's activities. Artists are often on hand to discuss their work with festival goers.

Art on Lark, Lark St., Albany, June 434-3861
Art in the Park, Congress Park, Saratoga Springs, July 584-4132
Ballston Spa Art Walk, village of Ballston Spa, April 226-0898
Hudson-Mohawk Regional, changing locations, July-Aug. 462-4775
Rensselaerville Art Walk, Main St., Rensselaerville, July 797-3449
Riverfront Arts Fest, River St., Troy, June 273-0552

Many exceptional art galleries are within easy traveling distance of the Capital Region. The following galleries are described in the chapter Not Far Away.

LITERARY

New York State Writers Institute Visiting Writers Series, University at Albany, 135 Western Ave., presents American and international authors, poets and playwrights for readings and discussions. Founded by Pulitzer Prize-winning Albany novelist William Kennedy, and inaugurated in 1984 by Nobel Prize-winner Saul Bellow, the spring and fall series bring 30 to 35 of the greatest writers in the world to the intimacy of UAlbany's Page and Recital Halls. Norman Mailer, Seamus Heaney, Russell Banks, and William Styron are just a few of the literary lights who've shared their work and insight with local audiences. Free. 442-5620. www.edu/writers-inst/

Rensselaer Newman Chapel & Cultural Center, Burdett Ave., Troy, presents regularly scheduled readings from local and national authors of literature, poetry, and inspirational nonfiction. 274-7793. www.rpi.edu

Summer Writers Institute Series, 815 North Broadway, Saratoga Springs, brings leading literary lights such as Joyce Carol Oates, Robert Pinsky and Mary Gordon to the Skidmore College campus every July. 442-5620.

Many local bookstores present readings and signings by authors. The Book House at Stuyvesant Plaza in Albany (489-4761), and the Open Door Book Store in Schenectady (346-2719) hold these events regularly.

FILM

Film Festivals

Empire State Film Festival, the Egg at the Empire State Plaza, Albany, is an annual, 8-day festival of independent films from across New York State. Screened pre-release, usually in January, it's unlikely you'll see these dramas, documentaries, animated, and short films at the multiplex – unless one of them becomes a breakout hit. Presented by the Media Art Coalition, the festival invites applications from filmmakers, sponsors and supporting members. Schedule and ticket information: (212) 802-4679. www.empirefilm.com

FilmColumbia, Crandell Theater, Main St., Chatham, is a high-caliber festival of films from the Hudson Valley region, held over a weekend in October. The screenings of independent films take place at the Crandell Theater and other downtown venues, and the involvement of writer-producer James Schamus – whose *Crouching Tiger, Hidden Dragon* was previewed at the festival before it became an international smash hit – is one indication of the excellence of the line-up. The festival also offers opportunities for audience members to meet the filmmakers. Schedule and ticket information: 766-5892. www.filmcolumbia.com

New York State Writers Institute Film Series, University at Albany, 135 Western Ave., is a weekly screening of domestic and international films of distinction. The biannual series (spring and fall) ranges from silent films to classics to recent independent films, including rare films obtained from archives and private collections. Screenings are usually at 7:30pm at Page Hall, and presentations are sometimes followed by talks from the filmmakers or readings by the screenwriters. Each series includes a one-week film festival exploring the cinema of a foreign country or the career of a notable director. Free. 442-5620. www.edu/writers-inst/

Movie Theaters

Off-Broadway Theater & Grille, 86 Congress St., Saratoga Springs, offers table and booth seating in three theatres. Dinner-and-a-movie combo prices are available. 587-3456.

Regal multiplex theaters are located in almost every shopping mall in the region and feature stadium seating. Patrons should keep in mind that Regal's admittance policy does not allow backpacks, shopping bags or large purses. Captioned screenings are held on a regular basis. 456-5678.

Scotia Cinema, 117 Mohawk Ave., Scotia, has been a neighborhood favorite since the 1930s, and its original balcony is still in use. The newly modernized theater screens second-run movies at bargain prices ($2-$4). 346-5055.

Spectrum 8 Theatres, 290 Delaware Ave., is a locally owned multiplex that mixes major-studio releases with independent, documentary, and foreign films. In addition to real buttered popcorn, the concession stand offers gourmet desserts and coffees and teas. The lobby displays local art exhibits. A monthly schedule is available. Tuesday discounts. 449-8995. www.spectrum8.com

In addition to movie theaters, film buffs can find a variety of screenings at the following venues:

Crandall Public Library, 251 Glen St., Glens Falls, screens award-winning foreign and independent films on a weekly basis. Free. 792-6508. www.crandalllibrary.org

Outdoor Movie Nights are occasionally held on summer evenings in Central Park in Schenectady. Free. 382-7890.

Proctor's, 432 State St., Schenectady, screens second-run and classic films on one of the last full-size screens left in the Northeast. Balcony seating and old-fashioned prices at the concession stand add to its Golden Age of Hollywood ambience. Virtuoso organists provide the scores for silent-screen classics by performing on "Goldie the Mighty Wurlitzer Organ," and usually there's an organ prelude for the 7:30 screening on Mondays. Tickets: $2, balcony seats $3. Movie hotline: 382-3231 x 68.

Saratoga Film Forum, the Arts Center, 320 Broadway, Saratoga Springs, screens classic movies and recent-release independent films on a regular basis. $6. 584-FILM.

Time & Space Limited, 434 Columbia St., Hudson, presents screenings of documentaries and classic movies on a regular basis. T&SL is often the only venue in the region to show critically acclaimed but limited-release foreign and political films. $3.50. Cinema Lux is T&SL's monthly curated film-and-filmmaker exhibition, $10. Schedules available. 822-8448.

Albany Pump Station, Albany

Photography by: Gary Gold

RESTAURANTS AND EATERIES

One of the more enjoyable adventures in life is exploring new restaurants. Visitors (and residents) looking to be surprised will find the region's dining scene to be as creative and diverse as that in any major city. Among the area's hundreds of eateries are several upscale establishments that are esteemed far beyond the area, Chez Sophie, Yono's, and Nicole's Bistro among them. Also waiting to be discovered are open-pit Florida barbecue (Everglades), authentic Southern-fried chicken (Hattie's), a patisserie seemingly airlifted from the Left Bank (Mrs. London's) and dozens of spots with scenic outdoor dining. The following entries – all of which received recommendations from several sources – represent only a smattering of the good eating to be found.

Due to the frequency of changes in hours and operations, it's advisable to call ahead. The chapter is organized in the following categories:

AMERICAN

Albany Pump Station
19 Quackenbush Square, Albany, 447-9000
Stylish microbrewery and restaurant in a lofty building – the old pump station – with a fireplace. The extensive menu ranges from meatloaf to calamari, with salads, sandwiches, pasta, and interesting veggie dishes. A changing variety of excellent house-brewed beers on tap, including an award-winning brown beer. Located behind the Visitor Center. Lunch and dinner daily.

Arlington House
3532 Rte. 43, West Sand Lake, 674-1880
Formerly the Arlington Hotel, this atmospheric building now serves American-fusion cuisine with an emphasis on seafood and seasonal ingredients. Standouts include duck in bing-cherry demi glace, grilled salmon in wasabi vinaigrette, and lamb osso buco. Homemade desserts, personable service. Dinner: Tues-Sat.

Barnsider
480 Sand Creek Rd., Colonie, 869-2448
A local favorite for steaks and seafood since 1967, this large and efficient eatery has a rustic, "barnboard" ambience that includes a fireplace and an open kitchen. The menu focuses on crowd-pleasing dishes such as chicken teriyaki, pork chops, shrimp scampi, fresh baked fish, and aged, handcut beef-from peppercorn steak to filet béarnaise. The Barnsider is famed for its salad bar and seasonal dining deck. Children's menu available. Dinner daily.

Bear's Steakhouse
Rte. 7, Duanesburg, 895-2509
This authentic steakhouse has been serving the very best beef – from prime rib to Chateaubriand – for over 40 years. Original owners Papa Bear and Mama Bear still preside over the unpretentious dining room. Dinner: Weds-Sat. Advance reservations required.

Century House
997 Rte. 9, Latham, 785-0834
American dining in a Federal-style farmhouse with a main dining room, a grand ballroom, three intimate rooms, and a tavern. The main room serves a formal menu (veal Oscar, rack of lamb, filet mignon) and a light menu (stuffed portabella mushrooms). Lunch: Mon-Fri. Dinner: daily.

Daisy Baker's
33 Second St., Troy, 266-9200
Eclectic gourmet fare focused on seafood, with pasta and vegetarian dishes. The menu changes often, but you can't go wrong by starting with the classic oysters Rockefeller and finishing with bourbon-pecan pie. The dining room is located in an 1892 brownstone redolent of Old Troy, with 1920s chandeliers, wooden booths, and a handsome bar. Lunch: Mon-Fri. Dinner: daily.

Dorato's
2050 Western Ave. (Star Plaza), Guilderland, 456-5774
The nouvelle-style menu of seafood, veal, and beef is noted for its tournedos and filet mignon. The friendly bar serves excellent pub fare. Lunch: Mon-Fri. Dinner: daily.

Everglades BBQ and Seafood
827 Saratoga Rd. (Rte. 9), Wilton, 580-9631
Florida-style baby-back ribs, spare ribs, and smoked and slow-roasted chicken, in addition to fresh fish (shark, mahi-mahi, catfish), coconut shrimp, and fried conch and gator. And Key Lime pie, homemade Southern style. Dinner daily.

Hattie's
45 Phila St., Saratoga Springs, 584-4790
Authentic Southern-regional cuisine since 1938. Very popular for its jambalaya, coconut shrimp, crab cakes, and legendary fried chicken with biscuits. Hattie's signature sweet-potato pie and banana pudding were featured on The Food Network. Family-style ambience, garden-patio dining in season. Dinner: Weds-Sun.

Jack's Oyster House
42 State St., Albany, 465-8854
Established in 1913 and operated by the founder's grandchildren, this Old Albany landmark is famed for its clubby ambience. Traditional favorites are augmented by a menu of contemporary interpretations from the master chef, with an emphasis on seafood. Signature items include clams casino, calves' liver, steak Diane, and a variety of oyster dishes. Lunch and dinner daily (expect crowds on holidays).

Justin's
301 Lark St., Albany, 436-7008
Adventurous, seasonal menus with strong ethnic accents, including a jerk chicken by which all others are judged. Intimate, downtown ambience with live jazz and a late-night café menu. Lunch: Mon-Sat. Dinner: daily.

Kirker's Steak and Seafood
959 Loudon Rd., Latham, 785-3653
Lots of steaks (porterhouse, Black Angus sirloin, superior prime rib) plus seafood and chicken. A mainstay for local carnivores for 50 years. Lunch: Mon-Fri. Dinner: daily.

Lake Ridge
35 Burlington Ave., Round Lake, 899-6000
Fine dining with seasonal menus that offer a new twist on old favorites: One signature dish is pork chop with crushed pecans and cherry sauce. Other menu regulars include duck breast veal roulade, Black Angus sirloin, and seafood. Beer and wine. Located in the charmingly Victoriana village of Round Lake. Lunch and dinner: Mon-Sat.

Lillian's
408 Broadway, Saratoga Springs, 587-7766
Steak and seafood (baked stuffed shrimp and scallops au gratin are specialties) with pasta and a light menu featuring a variety of stir-frys. Excellent specials, casual ambience. Lunch and dinner daily.

The Lodge
1 Nelson Ave., Saratoga Springs, 584-4030
This seasonal establishment, located in the former "hunting lodge" of Harry Payne Whitney, (a 1915 mansion in the Arts and Crafts fashion), promises to offer the ultimate dining experience. The dining room retains its historic, Old-Saratoga style, and the bar, converted from the "great hall" is stunning. The eclectic, American-fusion menu changes nightly; past favorites include foie gras in classical French and Asian preparations, butter-poached lobster tail and claws with tarragon frappe, and grilled venison chop in wild black-currant glaze. The Lodge is open during the six weeks of the Saratoga Race Track season (late July-Aug.) Dinner daily. Reservations required.

Olde Bryan Inn
123 Maple Ave., Saratoga Springs, 587-2990
Located in an 1825 stone house with a colonial ambience that includes fireplaces and a handsome tavern. Very popular for its large menu of American-rustic cuisine, extensive list of American wines, and moderate prices. Daily specials plus light items and salads and sandwiches. Garden dining in season. Lunch and dinner daily.

Old 499 House
499 Second Ave., North Troy, 238-0499
Historic Dutch building and ambience, featuring a classic steakhouse menu
with great ribs and seafood. Gracious service, weeknight early-bird menu.
Dinner: Tues-Sun.

Olde Kristel's Inn
654 Saratoga Rd., Burnt Hills, 399-7398
Old-fashioned favorites (chicken cordon bleu, meatloaf, pot roast, corn chowder)
from a new-cuisine chef. Country ambience with a large fireplace and views of
the countryside and nearby waterfall. Lunch: Mon-Sat. Dinner: daily.

Olde Shaker Inn
1171 Troy-Schenectady Rd., Latham, 783-6460
Atmospheric Shaker farmhouse serving an inventive, American-fusion menu
(Vermont duck with maple-sherry glaze, escargot with black-bean ragout).
Lunch: Mon-Sat. Dinner: daily.

Palmer House Café
1462 Main St., Rensselaerville, 797-3449
Located in a historic-village setting, this 1848 building maintains its old country
décor and original hand-painted murals. The café serves New-American cuisine
with a strong ethnic cachet (Brazilian seafood stew, Ropa Vieja, grilled swordfish
with nero risotto) all made from local and organic ingredients. Palmer House is
also known for its made-from-scratch desserts, including elegant pastries and a
variety of strudels. Moderately priced wine list, tavern room with pub menu.
Dinner: Weds-Sun. Sunday brunch.

River Street Café
429 River St., Troy, 273-2740
Attractively restored building on a historic street with views of the Hudson
River. The café's New-American menu is noted for its excellent sauces.
Dinner: Tues-Sat.

Scrimshaw at the Desmond
660 Albany-Shaker Rd., Albany, 869-8100
Colonial Williamsburg décor and a menu especially noted for steaks and
seafood (cedar-planked salmon, smoked sea bass, filet mignon). The extensive
(and pricey) wine cellar is the recipient of *Wine Spectator's* Award of Excellence.
Expect crowds during the holidays. Lunch: Mon-Fri. Dinner: Mon-Sat.

Van Dyke Restaurant & Brewery
237 Union St., Schenectady, 381-1111
Located in the historic Stockade neighborhood, this enlarged, 1820s house has several attractive dining rooms and a handsome bar serving delectable beers brewed on the premises. The extensive menu ranges from herb-roasted prime rib to saffron seafood paella, plus homemade ice cream. Food is also served in the upstairs jazz club. Late-night menu. Lunch and dinner: Tues-Sat.

Wishing Well
744 Saratoga Rd. (Rte. 9), Wilton, 584-7640
In business in a white clapboard house since 1936. The dining room has beamed ceilings and a fireplace, and serves hearty American cuisine with a French accent (triple-thick lamb chops, Long Island duck, Maryland soft-shell crabs). Ample, varied wine list, and a specially priced Sunday dinner menu (noon-4pm). Dinner: Tues-Sun.

ASIAN

Chinese

Dumpling House
120 Everett Rd., Albany, 458-7044
Extensive menu of dumplings, steamed or fried and available in combo platters. Chinese regional entrees including sa-chia pork, tangerine chicken, and squid in black-bean sauce. Ordinary décor, extraordinary food. Lunch and dinner daily.

Golden Dragon
2035 State St., Schenectady, 374-5773
Chinese regional dishes with American specials and a buffet. Lunch and dinner daily.

Ichiban
338 Central Ave., Albany, 432-0358
Authentic Chinese and Japanese cuisine, special combo platters, sushi bar and sushi lunch specials – an all-round excellent value. The small but appealing dining room serves beer, wine and sake. Lunch and dinner daily.

Pearl of the Orient
471 Albany-Shaker Rd., Loudonville, 459-0903
Mix of different Chinese regional styles (Hunan, Cantonese, Szechwan). Buffet lunch is available during the week, and a dinner buffet is offered on weekends. Good food, good value. Lunch and dinner daily.

Plum Blossom
685 Hoosick Rd., Troy, 272-0036
Beautiful dining room serving excellent Cantonese and Hong Kong dishes, plus Asian-American items. Lunch and dinner daily.

Tai Pan
Rte. 9, Half Moon, 383-8581
Exceptional pan-Asian cuisine with an extensive selection of Thai and Chinese dishes. Lunch and dinner daily, dim-sum brunch Sat-Sun.

Japanese

Hiro's
1933 Central Ave., Colonie, 456-1180
Japanese cuisine including sushi, sukiyaki and tempura, with skillful and entertaining hibachi table service. Dinner: Tues-Sun.

Mari's Japanese Cuisine
803 Saratoga Rd., Burnt Hills, 384-0924
Popular for its sushi bar, tempura, teriyaki and sukiuyaki; very busy on weekends. Lunch: Tues-Sat. Dinner: Tues-Sun.

Saso's Noodle House
218 Central Ave., Albany, 436-7789
Authentic Japanese cuisine with an extensive menu including noodles and soups. Artfully prepared sushi and sashimi, moderate prices, intimate ambience. Combo-box lunches to go. Lunch and dinner: Tues-Sat.

Yoshi Sushi
640 Loudon Rd., Latham, 783-6100
Good sushi for eat in or take-out, plus sushi ingredients and utensils. Lunch and dinner: Mon-Sat.

Vietnamese

My Linh
272 Delaware Ave., Albany, 465-8899
Vietnamese fine dining. Standouts include shrimp summer rolls, crispy pan-fried duck, and crepes in spicy curry sauce. Dinner: Tues-Sun.

Van's Vietnamese
137 Madison Ave., Albany, 436-1868
Classic, French-influenced Vietnamese cuisine in a lavender-painted, townhouse dining room. Generous portions, exceptional spring rolls, tofu steak, and spicy seafood dishes. Convenient to the Pepsi Arena. Lunch: Tues-Fri. Dinner: Tues-Sun.

CAFES AND BISTROS

Alibi's
1100 Madison Ave., Albany, 489-5972
Asian-American fusion menu with delectable spring rolls, crab puffs, and California potstickers. Extensive sushi menu and martini menu. Stylish ambience with tiki chairs and 1940s music (the dining area can be loud). Dinner: Mon-Sun.

Debbie's Kitchen
456 Madison Ave., Albany, 463-3829
Terrific gourmet sandwiches, salads and daily specials, and a creative selection of desserts. A good value. Mostly take-out, but there are four tables inside, and a couple more on the sidewalk during mild weather. Open Mon-Sat.

Four Corners Luncheonette
2 Grove St., Delmar, 439-0172
Old-fashioned eatery with booths and counter seats. Home-style breakfast and lunch, with a more ambitious dinner menu of old-time favorites (country-fried steak to eggplant parm). Breakfast and lunch: Mon-Sat. Dinner: Tues-Fri.

Ginger Man
234 Western Ave., Albany, 463-5963
The area's largest selection of wine by the glass. Light menu and full dinner specials, wine-tasting events. Sidewalk dining in season. Lunch and dinner daily.

Londonderry Café
Stuyvesant Plaza, 1475 Western Ave., Albany, 489-4288
Upscale bistro serving a fine-dining menu of pasta, chicken, and seafood dishes made from fresh ingredients. Wine and beer. The café is especially popular for its sidewalk dining in mild weather. Lunch and dinner: Mon-Sat. Sunday brunch.

Miss Albany Diner
893 Broadway, Menands, 465-9148
Authentic 1930s ambience (it was filmed as a location for Ironweed) with award-winning breakfasts (try the Irish-whiskey toast or homemade hash), creative lunch dishes, homemade pies, and a popular "poor man's tiramisu." Breakfast and lunch daily.

Mrs. London's Café
464 Broadway, Saratoga Springs, 581-1834
This haute patisserie is considered a regional treasure for its vintage ambience and Parisian-bistro menu. The café features made-from-scratch soups, breads (baguettes to panini), brioche, quiche, croques, and a wide selection of sandwiches, elegant pastries and decadent desserts. Beverages include gourmet coffees, teas, and hot chocolate. Open Tues-Sun.

Oliver's Café
181 Freeman's Bridge Rd., Glenville, 393-3060
Located close to the Schenectady County Airport, Oliver's is reputed far and wide for its fresh-beef burgers, fixin's, and hand-cut fries. Try the homemade soups and pies, too. Breakfast and lunch daily (cash only).

Peaches Café
Stuyvesant Plaza, 1475 Western Ave., Albany, 482-3677
Cozy, attractive café serving quiches, crepes, omelets, pasta, soup and sandwiches, plus luscious ice-cream desserts. Breakfast (including Belgium waffles) is served all day. Breakfast, lunch and dinner daily.

Ravenous
21 Phila St., Saratoga Springs, 581-0560
A European-style crepery featuring dinner crepes, vegetarian crepes, and dessert crepes, along with irresistible *pommes frites*, served in a paper cone with a choice of dipping sauces. Inexpensive, quick and delicious. Beverages include imported beer, wine, herbal teas, and espresso. Open Tues-Sat. Sunday brunch.

Scallions
404 Broadway, Saratoga Springs, 584-0192
This chic, storefront café with floral wallpaper serves healthy, homemade food with flair, including gourmet sandwiches and salads (one popular item is the farmer's market salad with organic greens, grilled eggplant, artichoke hearts, peppers, and goat-cheese croutons). Excellent dinner specials and desserts. Wine and beer. Open Mon-Sat.

Victory Café
10 Sheridan Ave., Albany, 463-9113
Downtown ambience, pub menu, daily specials, full bar. A short walk from Capital Repertory Theater and the Palace Theater. Open Mon-Sat.

Yellow Rock Café
Indian Ladder Farms, 342 Altamont Rd., Altamont, 765-2956
Farm-fresh soups and salads, gourmet sandwiches, hearty specials, and fresh-baked desserts and breads, all made from local ingredients. Scenic property with apple orchards and walking trails. Lunch: Weds-Sun. Closed Jan. and Feb.

CONTINENTAL

Auberge Suisse
1903 New Scotland Rd. (Rte. 5), Slingerlands, 439-3800
Regional Swiss-French cuisine featuring classics from coq au vin to beef Wellington. Intimate ambience, prix-fixe menu. Dinner: Tues-Sun.

Café Capriccio
49 Grand St., Albany, 465-0439
This renowned café is located in the basement of old townhouse and has an intimate dining room and an atmospheric bar. Capriccio serves unique, gourmet Italian-Mediterranean cuisine prepared from local and organic ingredients; signature dishes include Catalonian fish stew, calamari neri, and risotto with grilled quail. Attentive service and a well-selected wine list add to the café's repute, as does longtime owner Jim Rua, a local celebrity for his cookbooks and cooking seminars. Dinner daily.

Chez Sophie Bistro
2853 Rte. 9, Malta (Exit 13S off of I-87), 583-3538
Second-generation, family-owned French bistro in a vintage, stainless-steel diner. Exquisite, seasonal cuisine (quail in truffle butter, escargot de bourgogne, Canadian bison) applauded by the *New York Times*. The wine list features over 300 selections. Expensive, but complete prix-fixe dinners for $25 are available Tues-Thurs. Dinner: Tues-Sat.

Eartha's
60 Court St., Saratoga Springs, 583-0602
Intimate bistro with grille and mesquite menus specializing in fresh fish and prime meats, with excellent veal chops and rack of lamb. Consider the warm cremini-mushroom salad to start, and the chocolate nebula to finish. Dinner: Tues-Sat.

43 Phila Bistro
43 Phila St., Saratoga Springs, 584-2720
This stylish, peach-colored bistro serves inventive cuisine (Peking Duck with Asian roll, skillet-fried fillets of beef with smoked jack-cheese polanta) that has been featured in *Bon Appetit*. Delectable desserts, and an extensive, varied wine menu. Dinner daily.

George Mann Tory Tavern
Rtes. 30 and 443, Schoharie, 295-7128
Rustic-American cuisine in an authentic, Federal-era building with copper chandeliers and wait staff in Colonial garb. Dinner: Weds-Sun.

Georgian Room at the Gideon Putnam Hotel
Saratoga Spa Park, Rte. 9, 584-3000
The hotel's beautiful, rose-colored dining room is decorated with its original hand-painted murals from the 1930s – the Georgian Room really is Georgian in ambience, and an ideal setting for fine dining in the "timeless tradition." The Sunday brunch is legendary. Breakfast and lunch: Mon-Sat. Dinner daily (jacket required).

Glen Sanders Mansion Inn, see Lodging, pg. 228.

La Perla at the Gregory House
Rte. 43, Averill Park, 674-3774
Historic homestead with a country-villa ambience, three candlelit dining rooms, and an intimate pub. Italian-continental menu with wild-game dishes and lots of seafood: one standout is the smoked seafood trio. Interesting, Italian-oriented wine list. Lunch: Mon., Weds., Fri. Dinner: Weds-Mon.

La Serre
14 Green St., Albany, 463-6056
French-influenced cuisine from Black Angus steaks to Australian rack of lamb, plus nightly seafood specials. Greenhouse dining room, outdoor terrace in season. Lunch and dinner: Mon-Sat.

Longfellows Inn & Restaurant
500 Union St., Saratoga Springs, 587-0108
Located in a stylishly converted, 1915 dairy barn, the inn's restaurant serves seasonal menus of French-influenced, haute-American cuisine (sesame-dusted yellow-fin tuna, rack of lamb in port-wine sauce), plus mesquite items (gorgonzola-crusted NY strip steak), pasta dishes (gnocchi with arugula and artichoke hearts), and homemade desserts. Tavern and wine cellar. Dinner daily.

Mansion Hill Inn
115 Philip St., Albany, 465-2038
Intimate, country-inn ambience serving four-star American-continental cuisine, with award-winning adaptations of traditional favorites such as filet mignon with shallot demi-glace. Located in the old South End neighborhood, convenient to the Pepsi Arena. Dinner: Mon-Sat.

McGuire's
353 State St., Albany, 463-2100
Located in a stylishly renovated, 1930s barroom with high-backed booths and a handsome hotel bar, this classic city grill offers clubby entrees (hand-cut Delmonico steak in Madeira demi-glace, double-thick pork chops), along with innovative, pan-Pacific dishes such as ostrich potstickers, new Zealand venison, and Chilean sea bass in ginger-lime butter sauce. Desserts are sumptuous, and the far-ranging wine list offers good values and a large selection by the glass. For those who like to see and be seen, tables in back face the open kitchen on one side, and a streetside window on the other. Dinner: Mon-Sat. Valet parking available.

Nicole's Bistro at Quackenbush Square
351 Broadway, Albany, 465-1111
Inhabiting the historic Quackenbush House with atmospheric, Dutch-Colonial décor, Nicole's has become somewhat historic itself, serving sublime, French-influenced traditional and contemporary cuisine (duck in blueberry glaze, frogs-legs provencal, seafood cassoulet with crab claws). Enchanting garden dining in season. Convenient to the Palace Theater and Capital Repertory Theatre. Lunch: Mon-Fri. Dinner: Mon-Sat.

Provence
Stuyvesant Plaza, 1475 Western Ave., Albany, 689-7777
Colorfully stylish French bistro with a zinc bar, serving French and Mediterranean cuisine. Standouts include saffron-infused monkfish, bouillabaisse, and sea bass with polenta. Extensive wine list. Sidewalk dining in season. Lunch: Mon-Sat. Dinner: daily.

Sperry's
30 Caroline St., Saratoga Springs, 584-9618
Established in 1930, an era reflected in its Art Deco décor, Sperry's offers an upscale-eclectic menu with an emphasis on steaks (hand-cut steak au poivre) and seafood (Maryland crabcakes, fresh grilled fish), plus seasonal items such as soft-shell crabs (summer) and rack of venison (fall). Inventive specials, homemade desserts. Enclosed, year-round patio and cocktail garden. Dinner daily.

Springwater Bistro
139 Union Ave., Saratoga Springs, 584-6440
Located in a restored Victorian house on scenic Union Avenue, with a casual-chic dining room and bar. The upscale bistro menu blends classical French cooking with modern European cuisine (spit-roasted rabbit, braised lamb shank with polenta, veal-chop osso buco), based on fresh ingredients from local farms. The bar has a fireplace and serves tapas, appetizers and hors d'oeuvres. Dinner: Weds-Sun.

Stephanie's on the Park
462 Madison Ave., Albany, 449-2492
Creative, international cuisine (pork Jakarta, veal Florentine, shrimp curry, Bali chicken) in a romantic, townhouse dining room. Great desserts (don't miss the "chocolate bomb"), sophisticated yet personable service, a fun martini menu, and an exceptional Sunday brunch. Dinner: Tues-Sun.

Yono's
Armory Center (second floor), 64 Colvin Ave., Albany, 436-7747
Adventurous continental and Indonesian cuisine (sate campur to foie gras) from owner Yono Purnomo, a nationally recognized chef, and featuring exotic selections such as alligator haebler and ostrich Oleg. The decadent desserts are by Mrs. Purnomo. Recipient of *Wine Spectator's* Award of Excellence. Dinner: Weds-Sat.

GERMAN

Bavarian Chalet
5060 Western Turnpike (Rte. 20), Guilderland, 355-8005
A longtime favorite for its continental-influenced German cuisine and Old World charm. Wursts at their best, sauerbraten, schnitzels, superlative potato pancakes, and fresh seafood and game dishes. Microbrew beers on tap. Dinner: Weds-Sun.

Spa Brauhaus
East High St., Ballston Spa, 885-4311
A longtime regional favorite with an extensive German menu, plus steaks and seafood. Standouts include sauerbraten, wiener schnitzel, roulade of beef, and the homemade spetzel. Excellent veal butchered on the premises, plus homemade Black Forest cake and apple strudel. Dinner daily.

GREEK

The Chariot
5180 Western Turnpike, Guilderland, 356-1116
Consistently delicious traditional Greek cuisine. Dinner: Tues-Sun.

Taste of Greece
193 Lark St., Albany, 426-9000
This cheerful, sky-blue café serves inexpensive, well-seasoned Greek dishes ranging from shishkebab to grilled octopus, with saganaki as the house specialty. Many vegetarian selections, plus Greek beverages and wine. Open Mon-Sat.

INDIAN

Aashiana
118 Jay St., Schenectady, 370-3664.
Located in a storefront across from historic City Hall, this small café serves a Pakistani-Indian menu with many unusual items. Crowd favorites include chicken tikka Marsala and shrimp pakora. The lunch and dinner buffets are limited in selection but very inexpensive. Open Mon-Sat.

Shalimar
35 Central Ave., Albany, 434-0890, 405 Fulton St., Troy, 273-8744
Indian-Pakistani cuisine in a casual setting. Very popular for its chicken vindaloo, fresh tandoori bread and other stuffed breads, and large vegetarian selection. Open daily.

Sitar
1929 Central Ave., Colonie, 456-6670
Sizzling tandoori cuisine encompassing lamb, shrimp, chicken, and vegetarian dishes. Lunch: Mon-Fri. Dinner: daily. Sunday brunch.

ITALIAN

Bellini's
1366 New Scotland Rd., Slingerlands, 439-6022
Moderately priced, contemporary Italian restaurant serving a varied menu (from wood-fired pizzas to veal saltimbuca). Wine bar, cappuccino bar and homemade desserts, including cannoli, cheesecake, and mousse cake. Open daily.

Caffe Italia
662 Central Ave., Albany, 482-9433
Truly Old World in cuisine, ambience, and service. The menu has Calabrian
accents: two customer favorites are Roman saltimbuca and Chilean sea bass.
Dinner daily.

Carmine's
818 Central Ave., Albany, 458-8686
This stylish, Italian-influenced restaurant is the handiwork of Carmine Sprio
from the "Carmine's Table" cooking show. The chef's inventive interpretations
(pork with mango caponato, veal cacciatore with polenta crust, pistachio-encrusted
salmon) also encompass a wide selection of pastas. For starters, try the red-pepper
bisque, and for a grand finale, the fallen chocolate soufflé. Prices reflect its
celebrity ownership, and there's often a wait for reservations, but for good reasons.
(Located at the end of the strip mall behind Hollywood Video.) Lunch: Tues-Fri.
Dinner: daily.

Cavaleri's
334 Second Ave., Albany, 463-4320
Popular, inexpensive neighborhood restaurant known for its veal dishes.
Dinner: Weds-Sun.

Chianti II Ristorante
208 South Broadway, Saratoga Springs, 580-0025
Hearty Italian cuisine with a creative accent, served in a rustic dining room.
Popular dishes include seafood risotto, filet mignon in gorgonzola sauce,
the selection of carpaccios, and créme brûlée. The 250-choice wine list is the
recipient of *Wine Spectator's* Award of Excellence.

Citone's
457 Elk St., Albany, 463-6199
Very inexpensive and reliably good Italian meals, pizza, and more.
A mainstay for students, locals, and starving artists for decades. Beer and wine.
Dinner: Tues-Sun.

Cornell's Restaurant
1733 Van Vranken Ave., Schenectady, 370-3825
Homey, family-style dining. Specialties include clams casino, veal-and-lobster
francaise, stuffed steak, and homemade peanut-butter-fudge pie.
Dinner: Tues-Sun.

D'Raymond's
269 Osborne Rd., Loudonville, 459-6364
Upscale Northern-Italian cuisine, extensive menu (rigatoni with sausage in
vodka-cream sauce to shrimp Genovese, excellent antipastos), and personable
service. This second-generation, family-owned establishment has a loyal clientele;
expect a wait for prime-time seating. Lunch: Mon-Fri. Dinner: Mon-Sat.

Elda's
203 Lark St., 449-3532
Northern-Italian cuisine with continental offerings. Especially good homemade
pastas, eggplant parm, and tiramisu. Spacious, handsome dining room with
balcony seating and a lounge, plus sidewalk tables in season. Lunch: Mon-Fri.
Dinner: daily.

Elda's Trattoria
122 Fourth St., Troy, 274-3532
Italian favorites and daily specials, plus pizza, deli sandwiches and pub fare in a
candle-lit, Italian-style café. Full bar, take-out, deliveries 'til late. Open Mon-Sat.

Ferrari's
1254 Congress St., Schenectady, 382-8865
A local favorite for its friendly, family-style ambience, authentic Italian
cuisine, and generous portions. Specialties include veal in horseradish-cream
sauce, chicken in wine-and-mushroom sauce, and a variety of parmagianas.
Open Mon-Sat.

Le Caravelle
257 Washington Ave. Ext., Albany, 456-0292
The ristorante of the Italian-American Community Center knows how to do
Italian right. Lunch: Tues-Sat. Dinner: Tues-Sun.

Lombardo's
121 Madison Ave., Albany, 462-9180
This Old Albany establishment is the oldest restaurant in the city, and still retains
its original bar, wall murals, and booth seating. The extensive menu offers just
about every old-fashioned favorite (15 veal dishes alone), while the daily specials
lean toward Southern regional. A good value that packs 'em in. Lunch: Mon-Fri.
Dinner: Mon-Sat.

Lo Porto Ristorante
85 Fourth St., Troy, 273-8546
Sophisticated atmosphere, four-star Northern-Italian cuisine with Sicilian and
other regional accents (sole Veronique to scungilli fra diavolo). Filmmaker Martin
Scorsese ate here – and loved it. Dinner: Tues-Sat.

Mangi

1562 New Scotland Rd., Slingerlands, 439-5555,
Stuyvesant Plaza, 1475 Western Ave., Albany, 482-8000
Wood-fired, brick-oven gourmet pizzas, plus fresh pasta and world-cuisine
dishes. California-casual ambience. Open daily.

Milano

Newton Plaza, Rte. 9, Latham, 783-3334
This elegant bistro with cherrywood floors, aqua walls, and amphora urns
serves gourmet Northern-Italian cuisine ranging from wood-fired pizzas
to fresh-made pastas to inventive veal and seafood specialties. Extensive,
reasonably priced wine list, and homemade desserts including créme brûlée.
Lunch: Mon-Sat. Dinner: daily.

Nicole's

556 Delaware Ave., Albany, 436-4952
Northern- and Southern-Italian cuisine, with homemade pastas and great
seafood. Cozy, romantic ambience. Lunch: Tues-Fri. Dinner: Daily

Pagliacci's

44 South Pearl St., Albany, 465-1001
Northern-style menu with lots of seafood. Casual ambience, very popular for
before and after Pepsi Arena events. Seasonal rooftop dining. Lunch: Mon-Sat.
Dinner: daily.

Paolo Lombardi's

104 West Sand Lake, Rte. 150, Wynantskill, 283-0202
Outstanding Northern- and Southern-Italian cuisine; extensive menu with
specialty pastas, deluxe antipastos, and homemade tiramisu and cannolis.
Upscale ambience. Dinner: daily (Sundays from 1pm on).

Pennell's

284 Jefferson St., Saratoga Springs, 583-2423
Chef-owned and operated, this award-winning establishment has been
serving Northern- and Southern-Italian cuisine for over 80 years. Known for
its shrimp fra diavolo, lasagna, haddock francaise, and diverse nightly specials
(16-ounce Montreal steak to veal Marsala). Lively, friendly ambience, and a
bamboo outdoor patio. Dinner: Weds-Sun.

Petta's

134 Duane Ave., Schenectady, 346-7324
A family-owned local favorite for over 50 years. Italian-American menu
specializing in veal dishes. Lunch: Mon-Fri. Dinner: daily.

Romano's Family Restaurant
1475 Rte. 9, Halfmoon, 371-1650
Traditional Italian standards with an emphasis on pastas, served in a friendly,
casual ambience. Salad bar and a moderately priced wine list with a large
selection available by the glass. Open daily, 'til late on weekends.

Sam's Italian American
125 Southern Blvd., Albany, 463-3433
Longtime local favorite for its diverse Italian menu and cozy ambience.
Wine-list specials plus over a dozen wines by the glass. Children's and senior's
portions available. Lunch: Tues-Fri. Dinner: Tues-Sat.

Sorrento's
2544 Guilderland Ave., Schenectady, 377-2132
Old neighborhood mainstay, Italian-American menu, mid-week early-bird
specials, plus imported sorbets and homemade shortcakes. Lunch: Tues-Fri.
Dinner: Tues-Sun.

Spiak's
1 Archibald St., Watervliet, 273-9796
Good pizza and low prices keep this neighborhood eatery bustling.
Open Mon-Sat.

Wheat Fields
440 Broadway, Saratoga Springs, 587-0534
Known for its homemade pastas and extensive menu of usual and unusual
Italian dishes. The eggplant Pompeii is a consistent crowd pleaser. Lunch and
dinner daily.

MIDDLE EASTERN

Ali Baba
2243 15th St., Troy, 273-1170
Authentic Turkish cuisine in a very casual ambience. Popular for its kabobs and
Middle-Eastern pizza. Open Mon-Sat.

BFS's Restaurant
1736 Western Ave., Guilderland, 452-6342
Serving a diverse and healthy mix of Middle-Eastern and Mediterranean
cuisine, including Greek, Lebanese, Moroccan, Egyptian, and Italian dishes.
Beer and wine. Catering available. Open Mon-Sat (open for breakfast at 8am).

Mamoun's Mideast Café
206 Washington Ave., Albany, 434-3901
Tasty Middle-Eastern cuisine with lots of veggie dishes. Known for its delicious
Turkish coffee and baklava. Attractive, cozy atmosphere. Open daily.

SEAFOOD

Real Seafood Company
195 Wolf Rd., Colonie, 458-2068
Reliably good fresh-fish dishes (from stuffed flounder to Cajun catfish),
market-price lobster, and an excellent raw bar. Efficient service. Lunch: Mon-Sat.
Dinner: daily.

Seawave Fish Market
26 Picotte Dr., Albany, 438-1648
Fish fry to homemade crab cakes to surf-and-turf, plus a deli counter and fresh
produce. Cafeteria-style service and take-out. Open daily.

Weathervane Seafood
3368 South Broadway, Saratoga Springs, 584-8157
Inexpensive seafood including crab cakes, along with beef and chicken dishes,
and sandwiches. Raw bar. Open daily.

SPANISH/CARIBBEAN

Clayton's Caribbean & Spanish Cuisine
244 Washington Ave., Albany, 426-4360
This casual, colorful café serves spicy selections made from fresh ingredients,
including excellent goat curry and jerk chicken and shrimp, plus fried plantains,
oxtail, and beef roti. A good value made even better by the choice of large or
small portions, and a renowned lunch buffet. Open daily.

TEX/MEX

Bombers Burrito Bar
258 Lark St., Albany, 463-9636
Basement canteen with a fun, retro décor, serving a wide variety of tacos,
burritos, nachos, and French fries (from cheese to sweet potato). Vegetarian
friendly, and an ideal choice if you've got teenagers in tow. Open daily.

El Loco
465 Madison Ave., Albany, 436-1855
This excellent Tex-Mex café is a neighborhood staple that fills up early. The eclectic menu includes many vegetarian dishes (the spinach-artichoke burrito is especially recommended), and you can accompany the addictive blue-corn bread with a gourmet margarita made with blue agave. Open Tues-Sun.

El Mariachi
144 Washington Ave., Albany, 465-2568
"Homestyle Mexican cuisine" in a lively café setting. Known for its delicious, fresh-made sangria and exotic-fruit margaritas. The full bar offers 100 tequilas. Located across the street from the Albany Institute of History and Art. Open daily.

El Mariachi II
289 Hamilton St., Albany, 432-7580
This slightly more upscale offshoot serves authentic Spanish dishes, made from old family recipes from Pueblo, and including seafood and paellas. Located at the Empire Plaza end of historic Robinson Square. Open daily.

Mexican Connection
41 Nelson Ave., Saratoga Springs, 584-4666
The region's oldest Mexican restaurant has been serving authentic regional cuisine for two decades. Popular items include the burro grande, sour-cream enchiladas, spicy corn cakes, and any of the chimichangas. Daily specials, extensive microbrew and imported-beer selection, and more than 75 fine tequilas. Dinner: Weds-Sun.

VEGETARIAN

Antipasto's
1028 Rte. 146, Clifton Park, 383-1209
Vegetarian-Mediterranean menu with great use of fresh vegetables and cheeses (don't miss the Tex-Mex brie). Terrific veggie burgers and veggie pizzas, some with roasted-garlic crust; plus pastas, bruchetta, and tofu items. Colorful bistro ambience, wine bar with 50 selections by the glass. Open daily.

Shades of Green
187 Lark St., Albany, 434-1830
This cafeteria-style storefront café is almost constantly jammed with devotees of its diverse and innovative vegetarian cuisine, made from scratch from very fresh ingredients. Standouts include the hot tempeh sandwich, organic spinach fettuccine, and delicious energy shakes from the fresh-juice bar. Expect a wait at lunch, but this inexpensive mainstay is considered a "top dollar value" and orders can be called in ahead of time. Open Mon-Sat. Cash and checks only.

PUBS AND CASUAL FARE

Ale House
680 River St., Troy, 272-9740
Famed for its wings, especially the tequila-chipotle combo. The pub menu also includes real turkey dinners and homemade soups, chili, and desserts. The food is always fresh and the House is always busy. Open daily.

Broadway Joe's
86 Congress St., Saratoga Springs, 587-5637
Family-oriented ambience with sports memorabilia, a pool table, and a 25-foot, vintage shuffleboard. Large pub menu. Open daily.

Crazy Crab
50 Delaware Ave. (Van Schaick Island Marina), Cohoes, 235-4846
Colorful, roadhouse-style ambience inside a converted giant oil drum, serving pub grub and nightly specials. Live music, riverside outdoor patio in season. Open daily.

Daily Grind, (see Shopping/Coffee and Tea, pg. 140).

Deacon Blues
806 25 th St., Watervliet, 273-9888
This circa-1940s tavern and dining room serves a diverse and inexpensive menu with good beef and shrimp dishes. Open Tues-Sat.

Duncan's Dairy Bar
890 Hoosick St., Rte. 7, Brunswick, 279-9985
This old-fashioned roadside restaurant is a local institution for its home-style cooking and from-scratch bread, muffins, soups, and pies. Great coffee, too. Open daily (4am-2pm). Cash only.

Fountain Restaurant
283 New Scotland Ave., Albany, 482-9898
Full pub menu with pizza as the specialty. A good place for large groups.
Open daily.

Gateway Diner
899 Central Ave., Albany, 482-7557
An Albany mainstay for over 30 years. Good daily specials and homemade soups
and desserts. Early-bird and senior-citizen discounts. Wine, beer, and cocktails.
Open daily.

Holmes and Watson
450 Broadway, Troy, 273-8526
This English-style pub is located in a historic building with a cast-iron stove
and brick walls lined with Sherlock Holmes memorabilia. Famous for its 200
selections of beer, ale and stout, with a couple of dozen on tap. The pub menu
includes deli sandwiches, diverse specials, and steak and seafood dinners.
Outdoor dining in season. Open daily.

Kielty's Emerald Isle
41 Broad St., Waterford, 237-2829
Friendly, cheerful pub with Irish beers on tap and good fish and chips.
Open daily.

Krause's Restaurant and Grove
2 Beach Rd., Clifton Park, 371-8033
Scenic setting on the Mohawk River with outdoor picnic tables in season.
Clambakes, steaks, and pub fare. Open Weds-Sun. Closed in winter (Dec-April)
except for banquets.

Latham 76 Diner
722 New Loudon Rd. (Rte. 9), Latham, 785-3793
This expansive "dineraunt" has been a Rte. 9 waystation for decades. Full bar,
homemade pastries. Open 24 hours daily.

McGeary's
4 Clinton Square, Albany, 463-1455
Popular hangout for those who like hearty sandwiches, lots of beer, and live
music. Great wings and black-bean chili, and the dining room features an
impressive collection of political memorabilia. Close to the Palace Theater.
Open Mon-Sat.

Morette's King Steakhouse
1126 Erie Blvd., Schenectady, 370-0555
Serving kingly steak sandwiches since 1947. Beer only. Open Mon-Sat.

Orchard Tavern
68 North Manning Blvd., Albany, 482-5677
Good for families and softball teams. Burgers, pizza, dinner specials. Open daily.

Panera Bread, (see Shopping/Bakeries, pg. 138).

Parting Glass
42 Lake St., Saratoga Springs, 583-1916
Irish-pub menu known for its lamb stew and corned beef and cabbage, in addition to fried calamari, portobella platters, Black-Angus burgers, and more. Huge beer selection and an impressive single-malt scotch selection. Live Celtic music. Open daily.

Pinhead Susan's
38 North Broadway, Schenectady, 346-6431
Converted historic building with a full bar and a friendly ambience. Pub food with an emphasis on burgers: the house specialty is the "Guinness burger." Open Mon-Sat.

Plaza Grill
414 Broadway, Albany, 463-9439
Old Albany atmosphere, family owned since 1940. Full pub menu. Open Tues-Sat.

Purple Pub
2 Cohoes Rd., Watervliet, 273-9646
Popular gathering spot, extensive menu with great pizza and wings. Open Tues-Sat.

Quintessence
11 New Scotland Ave., Albany, 434-8186
Art-deco diner and bar (in a real diner car) serving salads, sandwiches, excellent teriyakis, and nightly international specials. Late-night grill menu, and a famous Sunday brunch. Live music on weekends. Open daily.

Smith's Tavern
112 Maple Ave. (Rte. 85A), Vooheesville, 765-4163
Established in 1945, this enduring regional favorite is known for its terrific pizza (distinguished by the dough and sauce). The menu also includes soups, salads and sandwiches, plus 40 beers and microbrews on tap. Cash and checks only.

Troy Pub & Brewery

417 River St., Troy, 273-2337
Located in a converted 1850s warehouse decorated with artifacts from famous Troy breweries of yesteryear, this two-story "public house" exudes a convivial ambience – especially around the bar. The microbrewery, which can be observed in operation, was awarded a gold medal by the Culinary Institute of America for its Trojan Pale Ale, one of a dozen handcrafted beers available (for takeout, too. They'll even fill a keg). The menu offers excellent pub fare plus dinners and homemade desserts. The festive riverside patio overlooks the Troy Marina. Open daily.

Vanilla Bean Baking Co., (see Shopping/Bakeries, pg. 139).

Zeeko's Charbroil

201 Continental Ave., Cohoes, 235-3940
BBQ ribs, hickory-smoked ribs, and smoked chicken. Grilled, barbecued, or slow-roasted sirloin or chicken. Philly cheese steaks and charbroiled burgers with all the fixin's. Garlic steak fries and dark-beer battered onion rings. And layered nachos grande, plus a children's menu. Open Tues-Sun.

PIZZERIAS

Cusato's

224 Quail St., Albany, 434-1068
A local favorite for two generations of family ownership. NYC-style pizza, Italian dishes-to-go, full deli, subs, and terrific fried raviolis. Takeout and delivery only. Open daily.

DeFazio's Pizzeria

266 Fourth St., Troy, 271-1111
One of the best pizzerias in the region, featuring wood-fired deluxe pizzas with fresh ingredients and delicious sauce. Open daily.

Fireside Pizzeria

1631 Eastern Parkway, Schenectady, 382-1616
Rustic ambience with a large fireplace and two floors for pizza, finger foods, and beer. Full bar. Open daily.

Gallo's

605A New Scotland Ave., Albany, 482-2248
An offshoot of Cusato's located across from St. Peter's Hospital. Pizza, Italian dishes-to-go, and deli items. Takeout and delivery only. Mon-Sat.

Lou-Bea's Pizza
376 Delaware Ave., Albany, 463-1992
A local favorite for its NYC-style pizza since 1965. Subs and Italian meals-to-go, limited eat-in space. Open daily.

Sovrano's
63 North Lake Ave., Albany, 465-0961
A local favorite for its Sicilian-style pizza and Italian meals. Deli counter. Takeout and delivery only. Open daily.

Spinner's Pizza and Subs
14 Picotte Dr., Albany, 482-7311
Good pizza and wings, plus sandwiches, munchies, and meals-to-go. Cafeteria-style service. Open daily.

DELIS

Bagel Bite
544 Delaware Ave., Albany, 449-1214
Bagels, omelets, sandwiches, and more, including a popular Middle-Eastern dinner menu. Wine and beer. Breakfast and lunch: Tues-Sun. Dinner: Thurs-Sun.

Center Stage Deli
2678 Hamburg St., Rotterdam, 355-7791
Sandwiches, gourmet subs, and good daily specials. Good soups, meatloaf, and puddings. Open Mon-Sat.

Deli Mill
33 Maiden Lane, Albany, 449-8340
Hot open sandwiches, daily deli special, meatloaf, and mac-and-cheese. Lunch: Mon-Fri.

Gershon's Deli & Caterers
1600 Union St., Schenectady, 393-0617
A real NYC-style deli known for its smoked whitefish, beef tongue, onion and garlic bagels, fresh lox, chopped liver, overstuffed sandwiches, and cheesecake direct from the Carnegie Deli. A local favorite since 1953. Open Mon-Fri.

Harvest Moon
2205 15th St., Troy, 271-8161
Inventive, inexpensive sandwiches (eggplant and gruyere on sourdough with garlic mayo, Cajun roast beef with chipotle mayo) plus salads, soups and homemade cookies. Close to RPI campus. Open Mon-Fri.

Sainato's Market
423 Quail St. (corner of New Scotland Ave.), Albany, 482-8595
Italian deli serving prepared pasta meals, good subs, sandwiches, antipastos, and salads (four-bean, artichoke, mushroom). Takeout only. Open Mon-Sat.

CHEAP EATS

Buttery Restaurant
111 Washington Ave., Albany, 445-9431
A bargain basement luncheonette for all the basics (grilled tomato-and-cheese, omelets, burgers, chicken salad, and lemon meringue pie). Breakfast and lunch: Mon-Fri.

Famous Lunch
111 Congress St., Troy, 272-9481
Memorable mini hot dogs (made by the Troy Pork Store) served with the works and slathered in Famous Zippy sauce. A local favorite since 1932. Open Mon-Sat.

Jimmy's Luncheonette
93 Congress St., Troy
Old-fashioned diner food at old-fashioned prices. Known for its tasty french fries and iced tea. Breakfast and lunch: Mon-Fri.

Jumpin' Jack's Drive-In
83 Schonowee Ave. (Collins Park), Scotia, 393-6101
This authentic 1950s roadside stand is a great place for kids of all ages. Fried clams, hot dogs, and ice cream are the specialties. Dozens of picnic tables with views of the Mohawk River. Open daily mid-April through Labor Day.

Scubber's
590 Loudon Rd., Latham, 786-1480
Legendary chicken wings. Open Mon-Sat.

Harbor House
1742 Rte. 9, Clifton Park, 371-3813
Good fish fry, fried clams and scallops, and fried chicken. Casual, cafeteria style, and close to Parkwood Plaza. Open Tues-Sun. (closed mid-Dec to early March).

Peter Pause Restaurant
535 Nott St., Schenectady, 382-9278
Homey Italian diner known for its homemade breads, soups and cheesecake, in addition to especially good eggplant parm. Open breakfast and lunch: Mon-Fri.

Cousins Fish Market Take-Out Counter
581 Livingston Ave., Albany, 449-1671
Excellent fried bluefish and catfish, plus fried clams, shrimp and scallops. Good soups and chowders. Roadside picnic tables and soft ice cream in summer. Open Mon-Sat.

Mabou, Saratoga Springs   *Photography by: Philip Caruso*

SHOPPING

Shopping in the Capital Region compares favorably with any major urban area – and with more bargains, to boot. The proximity to New York City and the area's many arts centers have the benefit of keeping the region filled with skilled artisans. Surrounding farmlands supply delectable fresh foods and homemade goods while the area's 19th-century ambience makes it a natural magnet for antique dealers. In addition, the area has more than its share of factory outlets and jumbo malls, including Crossgates Mall, one of the largest in the country. The following sections are just a sampling of the shops and services available, intended for newcomers and longtime residents alike. All entries are highly recommended; however, we'd like to emphasize that many praise-worthy merchants have been left out, and to remind the reader that even as we went to press, new stores were opening and others were closing or moving.

The chapter is organized in three parts: Goods (including malls and specialty stores), Clothing (pg. 129), and Food (pg. 155).

MALLS AND SHOPPING CENTERS

Clifton Park Centre
22 Clifton Country Rd. (Exit 9), Clifton Park, 371-0087
40 stores including Mega Marshall's, Boscov's, Pier One, and JCPenney.

Cor Retail Center
Rte. 7 and Forts Ferry Rd., Latham
Target, Babies "R" Us, and Sports Authority

Colonie Center
1425 Wolf Rd. (at the corner of Central Ave.), Colonie, 459-9020
120 stores and eateries including Macy's, the Gap, Sears, Boscov's, American Café, and the Christmas Tree Shops.

Crossgates Mall & Crossgates Commons
Washington Ave. Ext. and Western Ave., Albany, 869-9565
300 stores and eateries including JCPenney, Filene's, Best Buy, Ann Taylor, Banana Republic, Eddie Bauer, Pottery Barn, Tweeter, Etc., Home Depot and Old Navy.

Delaware Plaza
163 Delaware Ave., Delmar, 439-9030
30 stores and eateries including Hannaford, Priceless Kids, and Friar Tuck Book Shop.

Latham Farms
579 Troy-Schenectady Rd., Latham
Wal-Mart, Home Depot, CompUSA, Dick's Sporting Goods, All Star Wine & Spirits.

Mohawk Commons
Balltown Rd. and Rte. 5, Niskayuna
Lowe's, Marshall's, Target, Barnes & Noble, Panera Bread, Ruby Tuesday.

Northway Mall
1400 Central Ave., Colonie
Target, Marshall's, Thomasville Home Furnishings, Jo-Ann Fabrics.

Rensselaer County Plaza
Rte. 4, North of Exit 9 off I-90, East Greenbush
Wal-Mart Super Center. Target, Home Depot and Staples are all in close proximity to this plaza.

Rotterdam Square Mall
93 Campbell Rd., Schenectady, 374-3713
100 stores and services including Filene's, Sears, Zumiez, and the Gap.

Stuyvesant Plaza
1475 Western Ave. (at Fuller Rd.), Albany, 482-8986
60 specialty shops and services, including The Book House, Talbot's, Hippo's Home Entertainment, Jean Paul Spa & Hair, Ann Taylor Loft, and Different Drummer's Kitchen.

The Crossing
Rtes. 9 and 146, Clifton Park
Target, Home Depot, TJ Maxx, Kohl's, Linens 'N Things, and Michael's.

The Shops at Wilton
Rte. 50, Exit 15 off I-87N, Saratoga Springs
Best Buy, TJ Maxx, Bed, Bath, & Beyond, Pier One, Eastern Mountain Sports.

Town Center
Rte. 9W, Glenmont
Wal-Mart Super Center and Lowe's.

Wilton Mall
Rte. 50, Exit 15 off I-87N, Saratoga Springs, 581-5999
68 shops including Bon-Ton, JCPenney, Dick's Sporting Goods, and Sears.

Wilton Square
Rte. 50, Exit 15 off I-87N, Saratoga Springs, 587-7417
Target, Home Depot, Barnes & Noble, A.C. Moore, PETsMART.

OUTLET STORES

Factory Outlets of Lake George
Rte. 9, between Queensbury and Lake George, 949-5030.
You can shop-'till-you-drop at this gigantic complex of four adjacent outlet centers, known locally as the "million-dollar half-mile." The combined total of more than 70 stores includes Jones New York, Bass, Oneida Silver, Dansk, Nautica, Coach, Polo/Ralph Lauren, Timberland, Easy Spirit, Corning/Revere, Bali, Big Dogs Sportswear, Kay-Bee Toys, Samsonite, Kitchen Collection, Eddie Bauer, and Brand Name Closeouts. www.factoryoutletsoflakegeorge.com

Prime Outlets at Latham
400 Old Loudon Rd. (Rte. 9, north of the Latham Circle), 785-8200
Lenox, Dansk, Oneida Silver.

Rug & Carpet Outlet
320 Fifth St., North Troy, 235-7940
Quality remnants, 400 decorative area rugs in stock, imported woven rugs, braided rugs, outdoor carpeting, brand-name linoleum, and more.
www.rugandcarpetoutlet.com

Talbots Outlet
5 Metro Park Dr. #2 (off Wolf Rd.), Colonie, 482-4611
Women's clothing, shoes, accessories. Catalog overstocks and deep discounts on select inventory.

ANTIQUES

Art and Antiques
462 Broadway, Saratoga Springs, 584-4876
Group of 10 dealers specializing in American 18th- and 19th-century furnishings; rare books, textiles, and crystal.

Antiek LCC
Nassau Antique Center, 1 Church St. (Rte. 20), Nassau, 766-3445
This overstuffed shop offers mostly early American furniture with some German and English pieces, as well as china, lamps, a large selection of antique and vintage rugs, and a complete upholstery service. There's also another Antiek shop, a 15-room house arranged in period settings for serious antique collectors, and offering personalized service by proprietors Norman and Christine Young. Thurs-Mon.

Bournebrook Antiques
209 River St., Troy, 273-3027
Victorian-era antiques including marble-top tables, period settees; Old Hickory, Mission, and Thonet; and vintage tools, china, glassware, and Troy memorabilia. Bournebrook also operates a furniture restoration shop at 44 Tivoli St. in Albany (426-1066).

Forty Caroline Antiques
Downstreet Marketplace, Saratoga Springs, 584-4017
A "real-life curiosity shop" with a changing inventory of eclectic collectibles from around the globe. Also vintage toys and holiday items.

Gristmill Antique Center
2250 Rte. 7, Troy, 663-5115
Two floors housing over 50 vendors. Furniture from the 1800s-1960s; home décor, glass, tin, toys, and more. Open daily.

Holzman (Dennis) Antiques
240 Washington Ave., Albany, 449-5414
Furniture, paintings, autographs, prints, photographs, books; plus
political memorabilia.

Madison Art & Antiques
460 Madison Ave., Albany, 465-3735
Unusual 19th- and 20th-century furniture, paintings, art lamps, statues,
porcelain, fountains, garden bronzes, and Victoriana.

Metropolis Antiques
4 Vatrano Rd., Albany, 438-8277
Vintage jewelry, clothing and accessories from Victorian to 1960s. A good
place for unexpected finds such as a 1940s hatbox or 1950s fur-trimmed
cashmere sweater.

New Scotland Antiques
240 Washington Ave., Albany, 463-1323
General line of antiques; occasional tables, paintings, lamps, mirrors, statuary.

Regent Street Antique Center
153 Regent St., Saratoga Springs, 584-0107
Large, historic building housing 20 dealers of fine antiques, including Victorian
decorative art, jewelry, china, stoneware, silver, furniture, canes, music boxes,
and primitives. Weds-Sun.

Tuggonyx
1067 Broadway, Rensselaer, 436-8779
Antiques, collectibles, and "old junk." Will buy and sell anything old.

ARTS & CRAFTS

Arlene's Artist Material
57 Fuller Rd., Albany, 482-8881
A local institution known for its high-quality materials, discount prices, and
knowledgeable service. Inventory includes easels, drafting tables, paints,
airbrushes, block printing, frames, canvas, and children's supplies. Also art
books and magazines.

Ceramic Décor & More
2023 Oak Tree Lane, Schenectady, 862-1571
Ceramic mold pouring and a complete line of supplies, from glazes to
music-box mechanisms.

Crafts & Fabrics Beyond the Tollgate
1886 New Scotland Rd., Slingerlands, 439-5632
Loads of fabrics and fabric-related crafts supplies, including feathers, braid, ribbon, pom-poms, bells, wood items. Also Sculpey clays, miniatures, paints.

Kuma Beads
810 Saratoga Rd., Burnt Hills, 384-0110
Large selection of beads, supplies, and tools. Advice for beginners.

Michael's Arts & Crafts
Crossgates Commons, Washington Ave. Ext., Albany, 456-7015
Paints, silk and dried flowers, seasonal-décor supplies, stitchery, woodworking tools, clock-making items, beads.

Soave Faire Art & Office Supply
449 Broadway, Saratoga Springs, 587-8448
Complete art store for students, professionals and commercial artists. Supplies for fine art, graphics, drafting, blueprinting, framing, silk screening, and stained glass. Also scrapbooks, posters and prints. The gift section carries museum-style items.

Ye Olde Yarn & Gift Shoppe
1604 Union St., Schenectady, 393-2695
Yarns, needles and needlepoint patterns. Small selection of vintage yarn items and other gifts. Advice for beginners.

The Arts Center of the Capital Region offers an extensive schedule of arts and crafts classes. 273-0552.

BOOKSTORES

Barnes & Noble Booksellers
20 Wolf Rd., Albany, 459-8183, Mohawk Crossing, Niskayuna, 377-0349
3059 Rte. 50, Saratoga Springs, 583-7717
More serious titles than most chain bookstores, with excellent history and classic literature sections. Also a comprehensive magazine rack, large calendar selection, discount racks, customer-service desk, a music room, and a café.

Book House
Stuyvesant Plaza, 1475 Western Ave., Albany, 489-4761
Locally owned for over 25 years, with a large, well chosen, and easy-to-find inventory including an excellent section on regional interest and books by local authors. There's also art calendars, notebooks, local and world maps, and other inviting items for browsers, plus a children's "house" (see pg. 104). The store

is host to 30 book clubs and holds regularly scheduled readings by local and national authors. www.bhny.com

Book Mark
495 New Loudon Rd. (Newton Plaza), Latham, 785-7869
General bookstore with a large children's selection. Special orders.

Books Out Loud
251 River St., Troy, 272-3281
Wide selection of audiocassette books for sales and rentals. Special orders.

Borders Books & Music
59 Wolf Rd., Albany, 482-5800, 395 Broadway, Saratoga Springs, 583-1200
3 South Side Dr., Clifton Park, 383-2121
Books, CDs, and magazines from the global leader in book retailing (Borders is a subsidiary of K-Mart.) The Saratoga store displays art and photography exhibits; the Albany store has poetry readings and live music; and both stores have a café and hold writers' workshops and book signings. Open daily until 11pm.

Burnt Hills Books
772 Saratoga Rd. (Rte. 50), Burnt Hills, 399-7004
Full service, locally owned independent bookstore.

Empire State Plaza Book Outlet

(North Concourse), State St., Albany, 445-9446
General bookstore with good selection of African-American
fiction, non-fiction and children's titles.

Flights of Fantasy Books and Games

488 Albany-Shaker Rd., Loudonville, 435-9337
New and used fantasy, science fiction, and horror titles; huge inventory of
mystery and romance; book signings by prominent genre authors. Also games
and gaming accessories (see pg. 115).

Haven't Got A Clue

1823 Western Ave., Albany, 464-1135
Excellent selection of mystery, suspense, and espionage titles. Also used books
and children's mysteries and games.

Hodge-Podge Books

272 Lark St., Albany, 434-0238
This small, colorful store is just for youngsters (from kindergarten through
high school).

I Love Books

380 Delaware Ave., Delmar, 478-0715
Well-chosen book selections for children and parents. Great selection of cards
and inexpensive and whimsical gift items.

Little Bookhouse

Stuyvesant Plaza, 1475 Western Ave., Albany, 437-0101
Thousands of children's titles, including foreign-language books for youngsters,
plus an enthusiastic staff, a playful ambience, and storytelling on Saturdays.
www.bhny.com

Open Door Book Store

128 Jay St., Schenectady, 346-2719
This vibrant community book store offers more than books, although there's
plenty of those, including local-interest titles and books by regional authors, plus
a large children's section. The store also contains a unique gift gallery and a
learning-oriented toy shop (see pg. 112), and hosts regularly scheduled author's
readings and reading-and-writing activities for youngsters.

The Shop

Albany Institute of History and Art, 125 Washington Ave., Albany, 463-8190
Selection of books for adults and children relating to the history, art, and culture
of the upper Hudson River Valley, including books by regional authors.

Waldenbooks
Colonie Center, 1425 Wolf Rd. (corner of Central Ave.), Albany, 459-1588
Latham Circle Mall, Rte. 9, Latham, 783-0571
Waldenbooks is a mall-based chain owned by Borders. The Latham store has
a Waldenkids section.

Rare Books

Bibliomania
129 Jay St., Schenectady, 393-8069
Rare, old, and out-of-print books, plus autographs, literary ephemera,
and vintage stringed instruments.

Lyrical Ballad Bookstore
7 Phila St., Saratoga Springs, 584-8779
The labyrinth-like setting is a book browser's dream come true, especially since
it contains 75,000 titles, including regional interest and equine interest, plus first
editions and out-of-print stock. And vintage maps.

W. Somers Bookseller
841 Union St., Schenectady, 393-5266
Out-of-print and second-hand books, including regional-interest and fine-art titles.

Used Books

Book Barn
200 Troy-Schenectady Rd., Latham, 786-1368
A great big store with 80,000 (mostly used) books in 59 categories.

Book Outlet
71 Fourth St., Troy, 272-0010
Good selection of used books on a wide variety of subjects, including a worthwhile assortment of art books. Buying, selling and trading for over 20 years.

Dove & Hudson
296 Hudson Ave., Albany, 432-4518
A regional favorite located in an 1800s townhouse redolent with book-lover
ambience – and presided over by the book-lover owner. Excellent selection of
publisher's overstocks and like-new hardbacks on all serious topics, including
local interest, history, art, biography, and cooking. Also classic, modern and
world literature, with new stock arriving on a daily basis.

Lark Street Books
215 Lark St., Albany, 465-8126
Formerly the much-loved Byrn Mawr Bookstore, this neighborhood haven was saved from closure by local bookworms, who have spiffed up the store's junk-shop ambience while retaining its wide-ranging inventory of anything and everything, from $1 battered paperbacks to rare books and ephemera at bargain prices. Weekly local author's readings and music performances.

COUNTRY STORES

Fo'Castle Country Store
166 Kingsley Rd., Burnt Hills, 399-8322
Established in 1906, this is a big store with many small "shops" inside, all with an old-fashioned flavor. A sampling of its countryside offerings includes home-baked goods, regional food products, cookbooks, cards and paper goods, porcelain dolls at discount prices, and unusual home-décor items. Sunny coffee shop serving breakfast and lunch. Apples and apple picking.

Indian Ladder Farms
342 Altamont Rd. (Rte. 156), Altamont, 765-2956
Produce year-round (mostly local), cheeses, home-baked goods, teas and jams, clothing (including baby T-shirts), body-care products, pie plates, enamel ware, cookbooks, candles, hand-crafted toys and jewelry. Lunch café, scenic grounds for picnicking, fruit picking. Open daily. Closed January and February.

FLORISTS

Amaryllis
640 New Loudon Rd. (Rte. 9), Latham, 782-0241
Exotic flowers and elegant designs for weddings, galas, and other special events. Fresh calla lilies, scented candles, striking silk and dried flower arrangements.

Arkay Florists
3 South Pearl St., Albany, 463-4255
Over 90 years' experience. Sympathy flowers, silk and dried flowers, Holland flowers, locally grown roses, local delivery daily.

Doris Remis Flowers
1740 Union St., Schenectady, 346-1271
Traditional and contemporary arrangements, prepared to be long lasting. Also fresh-cut flowers and dish gardens.

Expressions Floral Design Studio
41 Lower Hudson Ave., Green Island, 272-1475
Family owned and operated studio offering friendly, attentive service and a large inventory of fresh flowers, tropicals and plants. High-style floral arrangements and dried-flower arrangements, dish gardens, children's designs, plus an extensive gift section.

Felthousen's Florist and Greenhouse
1537 Van Antwerp Rd., Schenectady, 373-4414
1711 Union St., Schenectady, 370-1212
250 Columbia Circle, Cohoes, 237-2100
Family-owned, full-service florists serving the greater Capital Region since 1950. The Schenectady store has houseplants and potted flowers. Delivery, international orders: (800) 278-2634

Fleur de Lis
15 Second St., Troy, 272-8120
Classic floral designs and personalized service, plus unique gifts.

Flower World
250 Broadway, Troy, 250-9308
Wholesale flowers for sale to the public.

Emil J. Nagengast
169 Ontario St., Albany, 434-1125
Stuyvesant Plaza, 1475 Western Ave., Albany, 489-1745
Huge selection of domestic and imported flowers, beautiful traditional designs, distinctive silk designs, exotic potted plants, personalized service for funerals and all occasions. Family owned since 1910. www.nagengast.com

Henry F. Clas
404 New Scotland Ave., Albany, 489-4764
Professional floral presentations for almost 50 years. Gourmet and fruit baskets, sympathy arrangements, balloons and cards. Located between Albany Medical Center and St. Peter's Hospital. www.clasflorist.com

Renaissance Floral Design
1561 Western Ave., Albany, 464-6002
Expert design services for all events large or small; from dinner parties to grand stylish weddings (free consultation). The floral showroom features unusual and stylish gifts, silk and dried arrangements, and fresh flowers.

Surroundings

145 Vly Rd. (Shaker Pine Mall), Schenectady, 464-1382
Beautiful flowers and artistic arrangements by award-winning
designers. Weddings, celebrations, and corporate events a specialty.
www.surroundingsfloral.com

GARDENING

Bill's Violets

548 Font Grove Rd., Slingerlands, 439-7369
Houseplant specialists; also perennials, shade plants.

Brizzell's Flowers

194 Maxwell Rd., Latham, 783-3131
Specializing in seasonal garden flowers, open seasonally including Easter and
Christmas (call for hours). Family-owned store with 30 years' experience.

Cedar Hill Iris Garden

Rte. 144, Bethlehem, 767-9608
Perennials, including peonies, irises and beautiful day lilies. You pick out the
plant, the proprietor digs it up. May-Oct.

Faddegon's Nursery

1140 Troy-Schenectady Rd., Latham, 785-6726
(just past the intersection of Albany-Shaker Rd. and Rte. 7)
This 40-acre, high-quality garden-supply center dates to 1920, when Johanas
Cornelius Faddegon planted some blue-spruce trees in Latham. The center is
still owned by Faddegons, and offers a helpful staff of experts along with a vast
inventory encompassing almost every gardening item under the sun. Plants
include annuals, perennials, dozens of rose species, orchids, two greenhouses
of houseplants (one for tropicals), and pond plants. Landscaping and indoor
"plantscaping" services available. The garden shop carries backyard and patio
items, from birdbaths to trellises.

Helderledge Farm

418 Picard Rd., Altamont, 765-4702
Specializing in day lilies and unusual perennials, plus herbs, trees, shrubs and
houseplants. Garden design services and display gardens, Christmas shop.
Pleasant location with benches for lingering.

Lark Street Flower Market

264 Lark St., Albany, 427-9466
House plants, inexpensive cut flowers, large selection of long-stem roses, plus
vases, baskets, garden accessories, cards, candles, and occasion balloons.

Price Greenleaf
14 Booth Rd., Delmar, 439-9212
Good selection of tools, flowers, houseplants, and outdoor bushes. Excellent selection of seeds, bulbs, vegetable starts, and herbs. Annual mid-summer sale.

Menands Regional Market
Broadway, Menands, 465-1023
Wholesale and retail garden plants. May-November. 6am-2pm.

White Birch Nursery and Florist
2004 Helderberg Ave., Schenectady, 355-1710
Family-owned, full-service gardening center including landscaping services, outdoor and indoor plants, greenhouse, florist shop, fruit baskets, and gifts.

Pigliavento's Greenhouses
3535 Lydius Rd., Schenectady, 356-9188
Annuals, perennials, herbs, vegetable plants.

Wells Nursery LLC
2557 Van Vranken Ave., Schenectady, 346-5104
A new nursery in the area with a large inventory of trees, bushes and plants. Design services available.

GIFT SHOPS

The below entries carry especially interesting, unusual or high-quality items.

Aurora's Willow Creek
165 River St., Troy, 266-1191
Antique and vintage clothing, furniture and pictures; home décor and Victoriana (dresser sets to hats), and a large, especially lovely selection of old and new jewelry. Located in an 1826 building, this charming shop is named after its resident "faerie spirit."

Celtic Treasures
456 Broadway, Saratoga, 583-9452
Huge selection of Irish music and books, also tin whistles and drums. Trollwork and other lines of artisan jewelry. Nicholas Mosse pottery and Belleck china. Clothing, Celtic crosses, foodstuffs, and more – all imported directly from Ireland by the owner.

Cottage Herb Farm Shop
311 State St., Albany, 465-1130
Three charming rooms stocked with every old-fashioned gift item imaginable, including delightful toys and puppets; home décor items such as dried flowers and wreaths; and scrapbook kits and fanciful gift wrap. Also teas, herbs and homemade jams.

Country Trunk
705 Columbia Tpke., East Greenbush, 479-7282
Original, New England-themed gift items for hearth and home, plus jewelry, homemade candies, Boyd's Bears, and women's fine apparel and accessories. The store has a cottage café serving lunch with homemade desserts and French-press tea service. No sales tax. Open daily (café is closed Sun.)

Clearly Yours
588 Newton Plaza (Rte. 9), Latham, 783-1212
Jam-packed with personalized and monogrammed gifts such as picture frames, photo albums, career accessories, glassware, stadium blankets, baby and wedding gifts.

Cravings
9 North Pearl St., Albany, 427-2912
You can find premium chocolates and nut clusters at other candy shops, but this "small space with big taste" also carries licorice mixes, wasabi peas, fresh-roasted peanuts, gourmet popcorn, rum cordials, savory sesame crunch, and more, any and all of which can be packed in a gift basket.

Dana Rudolph and Company
209 River St., Troy, 273-4532
Original jewelry by the owner and other local designers, plus a beadshop with an excellent selection of gemstone beads, bead necklaces for customizing, and beading tools. Also original local artworks and interesting gift items from around the world.

Destiny Threads
257 Delaware Ave., Delmar, 478-9467
Handmade woven products in original designs, including jackets, vests, scarves, rugs, quilts, pillows, and satchels. Also candles, puzzles, and gifts.

Elissa Halloran Designs
225 Lark St., Albany, 432-7090
Unique artist-designed jewelry, plus vintage jewelry and accessories. Beautifully handcrafted housewares and imaginative home-decor objects (stained-glass mobiles, rustic tin stars, miniature rococo mirrors). Artist owned and operated.

Faddegon's Nursery Garden Shop
1040 Troy-Schenectady Rd., Latham, 785-6726
(just past the intersection of Albany-Shaker Rd. and Rte. 7)
For the home that has everything, try the backyard: the gift shop carries birdhouses, window bird feeders, window flower boxes, fountains, arbors and trellises, statuary, wind chimes, plant stands, weather vanes, and dozens of wire topiary designs. There's also a home-accents shop and two greenhouses; one for houseplants and one for tropicals.

Gardener's Cottage at Boudreau
1208 Loudon Rd., Cohoes, 783-0628
This small but attractive shop specializes in holiday gifts and decorations (from Valentine's Day to Christmas) and floral arrangements (fresh, preserved, and silk) crafted by the owner.

Little Country Store
410 Kenwood Ave., Delmar, 475-9017
For 15 years, this unique shop has exclusively featured made-in-America products, carrying a wide selection of candles, tinware, pewter, pottery, quilts, old lace, and Americana items. The store is located in a Colonial house near the Four Corners off Delaware Ave.

Magic Moon
15 Phila St., Saratoga Springs, 583-2488
For the enchantress in everyone: Goddess clothing, sarongs, and handcrafted jewelry; plus tapestries, tarot cards, books and videos, magic tools, healing herbs, beaded curtains, incense, crystals, and essential oils.

Many Facets Rock Shop
438 New Karner Rd., Colonie, 456-0678
Fossils, gemstones, jewelry and jewelry-making supplies, silversmith equipment, and lapidary gifts.

Nest Home & Garden
578 New Loudon Rd., Loudonville, 785-6096
A house shop specializing in antique botanical prints, Nest's plants and gifts are displayed in homey settings, with a play room to keep little ones busy. Among the beautiful things to be found are blooming orchids, hyacinths, ferns, and ivies; Simon Pearce glassware; sterling-silver jewelry; Archipelago candles and bodycare; and children's prints. Fine chocolates, too. Open Tues-Sat.

Nostalgia

436 Broadway, Saratoga Springs, 584-4665
Elegant home décor and gift items in a romantic setting. Large selection of pillows, linens, tabletop items, decorative furnishings, and crystal candlesticks. Also fine toiletries, gift wrap and cards. Open till 9pm, Mon-Sat.

Open Door Book Store

128 Jay St., Schenectady, 346-2719
Within the Open Door (see pg. 104) is a gift gallery filled with whimsical and traditional items, including jewelry, autographed books, chimes, fountains, frames, pottery, and unusual items from around the world. There's also a learning-oriented toy shop with games, puzzles, imaginative puppets and stuffed animals, and more.

Pearl Grant Richman's

Stuyvesant Plaza, 1475 Western Ave., Albany, 438-8409
Bridal registry, china, linens, home decor, cookware, glassware, vintage collectibles, stationary, gourmet chocolate counter, charming toys, and an exceptional card selection. A good place to find "the perfect gift," such as an antique valise or a wine-and-cheese backpack complete with board, corkscrew, and serving utensils.

Phebe's Florist & Gifts

2026 Western Ave., Guilderland, 869-1036
High-quality flowers and fruit baskets, silk and dried flowers, dish gardens, gift section, and an "angel room" with hundreds of angel-themed products.

Romeo's Gifts

299 Lark St., Albany, 434-9014
Artist-made jewelry; gay-themed gift items and novelties; glassware, lamps, picture frames and other home décor items; plus gift wrap and cards. The upstairs holds vintage furnishings. Open until 10pm.

Schenectady Museum Shop

Nott Terrace Heights, Schenectady, 382-7890
The museum shop offers reproductions from around the world, along with books on nature, science and cooking, and museum souvenirs. The gallery shop features jewelry, home accessories, sculptures, pottery, embroidered clothing, and more, all crafted by select regional artisans.

Skinny and Sweet

181 Jay St., Schenectady, 377-7990
Fun gifts and fun candy, plus fine chocolates including Asher's from Pennsylvania.

Ten Thousand Villages
Stuyvesant Plaza, 1475 Western Ave., Albany, 435-9307
This socially responsible emporium is part of a volunteer retail network marketing fairly traded Third-World handicrafts. Many of these unusual gift and home-décor products reflect cultural traditions that add to their appeal. Among the colorful offerings are hand-printed, natural-fiber sarongs, scarves, curtains, and table linens; Middle-Eastern lamps and candlesticks; wonderful giant bug kites and ethnic-doll marionettes; mobiles, picture frames, and ceramics; Kwanzaa and Haukkah items; an extensive selections of baskets; plus cards, Arabica coffee, and world-music CDs. www.tenthousandvillages.org

The Balcony
1328 Van Antwerp Rd., Schenectady, 374-1333
Something for everyone, with gift ideas for baby, wedding and career; plus jewelry, stationery, crystal, tableware, and other home accessories.

The Shop
Albany Institute of History and Art, 125 Washington Ave., Albany, 463-8190
High-quality inventory reflecting the museum's collections and including jewelry, cards and paper goods, prints and posters, ceramic tiles, historic-building miniatures, and children's items. Also regional-interest books and books relating to the collections, plus arts and crafts by regional artisans.

Tipperary Trading at Tara Ltd.
RD3 Brunswick Rd., Troy, 279-3082
The largest and oldest Irish-import shop in upstate New York, with seven lines of Irish jewelry and an extensive selection of Belleck crystal. Glassware and other fine gift items, plus imported foodstuffs. (located off Rte. 2, next to Brunswick School District campus.)

Tri-City Luggage
1645 Central Ave., Colonie, 869-9221
Stuyvesant Plaza, 1475 Western Ave., Albany, 489-0211
Travel kits and accessories, leather goods (lots of wallets), clocks, deluxe pens, and desk sets. And luggage (Jack Georges, NX, Hartmann).

Turtle Pointe
351 Delaware Ave., Delmar, 439-8878
Unique, outdoor-themed gifts, home décor and lawn items, including vegetable-men marionettes, pumpkin lawn lanterns, country-style display cabinets, stuffed wild animals, whimsical toys, small Tiffany-style lamps, lovely cards, and more.

Verstandig's Florist Inc.

454 Delaware Ave., Delmar, 439-4946
Imported decorative items from Asia and Europe, plus silk arrangements,
glassware, figurines, stuffed animals, and framed pictures and prints. Distinctive
floral arrangements and quality plants since 1932.

Wit's End Giftique

Parkwood Plaza, Rte. 9, Clifton Park, 371-9273
A "wonderland" emporium of unique and enchanting gifts, with a turn-of-the-
century ambience that contains "stores within stores." Wide variety of antiques
and gift items (music boxes, crystal, dolls) in a range of prices.

HARDWARE STORES

The following stores are known to be particularly helpful for do-it-yourself and
fixer-upper types of customers.

Allerdice Building Supply

41 Walworth St., Saratoga Springs, 584-5533
One-stop shopping for all your home-repair and building needs, both interior
and exterior. The huge inventory includes power tools and hand tools, paints
and stains, lumber and sheet rock, hardwoods and specialty moldings, and
electrical and plumbing supplies. Within the store are a millwork shop for repair
and production, a metal shop for custom fabrication, and a lawn and garden
shop. Allerdice is owned and operated by a local family, and is known for its
helpful, well-trained staff. Open daily.

Country True Value

217 North Greenbush Rd. (Rte. 4), Troy, 283-6246
Hard-to-find items and personal attention.

A. Phillips Hardware

1157 Central Ave., Albany, 459-2300
Good general line for home projects.

Bridgeford Hardware

388 Delaware Ave., Albany, 465-8276
Expert advice. Screen repairs a specialty.

Menands True Value

359 Broadway, Menands, 465-7496
Good selection including masonry supplies. Glass cutting, paint mixing,
and lawn-mower repair.

Shaker Ace Hardware
607 Watervliet-Shaker Rd. (Rte. 155), Latham, 785-9052
Good general line, carpet-cleaner rentals.

Trojan Hardware Co.
96 Congress St., Troy, 272-7330
Hard-to-find tools and household items. Attentive service. Residential contracting services including plumbing, heating, air conditioning, electrical, and a 24-hour emergency service.

HOBBIES

Alfred's Fabric Center
Stuyvesant Plaza, 1475 Western Ave., Albany, 489-6700
898 New Loudon Rd., Latham, 783-1700
Over 1,200 bolts of fabrics, from faux lace to flannel and including upholstery materials. Huge selection of patterns; plus braids, ribbons, buttons, frogs, appliques, and trims of every description.

All-Sports Collectibles
1403 Rte. 9, Halfmoon, 383-8400
Classic baseball cards and new collectible cards.

Backyard Birds Nature Shop
Town Center Plaza, Rte. 9, Clifton Park, 383-4048
Everything pertaining to the backyard bird: seed, squirrel-proof feeders, copper birdbaths, hand-blown globes, hand-painted birdhouses, bird books and tapes. Personable service provided by the owner.

Davy Jones Locker
386 Delaware Ave., Albany, 436-4810
Specializing in freshwater tropical fish. Aquarium supplies, knowledgeable service, house calls.

Flights of Fantasy Books & Games
488 Albany-Shaker Rd., Loudonville, 435-9337
The area's grand central of gaming, with an extensive selection of role-playing games, war games, collectable-card games, and board games. All kinds of gaming accessories and miniatures. New and used books in fantasy, sci-fi, mystery, and horror. This haven for teenagers also hosts in-store gaming and tournaments. Open until 10pm on weekends. www.fof.net

Hobbytown USA
12 Wolf Rd., Albany, 435-9961
Supplying hobbyists of all kinds with an extensive inventory of model kits, trains and tracks; radio-controlled cars, boats and airplanes; board games and eye-hand learning games; plus die-casting, kites, puzzles, and science projects.

Lady Melissa's Miniatures
7 King Arthur's Court, Saratoga Springs, 581-7677
Specializing in handcrafted miniatures, including original 1-inch dollhouses. Large selection of miniature furniture and other items from major lines including Earth and Tree and Bespaq. Dollhouse restoration, landscaping and lighting, plus hundreds of wallpaper patterns.

Mohawk Valley Railroad Co.
2037 Hamburg St., Schenectady, 372-9124
Operating layout, model-train supplies, railroad-related merchandise.

HOME DÉCOR

Certified Framing & Gallery
475 Albany-Shaker Rd., Loudonville, 438-9471
The owner specializes in French (hand-painted) matting, and artistic framings such as three-dimensional framing for textiles. The selection of unusual frames includes 24-carat gold-leaf molding, and antique bead board. The gallery carries unique home-décor items, among them handcrafted pewter candlesticks, over-sized ceramics, reproduction Hudson River School oil paintings (by the shop's own painter), and plaster house parts from finials to columns. Open Mon-Sat.

Clement Frame and Art Shop
201 Broadway, Troy, 272-6811, 204 Washington Ave., Albany, 465-4558
Large frame selection with 50 years' experience in framing and matting. Also regional and antique art and prints.

Deitcher's Wallpaper Factory Outlet & Design Center
188 Remsen St., Cohoes, 237-9260
Huge selection of quality wallpaper at a discount; some patterns with matching fabrics and borders. Complete interior-design services including framing, carpeting, upholstering, window treatments, flooring, and custom-ordered and custom-made paints, plus Martin Senour paints.

Experience & Creative Design Ltd.
510 Union St., Schenectady, 374-6885
This huge, upscale home-decor store and interior-design service features stunning, one-of-kind items imported from around the world, including accent furniture, sculpture, paintings, lamps, tapestries, window treatments, silver, glassware, pottery, and floral arrangements. Five designers (including a specialist in customized drapery) are available by appointment; holiday decorating a specialty. The jam-packed store also sells locally designed Adirondack furniture.

Gerard Stowell Gallery
290 River St., Troy, 272-0983
Gorgeous pottery and fine crafts by more than 50 regional artists.

Harbrook Windows and Doors
47 Railroad Ave., Albany, 437-0016
A supplier of windows, doors and fine hardware to great estates, historic homes, and ordinary residences. Harbrook offers design advice and innovative solutions based on 50 years of experience. In addition to selling and installing windows, doors, architectural columns and skylights, the store also offers a terrific selection of doorfronts, knobs, and locksets, in styles from contemporary to rustic to Craftsman.

Historic Albany Foundation Parts Warehouse
83 Lexington Ave., Albany, 465-0876
Salvaged vintage parts for restoration, including mantels, columns, doors, brass hardware, architectural and decorative parts, and the occasional fantastic find. Technical and aesthetic assistance from the staff.

Historic Home Supply Corp.
213 River St., Troy, 266-0675
Architectural salvage merchandise, including house parts and decorative accessories. Home hardware and lighting repair. Knowledgeable staff.

Miller Paint
296 Central Ave., Albany, 465-1526
1693 Central Ave., Albany, 862-9432
1675 Rte. 9, Clifton Park, 371-1649
Benjamin Moore and Muralo paints and stains. Wallpaper, window treatments, and most other home-decorating supplies. Spray equipment sales, rentals and repairs. Free delivery.

Northeast Framing
243 Delaware Ave., Delmar, 439-7913
Wide selection of frames and expert matting including poster matting.

Passonno Paint
1438 Western Ave., Albany, 489-1910, 1729 Union St., Schenectady, 346-4383, 500 Broadway, Watervliet, 273-3822, 63 Excelsior Ave., Saratoga Springs, 580-0772
Locally manufactured and nationally recognized acrylic latex paints, oil paints, stains, and architectural coatings and varnishes. Large wallpaper selection. Over 70 years' experience.

Pearl Grant Richman's
Stuyvesant Plaza, 1475 Western Ave., Albany, 438-8409
Bed and bath accessories, linen, china, crystal, quilts, picture frames, fine kitchenware, vintage items, and decorative furnishings.

Visual Creations
205 River St., Troy, 274-5020
A wonderland of unique items, including ornate mirrors, hand-painted screens, original artworks by regional artists, Depression glass, porcelains, original-design indoor fountains, unusual lighting fixtures, stained-glass jewelry boxes and candle holders, artist-designed window displays, and more. New merchandise weekly.

HOME FURNISHINGS

CJ Designs
215 Old Loudon Rd., Latham, 782-0206
Unique children's furniture, design services available.

D. A. Rubin Oriental Rug Gallery
42 Caroline St., Saratoga Springs, 226-0014
Antique and vintage oriental carpets, plus "ethically-made" new rugs in striking tribal and folk-art designs.

Furniture House
1254 Rte. P (on Saratoga Lake), Saratoga Springs, 587-9865
Fine reproductions in Mission, Traditional, Queen Anne, Shaker, and Old World styles, plus lamps, rugs, and room accessories. The 20,000-square-foot showroom is staffed by design consultants.

Georgia Mills Direct Ltd.
28 Clinton St., Saratoga, 587-2200
All major brands and styles of residential (and commercial) fine flooring, up to 50-percent off. Hours by appointment.

Huck Finn's Warehouse

Erie Blvd. (off Broadway), Albany, 465-3373

Factory-direct prices on a huge selection of furniture (including unfinished pieces), plus lamps, rugs, and thousands of décor items.

Jacobsen Oriental Rugs

268 Broadway, Saratoga Springs, 584-1024

"America's home for Oriental rugs since 1924."

Kermani Oriental Rugs

3905 State St., Schenectady, 393-6884

Large selection of hand-made oriental carpets.

Mabou

468 Broadway, Saratoga Springs, 581-0424

Since 1971, the owners have been traveling the world and personally selecting decorative treasures, antiques, and home furnishings of every description. Located in an old hotel, this adventure in shopping offers three floors of "galleries" filled with rich woods and leathers, and exotic accessories from far-flung places. Mabou attracts a clientele from several states, and there's a basement clearance boutique for bargain hunters.

New Old Stuff

615 Pawling Ave., Troy, 274-3221

Large selection of reproduction antiques from quality manufacturers; Country, Victorian, and Shaker styles. Also lighting, picture frames, upholstery, lace, and Americana items, plus a sweets shop. Open daily.

Riverside Sales and Upholstering Co.

683 Broadway, Watervliet, 274-6442

Custom upholstering and furniture repair.

Schuyler Pond

727 Rte. 29, Saratoga, 581-8422

A restored barn showcasing an eclectic collection of furnishings for the home and garden. Featuring primitive and Victorian furniture, plus décor items from French linens to Claire Murray hooked rugs.

Stickley, Audi & Co.

151 Wolf Rd., 458-1846

Fine furniture by Stickley, Baker, Hickory Chair, and Ralph Lauren, plus leather and other fine upholstery, window treatments, lamps, and accessories. Complimentary interior-design service.

Troy Light Co.
85 Congress St., Troy, 274-6931
Standing lamps, table lamps, hanging lamps, wall sconces, shades, and beautiful Tiffany reproductions.

Visual Creations
205 River St., Troy, 274-5020
Stunning "fantasy" furniture, high-quality antique reproductions, moderately priced antique furniture, hand-carved marble and wood tables. New merchandise weekly.

HOUSEHOLD APPLIANCES

Algen Sales and Service
300 Kenwood Ave., Delmar, 439-3323
Appliance sales and major-appliance repairs

Cocca's Appliances
158 Railroad Ave. Ext., Colonie, 453-6100
All large appliances, plus home electronics. Large selection of models for special order, low prices, extended warranties, friendly service. (Located behind Target off Central Avenue).

Cornwell Appliance Company Inc.
1357 Central Ave., Colonie, 459-3700
New and used major appliance sales and repairs, over 60 years' experience.

Green's Appliance Direct
1207 Central Ave., Albany, 458-7994
Major household appliances at low prices.

Lexington Vacuum
562 Central Ave., Albany, 482-4427
Selling and servicing all makes of vacuum cleaners since 1946; large inventory of models, bags and parts. Trade-ins.

JEWELRY

Carr Mfg. Jewelers Inc.
637 New Loudon Rd., Latham, 783-2277
Specializing in gold jewelry, on-premises repairs, and buying and selling estate jewelry. Staff gemologist.

Drue Sanders Custom Jewelers
1675 Western Ave., Albany, 464-9636
Original and custom-design jewelry; precious gems and metals.

Elissa Halloran Designs
225 Lark St., Albany, 432-7090
Uniquely stunning artist-designed jewelry including coral, freshwater pearls, tourmaline, peridot, and silver. Moderately priced vintage jewelry, plus whimsical handcrafted home-décor items.

Frank Adams
1475 Stuyvesant Plaza, Western Ave., Albany, 435-0075
Gold and platinum jewelry, Rolex watches, custom-made wedding rings, estate jewelry. Gemologist and silversmith on staff, expert repairs, superlative service.

Harold Finkle
1585 Central Ave., Albany, 456-6800
Custom-made wedding rings, large selection of diamonds, estate jewelry. Gemologist on premises, repairs.

Hummingbird Designs
29 Third St., Troy, 272-1807
Original and custom fine jewelry; goldsmith and gemologist on staff.

Kaye's Jewelry Boutique
454 Broadway, Saratoga Springs, 584-1420
"The best earring selection in the Northeast," according to Travel & Leisure magazine. Artist-design jewelry from Ed Levin, Baltic Amber, Laurel Burch, Silver Forest of Vermont, Tabra, and more. Extensive necklace selection and Skagen watches and pens from Denmark.

Romanation Jewelers
48 Third St., Troy, 272-0643
Unique and antique fine jewelry; watches, clocks, and repairs.

Singer's Watchmakers & Jewelers
1704 Western Ave., Albany, 464-4748
Classic and contemporary jewelry; 50 years' experience with expert, on-premises repairs; master watchmaker and gemologist on staff.

MUSIC

CDs and Records

Blue Note Record Shop
156 Central Ave., Albany, 462-0221
Established in 1948 and staffed by second-generation owners. Inventory includes almost every hit record from the 1940s to the present (no used). LPs, '45s, oldies on CD and cassette, sing-along tapes, needles.

Last Vestige
173 Quail St., Albany, 432-7736, 437 Broadway, Saratoga Springs, 226-0811
Huge selection of used CDs (mostly rock) for about half the price of new. Rare, collectable, and cheap vinyl records in all music categories. New stock daily, buy-sell-trade, knowledgeable staff. Also used turntables, phono cartridges, and memorabilia. www.lastvestige.com

Music Shack
65 Central Ave., Albany, 436-4581
Alternative music, pop, reggae, hip-hop, and hard-rock CD's; select titles on vinyl. Good used section, also T-shirts, jackets, and magazines.

Mom's Digital Discs
3905 State St., Niskayuna, 393-4677
Specializing in 20th-century classical, plus unusual classical titles. Excellent historic-recordings section including vocal, piano and opera performances.

Musical Instruments & Accessories

Cathedral Music
1813 Fifth Ave., Troy, 273-5138
Handcrafted acoustic guitars; selection of tonewoods, quality craftsmanship, top designers and builders. Attentive service. Also production guitars (Rainsong, Tacoma, Seagull) and vintage guitars.

Cole's Woodwind & Brass
143 Troy-Schenectady Rd., Watervliet, 273-4711
Sales of new and used instruments, from bassoons to oboes. Small, personalized shop with over 25 years' experience in repairs; among the clientele are symphony-orchestra musicians.

Drome Sound
3486 State St., Schenectady, 370-3701
Keyboard instruments, drums, guitars, recording equipment, amplifiers, PA's; plus trade-ins, rentals, and repairs. A staple for area rock musicians.

Hermie's
727 State St., Schenectady, 374-7433
A local favorite since 1945. Instruments (new, used, vintage, and hard-to-find), sheet music, music books, friendly service.

John Keal Music Company
819 Livingston Ave., Albany, 482-4405
Big band and orchestral instrument rentals, sales and repairs. Specializing in outfitting school bands.

Saratoga Music Center
45 Phila St., Saratoga Springs, 584-9312
Excellent print-music selection in classical, folk, jazz, and Broadway. Hundreds of lesson books for piano to tin whistle, plus harmonicas, strings, reeds, and music accessories. www.saratogamusic.com

Schenectady Van Curler Music
Proctor's Arcade, 440 State St., Schenectady, 374-5318
Sheet music specialists; also music books, karaoke tapes, metronomes, music-writing supplies. Special orders.

Van Curler Music Company
1811 Western Ave., Albany, 862-1885
Sheet music plus reeds, strings, and music accessories. Special orders.

NEWS STANDS

Coulson's News Centers
420 Broadway, Albany, 449-7577 (open until midnight)
Coulson's News and Variety, Newton Plaza, Rte. 9, Latham, 785-6499
Extensive magazine selection.

Friar Tuck's Book Shop and News
Delaware Plaza, Delaware Ave., Delmar, 439-3742
Large selection of magazines, also whimsical toys, games, and gifts.

Ned Abbot Newsroom
185 Hoosick St., Troy, 272-9753

Nite Owl News
400 Fulton St., Troy, 272-8586

Saratoga News Stand
382 Broadway, Saratoga Springs, 581-0133
Friendly, locally owned shop specializing in racing news. Food-to-go.

Taylor News Service
81A McKown Rd., Albany, 482-1730
Newspapers from New York City delivered

Westmere News and Variety
1823 Western Ave., Albany, 456-4223

PARTY SUPPLIES & SERVICE

Cookie Bouquet
31 Broadway, Waterford, 238-1673
Cookies made-to-order, including unusual forms such as long-stem roses
or floral arrangements. Delivery.

Beyond Balloonmatics
454 Broadway, Saratoga Springs, 584-6134
Balloon services including delivery, custom imprints, and decorating. Fun gift
shop, open daily.

Have Puppets Will Travel
618 Rankin Ave., Schenectady, 382-0256
Professional, educational, and fun family entertainment.

Party Warehouse
76 Fuller Rd., Albany, 458-1144,
Shoppers World Plaza, Rte. 146, Clifton Park, 383-6146
Thousands of party-supply items at a discount, plus umbrella and wishing-well
rentals, decorating and balloon services, customized party invitations.

Tablecloths For Granted
1956 Watt St., Schenectady, 346-7647
Rental tablecloths and napkins.

SPORTING GOODS

Adirondack Paddle-N-Pole
2123 Central Ave., Colonie, 346-3180
Canoes, kayaks, cross-country skis, outdoor gear, and snowshoe rentals.

Anaconda Kaye Sports Inc.
44 State St., Schenectady, 382-2061
Team sports specialists (soccer, lacrosse, volleyball) and school-team outfitters.
Good selection of under armor. The discount-outlet store next door carries sports
clothing and shoes.

All Outdoors
35 Van Dam St., Saratoga Springs, 587-0455
Specializing in mountain bikes, including heavy-weight "machines" such as
Freeride and DH, plus large selection of BMX. Also hiking, climbing, and
snowboarding equipment. Repairs, customizing, knowledgeable staff, organized
outings and races.

Blue Sky Bicycles
71 Church St., Saratoga Springs,
Specializing in Schwinn and Cannondale. Repair shop. Open till 8pm weekdays.

Cahill's
26 Fourth St., Troy, 272-0991
General sporting goods, team sports, clothing.

Down Tube Cycle Shop
466 Madison Ave., Albany, 434-1711
Rated in the top 100 bike stores in the nation. Recreational-bike specialists
with large selections of Trek and Fisher. Expert repairs, serious accessories,
knowledgeable, personable staff. Good selection of children's bikes. Test
drives available in nearby Washington Park.

Eastern Mountain Sports
Stuyvesant Plaza, 1475 Western Ave., Albany, 452-9440
Mohawk Commons, 388-2700
Specializing in technical outdoor clothing and equipment, from paddling racks to camping tents to hiking poles.

Goldstock's Sporting Goods
98 Freeman's Bridge, Scotia, 382-2037
Longtime favorite established in 1896. High-quality, moderately priced sporting goods for team and individual activities. Friendly, knowledgeable service.

Kemp's Hockey Shop
Rte. 9, Latham, 785-5297
Specializing in hockey, also in-line and figure skates. Used skates, sharpening.

Klarsfeld's Cyclery
1370 Central Ave., Albany, 459-3272
Specializing in mountain and racing bikes. Large selections of Kona, Haro, Raleigh. Also clothing and accessories, repairs.

High Adventure
1057 Troy-Schenectady Rd., Latham, 785-0501
Full line of ski equipment, with large selection of Atomic. In summer, the store carries outdoor furniture.

Play It Again Sports
952 Troy-Schenectady Rd., Latham, 785-6587
New and used sports equipment for all sports. Great bargains and a trade-in policy that's good news for parents with growing youngsters.

Soccer Unlimited
1272 Central Ave., Albany, 458-8326, 1520 Rte. 9, Clifton Park, 383-1026
Extensive selection of soccer equipment and clothing.

Taylor & Vadney Sporting Goods
3071 Broadway, Schenectady, 374-3030
Longtime specialists in hunting and fishing gear.

Tough Traveler
1476 State St., Schenectady, 393-0168
Well-regarded local manufacturer of luggage, backpacks and carryalls for adults and children. Upscale outdoor clothing; camping, climbing and hiking equipment.

Waves Swimwear
454 Broadway (Downtstreet Marketplace), Saratoga Springs, 584-0169
The largest selection of swimsuits and beachwear in the Northeast. Women's, junior's, men's, children's, and plus sizes.

STATIONERY

Hill's Stationery
451 Broadway, Troy, 274-3191
Office stationery and supplies; copy services, fax, custom framing, plate engraving, shipping services.

Kinko's Copies
100 State St., Albany, 465-5656
Professional stationery (including Crane), cards, office paper of all kinds, and photocopy services in a beautiful, historic building.

Paper Mill
Delaware Plaza, Delaware Ave., Delmar, 439-8123
Fine stationery, thank-you notes, party invitations, cards, special orders.

Pearl Grant Richman's
Stuyvesant Plaza, 1475 Western Ave., Albany, 438-8409
A full wall of fine stationery selections, including Crane and William Arthur. Custom-order engraving. Also high-quality notepapers, invitations, and beautiful cards of all kinds.

TOYS

G. Willikers
461 Broadway, Saratoga Springs, 587-2143
A charming emporium of distinctive toys, including learning toys for children and classic toys for all ages. Also animal puppets, Corolle baby dolls, metal soldiers, kites, stuffed animals, games and puzzles.

Open Door Book Store
126 Jay St., Schenectady, 346-2719
Challenging games and puzzles, ant farms, stuffed animals from the pages of beloved children's books, arts and crafts supplies, imaginative puppets.

Poppychop Toys
66 Dayfoot Rd., Petersburgh, 658-2658
Handcrafted, original-design wooden toys, fully guaranteed.

Toy Maker
Stuyvesant Plaza, 1475 Western Ave., Albany, 458-8830
Newton Plaza, 594 New Loudon Rd., Latham, 220-9838
Brand-name playthings – Playmobil, Breyer, Gund, Creativity for Kids, Madame Alexander, and Corolle baby dolls – share the aisles with fun clothing items such as wizard hats and fairy skirts. Wonderful selection of stuffed animals, including enchanting, artist-designed puppets from unicorns to horned beetles.

Two Tin Soldiers
19 Third St., Troy, 271-6585
Largest selection of toy soldiers in the Northeast. All makes and eras, plus war-game armies from Old Glory, Essex, Battle Honors and more; Osprey books, paints and brushes. In-house war games.

WINE SHOPS

All Star Wine & Spirits
Latham Farms Plaza, Latham, 220-9463
Incredible selection, ranging from $10 bargains to rare and hard-to-find wines. Service-oriented staff, wine tastings. Wine classes available. www.allstarwine.com

Capital Wine & Spirits
State and Lark St., Albany, 434-5776
Good specials, free neighborhood delivery.

Delaware Plaza Liquor Store
27 Plaza, Elsmere, 439-4361
Good selection of high-quality wines. Enthusiastic service.

Delmar Wine & Liquor
340 Delaware Ave., Delmar, 439-1725
Small-town store ambience with a large selection and personalized service.

Wine Shop
265 New Scotland Ave., Albany, 438-1116
Established in 1935, the shop's ambience compares to a private wine cellar. Extensive wine selection with esoteric choices and excellent values, plus helpful signage. Also unusual liqueurs and largest selection of single-malts and small-batch bourbons in the area. Knowledgeable owner.

Wine-Skill Wine and Spirits
130 Main Ave., Wyantskill, 283-5477
Excellent discount prices.

Saratoga Wine Exchange
42 Phila St., Saratoga Springs, 580-9891
Upscale selection of fine wines and spirits, relaxing ambience (with art gallery)
and knowledgeable service. Free wine tastings and wine classes available.

CLOTHING

Men's

Broadway Clothiers
358 Broadway, Saratoga Springs, 583-6800
Upscale menswear in a relaxed environment with personalized service.
Specializing in distinctive, fashionable apparel; business, casual, and
dress clothes.

Casual Male Big & Tall
110 Wolf Rd., Colonie, 459-8540
Pocket tees to dress shirts and everything in between, from 2X-6X to LT-5XT.

Futia's Formal Wear & Custom Tailors
251 Central Ave., Albany, 436-7177
Tuxedos and special-occasion clothes, plus formal accessories from ties to shoes.
Expert alterations and tailoring with 40 years' experience in personalized service.

Jos. A. Bank Clothiers
Stuyvesant Plaza, 1475 Western Ave., Albany, 435-0056
Classic men's haberdashery since 1905. Pajamas to tuxedos, with a focus on dress
and dress-casual clothes. Full line of accessories, personalized service, tailoring.

Kelly Clothes Inc.
Latham Farms, Rte. 9, Latham, 785-3796
Full line of upscale clothing, from recreational to formal wear, men's and boy's,
and big and tall. Expert alterations.

Rodino's
348 Congress St., Troy, 274-1151
Suits and formal wear, expert tailoring.

Rudnick's Uniforms & Clothing
308 State St., Schenectady, 372-6486
Good selection of heavyweight jeans and work clothes (Levi's, Carhartt, Woolrich), plus T-shirts to boots.

Saratoga Army Navy
640 Central Ave., Albany, 482-7073
Good selection of jeans, T-shirts, winter wear (including thermal undies), work clothes, sweatshirts, flak jackets, pea coats, and flannel shirts. Good boot and shoe department (Wolverine and Chippera boots, Minnetonka moccasins, Red Wing shoes).

Simon's Men's Wear
1671 Union St., Schenectady, 377-1182
A local staple for 30 years. Full line from socks to suits; sportswear, some formal wear, big and tall section.

Waldorf Tuxedo
Lark St. at Lancaster St., Albany, 449-5011
Established in 1936 and located in an elegant brownstone, this family-owned and operated shop offers expert, personal service in addition to an extensive in-house inventory. Styles range from traditional to the latest fashions, from "single-breasted peak lapel" to "Savoy long coat." Also vests, shirts, ties, shoes, cufflinks and studs. Rentals and sales.

Women's

Casual Set
Stuyvesant Plaza, 1475 Western Ave., Albany, 482-7136
High-quality career separates, weekend wear, and casual-dress clothes.

Catherine's Plus Sizes, Stuyvesant Plaza
1475 Western Ave., Albany, 459-5506
Fashionable clothing in sizes 18-32, with some 34 and 5X. Casual, career, and special-occasion clothes, plus loungewear and sleepwear, pantyhose, and accessories.

Circles
Stuyvesant Plaza, 1475 Western Ave., Albany, 482-2554
Upscale fashion straight off the runways and in all categories, from casual to drop-dead glamorous – with shoes and accessories to match. Theory Jeans, Nicole Miller, Trina Turk, BCBG, Tony and Tina cosmetics. Personalized service, on-premises alterations.

Clothes Horse
322 Broadway, Saratoga Springs, 587-9667
Sportswear to eveningwear, moderately priced. Hats, scarves and jewelry.

Jean Lewis Maloy Studio
59 Loudon Rd., Latham, 783-5772
Casual clothes and designer dresses (Roza Nichols, Ghost).
High-quality accessories.

Mme. Pirie's Famise Corset and Lingerie Shop
1660 Western Ave., Guilderland, 434-2600
In business for 60 years, this old-fashioned undergarments shop attracts a loyal
clientele from all over the Northeast. Some of the favorites are French lingerie,
comfy cotton nightgowns, sexy designer nightgowns, Wacoal minimizing bras,
Goddess bras (up to 48 DDD), and clingy peignoir sets. Expert measuring by
owner Mme. Rosa.

Saratoga Trunk
487 Broadway, Saratoga Springs, 584-3543
Fantastic (and fantastical) designer hats for weddings, garden parties, and most
especially, a day at the Saratoga Race Track.

Visual Creations
205 River St., Troy, 274-5020
One-of-a-kind and original designs in evening gowns, coats, handbags, and hats.
Large selection of vintage clothing, including handcrafted handbags. Fur coats
in many different styles and pelts, with fur muffs, hats, and headbands. Vintage
and artist-designed scarves and shawls. Also original fine jewelry and vintage
costume jewelry.

Men's and Women's

Amore Clothing
123 State St., Albany, 434-4054
Custom-tailored and ready-made fine apparel including dress shirts and men's
and women's suits. Joseph Cheany and Alden shoes, exclusive collections of ties
and accessories.

Counties of Ireland
13 Second St., Troy, 687-0054
Unique lines of imported and domestic Irish clothing, from traditional to
contemporary. Jewelry, accessories, and gift items.

Peter Harris Plus
952 Troy-Schenectady Rd., Latham, 783-1938
Big, tall and full sizes for men and women. Mostly casual clothes plus dress
pants, sports jackets, and career separates.

Spectors
Colonie Center, 1425 Wolf Rd., Colonie, 482-2343
Upscale suits, career and dress clothes. Luxurious accessories, expert tailoring.

Sweater Venture
700 Columbia Tpke., East Greenbush, 477-9317
Sweaters, sweater accessories (gloves, scarves) and other handknit woolens from
around the world, and including alpaca. Over 20 years' experience in independent
production and design. Also ethnic gifts from pottery to tapestries.

Children's

Baby Depot
Latham Circle Mall (second floor of Burlington Coat Factory),
Rte. 9, Latham, 783-0464
Everything a baby could need (clothes, cribs, strollers, car seats) to everything a
baby could want (swings and toys).

Babyland
1400 Central Ave., Albany, 459-7706
Everything from A to Z for infants and toddlers.

Cripple Creek Trading Company
135 Jay St., Schenectady, 377-7968
Discount outlet for designer children's clothing.

Gymboree
Crossgates Mall, Albany, 452-3034
Fashion and recreational clothes for babies to big boys and girls. Accessories, too.

Lion's Rose
19 Phila St., Saratoga Springs, 583-0751
A unique children's outlet offering new clothing, off-priced clothing, and
like-new clothing, plus second-hand toys, furniture, books, and accessories –
all in excellent condition.

Lollipops Children's Shop
Newton Plaza, Rte. 9, Latham, 786-0379
A boutique of unique clothing, shoes, and accessories for little ones, from infants to girl's size 5 and boy's size 7. Cheerful service and special ordering for cribs.

Rugged Bear
Stuyvesant Plaza, 1475 Western Ave., Albany, 482-8325
Recreational clothes for infants to juniors, plus schoolbags and playtime accessories.

Clothing for the Family

B. Lodge & Co.
75 North Pearl St., Albany, 463-4646
Established in 1867, Albany's oldest store offers the basics-blue jeans, button-down shirts, shoes and socks, underwear, bathrobes, plus backpacks, kid's play clothes, Hawaiian shirts, and an especially good selection of men's and boy's T-shirts. You'll also find useful items from decades past, such as old-fashioned housedresses, nightgowns, and aprons. The prices are from a previous era, too.

Burlington Coat Factory
664 Loudon Rd., Latham Circle Mall, 783-0464
Huge selection of coats and jackets at discount prices.

CB Sports
490 Broadway, Saratoga Springs, 583-1113
Name-brand activewear and outerwear for the entire family.

Champion Factory Outlet Stores
Westgate Plaza, Central Ave., Albany, 489-8215
Crosstown Plaza, Schenectady, 381-4186
Athletic clothing and undergarments at low prices.

Cohoes Fashions
Crossgates Mall, Washington Ave. Ext., 452-7330
Designer-name clothing, shoes, and accessories at mark-down prices.

Peter Harris
574 Columbia Tpke., East Greenbush, 477-6837
Mayfair Shopping Center, Scotia, 399-7267
417 Kenwood Ave., Delmar, 439-9150
Moderately priced, quality clothing in every category, plus shoes.

Shoes

Delmar Bootery
Stuyvesant Plaza, 1475 Western Ave., Albany, 438-1717
376 Delaware Ave., Delmar, 439-1717
Small but very high-quality selection of men's and women's shoes and boots
(Le Donne, Alden). Large inventory of shoe accessories and shoe-care products.
Expert repairs.

Dexter Shoe Factory Outlet
1831 Central Ave., Colonie, 869-1048, Rte. 9, Latham, 785-5980
Men's and women's shoes at a discount

Saratoga Shoe Depot
255 Delaware Ave., Albany, 439-2262, 385 Broadway, Saratoga Springs, 584-1142
The latest fashions at reasonable prices, including men's shoes and Doc Martins.
Also handbags, belts, jewelry, and accessories galore.

Saratoga Soles
486 Broadway, Saratoga Springs, 587-6394
Upscale women's shoe and accessory boutique, specializing in designer footwear
(Jacqueline Levine, Tommy Bahama, Unsindo). Also jeweled hairpieces, tulle and
silk scarves, and other high-fashion accessories.

Shoe Repair and Dye
Empire Shoe Rebuilders
32 Maiden Lane, Albany, 465-3067
More than 50 years' experience in the repair, reconstruction and dying of shoes,
purses, and almost all other leather goods. Known for its old-fashioned, expert
shoe shines.

Troy Quick Shoe Repair Co.
81 Third St., Troy, 274-2431
Established in 1908, the company offers expert repairs of footwear, handbags,
and other leather goods, including baseball gloves. Dying and initialing, wide
selection of laces and shoe-care products. Also golf spikes, dance plates, gussets,
and luggage accessories.

SUPERMARKETS

There are two major supermarkets in the region, Hannaford and Price Chopper.

Hannaford Bros. started out as a fruit and vegetable stand in 1883 and expanded from its Maine roots to become an upscale grocer with over 150 stores throughout New England, New York, and Vermont. Produce continues to be a major focus at the chain, as are expansive meat sections, natural-foods products, and Hannaford's quality private-label items. In 2001, the company was purchased by Delhaize America (parent of Food Lion), which in turn is owned by Belgium's Delhaize "Le Lion." For store locations: www.hannaford.com

Price Chopper, a Schenectady-based company with over 100 stores throughout upstate New York and the surrounding areas, dates to the early 1900s, when Lewis Golub, an immigrant grocer, settled in Schenectady. In 1933, his sons opened the Central Market – named for nearby Central Park – and offered "one-stop shopping" that introduced the region to the "supermarket" concept. More stores followed, with the Golubs' commitment to local farms and produce helping to fuel the company's growth. The name was changed to Price Chopper in 1973 but the chain is still owned and operated by Golub family members. The chain offers in-store scratch bakeries, cut-to-order meat shops, and fresh-seafood departments. For store locations and general information: 355-5000 or www.pricechopper.com

FOOD MARKETS

Arthur's Food Market
35 North Ferry St., Schenectady, 372-4141
Good deli, general groceries, sidewalk café in season.

Cardona's Market
340 Delaware Ave., Albany, 434-4838
Italian-import deli, free-range chicken, meat counter with fresh-made sausages and meatballs, grocery items, takeout Italian meals.

Delmar Marketplace
406 Kenwood Ave. (off Delaware Ave.), Delmar, 439-3936
Complete market including Elmhurst Dairy products, sushi, takeout meals, and fresh meats and seafood from the Village Butcher.

Greulich's Market
3403 Carman Rd., Schenectady, 355-1530
Fresh produce and dairy products, meat department with fresh lamb and chicken.

Pede & Sons Cash & Carry
582 Duanesburg Rd., Rotterdam, 356-3042
Pede Bros. is a local, family-owned Italian-foods company known for its stuffed pastas and all-purpose spaghetti sauce. This factory-outlet store sells the company's "macaroni" (ravioli, manicotti, gnocchi, cavatelli) and sauce at a discount, plus cold cuts and imported Italian specialties (olive oils, gourmet desserts). Open daily.

Putnam Street Marketplace
435 Broadway, Saratoga Springs, 587-3663
High-quality food and ingredients, carefully selected by the helpful staff. The store's offerings encompass babka from Brooklyn, cheeses from France and England, organic olive oils from Spain, chocolates from Vermont, and sandwiches and baked goods from Saratoga. The marketplace includes a wine shop. www.putnammarket.com

Stewart's Ice Cream Company, Saratoga Springs, has over 300 convenience shops in the greater Capital Region. Privately held by the Dake family, makers of ice cream since 1921, the company is one-third employee owned. Many shops offer breakfast and lunch items to eat-in or take-out, but Stewart's is best known for its fresh milk and dozens of flavors of ice cream. Made from ingredients from Saratoga County farms, the company's dairy products are an especially good value. Stewart's also markets its own sodas, juices and bakery products. The shops' self-serve coffee is an area staple, and the make-your-own-sundae counters serve as popular neighborhood gathering spots in warm weather. For store locations and general information: 581-1200 or www.stewartsicecream.com

W.F. Ryan
114 Railroad Ave., Albany, 459-5775
Broad selection of seasonal produce, low prices.

WHOLESALE FOOD WAREHOUSES

B.J. Wholesale Club Inc.
1440 Central Ave., Colonie, 438-1400
Goods and foodstuffs at discount prices for an annual membership fee (membership cards may be purchased at the door). Open daily.

Deli Warehouse
132 Railroad Ave. Ext., Albany, 482-5732
Wholesale/retail, cold cuts, party platters, cheese boards, salads, Italian trays and more.

BAKERIES

Alfred Bakery
1600 Altamont Ave., Schenectady, 355-5170
Authentic German baked goods; Black Forest and other specialty cakes including mousse cakes, rum cakes, torts, and fruit fillings.

Bella Napoli
672 New Loudon Rd., Latham, 783-0196, 721 River St., Troy, 274-8277
Fine Italian cakes and pastries and bread and rolls, plus Italian ice cream. Famed for its cannoli.

Bread Basket
65 Spring St., Saratoga Springs, 587-4233
All kinds of breads including tea breads; also cakes, pies, cookies, brownies, and a variety of danish. All goods baked from scratch daily. Coffee available.

Bountiful Bread
Stuyvesant Plaza, 1475 Western Ave., Albany, 438-3540
Whole-grain gourmet breads baked from scratch daily, including maple oat, apple pecan, dill rye, challah, cinnamon swirl, honey wheat, cranberry walnut, garlic asiago, and five-cheese French bread. Good soups, too, plus brownies, scones, muffins and sour-cream coffee cake. Bountiful's giant peanut-butter-oat-meal-chocolate-chip cookie is the cookie to have when you're having only one.

Carosello Bakery
573 New Scotland Ave., Albany, 435-9070, 72 Hurlbut St., Albany, 434-2449
Italian breads, cookies, and desserts, including pasticiotti, tiramisu, several kinds of bear claws, and especially yummy almond horns.

Civitello's Pastry Shop
42 North Jay St., Schenectady, 381-6165
Old-world Italian pastries, cookies, rum cakes, and wedding cakes. Known for their spumoni and tortoni.

Fiorello Bakery
1180A Western Ave., Albany, 482-8171
Excellent, crisp-crust Italian bread and rolls.

Grandma's Pie Shop
1273 Central Ave., Albany, 459-4585
Good pies baked daily, 35 varieties including seasonal pies.

J & S Watkins Homebaked Desserts
1675 Rte. 9 (off I-87), Clifton Park, 383-1148
In addition to its famous New York City-style cheesecakes, Watkins carries over 50 other kinds of cakes, from carrot cake to Black Satin, as well as a variety of mousse torts. Also pecan, lemon meringue and Key Lime pies, and tiramisu.

Leo's Bakery
28 Maple Ave. (corner of Quail St.), Albany, 482-7902
Full line of kosher baked goods; known for their whipped-cream-icing cakes.

Mrs. London's Cafe
464 Broadway, Saratoga Springs, 581-1834
An haute patisserie and café (see "Restaurants," pg. 77) featuring made-from-scratch breads (baguettes to panini) and a lavish selection of elegant pastries and decadent desserts.

Nino's Bakery
718 Central Ave., Albany, 489-6640
Thick and tasty Italian breads and rolls.

Panera Bread Co.
County Rte., 50, Wilton, 226-0095
Crossgates Commons, Washington Ave. Ext., Albany, 862-9281
Mohawk Commons, Niskayuna, 377-9808
The Crossing, 6018 Troy-Schenectady Rd., Latham, 783-5980
This national chain of bakery cafes features dozens of baked-daily breads made from fresh, preservative-free dough. Also bagels, brownies, croissants, and muffins. Also serves excellent soups, salads and sandwiches.

Perreca's
33 North Jay St., Schenectady, 372-1874
Exceptional Italian bread from coal-fired ovens. Arrive early – everyone else does.

Prinzo's Bakery
344 Delaware Ave., Albany, 463-4904
Popular neighborhood bakery with a good assortment of rolls and rye breads.

Schuyler Bakery Inc.
637 Third Ave., Watervliet, 237-0142
Specializing in wedding and birthday cakes for 45 years. Also known for their pies, "midget" desserts, hearty donuts, and rolls.

Vanilla Bean Baking Co.
521 Troy-Schenectady Rd., Latham, 783-2326, 216 Fourth St., Troy, 272-8605
Assorted breads, cakes, pastries, specialty desserts, and a wide variety of cookies.
Light meals available, in Latham.

Villa Italia Pasticceria
3028 Hamburg St., Rotterdam, 355-1144, St. James Sq., Nott St., Niskayuna, 382-1144
A third-generation Italian sweets shop serving fine specialty cakes and cookies.
Wonderful selection of pastries and desserts, including chocolate cannolis, lemon
rolls, fresh-fruit tarts, "mousse mice," and cassata cake. Creative wedding cakes
(brochure available), and mail-order: 1-800-631-1442. www.villaitaliabakery.com

CANDY (HOMEMADE)

Candy-Kraft
2575 Western Ave., Guilderland, 355-1860
Famous peanut-butter ribbon candy and molded candies.

Chocolate Gecko
540 Delaware Ave., Albany, 436-0866
Award-winning, gourmet chocolates available for purchase online, by mail
order, or at this homey store. Favorites include Galapagos Turtles (cream
caramel and fresh pecans) and Komodo Crunch (toffee and crunchy nuts).
Also chocolate-dipped fruits and imaginative custom designs for all occasions.
www.chocolategecko.com

Krause's Homemade Candy
622 Central Ave., Albany, 458-7855
Established in Saugerties in 1929 by a German immigrant, the business is still
operated by Krauses, who continue to use the founder's recipes (and vintage
molds) for hand-dipped candies, fudge, peanut brittle, and caramels. Favorites
of the devoted clientele include peanut-butter malt balls, Grand Marnier truffles,
dark chocolates, and giant peppermint patties.

Peanut Principle
Rte. 9, Latham (3 miles north of traffic circle), 783-8239
Every kind of candy from truffles to spice candies, most of it homemade,
plus a variety of nut clusters and the house specialty, peanut brittle.

Saratoga Sweets
1733 Rte. 9, Clifton Park, 373-007
Full-service confectionery specializing in horse-related chocolates and custom
chocolates for any occasion. Home of the deliciously short-lived Peppermint Pig, a
popular holiday treat made from an old family recipe and available only in winter.

COFFEE AND TEA

Cottage Herb Farm Shop
311 State St., Albany, 465-1130
Charming gift store with teas and homemade jams.

Daily Grind
204 Lark St., Albany, 434-1482, 258 Broadway, Troy, 272-8658
Fresh-roast coffees in 20 varieties, including international flavors, plus a
wide variety of teas at the Albany store, which has café tables and serves
light foods, pastries and desserts. The Albany Grind also sells cappuccino
and espresso machines.

Earthly Delights Natural Foods
162 Jay St., Schenectady, 372-7580
Organic and regular coffee beans, specialty blends, international blends, and
espresso. Huge variety of black teas, good variety of green teas and fruit teas.
Bulk sizes available. Lunch café.

Uncle Sam's Good Natural Products
77 Fourth St., Troy, 271-7299
Variety of organic coffee beans, large selection of teas, good prices.

FARM STORES

Cichy Fruit & Vegetable Market
1717 State St., Schenectady, 374-2824
Open year-round.

Golden Harvest Farms
Rte. 9, Valatie (between Kinderhook and Niverville), 758-7683
Famed for their apples (including hard-to-find spy apples) and apple products,
particularly their delicious apple cider and cider donuts. Seasonal produce
with excellent peaches available early on, plus apple picking and pumpkins.
Also jam, eggs, honey, maple syrup, vegetables, plants, and baked goods.
Open daily Aug-Nov.

Goold Orchards
Brookview Station Rd., (off Rte.150), Schodack, 732-7317
This apple orchard and farm has been in the Goold family since 1910. The
store offers many varieties of apples and frozen or baked-to-order fruit pies,
plus honey and jams, apple cider and cider donuts in autumn, and maple
syrup in spring. Pick-your-own strawberries, raspberries, apples, and

pumpkins in season. Goold's holds a popular Apple Festival every Columbus Day weekend ($6). Open daily year-round.

Indian Ladder Farms
342 Altamont Rd., Altamont, 765-2956
Fresh produce (especially apples), cider, homemade baked goods, cheeses, jams, and gift baskets (see pg. 106). Open daily. Closed January and February.

Shaker Shed
945 Watervliet-Shaker Rd., Colonie, 869-3662
Fresh fruits and vegetables plus seasonal items (from flowers to pumpkins to Christmas trees). Deli, home-baked goods (pies baked daily), outdoor plants. Open daily mid-April-Dec. 24.

Schoharie Valley Carrot Barn
Rte. 30 (2 miles south of Schoharie), 295-7139.
The barn's bakery is famed for its carrot cake. Also local crafts and locally grown produce of every kind, including honey, maple syrup, and candies. Open daily March-Dec. 24. 295-7139.

Yonder Farms Cider Hill and Bake Shoppe
Rte. 155 at 4301 Albany St., Albany, 456-6823
Fresh fruit and produce, homebaked goods, cheeses, BGH-free milk, gourmet foods, plants, flowers, and gifts. Open year-round, Mon-Sat.

Farmer's markets and farm stands are listed at the end of the chapter.

ICE CREAM

Aromi d'Italia Café
205 Western Ave. (Star Plaza), Guilderland, 452-9200
Authentic Italian café famed for its gelato (Italian ice cream). Dozens of flavors made on-premises from imported ingredients. Open daily.

Ben & Jerry's homemade products and "scoop shops" can be found all over the Capital Region. The Vermont-based manufacturer of ice cream, frozen yogurt, and sorbet was founded in 1978 in a renovated gas station in Burlington. The company, which is now international, quickly became popular for its innovative flavors, made from fresh Vermont milk and cream. Tours of the company headquarters in the Green Mountains (just north of Waterbury) are open to the public daily, and offer free samples and a "moo-vie" on how Ben and Jerry created their socially responsible ice-cream empire. 866-BJ-Tour.

Carvel
590 Newton Plaza (Rte. 9), Latham, 785-4962
Ice-cream cakes and whimsical frozen treats.

Civitello's Spumoni Shop
42 North Jay St., Schenectady, 381-6165
Old-world pastry shop specializing in spumoni, bisque tortoni, and Italian ices.

Gina's Gourmet Italian Ice Cream
1841 Van Vranken Ave., Schenectady, 370-7941
Ice-cream cakes, spumoni, tortoni, and assorted frozen and non-frozen desserts.

Kurver Kreme
1349 Central Ave., Albany, 459-4120
A summertime roadside stand that draws big crowds.

People's Choice
1836 Columbia Tpke., Schodack, 477-7867
A popular stand with a wide variety of flavors.

Snowman
531 Fifth Ave., Troy, 233-1714
Ice-cream specialists for 50 years; hard and soft in 50 flavors. Open daily weather permitting.

Toll Gate Restaurant
1569 New Scotland Rd., Slingerlands, 439-9824
Handpacked, homemade ice cream and sherbet – a family-owned area favorite since 1949. Great flavors (banana ice cream, rootbeer sherbet) and fresh-baked brownie sundaes.

IMPORTED FOODS

Adventure in Food
84 Montgomery St., Albany, 436-7603
Truly an adventure in eating, offering snake and kangaroo meat, bison burgers, wild boar, exotic cheeses, pates, caviar, and more. (Located next to the Albany Pump Station, behind Quackenbush Square.)

BFS Deli Imports
1754 Western Ave., Albany, 452-6342
Full deli plus Mediterranean and Middle-Eastern specialties including shish-kebobs, kibbe balls, tabouli and other salads.

Kim's Oriental Shop
1649 Central Ave., Albany, 869-9981
Asian staples (noodles, rice) and Korean and Japanese specialties. Fish stock, chili pastes, all varieties of dumplings, heat-at-home dinners, Asian-style meat section.

India Bazaar
1321 Central Ave., Albany, 459-3108
Indian groceries including spices, produce, flours, rice, and specialty items.

Lee's Market
1170 Central Ave., Albany, 459-5250
Chinese dried and canned goods; high-quality Asian vegetables from bok choy to choy sum; seasonal items such as champagne mangoes.

Mona Lissa Fine Spices & Herbs
1 Third St., Troy, 266-9054
This pretty, sunlit shop is filled to the rafters with spices (140 and counting) in preserve jars and decorative canisters, or for bulk sales of any size. Raw ingredients are imported from around the world, and blended in-house by the culinarian owner, a licensed refiner. The shop also sells herbs, teas, dried fruits and nuts, custom-made oils and vinegars, and gift baskets.

Rolf's Pork Store
70 Lexington Ave., Albany, 463-0185
Over 200 kinds of German-import foodstuffs. A sampling includes breads (pumpernickels, ryes, whole-grain, and 10-lb. loaves sliced-to-order); canned fish from caviar to sardines; cookies, cakes, strudels, and other German desserts; baking ingredients such as glazes, extracts, and vanilla sugars; soups, pickles, and more.

Italian Imports

Between the late 1800s and 1922, large numbers of Italians – predominantly from Sicily, Naples, and Calabria – immigrated to the Capital Region for jobs created by the industrial revolution. This vibrant Italian-American heritage is especially noticeable in the area's many fine Italian bakeries, restaurants, and imported-food shops.

Andy's and Sons
256 Delaware Ave., Albany 463-2754
Full deli, delicious overstuffed sandwiches, and meals-to-go.

De Fazio Imports
264 Fourth St., Troy, 274-8866
Foccacia breads, 17 regional Italian sausages.

F. Cappiello Dairy Products
510 Broadway, Schenectady, 382-9045
Full Italian deli with the company's own Italian cheeses, plus imported pastas and other food items, and homemade cannoli.

Fiorello Importing Co.
1182 Western Ave., Albany, 489-7067

Genoa Importing
435 Loudon Rd., Loudonville, 427-0078
Every kind of prepared Italian meal; upscale import items at reasonable prices, including aged balsamic vinegars and specially-pressed olive oils.

Pellegrino Importing Co.
1197 Central Ave., Albany, 459-4472
Fresh sausages, imported oils and cheeses.

Ragonese Italian Import
409 New Scotland Ave., Albany, 482-2358
Good selection of olive oils, olives and all kinds of pastas; plus homemade sausages and cannoli, Greek items, and a full-service Italian deli.

Ricciardi Produce and Italian Imports
1599 Union St., Schenectady, 374-7448
High-quality, especially fresh Italian meats: Genoa salami, hot hams and peppered hams, and excellent prosciutto and mortadella.

Roma Importing Co.
9 Cobbee Rd., Latham, 785-7480
131 South Broadway, Saratoga Springs, 587-6004
Full deli plus sauces and prepared Italian dishes, homebaked roast beef and veal, homemade sausages, fresh mozzarella.

MEAT

Adventures in Food
601 New Loudon Rd., Latham, 783-4907
Wild game meats including bison burgers.

Falvo Meats
Rte. 85A, Slingerlands, 439-9273
Full line of prime meats. Variety of homemade sausages including bratwurst, andouille, and chorizo, plus fresh-ground patties and good weekly specials.

Helmbold's
12 Industrial Park Rd., Troy, 273-0810
A longtime Troy establishment known for its homemade hot dogs and sausages. Range of fresh meats, plus deli products.

Guertze Farm Market
Rte. 9W, Selkirk, 767-3345
Fresh chicken, eggs, lamb.

Rolf's Pork Store
70 Lexington Ave., Albany, 463-0185
Fourth-generation German specialty store and a local favorite. Old-fashioned sausages, home-smoked meats, wursts and cold cuts. Knowledgeable service, delivery.

Troy Pork Store
158 Fourth St., Troy, 272-8291
Every kind of German meat product, including smoked pork chops, baby-back ribs, ground sirloin, kielbasa, sauerkrauts, canned German imports and fish products, and homemade mustard. Excellent service.

Village Butcher
406 Kenwood Ave., Delmar, 478-9651
Old-fashioned, family-owned butcher shop within a village grocery store. Beef, pork, lamb, chicken, and very fresh seafood. Fast, friendly service.

NATURAL FOODS

Apothecary Rose Shed
Rte. 160, Amsterdam, 867-2035
The largest herb farm in the region, featuring hundreds of varieties and specializing in unusual and specialty herbs and spices. Knowledgeable, friendly proprietors.

Earthly Delights Natural Foods
162 Jay St., Schenectady, 372-7580
Organically grown produce, spices, medicinal and fresh herbs, fine coffees and teas, vitamins.

Four Seasons Natural Foods Store & Café
33 Phila St., Saratoga Springs, 584-4670
Organic produce, herbs, bulk foods and spices, Irish cereals, vitamins, books, and bodycare products. The café serves ethnic vegetarian foods for eat-in or takeout.

Honest Weight Food Co-Op
484 Central Ave., Albany, 482-2667
Healthy-foods grocery store with organic and locally grown produce. Bulk quantities; regional cheeses, breads and dairy; excellent selection of nuts, seeds, grains and pastas; fresh herbs in season; natural cleaning products and pet supplies, plus food-to-go. Open daily. www.hwfc.com

Magik Herb
138 Jay St., Schenectady, 377-2873
Huge selection of herbs, also books on herb lore, teas, and minerals and crystals.

Niskayuna Consumers Co-Op
2227 Nott St., Schenectady, 374-1362
General market with organic foods, fresh fish, full deli and meat counter. Meals-to-go. Open daily.

Uncle Sam's Good Natural Products
77 Fourth St., Troy, 271-7299
Organic produce and foodstuffs.

SEAFOOD

Captain Lee's Fish Market
9 Cobbee Rd., Latham, 783-1047
Specializing in New England shellfish, brought in daily. Also homemade chowders and bisques. Excellent service.

Off Shore Pier Fish Market
Rte. 4 at Third Ext., Rensselaer, 283-9880
Full line of fish from North Atlantic waters; lobster tails, special-order lobsters, prepared seafood meals and salads.

Two Cousins Fish Market
581 Livingston Ave., Albany, 449-8830, 1702 Chrisler Ave., Schenectady, 346-1798
Full line of fish and seafood preparations. The Albany store has a fish-fry takeout counter.

FARMER'S MARKETS AND FARM STANDS

The following list of farm markets are known for the freshness and variety of their offerings. In summer, many farm stands carry exotica such as Hand melons, which are harvested and sold only during August. These lush fruits mature just as the racetrack opens in Saratoga, linking them indelibly with racing season. Other area delicacies not to be missed are apple-cider donuts, and sweet corn – the region's cool, summer nights produce some of the best corn in the country.

Albany County

Armory Center Market
Colvin Ave. (just off Central Ave.), Albany
Sun., mid-June-Nov. 10am-3pm.

Best Berry Farm
1078 Best Rd., East Greenbush (between Rtes. 4 and 150) 286-0607
Pick your own apples and strawberries. Also sweet corn and baled straw.

Broadway and Maiden Lane
Albany
Ranked as one of the best markets in the state. Locally grown produce, fresh and dried flowers, crafts. Thurs., May-Oct., 11am-2pm.

Engel's Farm & Market
681 Albany-Shaker Rd., Loudonville (opposite Desmond Hotel), 869-5653
Known for its corn and wide variety of fruits and vegetables. Also homemade baked goods and jams, Oscar's meats, outdoor plants, houseplants, cut flowers. Open daily late-April-Thanksgiving.

Empire State Plaza Farmer's Market
North end (near Legislative Office building).
Summer and winter; Weds. and Fri., 11am-2pm.

George Vogt
760 Troy-Schenectady Rd., Latham, 785-0031
Garden vegetables, plants and flowers.

Indian Ladder Farms
342 Altamont Rd. (Rte. 156), Altamont, 765-2956
Seasonal farm stand in addition to the farm store. Also pick-your-own berries, apples, and pumpkins and homemade baked goods.

Kolber Deerfield Farm
Rte. 9, Selkirk, 767-3046
Fruits and vegetables, annuals, perennials, vegetable plants

Krugs Farm Stand
65 Everett Rd., Albany, 482-5406
Excellent corn, also fruits and vegetables.

Rensselaer County

Goold Orchards
Brookview Station Rd. (off Rte. 150), Schodack, 732-7317
Farm stand with many varieties of apples, plus apple cider, cider donuts, and fruit pies during autumn. Pick-your-own strawberries (June), raspberries (Aug-Sept.), apples (Sept-Oct.), and pumpkins (Oct.). Open daily year-round.

Hilltown Farmer's Market
1462 Main St., Rensselaerville, 797-3449
Held in front of the Palmer House Café, the market features made-from-scratch bakery goods from the café, plus farm-raised poultry, grass-fed beef, and local produce. The café serves a fabulous brunch at the same time. Sat., June-Oct., 10am-1pm.

Troy Waterfront Farmer's Market
433 River St. (Troy Dock and Marina, watch for signs), 785-7054
This sociable open-air market doubles as a festival: each week features chef's demos and kid's activities (sometimes with baby farm animals) plus live music, dancing, or an art event. Dozens of producer-only vendors offer superfresh fruits and vegetables (including unusual varieties), natural meats and eggs, jams and honeys, herbs and flowers, plus home-baked goods (fruit pies to sweet rolls) and handmade crafts (knits to stoneware). Sat., mid-May to late-Oct., 9am-1pm, rain or shine. www.troymarket.org

Uncle Sam Pavilion
Broadway between Third and Fourth St., Troy, 692-7312
Weds., 10am-2pm., March-Dec.

Schenectady County

Burhmaster Farms
Saratoga Rd., Scotia, 399-5931
Fresh fruits and vegetables, cider, cider donuts, flowers; Christmas trees during December.

City Hall Market
105 Jay St., Schenectady
May-early-Sept., Thurs., 10am-3pm.

Jolly Farmer's Market
St. Luke's Church, 1241 State St., Schenectady
May-Oct., Tues., 10am-6pm.

Saratoga County

Hayner Farm Stand
148 Rte. 236, Clifton Park, 664-2412

High Rock Park Market
High Rock Park Ave. (community pavilions), Saratoga Springs
Huge number of local producers offering hanging plants, flowers, baked goods, honey, crafts, meats, eggs, and more. May-Oct., Weds. 3pm-6pm; May-Nov., Sat. 9am-1pm.

Oronacah Farm
Vischers Ferry Rd. (south of Rte. 146), Clifton Park, 383-6438
Fields of wild flowers for picking, 30 acres of berries of all varieties.

Schoharie County

Schoharie Valley Carrot Barn
Rte. 30 (2 miles south of Schoharie, Exit 23, I-88), 295-7139
Asparagus and raspberry picking.

Photography by: Gary Gold

RECREATION AND SPORTS

The location of the Capital Region at the confluence of the Hudson and Mohawk rivers, and within an hour's drive to the Adirondack, Catskill, and Berkshire Mountains, makes it a natural paradise for sports enthusiasts. Numerous lakes and ponds allow for myriad water activities (sailing to ice fishing), and hundreds of acres of woodland provide for additional sport (hunting to snowshoeing). The Pepsi Arena in Albany plays host to a wide variety of athletic events, including prestigious championships, while the fieldhouses and playing fields of area colleges add to the roster of exciting spectator sports. City parks and local preserves are devotedly conserved, and the continually expanding network of New York State recreational sites is one of the best in the nation.

The chapter has two parts. The first part describes general recreation and outdoor activities. The second part covers sports and sporting venues (pg. 161), listed alphabetically from auto racing to yoga.

GENERAL RECREATION

Because they are the location of so many sporting and recreational opportunities, the region's state and city parks are listed ahead of the alphabetical sections of camping, cruises, fitness facilities, and nature preserves.

New York State Office of Parks, Recreation and Historic Preservation, Empire State Plaza, Albany, operates dozens of parks and preserves. All are located in beautiful areas and are attentively maintained for ease of usage. A free guide is available from the office. State park entrance fees are usually $5 to $6 per car, with small additional fees for pools and other amenities. 474-0456. www.nysparks.state.ny.us

Empire Passport offers unlimited year-round entry to all NYS parks and recreational facilities. The one-year pass (April 1-March 31) is $49, and can be purchased at all state-park offices, or by mail from Empire Passports, New York State Parks, Albany, 12238. A printable application is available on the Web site. The Golden Park Pass provides free admission to NYS residents age 62 and over (excluding holidays). The Access Pass is for NYS residents with permanent physical disabilities, and provides free vehicle access to state parks and historical and recreational facilities. 474-0456. www.nysparks.state.ny.us

Opening the Outdoors to People with Disabilities is a free guide to all handicapped-access parks in the state. (607) 652-7365.

Sporting Licenses for hunting, trapping, and fishing may be purchased over the counter at license-issuing outlets such as sporting-goods stores, town-clerk offices, some major discount stores, or by mail or in person from the sales office of the New York State Environmental Conservation Department, 625 Broadway, Albany, 12233-4790. 457-1860. www.dec.state.ny.

State Parks

Grafton Lakes State Park, Rte. 2 (12 miles east of Troy), has five lakes and 20 miles of trails for hiking, mountain biking, horseback riding, skiing, and snowmobiling. Anglers can cast for trout, perch, bass, walleye and pickerel among the five lakes. The lakes have launch facilities for canoes and sailboats, and rowboats and paddleboats are available for rental. Motor boats are allowed on Long Pond, which also has a 1,200-foot sandy beach for swimming. Friends of Grafton Lakes provides seasonal environmental programs. Open year-round, 8am-9pm. 279-1155.

John Boyd Thacher State Park, 1 Hailes Cave Rd., Voorheesville (Rte. 157), is part of the Helderberg Escarpment – an area described by geologists as one of the richest fossil-bearing formations in the world. The park's limestone cliffside provides magnificent views of the Hudson-Mohawk Valley and the peaks of the Adirondack, Taconic, and Green Mountains. Thatcher's 1,844 acres also offer numerous picnic areas with reservable shelters; woodlands and open meadows; and playing fields, a volleyball court, playgrounds, and an Olympic-size swimming pool. The most popular attraction, however, is the spectacular Indian Ladder Trail, a naturally formed ledge with caves, rocky slopes, and waterfalls. The forested Outlook Trail is also recommended for its stunning views of the escarpment. In winter, the park is open for skiing, snowshoeing, tobogganing, and snowmobiling, with heated comfort stations along the trails. Open year-round 8am-dusk, except for the Indian Ladder trail, open May-Nov.15. 872-1237.

Moreau Lake State Park, Old Saratoga Rd., Gansevoort, is located in Glens Falls in the Adirondack foothills (Rte. 7S). The park's hardwood forests, pine stands, and rocky ridges provide a diverse natural terrain for hiking and cross-country skiing. The lake has a pavilion and a sandy beach, and offers swimming, fishing, and boating (boats available for rental). The park's proximity to Saratoga Lake and Lake George, combined with its secluded campsites and trailer areas, make it especially appealing for campers. For information and camp reservations: 793-0511. Open year-round but vehicle access in winter can be difficult. 761-6843.

Peebles Island State Park, Cohoes (access by Delaware Ave.), is a 157-acre park at the confluence of the Hudson and Mohawk rivers, and offers spectacular views of river rapids along miles of wooded paths with picnic areas and fishing spots. Wildflowers and waterfowl are abundant, and the park's many oak trees make it a good place for fall leaf peeping. In winter, visitors can cross-country ski and snowshoe. The Matton Shipyard, on adjacent Van Schaick Island, was acquired in 1990 as additional parkland. Peebles Island is also the headquarters of the Bureau of Historic Sites and Bureau of Historic Preservation Field Services. No motorized vehicles or bicycles allowed. Open year-round, 8am-dusk. 237-8643.

Saratoga Spa State Park, 19 Roosevelt Dr., Saratoga Springs (between Rtes. 9 and 50), is entered through an "avenue of the pines" that makes a fittingly impressive gateway to this historic landscape. Aside from the grandeur of its ambience, the park offers a full range of seasonal activities, including two golf courses (a championship 18-hole course and a challenging 9-hole course), two swimming pools, tennis courts, a running course and streamside walking paths; and a dozen idyllic picnic spots. In winter, the park offers ice-skating and ice-hockey rinks, and 12 miles of cross-country ski trails. Open year-round. 584-2535.

For information on the Saratoga Performing Arts Center and the park's other cultural attractions, see Arts and Venues, pgs. 47, 52, 53, 56, 60.

The Spa is also famed for its two bathhouses, which offer herbal-infused mineral baths, full-body massages, aromatherapy, Moor mud wraps, and European facials. Advance reservations required during the busy July-Aug. season.

Roosevelt Bath Pavilion (open year-round): 584-2011.

Lincoln Baths (open July-Aug.): 583-2880.

Schodack Island State Park, Schodack Landing (Rte. 9J), was opened in June of 2002. The 1,050-acre site is bound by seven miles of the Schodack Creek and Hudson River shorelines, and provides the only public boat launch on the east side of the river between Rensselaer and Hudson. The island is a state estuary and conservation area, and shelters a bird area that is home to bald eagles, cerulean warblers, and blue herons. The park also has eight miles of multi-use trails, a paved bike path, floating docks, and picnic tables and grills. Interpretive signage highlights the area's historic and environmental significance. Open year-round. 732-0187.

Thompson's Lake State Park, Rte. 157, East Berne (SW of Albany), is just four miles from the spectacular Helderberg Escarpment, with breathtaking views from most vantage points. This popular recreational area is composed of mixed hardwood and conifer forests, limestone outcroppings, and open fields, and offers a sandy beach, 140 wooded campsites, fishing, a volleyball court, horseshoe pits, a playing field, carry-in boat access, and rental rowboats.

During winter, visitors can cross-country ski and ice fish. The park contains the Emma Treadwell Thacher Nature Center (see Parents and Children, pg. 207). Open year-round. 872-1674.

City Parks

The cities and towns of the region maintain dozens of parks and playgrounds for group activities as well as personal leisure; employees organize and supervise lessons and leagues throughout the year. Information on facilities and schedules is available from the park offices listed in the blue pages of the telephone book. The principal numbers for the four cities are as follows:

Albany 434-5699
Schenectady 382-5151
Troy 270-4600
Saratoga 885-2213

Albany

Washington Park, between State St. and Madison Ave., is a 19th-century park on 90 beautifully landscaped acres (see Points of Interest, pg. 13). It's also a modern urban oasis, with picnic tables, playgrounds, basketball courts, tennis courts, dog runs, and walkways for serious jogging or scenic ambling. Winter offers ice skating on the lake and tobogganing. In summer, when the park's concert, festival, and lakehouse-theater schedules are in full swing, this downtown greenery becomes an open-air arts center.

Lincoln Park, Morton Ave. (between Eagle St. and Delaware Ave.), is a spacious landscape set in a wide basin rimmed by towering blue and green spruce trees, situated just beyond the State Education Cultural Center. The park offers basketball and handball courts, tennis courts, a playground, large playing fields, and an enormous swimming pool with a grand bathhouse. 434-5699.

Corning Riverfront Park runs along the west bank of the Hudson all the way to the city line. It features a paved pedestrian/bike path, picnic tables, a beaver pond, a boat launch, a playground, fishing spots, and an amphitheater for summer concerts. Built in 2002, the picturesque Hudson River Way pedestrian bridge at Maiden Lane allows for easy access. 427-7480.

Westland Hills Park, Colvin Ave. (between Central Ave. and Lincoln Ave.), maintains eight diamonds to serve its Little League program of over 2,000 participants. It also has lighted tennis courts, a supervised junior swimming pool, and a multi-level playground. 459-6320.

Troy

Frear Park, Park Dr., was donated to the city by William Frear in 1917. The park's 247 acres offer ball diamonds, playing fields, picnic areas, walkways, two lakes, indoor ice rink, tennis courts, and an 18-hole golf course. 266-0023.

Knickerbacker Park, 103 8th Ave., Troy, has just about everything a sports enthusiast could want: baseball field, lighted softball field, tennis courts (with practice wall), basketball courts, soccer field, an outdoor swimming pool, a playground, a volleyball sand court, an outdoor oval for running, walking, and in-line skating; plus an outdoor roller-hockey rink, a bike path, even a bocce-ball court. And that's not to mention the year-round ice arena. 235-7761. www.troynet.net

Prospect Park, off Congress St. (turn right at St. Francis Church), is 273 acres encompassing lovely landscaped areas with rare trees; basketball and tennis courts (with practice walls); a one-mile trail with a comfort station; and a summit outlook with picnic grills and a 20-mile vista of the Hudson River. Created by the city in 1903, Prospect was designed by RPI's first African-American graduate, landscape architect Garnet D. Baltimore. This historic park is being restored by Friends of Prospect Park (273-1500), which holds guided walks and tennis events. 270-8292.

Riverfront Park, River St. runs along the downtown banks of the Hudson with a riverside walkway-bikeway. It's also the site of arts festivals, summer concerts, and many other cultural activities. For information and an event schedule, call the Riverspark Visitor Center: 270-8667.

Schenectady

Central Park, Fehr Ave. off State St., is the largest of Schenectady's parks, with 500 acres of rolling hills, small lakes, and open fields. This scenic, sprawling landscape offers an abundance of activities: 26 tennis courts, several ball fields, marathon routes, and an extra-large swimming pool. The imaginative playground, duck pond, and train ride make it an ideal outing for families. In winter, the slopes are perfect for tobogganing, tubing, and cross-country skiing. In warmer months, visitors can enjoy the beautiful garden, where thousands of roses in 200 varieties bloom from early spring until first frost. The park also contains a picnic pavilion and an excellent outdoor stage, the Agnes B. Macdonald Music Haven (see Arts and Venues, pg. 55). 292-0368.

Other parks in the city are Hillhurst, Rotunda, Steinmetz, Quackenbush, and Woodlawn (Hillhurst, Quackenbush and Woodlawn have pools). For information, call the Schenectady City Parks Dept. at 382-5152.

Collins Park, Schonowee Ave., Scotia, is bordered by the Mohawk River and offers just about everything for a delightful family outing: a picnic pavilion, playground, tennis and basketball courts, a ball field, and swimming in Collins lake – which also offers excellent fishing. If you forget the picnic hamper, Jumpin' Jack's Drive-In is a short walk away. During July, the Coors Light Water Ski Show Team practices within view on the river. 374-8611.

Gateway Landing-Rotary Park, Rotterdam, is located on the Mohawk River (one mile west of the Schenectady Stockade District) and provides river access for car-top boats and docking space for small boats. A good fishing spot, it also connects to the Mohawk-Hudson Bikeway. Open 7am-dusk. 386-2225.

Camping

NYS Office of Parks, Recreation, and Historic Preservation, Agency
Bldg. 1, Empire State Plaza, oversees all campsites in the Capital Region, and provides a pamphlet on state camping and cabins (call 474-0456). Reservations are recommended; sites are available on a first-come-first-served basis. Call 1-800-456-CAMP (with credit card) or visit the web site: www.reserveamerica.com.

Camping in the Catskill and Adirondack Forest Preserves is supervised by the Department of Environmental Conservation, 625 Broadway, Albany, 457-1860. www.dec.state.ny.

Camping is available on 50 state-owned islands on Lake George – a 32-mile paradise for campers who like to kayak, canoe, and motorboat. For more information, contact the Lake George Chamber of Commerce, 800-705-0059. www.lgchamber.org

The following is a sampling of area campgrounds that offer swimming and fishing:

Alps Family Campground
Rte. 43, Averill Park
95 sites (86 with electricity), swimming and fishing, showers, camp store, laundry, ice. May-Oct. 674-5565.

Frosty Acres
Skyline Dr., Schenectady
250 sites (100 with electricity), showers, camp store, laundry, ice. May-Nov. 864-5352.

Lee's Park
1464 Rte. 9P, Saratoga Lake
30 sites (20 with electricity), showers, boat launch, store, ice. May-Oct. 584-1951.

Rustic Barn Campsites
4757 Rte. 9N (I-87, Exit 15), Corinth
55 sites (37 with electricity), family ambience, free showers, bike trails, recreation building. Located halfway between Saratoga and Lake George. Mid-May-Sept. 654-6588.

Thompson's Lake State Campsite
RD 1, Rte. 157 (off Rte. 85), East Berne
140 sites, swimming and fishing, recreation building, showers, ice. Mid-May-Oct. 872-1674.

Cruises

Capt. J.P. Cruise Line
278 River St., Troy
This Mississippi paddle-wheeler (with central air and heat) tours the Hudson River for brunch, lunch, and dinner-and-dancing cruises, in addition to cocktail and buffet cruises, family cruises, and narrated lock cruises. Excursions average three hours. A private deck is available, and so are private charters. The ship is anchored behind Troy City Hall at Riverfront Park; free parking is available in the City Hall lower level parking lot after 5pm weekdays and all day Sat-Sun. Cruises held daily summer through fall. $6 (for children) to $110 (New York City cruise). 279-1901.

Crescent Cruise Line
Terminal Rd., Rte. 9 at Crescent Bridge, Halfmoon
Sightseeing, lunch, and dinner cruises on the famous Erie Canal. Special overnight tours available. May-Oct. 373-1070.

Dutch Apple Cruises
Albany-Castleton
This authentically styled, 65-foot-long ferry (with fully enclosed, heated decks) tours the Hudson River for narrated sightseeing cruises, in addition to a champagne brunch cruise, a sunset hors d'oeuvre cruise, lunch and dinner cruises, and various music and entertainment cruises, plus an Erie Canal cruise that passes through the federal dam and lock. Group tours and private charters are available. The ship is anchored at the Albany Snow Dock at Broadway and Madison Ave. (under the overpass adjacent to the U-Haul building). $6 (children) to $28 (dinner and entertainment). Cruises held daily April-Oct. 463-0220.

Fitness Facilities

Jewish Community Centers of Albany and Schenectady are non-sectarian recreational and educational facilities that seek to promote the well being of the Jewish community, and the community as a whole. They also offer cultural events, youth and senior programs, and child care. Both centers are multi-purpose complexes with pools, gyms, weight rooms, Cybex equipment, saunas, and more. The Albany center has a whirlpool spa; the recently expanded Schenectady center has an outdoor pool and playing fields. Fitness activities range from belly dancing to baseball, in addition to Red Cross swimming programs.

Albany, 340 Whitehall Rd. 438-6651
Schenectady, 2565 Balltown Rd. (Rte. 146) 377-8803

YMCAs have benefited the minds and bodies of regional residents for more than 150 years. The 1990 formation of the Capital District YMCA signified a resurgence of high-quality services for more than 38,000 members. Membership fees can be paid monthly or annually, and confidential financial assistance is available. With some variation, these climate-controlled, full-service facilities offer aerobic classes, Cybex strength-training and cardiovascular-fitness equipment, treadmills, Ergometers, stationary bikes, rowers, EFX Cross-Trainers, indoor swimming pools, racquetball courts, saunas and steam rooms, weight rooms, running tracks, and every type of fitness class imaginable. CD-YMCAs also offer child care, after-school programs, and teen activities. www.cdymca.org

Albany YMCA, 274 Washington Ave. 449-7169
East Greenbush YMCA, 22 Community Way 477-2570
Guilderland YMCA, 250 Winding Brook Rd. 456-3634
Parkside Family YMCA, 127 Droms Rd., Glenville 399-8118
Schenectady YMCA, 13 State St. 374-9136
Southern Saratoga County YMCA, 1 Wall St., Clifton Park 371-2139
Troy Family YMCA, 2500 21st St. 272-5900
YMCA Racquet & Fitness, 20 Old Gick Rd., Saratoga Springs 587-3000

Nature Preserves

Albany Pine Bush Preserve, Madison Ave. Ext., is a relaxing suburban oasis located just past monolithic Crossgates Mall and the roar of traffic. An inland, pitch-pine scrub-oak barrens, this wondrous preserve is one of the rarest landscapes in the country, and harbors many unusual and endangered species, including the federally endangered Karner blue butterfly and 14 other rare insects, along with endangered reptiles. There's also a variety of mammals, including coyotes. The Pine Bush is a multi-use preserve, with 20 miles of scenic walking, biking, and horseback-riding trails, as well as seasonal fishing (Rensselaer Lake is stocked annually), trapping, and limited small-game hunting in designated areas. Although fluttering Karners may be elusive, the stands of restored native flora such as wild blue lupine are easy to find, and guided field trips are held regularly. The preserve is protected by a private-public partnership; since the first 365 acres were purchased in 1974, more than 2,600 acres have been added. The Pine Bush is located between Colonie and Guilderland; trailheads can be accessed from Rte. 155, and the end of Washington Ave. Ext. (look for signs). The Rensselaer Lake park area can be reached from Fuller Rd. across from the I-87 ramp. A preserve guide and trail map is available by calling 785-1800 x 211. www.albanypinebush.org

Barberville Falls, Plank Rd. (County 40 off Rte. 66), Poestenkill, is a scenic, 90-feet-high waterfall with a large pool at the bottom beyond which a stream flows through a deep gorge. Along the ridge and creek trails in the valley can be found many varieties of wild flowers, including starflowers, painted trillium, trout lily, and cardinal flower. The preserve is located across from the Broadside Cemetery. 785-1800.

Dyken Pond Environmental Education Center, 475 Dyken Pond Rd. (Rte. 2), Cropseyville, is an 85-acre conservation area located at the headwaters of the Poestenkill Falls. The preserve contains beech-maple forest, lakes, spruce-fir swamps and vernal pools, and an abundance of wildlife, including red fox, porcupines, beavers, and black bears. The preserve is for low-impact recreation only; allowable activities are hiking, cross-country skiing, non-motor boating (there is a launch), fishing, and ice fishing. Guided hikes range from wildlife sighting to fall foliage, plus moonlight hiking and skiing treks. Open dawn-dusk. Schedules available. 658-2055. www.dykenpond.org

Five Rivers Environmental Center, Game Farm Rd. (off Rte. 44), Delmar, presents educational opportunities for all ages to learn about the natural world. The 330-acre center (which has been honored with a National Park Service award) has five trails winding through woodlands and fields, ponds and streams, and an abandoned orchard. Walking-tour pamphlets can be found at the start of each trail; guided tours are available on weekends. The intrepid explorer might come across foxes and weasels in the woods, or turtles and blue herons in the wetlands. The center can accommodate most physically challenged visitors and two of the trails are wheelchair accessible. The Interpretive Building has exhibits and holds workshops. There's also an amphitheater, picnic shelters, and an enchanting wildlife garden. The center publishes a free newsletter, The Tributary, with schedules of its many wonderful activities. Open dawn to dusk. The Interpretive Building is open Mon-Sat., 9am-4:30pm; Sun. 1pm-5pm. 475-0291. www.fiverivers.8m.com

Tivoli Lake Park, Albany (entrances at Judson St. and Manning Blvd.) is an urban wilderness refuge hidden away in Albany's historic and predominantly African-American Arbor Hill neighborhood. An 80-acre park of wetlands, flowering fields, and woodland, Tivoli is home to assorted wild animals and over 50 species of birds, including herons. Once neglected and used as an illegal dump, this important community resource is being restored by the efforts of the New York Audubon Society, in partnership with the City of Albany and local volunteers.

Schenectady County contains five nature preserves; for more information, call 370-4125. www.schenectadychamber.org

Schenectady County Forest, Lake Rd., Duanesburg (remains of James Duane's colonial settlement, including a family cemetery).

Indian Kill Nature Preserve, Glenville (hardwood and conifer forest, wetlands, and streams stocked with rainbow trout)

Plotter Kill Nature Preserve, Rotterdam (three beautiful waterfalls)

Amy Lemaire Woods, Niskayuna

Schenectady Museum Nature Preserve

Edmund Niles Huyck Preserve, Village of Rensselaerville (off County Rte. 85), is a 2,000-acre natural laboratory of woodlands, fields, swamp bogs, streams and lakes. This environmental center is open to the public year-round for picnicking, fishing, canoeing, rowboating, and bird watching – avian sights include loons, bald eagles, warblers and wild turkeys. The creek trail has a waterfall; trail maps can be obtained at the Mill House Visitors Center (next to bridge on Main St.). Guided hikes are held on Sunday afternoons from mid-May to mid-September. 797-3440.

Lester Park, Lester Park Rd., Saratoga Springs, is a geological park operated by the New York State Museum. This 490-million-year-old sea floor provides a great opportunity to see important fossils and minerals right where they were discovered, and it's a good spot for autumn leaf peeping, too. Open year-round. 474-5877.

Lock 4 Canal Park, Schaghticoke (opposite the village of Stillwater), has shale buffs that overlook the Hoosick River as it flows over a series of rapids. This highly scenic park is a significant botanical habitat, with more than 400 plant species including some state-listed rare species. The area is most impressive in spring, when visitors can watch boats "lock through" from the observation deck. The park also offers a canoe launch, picnic area, and a short nature walk. A fishing spot can be found at the tip of the peninsula at the end of the trail. Open May-November. 664-5261.

SPORTS VENUES

Bleecker Stadium, Clinton Ave. (below Manning Blvd.), Albany, is a multi-purpose, 10-acre sports complex with a professional-size baseball diamond, a football/soccer field, a softball field, and a large field house with lockers and showers. The stadium seats 7,000 for football and soccer, and 2,000 for baseball. Bleecker is the home of the Albany Twilight Baseball League and several youth and adult leagues. 438-2166.

Joseph L. Bruno Stadium, Hudson Valley Community College, 80 Vandenburgh Ave., Troy, was built in 2002 for $14 million and is the finest ballpark in the region. The 4,500-seat stadium (including luxury box seats) is known for its excellent visibility and comfortably wide main concourse. The site also has a picnic area and playground. *"The Joe"* is home to the nationally ranked Tri-City Valleycats. 629-2287. www.hvcc.edu

Pepsi Arena, 51 South Pearl St., Albany, has developed into a mecca for sports fans. The 17,000-seat multi-purpose venue is home to the Albany River Rats of the American Hockey League, the Albany Attack of the National Lacrosse League, Albany Conquest Arena Football, and Siena Saints Division I College Basketball. Other sporting events drawing spectators from near and far include the NBA Classic, the NHL Face-Off, world championship boxing, professional tennis, and the HSBC Metro Atlantic Athletic Conference (MAAC). The arena is also a regular host to premier NCAA championships and collegiate events. And as of 2002, you can add national wrestling and basketball play-offs to the arena's chock-full schedule. 487-2000. www.pepsiarena.com

Auto Racing

Albany Saratoga Speedway, Rte. 9, Malta, offers five divisions of stock-car races: street stock, hobby stock, sportsman, cruiser class, and modifieds. All divisions race almost every evening from late April to late October. Special events include bikers' nights and kids' nights, and a grand finale, "Halloween Havoc." 587-0220. www.newenglandracing.com

Lebanon Valley Speedway and Dragway, Rte. 20, West Lebanon, features stock-car races every Saturday evening and drag races every Sunday, from early April to early November. Novelty events such as demolition derbies and monster-truck rallies crank up the enthusiasm of spectators hooked on the excitement and the roar of engines. On Kiddy Ride Nights, youngsters can go for a spin around the clay track in a racecar. 794-9606. www.lebanonvalley.com

Ballooning

Adirondack Balloon Flights, 76 Helen Dr., Glens Falls, offers sensational one-hour, 10-mile rides over a valley between the Adirondacks and the Green Mountains. Plan on three hours round-trip from the pick-up point at Exit 19, I-87. Sunrise to sunset daily, from April-Nov. $175-$195 per person. 793-6342. www.adirondackballoonflights.com

Ballooning fans and flyers gather for a three-day, hot-air balloon festival every September at the Warren County Airport, Glens Falls. The parade of colorful balloons floating gracefully above the field creates an enchanting backdrop for picnics and family get-togethers. Free. 1-800-365-1050.

Baseball

Many city parks have baseball fields (see pg. 154), and every city and town has Little League and Babe Ruth leagues and dozens of semi-organized sandlot groups. Listings can be found in the yellow pages of the phone book.

Bleecker Stadium, Clinton Ave. (below Manning Blvd.), Albany, has a professional-size baseball diamond, a softball field, and a large field house with lockers and showers. The stadium seats 2,000 for games, and is the home of the Albany Twilight Baseball League and several youth and adult leagues. 438-2166.

Tri-City Valleycats, a Class A affiliate of the Houston Astros, recently relocated to Troy from Pittsfield, Mass. The 'Cats make their home at the Bruno Stadium (see pg. 161) and play an average of 75 games between mid-June and early September. The team holds an annual three-day baseball camp for children. 629-2287.

Westland Hills Park, Colvin Ave. (between Central Ave. and Lincoln Ave.), Albany, maintains eight diamonds to serve its Little League program of over 2,000 participants. 459-6320.

Basketball

Most of the region's city parks (see pg. 154) have basketball courts.

Adirondack Wildcats of the United States Basketball League make their home at the Glens Falls Civic Center, 1 Civic Center Plaza. The center seats 4,800. 798-0366.

Siena Saints Division I College Basketball is considered the region's top sporting event. Siena College's men's and women's basketball teams have established new heights in area attendance records, and each is well represented in the NCAA annual attendance report. The college's men's team makes its home at the Pepsi Arena, drawing an average of 6,500 loyal and wildly enthusiastic fans per game. For ticket information, call 487-2282.

Biking

Many area bike shops (see Shopping, pg. 125) provide information on local bike trails, events, and races. Capital Region Bike-Hike Map is available at the Albany Visitor Center, or by calling 458-2161.

Blue Sky Bicycles, 71 Church St., Saratoga Springs, rents bikes year-round. The shop is located near Broadway and the city's historic district, and stays open till 8pm during the week. Full day rental: $25, half-day: $20. 583-0600.

Colonie Town Park guides peddlers along its section of the Mohawk-Hudson Bikeway with an excellent booklet complete with identification of flowers, birds and wildlife likely to be encountered. The booklet is available in the park office, Rte. 9, Latham (2 1/2 miles north of Latham Traffic Circle, on the left). 783-2760.

Downtube Bike Shop, 466 Madison Ave., Albany, rents bikes year-round, weather permitting. The shop is located across the street from scenic Washington Park, adjacent to Lark Street, and an easy peddle to the Empire State Plaza and downtown historic districts. $25 per day. 434-1711.

Gideon Putnam Hotel, 24 Gideon Putnam Rd., Saratoga Spa State Park, rents bikes June-Sept., 9am-6pm (weather permitting). The terrain throughout the park is level and the surroundings are beautiful – an idyllic locale for sightseeing under one's own steam. $10-$15 per hour, $20-$90 per day (depending on bike). 584-3000.

Mohawk-Hudson Bikeway is 40 miles of asphalt trail running parallel to the Hudson and Mohawk rivers and connecting the cities of Albany, Troy and Schenectady. The bikeway – which also accommodates joggers, walkers and skaters – starts at Corning Riverfront Preserve in Albany and extends to Rotterdam Junction in Schenectady County, passing river banks, canal locks, and scenic countryside along the way. One popular access point is Colonie Town Park, a section that offers flowers, birds and wildlife. From Watervliet, you can meander south along the river to the Empire State Plaza. The bikeway is off-road, except for four miles between Amsterdam and Rotterdam Junction (Rte. 5S can be used to connect), and one mile in the city of Schenectady. Many sections follow along the old Erie Canal towpath; some of America's earliest mills, dams, bridges, and mansions were built along this route. The bikeway is justifiably famed statewide. Maps are available at the Albany and Troy Visitor Centers, or by download at www.nycanal.com

Mohawk-Hudson Cycling Club has 700 members and sponsors daily rides within a 60-mile radius in the Albany-Troy-Schenectady area. The rides are open to all, and geared for beginners through experienced cyclists. MHCC holds two major events every September: the Century (100-mile) Weekend in Saratoga Spa State Park, and the Mountain Bike Festival in Grafton Lakes State Park. The club also supplies information on road riding, mountain biking, and safety tips, and presents repair clinics and cycling courses. Meetings are held the first Thursday of each month at St. Michael's Church in Colonie. Membership is $15 per year, and includes a subscription to the *Bikeabout* newsletter. 439-6678. www.hudsonmohawkcycling.org

Riverspark Visitors Center, 251 River St., Troy, loans bikes for free (with a $20 deposit). This is a terrific way to tour the city's historic downtown and college campuses, or to peddle along the Hudson in nearby Riverfront Park. Summer hours: Tues-Fri., 10am-6pm (some Fridays 'till 8pm); Sat-Sun., 10am-5pm. 270-8667.

Saratoga Freewheelers Bicycle Club promotes bicycling in the Saratoga area and provides "fast" rides on weekday evenings at 6pm, and women's rides on Sundays. Free. Call Blue Sky Bicycles, 71 Church St., for more information. 583-0600.

Saratoga Mountain Bike Association leases pristine trails in Saratoga Springs. Meetings are held at the Saratoga Springs Public Library, 49 Henry St.; membership is $35 per year, and includes access to the trails and a subscription to the newsletter. Contact All Outdoors, 35 Van Dam St., for more information. 587-0455.

Uncle Sam Bikeway, North Troy and Lansingburgh, features three miles of paved pathway, with wildflowers, waterfalls and shale cliffs along the way. It provides excellent walking for handicapped persons and for pushing wheelchairs and strollers: Built on an 1800s railroad bed (the tracks were dismantled in 1973 and the bikeway was opened in 1981), the trail is mostly level with gentle curves. There's a wondrous variety of trees including oaks, cottonwood, sugar maple, black cherry, mulberry, elm, and locust, and in the fall the foliage is brilliant. At the culvert about one-quarter mile north of the monument at Knickerbacker Park is an unmarked trail that leads to scenic Oakwood Cemetery. Dusk to dawn. For more information, contact the Troy Recreation Dept. at 270-4600. [Directions: the bikeway is accessible from Rte. 142 (Northern Dr.), from the east end of 124th St.; from Cemetery Rd. at 119th St.; also from Gurley Ave. at 114th St.; also from Knickerbacker Park (by crossing the fields to the monument). Handicapped access is best from Rte. 142, Gurley Ave., and Cemetery Rd.].

Boating

The Capital Region is a haven for boating enthusiasts. Lake George and the Mohawk and Hudson rivers accommodate sizeable vessels, and lakes suitable for small craft abound (see State Parks, pg. 152).

Saratoga Lake State Boat Launch, Rte. 9P (four miles southeast of Saratoga Springs), is located at the north end of the lake and has parking capacity for 100 trailers. The lake has several private marinas, and allows sailing, rowing and motor boating. Open year-round.

Waterford Canal Visitor Center, Tugboat Alley, was recently renovated and expanded to accommodate the canal's growing number of pleasure boats. The two-story center contains small exhibits related to the Erie Canal, a boat launch and services for boaters (including showers), and a walking tour of the towpath. A schedule of festive canal-boating events is available. Open April-October, 7am-7pm. Off-season by appointment. 233-9123.

Information packets on other boat launches along the Erie Canal are available from the NYS Canal Corp., 436-2799. www.canals.state.ny.us

Hudson River public launches can be found at the Corning Riverfront Preserve, under the I-787 bridge.

Mohawk River public launches can be found at:

Freemans Bridge, Freemans Bridge Rd., Glenville

Quist Rd., one mile east of the city of Amsterdam

Rotterdam Junction, Rte. 5S, just past the Exit 26 toll station.

Waterford Battery Park below Lock #2.

For more information and a complete list of state boat-launch sites, contact the New York State Environmental Conservation Department, 625 Broadway, Albany, 457-1860. www.dec.state.ny

The following sites are just a sampling of the region's many marinas. Services vary, although most include transient and overnight dockage, electricity, water, and pump-outs. It's advisable to call in advance to determine availability of dock space, specific services, and hours of operation.

Hudson River
Albany Marine Service, 1395 New Loudon Rd., Cohoes, 783-5333

Schuyler Yacht Basin, 1 Ferry St., Schuylerville, 695-3193

Troy Town Dock and Marina, 427 River St., Troy, 272-5341

Van Schaick Marina, 50 Delaware Ave., Cohoes, 237-2681

Erie Canal
Blaine's Bay Marina, 1 Dunsback Ferry Rd., Cohoes, 785-6785

Schenectady Yacht Club, Rexford (Rte. 146), 384-9971

Wilson's Marine Service, 4 Freeman's Bridge Rd., Scotia, 382-0077

Canal Boating

Erie Canal Cruise Lines offers fully equipped, easy-to-operate canal boats for week-long or weekend charters, May through October. These roomy, 41-foot vessels contain full-size showers and beds, deluxe galleys, and almost everything else needed for a safe and comfortable cruise, including instruction on navigating canal locks. A sample seven-day itinerary starts in Waterford and cruises north on the Champlain Canal to Saratoga Springs, Schuylerville, and Fort Edward, with entry to Lake Champlain in Whitehall, Vt., and passage to Fort Ticonderoga, with the Adirondacks and Green Mountains in the background. Boaters can also head south on the Hudson River and tour the Hudson Valley from Waterford to West Point, or go west on the Erie Canal to Oneida Lake. A variety of self-captained boats are available, providing a unique way to experience the scenic beauty and historic attractions of the region. One-way, seven-day cruise: $2,200 (up to four passengers, $100 fee for each additional passenger). 1-800-962-1771.

Canoeing, Kayaking & Rowing

Albany Rowing Center, Boat House, Corning Riverfront Preserve (under the I-787 underpass), has an ideal location: The riverfront boat launch offers direct access to the Hudson River, a ramp, plenty of parking, and proximity to the Hudson-Mohawk bike path. The center offers four competitive and recreational rowing programs for all levels of ability. March-Oct. 446-6282

The Boat House, 2855 Aqueduct Rd. (Balltown Rd. at Rexford Bridge), Schenectady, is located on the Mohawk River and rents canoes and kayaks by the hour or by the day, from April to November. These lightweight boats are easy to handle and transport by car top, and classes are available. The boat house also sells canoes, kayaks, rowing shells, and all accessories, including car racks and portage dollies. Close to the historic Rexford Aqueduct, this part of the Mohawk is known for its bass fishing. $25-$35 per day. 393-5711. www.boathousecanoeskayaks.com

Rising Tide Touring Company offers scenic perspectives on the Hudson River, as well as the opportunity to learn new watercraft skills. Kayak trips start at the Port of Albany – with views of the urban skyline – and continue past Kinderhook and Stockport to the grand landscapes of the Catskill Mountains. 784-2342.

Saratoga Outfitters, 268 Broadway, Saratoga Springs, offers customized kayak trips, rentals, and instruction on Saratoga Lake and the Hudson River. 584-3932.

Curling

Curling, the sport in which two teams of four players strategically slide "stones" over a stretch of ice toward a circular target, has grown in popularity since becoming an official Olympic competition in 1998.

Albany Curling Club, 117 McKown Rd. (just off Western Ave.), McKownville, offers curling activities for all ages and levels of abilities from Nov-April. 456-6272.

Schenectady Curling Club, Balltown Rd., Niskayuna, has been in existence for 70 years. Free clinics for beginners are offered frequently. The club also hosts national competitions. 372-4063. www.members.localnet.com

Fishing

Good-to-excellent trout fishing can be found in the Hudson and Mohawk rivers. The Mohawk, especially, offers exceptional warm-water fishing: anglers can cast their rods for small-mouth bass, channel catfish, northern pike, Coho salmon or blueback herring. Areas around the canal locks are reputed to be the most bountiful. (A handicapped-adopted fishing-access facility can be found between Locks 6 and 7.) The upper Hudson offers the prized striped bass in springtime (don't forget the bloodworms!) and shad almost year-round. Salmon, small-mouth bass, trout, and pike can be fished from Lake George, while large-mouth bass are known to inhabit all the major lakes in the area, especially Saratoga Lake.

For information and equipment, contact:

Keith Bait & Tackle Store, 101 Clinton Ave., Albany.................. 449-1229
Nick's Field & Stream, 1513 Broadway, Schenectady................. 383-7908
Goldstock's Sporting Goods, 98 Freeman's Bridge Rd., Scotia.......... 382-2037

Battenkill Riversports & Camping, 937 Rte. 313, Cambridge, has seasonal river sites on the Battenkill – one of the best trout fishing areas in the country. The company offers fishing gear, instruction, licenses, and bait, in addition to canoe, kayak and tubing trips. Camp grounds available. 677-8868. www.brsac.com

Football

Albany Conquest Arena Football is hosted by the Pepsi Arena during its April-July season. The 'Quest, as this exciting team is called, features local talent from RPI and UAlbany. 487-2000. www.pepsiarena.com

New York Giants Summer Training, University Field, UAlbany, 1400 Washington Ave., Albany, takes place during July and August. Practice sessions are usually held 9am-11am and 3pm-5pm. Spectators are welcome, and the team plays several pre-season games during training, in addition to holding events such as the "Exhibition Program and Fan Rally," and the "Meet the Giants Fan Party." The university's superior playing fields and the accessibility of the players for autographs – combined with the fact that Giants' games sell out in advance – make these practices a great opportunity to see the team in action. $8 per day (includes parking). Tickets are available at the UAlbany Recreation Center, Mon-Fri., 9am-3pm, or by phone: 442-4683. Fan info-line: 442-7369. www.albany.edu/sports.giants

Golf

The following list of the area's many public courses is not all-inclusive. For additional listings of area golf courses call for the free booklet, The Capital Region Golfer, 1-800-I LOVE NY. www.iloveny.com

Capital Hills at Albany
65 O'Neill Rd. (off New Scotland Ave.), Albany
18 holes, par 72, 6,230 yards, pro shop, driving range, putting green.
Open April-Nov. 7, Mon-Fri. 9am-dusk; Sat-Sun. 6:30am-dusk. $24. 438-2208.

Eagle Crest Golf Club
Rte.146A, Ballston Lake
18 holes, 72 par, 6,814 yards, pro shop, driving range, putting green.
The layout features two-tiered greens and large greens with many undulations.
Open March 20-Nov., dawn to dusk. $13-$26. 877-7082.

Frear Park Golf Course
Oakwood Ave., Troy
18 holes, par 71, 6,234 yards, pro shop, putting green. Open mid-April-Nov., 7am-dusk. $11-$23. 270-4553.

Hiawatha Trails Golf Course
State Farm Rd. (Rte. 155), Guilderland
18 holes, 57 par, 2,331 yards, pro shop, putting green. The layout has a flat front 9 and a hilly back 9. Open April-Nov., 7 am-dusk, closed Mondays. $13. 456-9512.

Mill Road Acres
30 Mill Rd., Latham
18 holes, par 58, driving range, putting green. Open March-Nov., 7am-7pm.
$10-$18. 785-4653.

Orchard Creek Golf Club
6700 Dunnsville Rd. (Rte. 399), Altamont
18 holes, par 71, pro shop, grass driving range, putting green. The layout at this regional favorite is carved out of a mature apple orchard, and was featured in Golf Digest. Open April-Nov., 6:30am-8pm. $25-$30. 861-5000.

Stadium Golf Course
333 Jackson Ave., Schenectady
18 holes, par 71, 6,316 yards, pro shop, driving range, putting green. Open March-Nov., dawn-dusk. $13-$26. 374-9104.

Saratoga Lake Golf Course
Grace Moore Rd. (south end of lake, off County Rte. 76)
18 holes, par 72, 6,270 yards. The layout has significant elevation changes, undulating greens, and wetlands hazards. Driving range, putting range. Open April-Nov., 7am-dusk. $20-$30. 581-6616. www.saratogalakegolf.com

Saratoga National Golf Club
458 Union Ave. (Rte. 9P), Saratoga Springs
18 holes, 72 par, 7,237 yards, driving range, putting green. The world-class layout, considered the most challenging in the region, meanders through and around wetlands, ponds and lakes. Facilities include a multi-million-dollar clubhouse. Open April-Nov., 6:30am-9pm. $120. 583-4653.

Saratoga Spa Champion Golf Course
Roosevelt Dr. (Spa State Park), Saratoga Springs
18 holes, par 72, 7,078 yards, driving range, putting green. The layout is mostly flat and especially beautiful. J. Victor Skiff Executive is the spa park's 9-hole, par-29 course. Open mid-April-Nov. (till Dec 20, weather permitting), weekdays 7am-7pm; weekends 6am-7pm. $13-$25. 584-2006.

Schenectady Municipal
400 Oregon Ave., Schenectady
18 holes, par 72, 6, 560 yards, pro shop, driving range, putting green. Open mid-March to mid-Dec., 7am-dusk. $23. 382-5155.

Sycamore Country Club
Rte. 143, Ravena
18 holes, par 71, 6,528 yards, pro shop, practice range, putting green.
Open April-Oct., 7am-dusk. $14-$22. 756-6635.

Town of Colonie Golf Course
418 Consaul Rd., Colonie
36 holes, 72 par, 6,704 yards, driving range, putting green. The layout has
a new bridge over the Lishakill Creek. Open March-Dec. (weather permitting),
8am-7pm. $24. 374-4181.

Van Patton Golf Course
Main St., Clifton Park
27 holes, par 73, 6,640 yards, pro shop, putting green. The challenging
layout features mature trees, spacious greens, and wide, sloping fairways.
Open April-Nov.25, 6:30am-6:30pm. $13-$25. 877-5400.

Western Turnpike
Rte. 20, Guilderland
27 holes, 72 par, 6,336 yards, driving range, putting green. Open April-mid-Nov.,
7am-dusk. $25. 456-0786.

Whispering Pines Executive
2208 Helderberg Ave., Rotterdam
9 holes, par 55, 2,315 yards, pro shop, driving range, putting green.
Open April-Dec. (weather permitting), 8am-dusk. $15. 355-2724.

Capital District Skins Game is an annual tournament and benefit for Ellis
Hospital in Schenectady. The match is held in late June at a local golf course,
and features celebrity golfers such as Arnold Palmer, Lee Trevino, and Craig
Stadler. Over the past 10 years, the tournament has raised almost $2 million
for the hospital.

Capital Region Futures Classic tournament is an annual part of the LPGA's
official developmental tour. The match is held in early July at the Orchard Creek
Golf Club in Altamont. 861-5000. www.orchardcreek.com

Hockey

Adirondack Ice Hawks of the United Hockey League make their home at the Glens Falls Civic Center, I Civic Center Plaza. The center seats 4,800. 798-0366.

Albany County Hockey Training Facility, Albany Shaker Rd. (across from Albany International Airport), is a 40,000-square-foot facility that serves as home ice rink for the US Olympic team. A multi-purpose venue, it's available for speed and figure skating, hockey, and public skating. Rentals, sharpening. Open daily (closed May-June). Adults $3, youths and seniors $1-$2. Open hockey games $7. 452-7396.

Albany River Rats are an AHL team whose exploits are eagerly followed by local hockey fans. The team makes its home at the Pepsi Arena for the Oct-April season, and is considered one of the region's top sporting attractions. 487-2000. www.pepsiarena.com

Clifton Park Ice Arena, Clifton Commons (left on Vischer's Ferry Rd.), hosts hockey clubs and leagues. 383-5440.

Frear Park, Park Dr., Troy, 266-0023 (see pg. 155)

Houston Field House, RPI campus, Troy, is home to RPI's Men's and Women's hockey teams. It seats 5,000-7,000 and has a 185-by-85-foot ice rink. The arena was built after World War II out of a surplus Navy warehouse relocated from Rhode Island, and for many decades was popularly known as "the Madison Square Garden" of upstate New York. The field house was revamped in 1983, and today serves primarily as a hockey, figure-skating, and public-skating facility. Box-office: 276-6262. www.rpi.edu

Knickerbacker Ice Arena, 103 8th Ave., Troy, hosts hockey leagues and tournaments. The 180-by-100-foot rink has NHL regulation markings, while the wooden bleachers give over 2,000 spectators a bird's-eye view. Pro shop, lessons, skate rentals, sharpening. 235-7761. Year-round.

RPI Engineers, Rensselaer Polytechnic Institute's men's hockey team, has been in existence since 1901. After the construction of the Houston Field House, the team achieved national prominence – a tradition that continues to contribute to the excitement level of area hockey. Tickets are available through the field-house box office (see above entry) or through Ticketmaster at 476-1000.

Horseback Riding

The stables listed below offer boarding, training, and riding lessons (English saddle) for adults and children.

After Hours Farm, 711 Waite Rd., Clifton Park 399-3310
Dutch Manor, 2331 Western Ave., Guilderland 456-5010
Harlequin Farm, 383 Rte. 32, Schuylerville 587-9820
Hunter Creek Stables, Amsterdam 842-3800
Pine Bush Equestrian Club, 175 Rapp Rd., Albany 452-7755
Winter Glen Riding Academy, Farm County Line Rd., Schenectady 356-3364

Bailiwick Ranch, 1118 Castle Rd., Catskill, offers recreational horseback riding on scenic mountain trails. Hourly, all-day, and overnight camping excursions available year-round. Also four-wheelers for hire. Open daily April-Nov.; Dec-March on Sat-Sun. only, or by appointment. 678-5665.

Horseracing

Harness Racing

Saratoga Equine Sports Center, Nelson Ave. (Rte. 9), Saratoga Springs, was created in 1941 and is known for its intense wagering and intimate, 1/2 mile track – the clubhouse and glass-enclosed grandstand put fans right on top of the action. Live harness racing is featured 124 dates a year: weekend afternoons during winter, and evenings under the lights during spring and summer. Post time is generally 7:40 pm. The center also hosts polo, barrel racing, and team-roping competitions, and is currently undergoing a $5 million expansion to outfit the lower grandstand with video lottery terminals and convert the facility into "racino." Admission and parking are free. 584-2110. www.saratogaraceway.com

Thoroughbred Racing

Saratoga Race Track, Union Ave., Saratoga Springs, is the country's oldest and most beautiful racetrack (see Points of Interest, pg. 31). It's also renowned for its excellence: *Sports Illustrated* ranks the track as one of the "Top Ten Sports Venues in the World." The historic grounds, the aura of tradition, and the accessibility of the paddocks make a day at these races a greater experience than just handicapping the horses and betting on the outcome – although that alone is plenty exciting. Races are held daily (except Tuesdays) from July through early Sept. Post time is 1pm. The legendary Travers Stakes is run on the third Saturday in August. For many fans, the track's early-morning routine is as interesting as the racecard events. Between 7:30 to 9:30am, there are starting-gate demonstrations, a paddock show, and free tram tours of the barn area. Visitors may listen to expert commentary as they watch these beautiful animals take their warm-up laps. Breakfast is available on the clubhouse porch (without entrance fee).

The grounds are then cleared, and visitors must exit and re-enter for the day's races. Gates open at 11am weekdays, 10:30am weekends. General admission $3, clubhouse $5, children 12-and-under are free. Get there early – tickets for the grandstand are limited. 584-6200. www.nyracing.com/saratoga

Hunting

New York State Dept. of Environmental Conservation supervises several Wildlife Management Areas in the greater Capital Region. Hunting and fishing are allowed in the following areas:

Black Creek Marsh, Voorheesville, is 287 acres of wetland with hiking trails for bird watching, snowshoeing, hunting, fishing, and trapping. This WMA is located in the towns of Guilderland and New Scotland. To reach the area from Voorheesville, take Rte. 156 north, turn right on Kling Terrace, go to the end to reach state land or take Rte. 156 north two-and-a-half miles, turn right on County Rte. 202, go three-tenths of a mile to the state land. Parking lot.

Margaret Burke, Knox, is 246 acres of upland offering bird watching, cross-country skiing, snowshoeing, hunting and trapping. To reach the area from Knox, take Rte. 156 east two miles, turn right on County Rte. 254, go about eight-and-a-half miles to the state land. Parking lot.

Partridge Run, Sickle Hill Rd., Berne, is 4,600 acres of upland with hiking trails, birdwatching, cross-country skiing, snowshoeing, hunting, fishing and trapping. Recreationists are well advised not to use this area during big-game hunting season. To reach the area from Rensselaerville, take NYS Rte. 85N one mile, turn left on County Rte. 6, go three miles to state land.

For more information or to confirm directions, contact the Region 4 EnCon office at 357-2234. www.dec.state.ny.us.

Ice Skating/Indoors

It's advisable to call ahead for hours, which are limited and subject to interruption by hockey matches. Admission to the below entries averages $3-$4 for adults, a dollar or two less for children and seniors.

Albany County Hockey Facility
830 Albany-Shaker Rd., Albany
Rentals, lessons. Free learn-to-skate sessions, fall through winter on Saturday mornings (384-0488). Open year-round. 452-7396.

Clifton Park Ice Arena
Clifton Commons (off Vischer's Ferry Rd.)
Rentals, lessons. Open year-round. 383-5440.

Frear Park, Park Dr., Troy, 266-0023 (see pg. 155)

Houston Field House
RPI campus, Troy
Full-service pro shop, regularly scheduled public skates. Open year-round.
276-6262.

Hudson Valley Community College Ice Arena
80 Vandenburgh Ave., Troy
Instruction, rentals, sharpening, repairs. Oct-March. 629-4850.

Knickerbacker Ice Arena
103 8th Ave., Troy
The arena's 180 x 100 ice rink accommodates figure skating, speed skating and free style. Expert instruction, pro shop, rentals, sharpening, repairs. Open year-round. 235-7761.

Saratoga Springs Youth Community Rink
Excelsior and East Ave., Saratoga
Figure-skating club, adult-hockey club. Open Oct-March. 587-3550.

Saratoga Springs Ice Rink
Weibel Ave., Saratoga Springs
Rentals. Open year-round. 583-3462.

Schenectady County Ice Rink
Airport Rd. (off Rte. 50), Glenville
Skating and hockey. Rentals, classes. Open year-round. 384-0538.

Ice Skating/Outdoors
Albany
Buckingham Lake Park, Berkshire Blvd. and Colonial Ave.

Empire State Plaza, (near the Egg at the north end). Parking is free on weekends and after 2pm weekdays. The closest parking is on State St. (metered on weekdays). For ice conditions, call 474-8860.

Swinburne Park, Clinton Ave. at Manning Blvd., Albany, has an all-weather, protected rink for city residents. The YMCA offers a free after-school learn-to-skate program for kids and teenagers on Fridays and Saturdays. Rentals. Open Nov-March. 438-2406.

Washington Park Lake, Madison Ave. (south side of park).

Colonie
Colonie maintains 14 natural skating ponds. Ann Lee Pond, adjacent to the Albany International Airport, is one of the best in the area. For information and conditions for all Colonie sites call 785-4301.

Troy
Beldon's Pond, near the junction of Rtes. 2 and 66.

Knickerbacker Park, 103 8th Ave., Troy, 235-7761 (see pg. 155).

Schenectady
Iroquois Lake, Central Park, Fehr Ave. (off of State St.), 292-0368.

Steinmetz Lake, Steinmetz Park (near Lenox Rd.).

Saratoga
Saratoga Spa State Park, 19 Roosevelt Dr. (off Rte. 9), has a hockey rink and a recreational rink. Both have night lighting and offer round-the-clock skating hours. The large and scenic Avenue of the Pines rink (follow signs for Victoria Pool) is one of the most enjoyable in the region. Rentals, sharpening. Open mid-Nov-mid-March. 584-2535.

Mountain Climbing
Some of the tallest and most breathtaking mountains in the United States are located in the Adirondacks, between one and two hours drive from downtown Albany.

Adirondack Mountain Club, 814 Goggins Rd., Lake George, was founded in 1922 and has twenty-eight chapters. The Albany chapter is the oldest and largest, with 3,400 members who enjoy canoeing, camping and mountain hiking. The club takes a balanced approach to outdoor recreation and advocacy, and offers activities throughout the year including trips, seminars on wilderness skills, and volunteer conservation efforts. Members receive the quarterly magazine, *The Cloudsplitter*. Informal meetings are held the second Tuesday of the month, Oct-June, at St. Paul's Episcopal Church, 21 Hackett Blvd., Albany. The public is welcome to attend. 899-2725. www.adk.org

Parasailing

In this exciting sport, the bold-at-heart sail hundreds of feet above a body of water, held aloft by a parachute drawn by a motorboat. In the Lake George area, the views are especially spectacular.

Parasailing and Power Chuting Adventures
2 Kurosaka Lane, Lake George
Instruction provided. Daily May-late-Oct. 668-4644.

Sun Sports Parasailing, Chick's Marina
Bolton Landing (10 mi. north of Lake George Village on Rte. 9N)
Daily 10am-6pm. 644-3470.

Polo

Saratoga Polo, Whitney and Boswick Fields, Saratoga Springs, presents some of the best high-goal polo in the world. From June through September, top players from England, Argentina and the U.S. contend in sponsored cup matches, including the USDA President's Cup. The matches are played on fields famous for their quality. The association welcomes spectators, and picnic facilities are available. General admission: $5. 584-8108. www.saratogapolo.com

Rafting

The Hudson River Gorge in the Adirondack Mountains is one of America's premier white-water rivers.

Adirondack Wildwaters, Corinth, offers rafting trips on the Hudson River Gorge and the gentler Sacandaga River. 696-2953.

Hudson River Rafting Co., Rte. 9N to Rte. 28, North Creek (just before south entrance to North Creek, at Cunningham's Ski Barn), offers scenic rafting trips and whitewater adventures on four rivers, including the Hudson River Gorge, the Sacandaga River, and the challenging Moose River. Daily 9am-3pm, May-Oct. 696-2964. www.hudsonriverrafting.com

Whitewater Challengers, Rte. 28, 13th Lake, North Creek, offers whitewater rafting trips on the Hudson River Gorge. Reservations required. April-Columbus Day, 8am-9pm. 1-800-RAFT.

Rock Climbing/Indoor

Albany's Indoor Rockgym, 4C Vatrano Rd. (off Central Ave.), Albany, has the area's only indoor cave for spelunking. Designed for training or games, this labyrinth includes a Tyrolean traverse and "stalactites." The gym also has a realistic wall surface with overhangs, and provides instruction in climbing techniques and safety, rappelling, and caving games. Rentals and group rates available. Open 3pm-10pm weekdays, noon-10pm weekends. $16.50 (includes equipment). 459-7625.

Electric City Rock Climbing Gym, City Center Sportsplex, 433 State St., Schenectady, is a full-service facility featuring a 40-foot-high climbing wall, a transversing wall, and a challenging bouldering room. The gym offers instruction, rental gear, and memberships, and also sponsors outdoor trips for rock climbing, ice climbing and rappelling. Open Tues-Fri., 11am-9pm; Sat. noon-10pm, Sun. noon-7pm. $15 adults, $12 children (includes equipment). 388-2704.

Running

Runners can use college-campus facilities (see Education), and city bike and pedestrian paths, including:

Riverfront Park, Troy

Corning Riverfront Preserve, Albany

Central Park, Schenectady

Hudson Mohawk Road Runners Club is the region's largest running organization. Formed in 1971, the club has over 2,000 members – of all running styles and speeds – and organizes nearly 30 running events. Club races are held at many different locations in the region, offering something for novices and veterans alike, including European-style cross-country races. Popular races include the annual marathon held in February; the Schenectady Stockade-athon held in mid-November, and Indian Ladder trail race and barbecue at Thatcher Park in July. HMRRC also publishes a monthly newsletter, The Pace Setter. For race information: 435-4500. www.hmrrc.com

Freihofer's Run for Women is a 5-K race held in downtown Albany every spring, and is one of the most important races in America for female runners. A 20-year tradition, the event has grown to involve the entire community with the inclusion of recreational races, walking events, and a Kid's Run. 434-2032. www.albanyevents.org

Saratoga Spa State Park, 19 Roosevelt Dr., Saratoga Springs (between Rte. 9 and 50), has shady streamside trails for casual running and nature walks, and a certified running course for use by athletes. 584-2535.

Troy Turkey Trot, Knickerbacker Recreational Facility, 191 103 St., Troy, holds a benefit running and walking event every Thanksgiving morning. A series of trophy road races for all ages is augmented by the 1.5-mile Turkey Walk, a turkey-day tradition since 1964. 235-7761. www.coolrunning.com

Skiing/Downhill

Surrounded by four mountain ranges, the Capital Region is conveniently adjacent to numerous ski facilities within an hour's drive or less, and suiting every budget and skill level. For a free guide to New York State ski centers, call 1 (800) CALL NYS. www.iloveny.com

For current ski conditions, call:

New York State . . . . 1 (800) CALLNYS
Catskills 1 (800) 852-5500
Massachusetts 1 (800) 342-1840
Vermont 1 (800) 229-0531

Ski season is generally mid-November through early April. Rentals, lessons, and snow making are standard at the below entries. Facilities with lighted trails for night skiing are preceded by an asterisk [*].

*Bousquet Ski Area
101 Dan Fox Dr., Pittsfield, Mass.
This is an accessibly sized, family-oriented ski area located in the beautiful Berkshires. 21 trails (13 lighted), 750-foot vertical drop, snowtubing park. Open Mon-Fri., 10am-10pm; Sat. 9am-10pm; Sun. 9am-4pm. $15-$25. (413) 442-8316. www.bousquets.com [I-90E to Exit 11E, follow Rte. 20 for 15 mi. into Hancock, turn right at Friendly's onto Barker Rd., then left on Tamarack Rd.]

Brodie Mountain
Rte. 7, New Ashford, Mass.
In 1999, Brodie was purchased by nearby Jiminy Peak, which put a new emphasis on family fun with expanded snow-tubing areas and snowshoeing trails. As of winter 2003, Brodie suspended downhill skiing indefinitely. Open Fri. evening; Sat-Sun; and holidays. Rates for snowshoe rentals and tubing (includes advanced tubes and chairlifts) are $12 per 90-minute session. (413) 443-4752. www.skibrodie.com

*Catamount Ski Area
Rte. 23 between Hillsdale and South Egremont, Mass.
Located atop the N.Y. and Mass. border, Catamount has skiing terrain on both the Berkshires and the Taconic Range, holding a special attraction for skiers. The ski area's more than 110 acres offer challenges for beginners to experts – the double black diamond "Catapult" trail is the steepest in the Berkshires. 28 trails, 1,000-foot vertical drop. Open daily 9am-4pm; Weds-Sat., 5pm-10pm. $21-$42. 724-1846. [Taconic State Parkway south to Hillsdale Exit, onto 23 East; 11 miles to Catamount.]

Hunter Mountain Ski Bowl
Hunter
This three-mountain facility for beginners to extreme skiers recently made over $7 million in improvements, adding a state-of-the-art learning center, a terrain park and pipe, and advanced snow-making equipment – Hunter is famed for having the deepest snow base in the East. 53 trails (4 of them double-black diamond), 1,600 vertical drop. The ski bowl's season begins early and ends late. Open daily, 8am-4:30pm. $38-$46. 1-(888)-HunterMTN. [NYS Thruway Exit 21] www.huntermtn.com

*Jiminy Peak Ski Resort
Hancock, Mass.
The largest ski and snowboard resort in the region, Jiminy is also one of the most inexpensive, flexible, and fun. 40 trails (18 lighted), 1,150-foot vertical drop, and the scenic "Berkshire Express" 5-minute lift. $28-$49. (413) 738-5500. [I-90 East to Exit 7 (Defreestville); left on Rte. 43 to Hancock; right at sign; Jiminy is 1/4 mile on right]. www.jiminypeak.com

*Maple Ski Ridge
Mariaville Rd., Rotterdam
This former family farm retains its family atmosphere, and non-skiing parents can watch their children from a large window in the lodge. Excellent lessons are offered by the Schenectady Ski School (377-3730). Five miles of trails for beginners to intermediate, 400-foot vertical drop, double- and triple-chair lifts. $12-$21. 381-4700. [Rte. 159, 4 mi. west of Schenectady]. www.mapleridge.com

Ski Plattekill
Plattekill Mountain Rd., Roxbury
An all-ages, all-skill-levels adventure, Plattekill offers a "Tubalooza Snowtubing Park" in addition to its recently expanded snow-making and grooming capabilities. 32 trails and slopes, 1,000 vertical drop. Open Fri-Sun., plus holidays and Christmas week, 8:45am-4:15pm. Also open midweek after a snowstorm. $24-$35. (607) 326-3500. [Exit 19 off I-87N]. www.skiplattekill.com

*West Mountain Ski Center
59 West Mt. Rd., Glens Falls
Located in the Adirondacks, West offers breathtaking views of the Hudson
Valley, Lake George, and the surrounding mountains. 22 forest trails, 1,010-foot
vertical drop, snowboard park. Open Mon-Fri., 9:30am-10:30pm, Sat-Sun.,
8:30am-6:30pm. $18-$35. 793-9431. [I-87N to Exit 18; left on Corinth Rd., 3 miles
to sign on right, entrance is 3/4 mile on left]. www.westmountain.com

*Willard Mountain
77 Intervale Rd., Greenwich
Generations of area residents learned to ski at this convenient, beginner-friendly
ski area, which sits atop the serenely resplendent hills of Washington County.
14 trails, 508-foot vertical drop, tubing park, sled-dog rentals. $18-$25. Open daily
9am-10pm. 692-7337. [Rte. 40N straight ahead; 8 mi. north of Schaighticoke, look
for signs]. www.willardmountain.com

*Windham Mountain
Lane Rd., Windham
Located in the stunning Great Northern Catskill Mountains, Windham is a
premier ski facility offering every amenity and accommodating all skill levels.
39 trails 1,600-foot vertical drop on two mountain peaks, terrain parks with a
lighted park and ski and tubing trails. Open daily 9am-4pm, weekends and
holidays 8am-4pm. Lighted trails till 10pm. $20-$46. 734-4300. [NYS Thruway
to Exit 21; then take Rte. 23 West directly to Windham]. wwwskiwindham.com

Not Far Away
Belleayre Ski Center
Bellayre Mountain Rd., Highmount (87 mi.)
Located in the beautiful heart of the Catskill Forest Preserve, Belleayre is an
especially scenic mountain with pristine, forested trails and a glade trail. Owned
by EnCon, the ski center is family-oriented (free lessons for first-timers) and
accommodates all levels. 35 trails, 1,404-foot vertical drop, snowboard park.
Open 9am-4pm. $30-$39. During winter discount week (Jan.27-Feb.3) lift tickets
are discounted to $10. (845) 254-5600. www.belleayre.com

Bromley Mountain
3984 Rte. 11, Manchester, Vt. (75 mi.)
Sunny Bromley is described as a "big, classic New England mountain," with
varied terrain for all skill levels. 43 trails, 1,334-foot vertical drop, high-speed
quad lift. Open weekdays, 9am-4pm, weekends and holidays, 8:30am-4pm.
$31-$51. (802)-824-5522. www.bromley.com

Gore Mountain Ski Center
Peaceful Valley Rd., North Creek (90 mi.)
This Adirondack ski resort is routinely rated in the top five of Northeast ski facilities. Gore's three mountains of skiing and snowboarding include every variety of trail, from gentle glides to dizzying vertical drops. And the Northwoods Gondola ride, with its views of the high peaks, is worth the trip even for non-skiers. 75 trails, 2,100 vertical drop, ski school and clinics. Open 8:30am-4pm. $26-$52. Under-6 and over-70 are free. 251-2411. Snow conditions: (800) 342-1234. www.goremountain.com

Stratton Mountain
Bondville (near Manchester), Vt. (81 mi.)
Stratton is known for its snow cover and advanced snowmaking capabilities. This 600-acre ski resort (with lodging village) offers "the ultimate in uphill capacity," with 16 lifts including four high-speed, six-passenger lifts and a high-speed, 12-passenger summit gondola. 90 trails, 2,003 vertical drop, ski and snowboard schools, award-winning terrain parks. Open 8:30am-4pm. $46-$72. (800) STRATTON. www.stratton.com

Skiing/Cross-Country
Capital Hills at Albany Golf Course
New Scotland Ave., Albany
Gentle slopes. Free. 438-2208.

Dyken Pond Environmental Center
Dyken Pond Rd. (off Rte. 2), Cropseyville
7 miles of varied-terrain nature trails – you just might shoosh past a red fox, coyote or porcupine. Guided moonlight ski treks. Free. 658-2055.

Featherstonhaugh State Forest
Rotterdam Junction (9 mi. west of Schenectady near Mariaville)
2 miles of flat trails, 2 miles of hilly trails; good for novices. Free. 370-4125.

Five Rivers Environmental Education Center
56 Game Farm Rd. (off Rte. 443), Delmar
10 km of trails, open daily 9am-4:30pm. Free. 475-0291.

Grafton Lakes State Park
Rte. 2, Grafton
15 km of trails. Free. 279-1155.

Indian Ladder Farms
242 Altamont Rd., Altamont
7 miles of groomed trails, homemade hot cider and warm cider donuts in the
barn. Open Weds-Sun., 9am-5pm. $5. 765-2956.

John Boyd Thacher State Park
Rte. 157, Voorheesville
6 miles of ungroomed trails, heated comfort stations. Free. 872-1237.

Kims Road Park
Kims Rd. (off Rte. 9), Clifton Park
12 km of trails. Free. 371-6667.

Owl Hill Farms Cross Country Ski Center
Owl Hill Rd., Esperance (past intersection of Rtes. 20 and 30)
30 km of groomed, track-set trails that wind through 500 acres of woods, orchards
and fields, with panoramic views. Trails accommodate beginners to experts.
Lessons, rentals, lodge with fireplace. Open daily in season, 9:30am-4:30pm.
Adults $9, children (6-12) $3, under six are free. 875-6700. www.oakhillxc.com

Peebles Island State Park
Delaware Ave. (off Ontario St.), Cohoes
5 km of trails. Free. 237-8643.

Pineridge Cross Country Ski Center
Plank Rd. (County Rte. 40, 12 miles east of Troy), Poestenkill
33 km of groomed trails, some lighted; warming station, 10 km of ungroomed
snowshoe and skating trails, rentals, lodge. Open daily 9am-4pm; lighted trails
Tues-Thurs., 6pm-10pm. $10. 283-3652.

Saratoga National Historical Park
(between Rte. 4 and Rte. 32), Stillwater
8 km of trails, open daily except major holidays. Free. 664-9821.

Saratoga Spa State Park
(Rte. 9), Saratoga Springs
20 km of groomed trails. Open daily. Free. 584-2535.

Schenectady Municipal Golf Course
Oregon Ave., Schenectady
Lighted trails, open daily till 10pm. Free. 382-5153.

Town of Colonie Golf Course,
418 Consaul Rd., Schenectady
Well-groomed trails, free except for small fee for adults on weekends.
346-5940 or 783-2760.

Sky Diving

Sky diving is an exhilarating activity that sends adult daredevils plummeting to earth at 120 miles per hour. The below entries provide instruction (from one to eight hours, depending on the style of dive) by certified staff. Reservations and a $50 deposit required.

Duanesburg Skydiving Club, Duanesburg Airport (intersection of Rtes. 7 and 20), offers tandem, static line, and accelerated-freefall dives. Parachute rides fall over the scenic Hudson Valley with views of the Berkshires and Catskills. Must be 18 years old and over (16- and 17-year-olds need parental consent). May-Oct. $150-$185. 895-8140. www.duanesburgskydiving.com

Mohawk Valley Skydiving, 4281 Amsterdam Rd. (Rte. 5), Scotia, offers tandem, static-line and accelerated-freefall dives. Parachute rides fall over the Mohawk Valley basin with views of the Catskill and Adirondack Mountains. $70-$300. 370-5867. mohawkvalleyskydiving.com

Saratoga Skydiving, Heber Airpark, Rte. 87 (Exit 16), offers dives in tandem and advanced freefall. Parachute rides fall over the beautiful Saratoga-Adirondack area. Open daily, must be 18-and-over. $170-$180. 374-5867. www.saratogaskydiving.com

Swimming

Outdoor swimming pools can be found at Lincoln Park in Albany, Knickerbacker Park in Troy, and Central Park in Schenectady (See City Parks, pg. 154)

Additional information on pools and swimming programs in the four cities is available at the following numbers:

Albany 438-2447
Schenectady 382-5152
Troy 270-4600
Saratoga . . . . 587-3550 x 2

Parks with Lakes and Pools: State Operated

(Call for directions, or visit www.nys.state.ny.us)

Grafton Lakes State Park, Rte. 2, Grafton, has 1,200-foot sandy beach on Long Pond. Open 10am-7pm daily, late-June-Labor Day. (CDTA runs a bus to and from the park during summer: 482-8822.) $6 per car. 279-1155.

John Boyd Thacher State Park, Voorheesville, has an Olympic-size pool. Open late-June to Labor Day, 10am-6pm; 10am-7pm Sat-Sun. $2 adults, $1 children. 872-1237.

Moreau Lake State Park, Old Saratoga Rd., Gansevoort (Rte. 7S), South Glens Falls, has a sandy beach and a lakeside pavilion surrounded by pine stands. Open Memorial Day to Labor Day. $6 per car. 793-0511.

Saratoga Spa State Park, Rte. 9 Saratoga Springs (Exit 13N off I-87), has two pools: fashionable Victoria Pool, which is surrounded by arched promenades, and the larger Peerless Pool, which has zero-depth entry and includes a slide pool and a children's wading pool with a mushroom fountain. Open late-June to Labor Day, 10am-6pm. Peerless: Adults $3, children $1.50; Victoria: Adults $6, children $3. Children under five are free at both pools. 584-2535.

Thompson's Lake State Park, Rte. 157, East Berne (18 miles SW of Albany, 3 miles NW of Thacher Park). Open daily late-May-Labor Day, 10am-5pm. $6 per car. 872-1674.

Parks with Lakes: Privately Operated

Brown's Beach, Rte. 9P, Saratoga Lake, has a public beach; also a marina, a restaurant and lodgings. June-Sept., 10am-6pm. $4 adults, $3 children. 587-8280.

Scholz-Zwicklbauer Beach, Warners Lake, Berne, has a public beach and a restaurant. Daily July 4-Labor Day, noon-6pm. $5 adults, $3 children. 872-9912.

Yoga

Yoga is a 5,000-year-old practice promoting the integration of mind, body and spirit. This holistic health system has many branches, and involves gentle stretching, relaxation techniques, and meditation.

Albany Kripalu Yoga Center, 6 Metro Park Rd., Colonie, has a mission to nurture healing and wellness through Kripalu yoga. To that end, it has been serving the community for 25 years with lectures and workshops as well as a wide range of classes at all levels. The center also offers Ashtanga, Iyengar, Qi Gong, Tai Chi, and other holistic-health modalities. AKYC has several satellite locations, including 40 Colvin Ave., Albany (rear entrance), and 1020 Barrett St., Schenectady (above the Costumer). The center offers a free introductory class for newcomers; drop-ins are on a space-available basis. Eight-week courses are $79, discounts with yearly membership ($35). 454-9642. akyc.org

Center For Body Mind Awareness, 4 Central Ave., Albany, offers a variety of yoga and movement disciplines in two studios: The In Town Yoga Studio, a spacious, wood-floored studio with natural lighting; and a contemplative studio (upstairs) for the expressive arts. Classes include Kripalu and Himalayan yoga, NIA technique, soul aerobics, movement therapy, meditation, and more. 233-1717. www.thecenterformindawareness.com

Joy of Yoga, 446 Hoosick St., Troy, 587-6882, 587 Broadway, Suite 8L (Arcade Building), Saratoga Springs, 587-6882. Soothing environment and comprehensive work-outs, with 13 years of experience in instruction. Beginner's classes provide a strong foundation in yogic principles.

Saratoga Yoga, 8 Phila St., Saratoga Springs, teaches yoga classes in a variety of disciplines including Ashtanga, Vinyasa, power, and therapeutic yoga, and also holds mantra, japa and silent meditation sessions. Open classes are scheduled in the morning, usually beginning at 9:30am. Prices from $15 for a walk-in class to $60 per hour for private instruction.

Washington Park Yoga, 747 Madison Ave. (entrance is on right side of the building), Albany, is dedicated to the teaching of Ashtanga Power yoga, in addition to Kripalu yoga and Pilates mat classes. Childrens' classes. Free introductory classes available. Prices from $15 for a drop-in class to $50 per hour for private instruction. 439-9612 or 433-1750. www.wpyoga.com

Yoga Room, Parade Ground Village, Rte. 9, Malta, specializes in Ashtanga yoga, complemented by yoga therapy, massage therapy, meditation, and reiki, and relaxation classes. 899-4372.

Albany Tulip Festival, State Street   *Photography by: Gary Gold*

SEASONAL

Each of the four seasons in the Capital Region brings a fresh bounty of interesting activities and exciting events. Many area happenings – from tugboat rides to concerts by national acts – are free of charge. The chapter is divided into four parts: Spring (pg. 187), Summer (pg. 191), Fall (pg. 196), and Winter (pg. 202).

Albany Mayor's Office of Special Events, 60 Orange St., sponsors city celebrations including the Tulip Festival, Lark Fest, and First Night. For a schedule, call 434-2032. www.albanyevents.org

Schenectady Chamber of Commerce, 306 State St., sponsors special events including festivals and performances held in Central Park. For a schedule, call 372-5656. www.schenectadychamber.org

SPRING

Maple sugaring, the laborious process of drawing sap and converting it to syrup, requires patience, skilled labor, and watchfulness – particularly in March when the sap is running. The below listed regional farms welcome visitors to tour their stands of "sugar bushes," observe the wood-fired sap processing, and to sample the syrup. Operations are dependent on the weather, so call ahead for hours.

Century Farm, Harris Rd., Corinth 654-9752
Maple Hill Farm, Tenantville Rd., Edinburg 863-4188

Maple Sugar Basics, Up Yonda Farm Environmental Center, Bolton Landing, teaches non-tappers the sticky traditional methods that result in sweet rewards. The workshop is held through the month of March, Sat-Sun., 11am and 1pm. $2 per class. 644-9767.

March

Albany Auto Show, Pepsi Arena, 51 South Pearl St., is an indoor auto show held the first weekend in March. Displays of over 170 vehicles include all four-wheel categories, in addition to auto-related exhibitions. Fri. 3pm-9pm, Sat. 10am-9pm, Sun. 11am-5pm. $6, children under 12 are free. 452-2584.

Capital District Garden and Flower Show, Hudson Valley Community College, 80 Vandenburg Ave., Troy, is held over four days in late March. Upstate New York's premier gardening exposition transforms the 60,000-square-foot Sports Complex into a colorful, fragrant and blooming wonderland. Over 150 booths and exhibits on flowers, landscapes, ponds, and plant supplies provide the materials to turn any backyard into a garden paradise, while dozens of lectures and demos by experts help inexperienced thumbs turn green. The landscape and floral displays are noted for their creativity; this popular event also offers an excellent garden marketplace, a garden café, and a kid's playland. Proceeds benefit the Wildwood Program. Thurs-Sun., 10am-8pm. $7, children under 10 are free. 786-1529.

Northeast Great Outdoors Show, Empire State Plaza Concourse, Albany, is held in mid-March and offers displays on fishing, hunting, and camping; plus turkey-calling and deer-calling contests, scoring sessions by the Northeast Big Buck Club, an archery tournament with cash prizes, and exhibits of predatory animals. Fri. 4pm-9pm, Sat. 9am-6pm, Sun.10am-6pm. $6, 12-and-under $4. 383-6183.

Woodworkers Showcase, Saratoga Springs City Center, 522 Broadway, is held for two days in late March by the Northeastern Woodworkers Association. This nationally recognized fine-woodworking fair displays over 500 wood creations by the region's most talented woodworkers, including furniture, toys, decorative objects, musical instruments, miniatures, and sports equipment. These handcrafted objects are entered into a competition; one of the more interesting categories is "Intarsia, Inlay and Marquetry." The fair also offers information booths and exhibits from a wide variety of merchants and service providers, such as specialized tool companies and tree nurseries. The showcase is highly regarded for its extensive schedule of free lectures and demonstrations by renowned craftsmen; topics have included "Making Drawers: Dovetails and Veneers," "Basics of Wood Identification," and "Scroll Saw Magic." Each fair follows a theme, with all-day seminars available for $10. A raffle completes this unique event. Sat-Sun., 10am-5pm. $5, children under 12 are free. 371-9145. www.woodworkers.org

April

Country Folk Art and Craft Show, Saratoga Equine Sports Center, Crescent Ave., is held in mid-April and features the handcrafted works of artisans from across the country. Fri. 5pm-9pm, Sat.10am-5pm, Sun. 10am-4pm. $6. 634-4151.

Fur Ball, Observation Level, Albany International Airport, Albany, is the annual benefit for Whiskers Animal Benevolent League. Expect live music, a light buffet, a weekend-getaway raffle, door prizes, a humanitarian award ceremony, and lots of pet talk. All proceeds go to the four-legged residents of Whisker's no-kill shelter. $35. 448-9565.

Half Moon Arrival, Water Pumping Station (behind the Quackenbush Visitor Center) Albany, allows visitors to board the Half Moon, an 85-foot, authentic replica of the Dutch ship that explorer Henry Hudson used to sail the Hudson River in 1609. Crew members in period garb enact life aboard the ship as it was 400 years ago, demonstrating how the crew survived for months at sea at a time, and how they fired cannons, set sail, and navigated across the ocean with very simple tools. April 21-May 13. $5. 443-1609.

Kite Day, Shaker Museum & Library, Old Chatham, is the day in late April when the museum takes to the skies with kite-flying demonstrations. Free. 794-9100.

May

Albany Tulip Festival is held the second weekend in May in Washington Park. This beloved event has been a harbinger of spring for more than 50 years, and commemorates Albany's Dutch heritage with the blooming of thousands of tulips in a kaleidoscope of colors. The three-day revel begins Friday (11am) with a carillon concert, an opening ceremony marshaled by the mayor, and a raft of residents in Dutch garb scrubbing historic State Street with traditional broad brooms. The Tulip Pageant begins Saturday (11am) with a procession from Willett Street to the crowning of the new Tulip Queen in the park. On Saturday and Sunday, the outdoor festival known as Pinksterfest takes over the park with national and regional music and dance performances, along with roving entertainers, crafts booths, gardening demos, and a Kinderkermis (children's carnival). Free. 434-2032. www.albanyevents.org

The weekend festival also includes the Royal Tulip Ball on Saturday night, followed on Sunday by the Tulip Luncheon. Both events are open to the public with the purchase of a ticket. 434-2032.

Albany Historic House and Garden Tour, held in mid-May by the Albany County Historical Association, is a walking tour of the exceptional architectural highlights, unique urban gardens, and interesting house interiors of the Ten Broeck Triangle historic district. The tour includes admission to the Ten Broeck Mansion, and concludes with hors d'oeuvres and music in the mansion garden. $12. 436-9826. www.tenbroeck.org

Am-Jam, Cobleskill Fairgrounds (off Rte. 7), is held each Memorial Day weekend for the enjoyment of motorcycle enthusiasts. Activities include cycle and novelty games, food vendors, live entertainment, an antique-motorcycle museum, and a $500,000 mobile show featuring chrome products and accessories for cycles. 346-0521.

Festival of Nations, Nott Terrace behind the Schenectady Museum, is a multi-ethnic festival hosted by the museum and held in mid May. For more than 30 years, the festival has celebrated the cultural richness of the people of Schenectady with international food, music, dance, storytelling, and arts activities. Expect to see citizens in ethnic and historical costume, as well as a lot of other people: this colorful event is one of the city's most popular. Free. 382-7890.

Grecian Cultural Festival, St. Sophia's Greek Orthodox Church, 440 Whitehall Rd., Albany, is held the third weekend in May. Thousands flock to this lively event, savoring fine Greek dining indoors or traditional Greek cuisine from the booths under the tent, and the accompaniment of live bouzouki music. Also among the offerings are folk dancers in ethnic dress from the Greek islands; tours of St. Sophia's stunning, Byzantine-style architecture, mosaics, and iconography; and in the evenings, "Greek night life," held in the taverna. In the parish house, parishioners display, explain, and sell imported Greek food, jewelry, clothing, icons, and crafts. Fri-Sun. Free. 489-4442.

Saratoga Antique & Classic Car Show, Saratoga Performing Arts Center (Rte. 9), revs the engines of spectators by featuring over 300 vehicles organized into 26 categories, with the newest one being "muscle cars." Showcased autos have included rare Rolls Royces, 1950s Chevy sedans, 1960s Studebakers, and a 1918 Detroit electric car. Trophies are awarded in each category, with a People's Choice award decided by the audience. The show is capped by the "Cruise Broadway" parade from the Spa Park to downtown Saratoga Springs. Proceeds benefit various Saratoga museums. Free. Sat., 9am-4pm, 587-1935.

Saratoga ARC Festival and Dressage, Saratoga Race Course (Rte. 9), Saratoga Springs, is held the three days of Memorial Day weekend. This benefit festival is regarded as one of the most prestigious events in the state. The glamorous dressage competition is augmented by four other horse shows (on both the racing and harness tracks), including the Carriage Classic, barrel racing, and an exotic All Breeds show. The festival also features Special Olympics riding demos, equestrian acrobatics, a llama and alpaca festival, Victorian carriages with costumed drivers, a master dog-agility contest, an antique-car show, live entertainment, and more than 200 craft and food vendors, many of them upscale. 9am-6pm. $5, kids $4, under-five are free. 587-0723 x115. www.saratogaarcfestival.org

    The Black Tie Gala precedes the festival on Friday evening at the Hall of Springs, and serves as the kick-off celebration for Saratoga's summer social season. $150 per person. www.saratogaarcfestival.org

Spring Smorgasbord, Hudson Valley Community College Cultural Center, 80 Vandenburg Ave., Troy, is a benefit brunch held in early May by Capital District Community Gardens. Participants can sample selections from over 100 local restaurants and supporting gardeners; the menu covers salads to desserts and everything in between. Prizes for the silent auction range from weeding tools to weekend getaways, and the childrens' activities are sponsored by the Junior Museum. Sun., 10am-2pm. $25 ($20 in advance); children under 10 are $5. 274-8685.

SUMMER

'Round these parts, summer in the city means a bonanza of music and drama – and most of it doesn't cost a dime. (Summer theater festivals are described in Arts and Venues, pg. 57.) It's also a time when the area's scenic fairgrounds burst into activity, offering a different kind of fair for almost every weekend.

Albany City Hall Carillon, Eagle St. (across from the Capitol), is a world-class, historic carillon of 49 bells weighing up to 11,000 pounds. On summer Sundays at 3pm, Friends of the Albany City Carillon present free concerts by international carilloneurs. East Capitol Park across the street provides a tranquil setting for listening, lounging and picnicking. 434-8036.

Alive at Five, Hudson River Way amphitheater (Maiden Lane off Broadway), Albany, is held each Thursday evening from late June through early August. The multi-cultural line-up includes swing, Cajun, blues, and classic rock and pop, performed by national and international bands as well as local bands. These popular concerts draw a large and lively crowd, and include food booths and a beer concession. Rain site is the Corning Preserve boat launch under the I-787 underpass. 5pm-8pm. Free. 434-2032.

Collar City Live!, Riverfront Park, downtown Troy, presents acoustic, folk, and children's concerts throughout the summer. 7pm. Free. 233-9123.

Empire State Plaza Summertime Concerts, Madison Ave., Albany, presents major rock, pop, R&B, and oldies bands throughout July and August. The opening acts, usually regional or up-and-coming bands, tend to be just as exciting as the headliners. Expect food vendors, beer carts, and very large crowds – get there early for a seat on the plaza stairs. Weds., 7pm. Free (free parking in the east garage). 434-2023.

Second Wind Productions is a summer concert series held at the Music Haven Stage in Central Park in Schenectady, and at the Park Playhouse in Washington Park in Albany. Second Wind's motto is "Traveling the world one concert at a time," and it's an apt one. The eclectic yet discerning schedule includes the best and brightest in world music, blues, folk, soul, and funk. These free concerts are not to be missed, especially since both outdoor stages offer excellent visibility and scenic surroundings for picnicking. July-Aug.; Sundays at 3pm in Central Park and Mondays at 7:30pm in Washington Park. (800) 776-2992. www.swconcerts.org

June

Aerosciences Museum Air Show, Schenectady County Airport, 250 Rudy Chase Dr. (off Rte. 50), Glenville, is a terrifically exciting showcase of aerodynamic daredevilry. The program features nationally famed air-acrobatic teams such as the Blue Angels and Iron Eagles, along with the Mohawk Valley Skydiving team. The sky-high attractions include a freestyle competition with international competitors, "a mass parachuting," aerial comedy acts, "mad bombers," and F-16 demos and other feats of flying by historic military aircraft. On the ground you'll find exhibits from the museum and food booths. Adults $15 ($10 in advance), youths (6-12) $5, children under 6 are free. 11:30 am. Gates open at 9am; expect heavy traffic. 383-6183.

Art on Lark, Lark St., Albany, is an annual street festival that displays the region's considerable artistic talents, as well as the bohemian ambience of this historic downtown neighborhood. More than 80 artists and crafters show and discuss their wares, from paintings to jewelry to ceramics. Activities include a "creative chaos" station that allows neophyte artists to try their skills with spin art and other challenges, and the People's Choice Art Show, held in the Trinity United Methodist Church where festival-goers can vote for their favorite artworks (winners are announced at 4pm). Free. Noon-5pm. 434-3861.

Freihofer's Jazz Festival, Saratoga Performing Arts Center, kicks off the SPAC concert season with a late-June weekend festival featuring the greatest jazz performers and ensembles in the world. The main stage is augmented by a pavilion stage featuring up-and-coming acts, and an exhibit of jury-selected fine arts, jewelry and pottery on the lawn. The combination of venue (the amphitheater is within beautiful Saratoga Spa Park) and talent makes the festival one of the region's most worthwhile summer events. $15 to $50. 587-3330.

Freihofer's Run for Women, Madison Ave., Albany, is a 5-K run and one of the most important races in America for female runners, attracting Olympic-level competitors. A 20-year tradition, the race has grown to involve the entire community through the inclusion of thousands of recreational runners – with thousands more cheering from the roadside. 434-2032. www.albanyevents.org

History Hikes, Saratoga Battlefield National Historical Park, are held each weekend in June, when park guides and volunteers lead walking and caravan tours to American and British positions on the Saratoga Battlefield. Sat., 10am-11:30pm. Free. 664-9821.

Latin Fest, Washington Park, Albany, is held on a Saturday in June to celebrate Latin culture, heritage and music. Expect a stellar line-up of Latin pop and folk acts, along with kids' rides and games, and lots of food. Free. 434-2023.

Lobster Fest, Washington Park, Albany, is held every Father's Day and offers twin lobsters or 14 oz. steak dinners (available onsite or for take-out), in addition to burgers and other grill items. The while-u-eat entertainment includes historical re-enactments and a lively concert line-up. $25 for dinner, the festivities are free. 434-5412.

Old Songs Festival of Traditional Music and Dance, Altamont Fairgrounds (Rte. 146), is held over an entire weekend in mid June and features an average of 60 performers on nine stages. As the name implies, the foot-stomping line-up leans toward seasoned veterans and young interpreters of traditional songcraft, as well as one or two living legends. The festival draws acclaimed folkies from all over: Don't be surprised to find Appalachian gospel singers, highland pipers, Italian dulcimer players, or Senegalese drummers on the bill. The schedule also includes songwriting workshops conducted by the performers; storytelling; "mini-concerts" on a theme, such as the Sunday-morning family concert; and folk dancing, in addition to craft booths (including handcrafted musical instruments), food stands, and camping out. $20 per segment or $70 for a three-day, all-inclusive pass. Children 12-and-under are free. 765-2815.

Opera on the Lake, Lake George, is presented on a weekend evening in mid June by the Lake George Opera Festival, which performs selections from great operas and musicals aboard a Lake George steamboat cruise. 6:30pm, $25. 584-6018.

Riverfront Arts Fest, Riverfront Park, Troy, held the third weekend in June, is the longest running multi-arts festival in the region. A celebration of visual arts and fine crafts, the event also offers an abundance of music and dance performances, along with spoken-word readings, ethnic-food booths, tumblers, tarot-card readers, and hands-on activities for all ages. One of the most popular attractions is the street-painting competition on River Street, which draws thousands of viewers. Local artists compete in a juried show; the winning artworks are shown in the following weeks at the Arts Center of the Capital Region. A recent addition to the event is the 5K race, which is divided into several prize categories for competitive and recreational runners alike (9:30am Sun.). Free. Schedules available. 273-0552.

Round Lake Antique Festival, Round Lake (I-87, Exit 11), is held on a weekend in late June, when 300 or so exhibitors take over the parks and greens of this picturesquely Victorian village. 10am-5pm. Free. 899-2800.

July

Cappiello Festa Italiana, Central Park, Schenectady, is held in mid July in a celebration of all things Italian, including boccie ball, traditional story-telling, opera singing, and displays on the contributions of Italian Americans to the city presented by the Schenectady Museum. Among the festivities are puppetry, cookie-baking contests, homemade-wine contests, genealogy demos, casino games, and, of course, Italian food. Reputedly, Cappiello offers the best festival food to be had all summer. Proceeds benefit the park's Music Haven. Fri. 4pm-10pm., Sat. noon-10pm, Sun. noon-8pm. Free. 372-5656. www.schenectadychamber.org

Fabulous Fourth Festival, Empire State Plaza, Albany, is the region's biggest Fourth-of-July celebration. Presented by Price Chopper, it's more of an extravaganza than a festival, featuring spectacular fireworks and big-name rock-and-pop performers. The plaza is an ideal stage: The tower windows reflect the exploding lights, and the modernist architecture echoes the collective "ooohs" of delighted spectators. Food vendors and street entertainers add to the carnival-like atmosphere. The platform accommodates crowds but it's advisable to get there early, as this well-known festival attracts a crowd in the tens of thousands. Free. 4pm-10pm. 473-0559.

Fleet Blues Fest, Empire State Plaza, Madison Ave., Albany, is held on four stages for one evening in July. The main stage features acclaimed traditional, acoustic, contemporary, and rock acts. The north stage presents up-and-coming and regional bands; the acoustic stage offers unplugged performers; and the workshop stage provides an opportunity to learn from the artists. The event includes a kids' zone, food and beer stands, and lots of tuneful revelry. Noon-10pm. Free (free parking in the east garage). 473-0559.

GE Kids' Day, Empire State Plaza, Madison Ave., is an annual event held in late July – and is the one summer festival where "kids' activities" are the whole shebang instead of just a sideline. Offerings include a petting zoo, professional storytellers and interactive "story acting," magic shows, live music, puppeteers, family arts-and-crafts projects, food booths, inflatable "bounces," clowns, face-painting, pony rides, jugglers, balloons, and more. Free. 1pm-5pm. 473-0559. www.ogs.state.ny.us/plaza

Hidden City Home & Garden Tour, Albany, is held one evening in early July by Historic Albany Foundation. For locals who want to experience the stunning interiors behind the city's renowned facades, or for out-of-towners wishing to explore the historic architecture of a 300-year-old downtown, or for anyone at all who appreciates the art of urban gardening, this well-planned walking tour is a must-see. Patrons go at their own pace through townhouses and courtyards, viewing the creative adaptations of the city's most distinctive private residences. Free rides from the Albany City Trolley for the duration. $15. 465-0876.

New York Giants Exhibition Program and Fan Rally, UAlbany, University Field, 1400 Washington Ave., Albany, is a celebration of the football team's summer training season at the University of Albany (see Sports, pg. 168). 6pm-8pm, $10. The exhibition program is preceded by a barbecue, $25 extra. 442-7369.

Saratoga County Fair, 162 Prospect St. (off I-87), Ballston Spa, is a 160-year old tradition held the last full week of July by the Saratoga County Agricultural Society. More than 80,000 fairgoers are entertained by its diverse offerings – everything from see-through beehives to draft horses to fine-art exhibits to maximum-G-force thrill rides. With a 32-ride midway, Farmer's Olympics, beer garden, dozens of animal exhibits (over 150 breeds of rabbits alone!), a petting barn, 4-H demos, pony rides, and artisan-crafts booths, the Saratoga Fair is not only the first fair in the state, but also one of the best. Six days, 9am-midnight. $3-$7. 885-9701. www.saratogafair.org

Saratoga Shakespeare Company, Congress Park, Saratoga Springs, was founded in 1999 to provide "a Shakespeare for the enjoyment of everyone of every age." The company of local and national actors performs physically exuberant stagings of a comedy by the Bard during the last week of July and the first week of August, Weds-Sat. evenings. Bring a blanket and a picnic basket, enjoy the beautiful park, and be prepared to roll in the grass laughing. Free. 884-4947.

Shaker Craft & Herb Fair, 875 Watervliet Shaker Rd., Albany (across from the Albany International Airport), is held on the site of the country's first Shaker settlement, in celebration of the sect's unique craftsmanship and herb lore. Plants from the heritage herb garden are for sale, along with Shaker reproductions. The 1848 meetinghouse hosts 25 crafters, in addition to 75 booths on the grounds. Among the offerings are made-to-order meals, refreshments, and fresh-baked pies. Guided tours are included, and youngsters can visit with the society's two pet oxen. Sat-Sun., 10am-4pm. $4 for both days, children under 12 are free. 456-7890.

Steamboat Cruises, Lake George, (see Not Far Away, pg. 243), offers a fireworks cruise on the Fourth-of-July and other summer evenings. 668-5777. www.lakegeorgesteamboat.com

Street Fair, River Street, Troy, is presented on a Saturday in July by the merchants of River Street, along with the dealers of the city's antiques district, local gallery owners, Troy artists and crafters, and local food purveyors. The fair includes a Victorian fashion exhibit, puppetry, a sidewalk pianist, clowns, and more. Free. Free parking in city garages for the duration. 270-8667.

August

Altamont Fair is held on the Altamont Fairgrounds (naturally enough), in the picturesque Helderberg village of Altamont (Rte. 146). This tri-county festival combines an authentic country fair – including cooking competitions, 4-H exhibits, animal-husbandry contests, and sheep-shearing demos – with a huge midway, live music by top local bands, horse and pony shows, an antique-vehicles show, a demolition derby, a circus museum, a fire-equipment museum, art and flower displays, and last but not least, "great eats." This fair has a reputation for being one of the best in the region – and the pig races clinch it. 8am-midnight. $4-$8. 861-6671. www.altamontfair.com

Hancock Shaker Village Antiques Show, Rte. 20, Pittsfield, is held in late August in the historic Round Stone Barn (see Not Far Away, pg. 266), and offers high-quality antiques and Americana, including paintings, prints, country furniture, decorative housewares, garden and sports antiquary, folk art, glass, and estate jewelry, all from prominent dealers from a 10-state radius. $6 for the antique show, admission to the show with a tour of the 21-building village and its exhibits is $13.50. 861-547. www.hancockshakervillage.org

Tuesday in the Park, Central Park, Schenectady, is held the first Tuesday of August. This popular community fair features multi-ethnic live music, a performance by the Schenectady Symphony Orchestra, food booths, rides, children's activities, a 5K race, and fireworks. Free. 382-5147.

FALL

Apple-picking forays are an annual tradition in the Capital Region: New York State is one of the country's top producers of apples. Many local orchards allow patrons to climb their trees to obtain the freshest Empire, Macintosh, Macoun or Red Delicious apples. September is the prime picking month, and Saratoga County in particular has a bounty of orchards that welcome the public. For a complete Saratoga listing, call the Cornell Cooperative Extension at 885-8995. www.ccesaratoga.org

These pick-your-own orchards also offer pumpkins, plants, baked goods, cheese, maple syrup, and more.

Bowman Orchards, 141 Sugar Hill Rd., Rexford 371-2042
Bowman Orchard North, Van Aermen Rd., Malta. 885-8888
DeVoe's Rainbow Orchard, 1569 Rte. 9, Clifton Park 371-8397
Fo'Castle Country Store, 166 Kingsley Rd., Burnt Hills 399-8322
Goold Orchard, Brookview Station Rd., Schodack 732-7317
Indian Ladder Farms, 342 Altamont Rd., Altamont. 765-2956
Saratoga Apple, Saratoga (near the National Battlefield). 695-3131

Fall foliage tours are a regional ritual and a celebration of the area's gloriously colored leafage. Although exact dates depend on the summer rainfall, the northern counties generally peak in the last week of September; the Capital Region (including the Helderbergs) in the middle two weeks of October; and the Catskills during the last two weeks of October. A foliage brochure is available from the Department of Economic Development, 1 Commerce Plaza, Albany, or by calling 1-800-CALLNYS. One of the region's most spectacular tours is the three-state triangle of the Capital Region, Bennington, Vt., and Williamstown, Mass.

September

Capital District Scottish Games, Altamont Fairgrounds, Rte. 146, is held Labor Day weekend, bringing the pageantry and spectacle of Brigadoon to the green hills of the Helderbergs. To say this colorful, athletic, and jam-packed gathering offers something (Scottish) for everyone is an understatement: the fun and games include pipe and drum competitions; marches, reels, and Scottish "classical" music; highland-dance demos from the Highland Fling to the Sword Dance (some dances date to the 1200s); caber-toss contests and a children's hay pile; and the very popular (except with the sheep) Border Collie sheep-herding competitions. And that's not to mention stage performances by Celtic-music bands and step dancers, Scottish food and imported beer, and lively military-history displays. Fair-goers can rub elbows with representatives from over 100 Scottish clans, and marvel at the authentic tartan garb of the participants. Adults $12, children $3, children under six are free. 785-5951. www.scotgames.com

Grafton Lakes Mountain-Bike Festival, Grafton Lakes State Park (beach entrance) Grafton, is held in mid-September in conjunction with the annual Bike-a-Thon benefit. The festival offers rides for all levels of ability, plus childrens' rides, skill clinics, a rock-garden challenge, and more. $6. 279-1155. www.mohawkhudsoncycling.org.

Fireplug 500 Walk for Animals, Central Park Pavilion, Schenectady, is an annual fund-raiser for the Animal Protective Foundation. The two-mile, scenic walk through the park (four-legged companion not required) is followed by live music, an amateur animal-variety show, "Silly Pet Tricks," and a Blessing of the Animals ceremony that bestows each pet with a St. Francis medal. The event ends with an awards presentation honoring the top walkers. For more information and/or a registration form, contact the foundation. 374-3944. www.animalprotective.org

Half Moon Arrival, Water Pumping Station (behind the Quackenbush Visitor Center) Albany, is the autumn return of the authentic replica of the Dutch ship that explorer Henry Hudson used to sail the Hudson River in 1609 (see pg. 189). Sept. 19-Oct. 13. $5. 443-1609.

Hudson Valley Garlic Festival, Cantina Field, Saugerties, is held the last full weekend of September but two days is barely enough time for this huge – and hugely popular – community celebration of locally grown garlic in all its glory. Chef demonstrations (from Culinary Institute chefs), cooking classes, a lecture tent, and a farmer's market are only a sampling of the festivities. The grounds feature 30 garlicky food booths, 70 widely diverse crafts booths, five stages of music and dance (with an emphasis on ethnic and folk), giant puppets, and more. Try the garlic ice cream, if you dare. A free shuttle bus runs from Main Street to the festival grounds. Free. 845-246-3090.

Irish 2000 Music and Arts Festival, Altamont Fairgrounds, Rte. 146, is a nonprofit gala of Irish arts and culture held in late September. One of the largest Irish fests in the country, the event features Irish music from traditional to Celtic rock and everything in between, with more than 25 bands and performers on three stages. The line-up usually includes some of the finest Irish musicians in the world. The festival also offers step dancing, storytelling, and theater competitions, plus a tug-'o-war and a family-fun area, in addition to Irish food, beer, and crafts vendors. Sat., 10am till the wee hours. $15. (888) 414-3378. A shuttle bus runs a continuous loop between downtown Albany, Guilderland, and the fairgrounds, noon-midnight. $5.

Iroquois Festival, Cavern's Rd., Howe's Cave, occurs over Labor Day weekend (rain or shine) in celebration of the creativity and cultural survival of the Five Nations. Held on the grounds of the Iroquois Indian Museum, the festival features Iroquois performing artists, guest speakers, and storytellers, along with handicrafts, cornbread making, cooking demos and recipes, nature walks, wildlife presentations, an Iroquois art market, a children's tent, and genealogy and archeology stations. On other summer weekends, the museum holds crafts classes including basket making, bead working and bark working. 10am-6pm each day. $4-$10. 296-8949. www.iroquoismuseum.org

Knickerbocker Mansion Harvest Festival, Knickerbocker Rd. (off Rte. 67), Schaghticoke, is held in late September on the grounds of this 1770s brick mansion, which is undergoing a grass-roots restoration. The festival celebrates the area's early-Dutch history with tours of the mansion and its family cemetery (led by Knickerbocker descendents), costumed re-enactors and living-history displays, handcrafted "Knick-knacks," autumn produce, fresh-pressed cider, homebaked goods, and an all-day ox roast (Sat./Sun.) and a pancake breakfast (Sun.). Sat. noon-5pm, Sun. 8am-4pm. The festival is free, except for the breakfast ($3-$5) and ox roast ($4-$8). 677-3807.

Lark Fest, Lark St., Albany, held on the third Saturday of September, is one of the state's largest street festivals, attracting over 40,000 revelers in good weather. The long-running festival closes off historic Lark Street from Central Ave. to Madison Ave., transforming the street into an urban fair ground. More than 100 vendors – including the street's merchants and eateries – set up sidewalk booths alongside of regional artists and crafters displaying their wares and demonstrating their artistry. Popular local bands in every musical style perform on three stages (rock, acoustic and jazz), and there's plenty a-goin'-on for youngsters, too, from the Kidsfest stage to a virtual amusement park. Free. 10:30am-dusk. 434-3861. www.albanyevents.org

Saratoga Wine & Food Festival, Saratoga Performing Arts Center (Rte. 9), Saratoga Springs, is an epicurean benefit bash (proceeds go to SPAC) held in mid-September. Three elegant evenings of dining and wine drinking are augmented by one enlightening afternoon of learning about the subtleties of fine wines and delectables. The first night is held at area restaurants, the second two nights at the Hall of Springs and the Spa grounds. The event includes seminars by gastronomic experts, presentations by vintners, samplings of wines and champagnes from around the world, and a silent auction. Tickets range from $60 for the afternoon seminars to $300 for the entire event. 587-3330.

Stockade Villagers' Outdoor Art Show, Stockade District (junction of Ferry St. and Front St.), Schenectady, has been an annual event for over 50 years. The informal, sales-oriented show is a local favorite for its friendly bartering and arts gossiping. Potential buyers can meet and talk with the artists, and a juried segment is held by the show's organizers, who select the best paintings for exhibit in the following weeks at the Schenectady Museum. Free. 382-7890.

Stockade Walkabout, Stockade District (junction of Ferry St. and Front St.), Schenectady, is a celebration of the state's oldest historic district, conducted by the Schenectady County Historical Society and the Stockade Association. Participants receive an illustrated map and brochure to guide them through the architecturally diverse homes, churches, and buildings of the 300-year-old Stockade area (see Points of Interest, pg. 23), along with the interiors of elegant private residences. Costumed re-enactors of "famous people from Olde Schenectady" are on hand to lead tours and provide information. The event also includes an antique-car show, food booths from local restaurants, colonial games for children, and live music. If you don't want to walkabout the entire Stockade, carriage and trolley rides are available; 10am-5pm. $15. 377-9430. www.historicstockade.com

Waterford Tugboat Round-up, Waterford Waterfront, is held over a weekend in early September and begins on Friday afternoon with a parade of historic tugboats chugging from the Port of Albany to Waterford Harbor, where they're moored for the weekend. These colorful "gentle giants" can be boarded for informative tours and boat rides, while onshore the festivities include a "Blessing of the Fleet" ceremony on Saturday morning, a celebrated chicken barbecue in the afternoon, tugboat exhibits and lectures at the Waterford Visitor Center, roving entertainers, and a grand fireworks display with a tugboat "send-off" on Saturday night. Free. 233-9123 or 674-2512.

The tug parade can also be viewed from the Corning Riverfront Preserve, the Troy Town Dock, and Peebles Island State Park.

October

Columbus Day Parade & Italian Festival, downtown Albany, is held the second weekend in October in celebration of the region's Italian-American heritage. Led by the Grand Marshall, the parade of floats, marching bands, antique cars, and clowns travels down Washington Ave. from Partridge St. to Washington Park, where the bleacher area is transformed into an Italian street fair modeled on New York City's San Gennaro festival. New as of 2002 is the use of the lakehouse as an exhibit space for Italian-immigration memorabilia. One of the largest of its kind in the state, the festival includes Italian singing, music and dance (expect hordes of Tarantella dancers), childrens' games and rides, and excellent Italian cuisine. Free. 1pm-6pm. 436-0402. www.columbusdayalbanyny.com

Festival of Nations, Empire State Convention Center (below the Egg), Albany, is held in late October in celebration of over 20 cultures, from Argentina to the Ukraine (recent additions are Puerto Rico and Armenia). The festival features food booths offering cuisine from around the world, ethnic music and dance performances, ethnic crafts, a parade, and a crowning ceremony for the winner of the Miss Festival of Nations pageant. Free.

Fiber Tour of Saratoga County, various farm locations, is held the first Sunday in October, and features llama, alpaca, sheep, and angora-rabbit farms. Located in the bucolic hamlet of Bacon Hill (see Points of Interest, pg. 29) each farm does its own presentation, and youngsters will be delighted by their wooly hosts. Free. 11am-4pm. 885-8995. www.ccesaratoga.org

Knick At Night, Knickerbocker Mansion (off Rte. 67), Schaghticoke, is a candlelit tour of the 1770s mansion held the last weekend in October, at which time the Georgian-style house is inhabited by the "ghosts" of former occupants and important visitors from 200 years of its history. The early-Dutch building and family cemetery are well suited to the Halloween season: the Knickerbockers are believed to have been the inspiration for the Van Tassles of Washington Irving's *The Legend of Sleepy Hollow.* Refreshments, snack booth. $5. A homemade dinner is available for an additional $5. 6pm-9pm. 677-3807.

Medieval Faire at All Saints Cathedral, 63 Swan St., Albany, is held on a Friday (4pm-9pm) and Saturday (10am-5pm) in late October. This atmospheric, 19th-century Gothic cathedral (see Points of Interest, pg. 12) is the ideal place for recreating an Old World harvest festival, especially since its vast interior harkens to the time when cathedrals also served as town hall and market place. The variety of the faire's offerings – madrigal singers, calligraphy, early-music concerts, period-dance performances, a wonderful Punch-and-Judy show, food ("dragon wings" are the house specialty), medieval crafts, and an authentic Crowning of the Boy Bishop ceremony – attracts living-history buffs as well as families and couples. Guided tours available with admission. $6. 465-1342. www.cathedralofallsaints.org

Saratoga Springs Fall House Tour is held on the first weekend of October by the Historical Society of Saratoga Springs. The walking tour highlights the city's award-winning preservation efforts, its High-Victorian architecture, and the interiors of several elegant private residences. Sun., 11am-4pm, $20.

Sc'ary County Harvest Festival, held on the grounds of the New York Power Authority, Rte. 30, North Blenheim, is a recently established annual festival celebrating the agricultural heritage of Schoharie County. Held the Saturday before Halloween, the event features live music, crafts, local-history displays, clowns, a petting zoo, horse-drawn wagon rides, and great food made from the bounty of the county (apple pie is the specialty). Free parking. 10am-4pm, $1, children under 12 are free. 295-7023.

Also on the grounds of the NYPA is the recently restored Lansing Manor, a 19th-century country estate with authentic furnishings. The manor's dairy barn houses the NYPA Visitor Center. Free. 10am-5pm.

The Sc'ary festival ties in with nearby Howe Caverns (see Not Far Away, pg. 256), which is "haunted" for the second half of October; and the Landis Arboretum in Esperance (pg. 254), which holds an evening "Owl Prowl" through its old-growth forest (7pm-9:30pm). While in Esperance you can also stop by the Pick-a-Pumpkin Patch on Creek Road and pick your own pumpkins, gourds and Indian corn, and walk through the farm maze. Free. 10am-8pm. 868-4893.

WINTER

Sleigh Rides are offered at several local farms, providing a picturesque way to enjoy the region's snowy drifts of winter. Call ahead for hours.

Indian Ladder Farms, 342 Altamont Rd., Altamont 765-2956
Rolling Meadows Farm, White Rd., Ballston Spa 885-1655
Viewmere Farm, Rte. 40, Schaghticoke 753-4630

The Capital Region also offers exceptionally scenic locations for cross-country skiing and snow shoeing (see Recreation and Sports, pg. 181).

November

Designer Crafts Festival, City Center Sportsplex, Schenectady, is held by the Designer Crafts Council, the oldest fine-crafts guild in the state. The council has been affiliated with the Schenectady Museum since 1965, and works to stimulate public interest in the fine crafts through programs, exhibits, and shows. Council artists are selected for membership based on innovative design, originality, and execution, and their products are known to "transcend the line between functional crafts and fine art." This popular event features woodcarved objects and sculpture, beaded and embroidered items, handmade clothing and pottery, and other useful artworks. Free parking off Jay St. behind the Sportsplex. Sat-Sun., 10am-5pm. Adults $4, children $1. 382-7890.

Saratoga Victorian Streetwalk, Saratoga Springs, is held in late November or early December in the downtown area, which is festively decorated to accent its Victoriana charm. This Yuletide evening of cheer includes live music, magic acts, dance performances, strolling entertainers – Santa and Mrs. Clause among them – horse-drawn trolley rides, and the Festival of Trees in the City Center on Broadway. Free. 6pm-10pm.

Shaker Heritage Christmas Craft Fair, 875 Watervliet-Shaker Rd., Albany, is a fund-raiser held from November 1 through Dec. 21. Featuring the wares of over 50 crafters and artisans, the fair is a highly anticipated event for holiday shoppers. 456-7890.

Schenectady Christmas Parade, State Street, is held the Friday evening after Thanksgiving, and is the largest evening parade in the Northeast. As the holiday brigade makes its merry way east on State Street to Lafayette Street, the flotilla of marching bands, clowns, floats, and gigantic helium balloons enchants a crowd in the tens of thousands. 372-5656.

December

Albany Berkshire Ballet, Palace Theater, 19 Clinton Ave., Albany, performs an annual holiday presentation of The Nutcracker Suite that is a cherished area tradition, and for which the company recruits local ballet students to complement the regular ensemble. $15-$30. 465-4663. www.berkshireballet.org

Holiday Greens Show at the Rensselaer County Historical Society, 57-59 Second St., Troy, is held over four days in early December. A cherished tradition for more than 45 years, the show consists of the architecturally stunning Hart-Cluett Mansion adorned with enchanting holiday greenery and decorations by the Van Rensselaer Garden Club. Music performances in the mansion and decorating workshops in the carriage house are held at regularly scheduled intervals. Thurs-Sat., adults $5, youths $2, children under 5 are free. 272-7232. www.rchsonline.org

Saratoga Springs Preservation Foundation, 6 Lake Ave., Saratoga Springs, holds an annual historic-homes tour the first Sunday of December. The tour of candlelit, decorated interiors is followed by a reception at the Canfield Casino. 7pm-10pm. $20-$45. 587-5030.

Troy Victorian Stroll, downtown Troy, is a sidewalk festival where the sights, sounds, and scents of a 19th-century Christmas come to life in stores, restaurants and public places. This distinctive, early-December event features costumed carolers, strolling minstrels, jugglers, period dancers, historic-homes tours, fresh popcorn and hot cider, a reindeer zoo, and a wide variety of performances in a multitude of locations. Strollers can also be squired about town in a horse-drawn carriage or vintage firetruck, or ride the free shuttlebus that departs from City Hall. Two attractions not be missed are the early-music concerts in St. Paul's Episcopal Church, a renowned "Tiffany Church," and tours of the Gilded-Age interior of the John Paine Mansion. Free. 272-8308. www.victorianstroll.com

Van Etton Christmas Tree Farms, Rte. 156, Altamont (5 miles west of the village), sell cut-to-order Christmas trees during December. 872-1895.

Yuletide Open House, Historic Cherry Hill, 523 1/2 South Pearl St., Albany, celebrates the holiday season in authentic style: Built in 1787 for Philip and Maria Van Rensselaer, the house was lived in continuously for five generations of descendents. Held the first weekend in December, the event features period music, refreshments made from Van Rensselaer family recipes, themed displays throughout the house, and holiday decorations, including a huge Christmas tree in the formal parlor. $3. 434-4791.

January

First Night Albany, downtown Albany, is a family-oriented and alcohol-free New Year's Eve celebration featuring arts and entertainment. The night begins at 6pm with a parade and the all-ages, 5K "Last Run" through Washington Park, which is decorated with holiday lights. At 6:30pm, a fireworks display kicks off a non-stop schedule of performances (dance, theater, music) at over 30 locations, including major concerts at the Palace Theater. All-access admittance buttons make the evening an excellent value, and include free shuttle-bus service, ice-cream sundaes from Ben & Jerry's, and other extras. Horse-drawn carriage rides are available, and street vendors and snack tables can be found at most locations. There's plenty on hand for youngsters, such as mask making, planetarium shows, and puppeteers. A fireworks extravaganza concludes the celebration at midnight. When the weather cooperates, First Night can be a truly joyous way to ring in the new year.

Programs are available prior to the event; buttons are available at local Price Chopper and Stewart's stores, City Hall, and many other locations. $12. Advance purchase, $10 (Dec.-Dec.25). Children under 5 are free. 434-2032. www.albanyevents.org

First Night Saratoga, Saratoga Springs, is a family-oriented New Year's celebration offering a full evening of entertainment – live bands, a magic-and-illusions act, Revolutionary War re-enactors, Shakespearean theater – presented at various downtown locations including the Children's Museum for children's activities. The night begins at 5:30pm with a 5K race at Skidmore College, and concludes with a fireworks display behind City Hall on Lake Avenue. And since it wouldn't be New Year's without resolutions, you can write yours on a moon rock at the Fleet Bank on Division Street. $12; $10 in advance. Children under five are free. 584-8266.

February

Dance Flurry, Saratoga Springs, held by Hudson-Mohawk Traditional Dances, Inc., is one of the largest dance parties in the country. Waltzes, squares, tango, swing, and English country are just a few of the dances that are performed by professionals, and made available to party goers in over 300 participatory classes. Regional bands, singers, and storytellers are also part of the three-day festival, which takes place in various downtown venues, including historic Canfield Casino. Tickets range from $14 for students and seniors to $65 for an all-access three-day pass. 292-0133. www.danceflurry.org

Mardi Gras Festival, Proctor's Theater, 432 State St., Schenectady, is held in early February and has been known to thaw the area's merciless February weather with a red-hot blast of revelry. The theater's charming arcade is turned into a New Orleans street fair (6pm) with booths for beads, masks, and catered Cajun and Creole food; followed by performances from living legends from the Big Easy playing zydeco, Cajun, Mississippi blues, and more (8pm). In between is a costume contest. $25. 346-6204.

New York in Bloom, State Museum, Madison Ave., Albany, is held the last weekend in February. Just when residents weary of gray skies and slush are ready for a lift, this annual fundraising display supplies one: exhibits from regional florists and flower designers are dispersed throughout the museum like unexpected bursts of springtime. The highly creative arrangements reflect themes from the galleries in which they are placed, often incorporating related artifacts and always to resplendent effect. Get there early for the fresh-flower market in South Hall – these blooms sell out quickly. Adults $3, children under 12 are free when accompanied by an adult. 474-5877.

Saratoga Winterfest is held over a three-day weekend in early February at various venues in downtown Saratoga Springs. This snowy extravaganza (decorated with ice carvings) runs the gamut from wine tastings at the Holiday Inn and games of chance at the Canfield Casino (a great opportunity to gamble in turn-of-the-century high style), to a chowderfest spread over 16 local restaurants. Other picturesque activities include cross-country skiing by candlelight on the Bog Meadow Trail, family-oriented dances at the National Museum of Dance, sledding in Congress Park, Victorian-themed ice skating, horse-drawn sleigh rides, a snowshoe race in Saratoga Spa State Park, and the Canfield Crafts Fair. Various fees. 584-2535.

Schenectady Colonial Festival, held in early February, celebrates the city's colonial heritage with re-enactments of colonial life, tours of historic houses, horse- and dog-cart rides, worship services, broom-making demos, a snowman contest, and additional activities for children at the Schenectady Museum. Free. 372-5656.
    A gala costume dinner is held at the Glen Sanders Mansion the evening before. $45. 374-7262.

Winter Arts & Crafts Show, Empire State Plaza (North Concourse), Albany, is a juried show featuring 50 professional crafts exhibitors from throughout the Northeast. 9:30am-3:30pm. Free. 786-1529. www.northeastshowpro.com

PARENTS AND CHILDREN

The children's' activities listed below have been chosen because they are educational or cultural as well as enjoyable. Parents should find these places and events just as engaging as youngsters will. Admission fees are subject to change.

IN AND AROUND ALBANY

Albany Heritage Area Visitors Center, 25 Quackenbush Square, holds imaginative, child-oriented events on a regular basis. One example is the "Christmas Kinderfest," which celebrates the holiday in the Dutch tradition with decoration making, storytelling, and sing-alongs. There's a Building Blocks of the City room, where the entire family can explore Albany's architecture, and both youngsters and parents will marvel at the exhibit of finely detailed scale models (circa 1920s) of historic buildings. Free. Open Mon-Fri., 9am-4pm; Sat-Sun., 10am-4pm. Free parking. 434-0405. www.albany.org

Henry Hudson Planetarium is located within the Visitors Center. The 30-foot-high domed theater presents magical "star shows" to light up a child's interest in astronomy. The custom-made shows are held Saturdays, 11:30am and 12:30pm. 434-0405.

Albany Institute of History & Art Explorers Gallery, 125 Washington Ave., is where visitors of all ages can explore images and reproductions relevant to the museum's collections. The six activity areas include an interactive computer-learning station; mystery boxes of unidentified objects; a costume corner with antique clothing for children and adults to try on; and a hands-on miniature museum with scale-model galleries and objects. In addition to regularly scheduled scavenger hunts are play-and-learn experiences such as "Curator For a Day," as well as art-making projects for children and parents to share. Families should also be sure to visit the Egyptology Room, a colorful burial chamber containing two mummies and antiquities of the Nile that will fascinate young and old alike. Open Wed-Sat., 10am-5pm; Sat-Sun., noon-5pm. Weds. until 8pm. Free with museum admission. 463-4478. www.albanyinstitute.org

Emma Treadwell Thacher Nature Center, 87 Nature Center Way (off Ketchum Rd., 17 miles southwest of Albany), Voorheesville, opened in Thompson's Lake State Park in 2002 with a mission of enchanting children with the wonders of nature. The center contains a natural-resources classroom and several marvelous exhibits, including a geologic model of the Helderberg Escarpment, a live honeybee observation hive, a wildlife viewing area, and fossils, furs and other hands-on collections. A beaver dam is a short walk away, and trails for hiking and skiing lead through woodlands and fields from the nature center to the lake. Open year-round, 10am to 6pm from Memorial Day to Labor Day; 9am-5pm the rest of the year. Closed Mondays and holidays. Free. 872-0800. www.nysparks.org

Empire State Plaza, Madison Ave., has many aspects that can provide for a pleasant family afternoon, including a playground (near the Swan St. entrance) of modernist beams set in sandy basins and surrounded by landscaping and comfortable seating. Nearby is the playground's counterpart, "Labyrinth," a child-friendly teakwood art installation by Francois Stahly. From this point you can look out over the rock wall facing the Cultural Center for an excellent view of the World War II memorial and its gigantic steel eagle. Within the plaza is a wide, brick promenade that's ideal for bicycling and rollerblading. And the picnic tables around the reflecting pool (toward State Street) allow for a scenic urban repast. In winter, the pool becomes an ice-skating rink. Open daily 6am-11pm. Free. 473-0559. www.ogs.state.ny.us/plaza

GE Kids' Day, Empire State Plaza, Madison Ave., is an annual event held in late July – and is the one summer festival where "kids' activities" are the whole shebang instead of just a sideline. Offerings include a petting zoo, professional storytellers and interactive "story acting," magic shows, live music, puppeteers, family arts and crafts projects, food booths, inflatable "bounces" and rides, face-painting, pony rides, clowns and jugglers, balloons, and more. Free. 1pm-5pm. 473-0559. www.ogs.state.ny.us/plaza

Hoffman's Playland, 608 New Loudon Rd., Latham, is a small amusement park that's not the least bit educational – it's just for fun, and lots of it. A local rite of childhood for 50 years, this old-fashioned park is especially suited to very young children, who will delight in its boat ride, small-fry Ferris Wheel (there's a larger one for older children), and "Jolly Caterpillar" locomotive. The playland's vintage bumper cars, skee-ball arcade, and diner-car food stand are well maintained, and the park has a relaxing, nostalgic ambience that parents will appreciate. The old-fashioned prices are fun, too: rides are $1. Open daily April-Sept., noon-9pm ('till 10pm on busy evenings). 785-7368.

Hoffman's Miniature Golf, 626 New Loudon Rd., is a challenging, 36-hole course with a charming layout of flower beds, huge old trees, and flaming torches. $3.50-$7.50. A driving range is located between the golf course and the playland. 785-9891.

Indian Ladder Farms, 342 Altamont Rd., Altamont, has lots of things to see and do for families. Among them are a baby farm-animal petting zoo and animal exhibits; nature hikes with dramatic views and picnic areas; tractor- and horse-drawn hayrides through the scenic orchard; pick your own berries (July), apples (Sept-Oct.) and pumpkins (Oct.), and fresh-pressed cider and cider doughnuts year-round. "Let's Feed Rosie" is the farm's educational activity, starring Rosie, a Scottish Highlander heifer who looks like a red buffalo. The farm hosts birthday parties for youngsters. Lunch café, farm-produce store, crafts shop. Open daily. 9am-5pm fall and winter; 10am-6pm spring and summer. Closed January and February. Hayrides need reservations. The grounds are free, other activities are $1 to $5. 765-2956.

New York State Museum Discovery Place, Madison Ave., is a hands-on learning gallery for children ages 3 to 12. This roomy space is full of fun things, such as dinosaur-bone puzzles, child-oriented changing exhibits, game-like computers, artwork projects, and an impressive bug display. Activities include Kids Collect, allowing youngsters to display their own exhibits, and Furry Tales and Touchables, an interactive storytelling hour held two Saturdays each month at 11am.

Windows on New York is interesting for all ages. This walk-around exhibit of colorful, interactive displays, representing each of the state's regions from Coney Island to the Adirondacks, is located in the Terrace Gallery (fourth floor), where floor-to-ceiling windows offer panoramic views.

1900 Dare Carousel is showcased in a custom-made glass pavilion in the Terrace Gallery. This unusually large and beautiful merry-go-round has 40 horses (and deer and donkeys) hand-carved by Charles Dare of Brooklyn in 1895; also a Neptune boat and a spinning "love tub" that is one of the last of its kind. An early "jumping" carousel, the Dare was painstakingly restored in 2001, right down to the German-marble eyes, real horsehair tails, and gold-painted decorations. Antique carousels are a rare item in museums, but what makes this one really special is that youngsters can ride it. The carousel is in operation noon-4pm Mon-Fri., and 10am-4pm Sat-Sun. Open daily 10am-5pm (closed major holidays). Suggested donation $2. 474-5877.

Shaker Learning Fair, Shaker Heritage Society, 875 Watervliet-Shaker Rd., is the society's major educational program. During summer workshops, ages 6-12 can learn about Shaker culture from costumed guides; activities include Shaker songs and dances, and hands-on demonstrations of crafts such as broom making, spinning, weaving, and soap making. Family Day is held in August, and features crafts, tours, and farm animals. 456-7890. www.shakerwv@crisny.org

Snow Tubing, Capital Hills at Albany Golf Course, 65 O'Neil Rd., is an exhilarating (and easy) winter sport for toddlers to teenagers. Parents can match one of the course's many hills to their child's age and ability. Free. Dawn to dusk. 489-3526. 438-2208.

Frear Park in Troy and Central Park in Schenectady are also good sites for a family tubing excursion (see Recreation and Sports pg. 155)

Steamer No. 10 Kid's Fare, Western Ave., is a series of children's theatrical entertainments, many of them written by the Steamer's award-winning troupe. Housed in a converted 19th-century fire station, the 120-seat theater resounds with madcap productions of fairy tales, children's literature, and local history. Stories are dramatized with an eye to imaginative, interactive stagings for three seasons yearly, with a Shakespeare production every summer. There's also a holiday program called "Vacation Daze" (named after the dazed expression of parents cooped up with restless youngsters), which features the most magical and whimsical of regional performers. The concession sells fresh popcorn and cider. 438-5503.

Sunday Symphonies for Families is presented by the Albany Symphony Orchestra (see Arts and Venues, pg. 51) to introduce younger audiences to the joy of classical music – and to build future symphony audiences – while providing families with a shared activity. The hour-long concerts are energetic, theatrically wacky affairs, featuring maestro David Alan Miller costumed as a historical figure or a figure from his own imagination. The programs, such as "Captain Dave in Nutcrackers in Outer Space," and especially, "Cowboy Dave's Excellent American Adventure" are hugely popular; in fact, other orchestras from around the country request the programs – and the maestro, too. There are three Sunday family symphonies presented yearly at the Palace Theater in Albany. Showtime is 3pm, call for dates. Adults $12, children (14 and under) $6. Group discounts. Box office: 465-4663. www.albanysymphony.com

IN AND AROUND TROY

Berkshire Bird Paradise Sanctuary, 43 Red Pond Rd., Grafton (3 miles east of Grafton Lakes State Park), is a non-profit bird sanctuary established in 1972 to provide care and a safe haven for injured and disabled birds. It's now one of the largest bird sanctuaries in the country, with more than a 150 species including bald eagles, peregrine falcons, peacocks, owls, exotic cranes, and red-tailed hawks. Natural habitats are customized to the needs of the avian residents, and the sanctuary has to its credit the rare accomplishment of breeding a golden eagle chick. ("Goldie" lives free and returns for visits.) The sanctuary offers a wonderful opportunity for children to see wild and endangered birds up close, and to learn about animal conservation. Open daily mid-May-Oct., 9am-5pm. Donation suggested. 279-3801. www.birdparadise.com

Flag Acres Zoo, Rowley Rd., Hoosick Falls (follow zoo signs from the village), is a non-profit, family-owned zoo with lions, tigers and bears. And lots of primates, from tiny marmosets to gibbons. And kangaroos and tortoises, and about 50 other species of hand-raised animals. Walking trails wind through 20 acres of habitat, including a picnic area. The zoo is an educational facility that presents animal programs at the Berkshire Museum (see below entry), and the staff welcomes questions. Open daily May 15-Sept.15, 10am-5pm. Adults $8, children $5. 686-3159.

Junior Museum, 105 Eighth St., Troy, is a learning playhouse of the arts, science and history for ages 2-12. In existence for 50 years, the museum recently underwent a $4.5 million relocation, expanding to four floors of exciting "adventures" and hands-on activities. In addition to the educational center on the top floor (from child-friendly computers to funhouse mirrors), it features a wide variety of animals (including exotic reptiles and tarantulas) and an animal nursery. The sophisticated Digistar II planetarium offers virtual-universe tours, and there's a log cabin and Native American gallery, as well as permanent and changing exhibits. The museum also offers family crafts projects and musical events. Open Weds-Fri., 11am-4pm, Sat-Sun., 10am-4pm (closed major holidays). All family members $5, children under three are free. 235-2120. www.juniormuseum.org

Rensselaer Railroad Heritage Center, RPI campus, Burdett Ave., Troy, contains an incredibly detailed, historically accurate HO-scale model railroad. Its 500-feet of hand-laid, "walk-around" track ranges from "South Troy" to "the Adirondacks," with lifelike pine trees, water towers, dairy cows, and architectural landmarks along the way. "The Berkshire Line" is based on the Delaware & Hudson and the Rutland (Vt.) railroad lines and is set in 1950, during "the twilight of America's great age of railroading." Begun in 1947, the railroad is a must-see for railroad buffs and modelers of all kinds. Children will be enchanted by this extraordinary miniature world, and parents will be amazed by its ingenuity. The railroad is located in the basement of Davison Hall and can be viewed during regularly scheduled open houses. 276-2764. http://railroad.union.rpi.edu

IN AND AROUND SCHENECTADY

Central Park, Fehr Ave., is chockablock with attractions for youngsters. A train ride, swimming pool, duck pond, and gentle hills for toboganing and tubing are just a few of the landscape's offerings. In summer, the park hosts almost weekly festivals or concerts, free family movie nights, and theater productions. Schedules are available at the Schenectady Chamber of Commerce, 306 State St. 372-5656.

Costumer, 1020 Barrett St., Schenectady, is an international supplier of theatrical costumes and accessories, and contains a "library" of approximately 60,000 costumes, most of them created in-house. A free workplace tour is available by appointment for groups of five or more. 374-7442.

Empire State Aerosciences Museum, 250 Rudy Chase Drive, Glenville, is a fun and educational facility that is truly for all ages. Located opposite the Air National Guard site on the Schenectady County Airport, the museum provides hands-on experiences in aviation science and technology. Building a rocket, piloting from the cockpit of an airplane, and guiding model aircraft in flight are only a few of its things to do. Interactive exhibits include a mock-up of a 1910 Von Pomer airplane, a model-airport landing board, and a Simulated Flight Reality Ride synchronized with an exciting video. Classes are offered ("Radio Control for Beginners," "Strategy Battle Games") during school vacations. An extensive aircraft collection contains historic fighter-bombers, an experimental glider and a "Flying Motorcycle" from France. Open April-Oct., Tues-Sat., 10am-4pm; Sun. noon-4pm. Nov-March, Thurs-Sat., 10am-4pm. Group tours by appointment. Adults $5, children $2, Reality Ride $2. 377-2191. www.esam@esam.org

Observatory Open House, Union College, is a collaborative program between Union and the Schenectady Museum, geared to family members of all ages. The museum's science educator and the college's observatory manager guide participants as they examine the night sky through Union's 20-inch-diameter telescope. On clear nights a variety of planets and stars are visible. Free. 6:30pm-8:30pm. For information and dates: 388-7100.

MVP Kid's Place, Schenectady Museum, Nott Terrace Heights, is an interactive area for youngsters ages four to nine, with a "Barney's Department Store," for dress-up, a 1970s play kitchen, and crafts projects. But the most unique fun comes from how the activities are plugged into the museum's focus on the technological and industrial achievements of Schenectady. Kids can "conduct an experiment" in the GE Research Lab, put on a puppet show in "the world's first television station," and "work" on an ALCO locomotive assembly line. Parents can enjoy the exhibits of ALCO tools, vintage toys, and early photographs from WRGB-TV while their child plays at being Thomas Edison. MVP Kid's Place is open during regular museum hours.

    The Schenectady Museum and Planetarium presents a variety of family planetarium programs Mon-Fri. during school vacations, with "Honey, I Shrunk the Solar System" and "Inter-Planetary Puppets in Space" being just two examples. Pre-registration not required. Schedules available. Open Tues-Fri., 10am-4:30pm. Closed major holidays. Adults $5, seniors $4, children (4-9) $3. (For museum with planetarium admission, add $1.50). 382-7890. www.schenectadymuseum.org

IN AND AROUND SARATOGA

Children's Museum, 69 Caroline St., provides positive opportunities for children ages 2-10 to learn about science, history, community living, and the arts. The two-story brick house (acquired in a $1.3 million relocation and expansion in 2001) features a variety of programs designed to encourage youngsters to make their own discoveries. The first floor has a replica of Congress Park, a duck pond, a fire truck, and a very popular bubble-making machine. Upstairs is a dress-up attic, and the yard outside has a garden and a performance space. Once a month, the museum offers Kid's Night Out: two-plus hours of chaperoned activities on a Friday or Saturday evening. Open Tues-Sat., 9:30am-4:30pm; Sun. noon-4:30pm. $4 per person, children under 1 are free. 584-5540. www.childrensmuseumatsaratoga.org

Circus Smirkus, Saratoga Spa State Park, is a three-day event held in mid-July by the Saratoga Arts Council. The Vermont troupe (who've been featured on the Disney Channel) practices the time-honored circus arts of juggling, clowning, acrobatics, sword swallowing, and flying through the air with the greatest of ease. The troupe's athletic aplomb may be attributed to their youth: each Smirkus performer is between 10 and 20 years old. Two performances daily. Adults $14, children $12. 584-4132.

Dakota Ridge Farm, 189 East High St., Ballston Spa, offers guided 1- and 2-hour llama hikes on groomed, woodland trails (you do the walking, the llamas carry lunch). Afterward, visitors are welcome to make the acquaintance of baby llamas, horses and goats, and to watch the llamas train on an obstacle course. Open spring-fall, Fri-Sun., 8am-5pm. Reservations required. Adults $20, youths (5-16) $10. 885-0756. www.llamaweb.com/llfarms/drf/

Fiber Tour of Saratoga County, Bacon Hill (various farm locations), is held the first Sunday in Oct. (11am-4pm), and features llama, alpaca, sheep, and angora-rabbit farms (see Points of Interest, pg. 29). Each farm does its own presentation, and small children especially will be enchanted by these appealing, gentle animals. You might even spot a camel! Free. A tour brochure is available. 885-8995. www.ccesaratoga.org

Maize at Liberty Ridge Farm, 29 Bevis Rd., Schaghticoke, invites visitors to get lost in a corny creation: a 10-acre corn maze for families and teenagers. Learn about agriculture while you try to find your way out. Open Aug-Oct., Mon-Fri., 4pm-10pm; Sat., 10am-10pm; Sun., noon-7pm. Adults $7, kids (4-11) $5, children under 3 are free. Halloween season turns the maze turns into a "Field of Screams," where frightful things go bump in the stalks ($1 extra). 664-1515. www.cornfieldmaze.com.

National Museum of Racing, 191 Union Ave., Saratoga Springs, is wonderfully entertaining for the whole family. Set up in a circle just like a racetrack, the museum has several programs for both very young and older children, including Horse Play, an interactive gallery where kids can try on jockey gear and "shoe a horse," and an Anatomy Room with a horse skeleton. Exhibits feature fine art, trophies, and educational displays on Saratoga's role in the growth of Thoroughbred racing in America. Open Mon-Sat.,10am-4:30pm, Sun 12-4:30pm; During racing season, Mon-Sun., 9am-5pm. Adults $7, seniors/students $5, children under 5 are free. 584-0400. www.racingmuseum.org

Petrified Sea Gardens, Lester Park Rd. (Rte 29), Saratoga Springs, is a sea-floor park full of interesting rock formations – and a prehistoric ambience that is almost magical. An acre of exposed Stromatolite fossils, approximately 500-million-years-old, form walking trails through what was once the ocean reef of a tropical sea. Along the walkways you'll see dinosaur tracks, a Native-American medicine wheel, towering pine trees, a sundial garden, and a limestone grotto – and if that isn't enough to explore, you can enter the labyrinth. Discovered by accident in the 1920s, this National Historic Landmark has an interesting history, too. The gift store specializes in fossils and minerals. Open late-April-early-Nov., 11am-4pm (weather permitting). Open daily July and Aug., 11am-5pm. Guided group tours by appointment. Adults $3, seniors/students $2, youngsters (6-16) $1.50, children under 6 are free. 584-7102. www.petrifiedseagardens.org

 Lester Park, a year-round geologic park, adjoins the Sea Gardens and is known as a good spot for fall leaf peeping. 474-5877.

Saratoga Shakespeare Company, Congress Park, Saratoga Springs, was founded in 1999 to provide "Shakespeare for the enjoyment of everyone of every age." The company of local and national actors performs physically exuberant stagings of a comedy by the Bard during the last week of July and the first week in August, Weds-Sat. evenings. Free. 884-4947.

Skating on the Canal, Fort Hardy Park, Schuylerville, occurs on several days in winter when the town of Schuylerville sets up skating areas along the Champlain canal – just as they do in Holland, where the Dutch skate along their canals like Americans drive the highways. Colonial-style winter games are put on by the Old Saratoga Historical Society, and free refreshments are served in the park's youth center. Call for dates. 695-4159.

NOT FAR AWAY

Camp Chingachgook, Pilot Knob Rd., Kattskill Bay, is a non-profit outdoor center (operated by the Schenectady YMCA) dedicated to the promotion of fitness, character-building and environmental awareness – as well as providing campers with a terrific time. The center is located by Lake George on 200 acres bordering the Adirondack Forest Preserve. Activities take place along the waterfront, in the mountains, and on 50 miles of trails, and include everything from archery to kayaking to rock-climbing. One- and two-week sessions are available. In addition to the summer camp, Chingachgook offers wonderful year-round retreats (for a day, a weekend, or one or two weeks) for all family members, including bicycling, hiking, climbing, and water trips for children and/or parents, organized by three levels of ability. A wide variety of teen adventure trips build survival and leadership skills. The center also offers "Y-Knot" sailing clinics (half-day) for people with disabilities and their able-bodied friends. 656-9462. www.chingachgook.org

Wild West Ranch, Bloody Pond Rd., Lake George, is a Western-Town tourist attraction during the summer. But in winter, it offers 45-minute horseback rides and horse-drawn sleigh or wagon rides through wooded trails on French Mountain, offering beautiful views of the Adirondack wilderness under cover of snow. Cowboy guides narrate the rides with historical anecdotes of the French and Indian War, colorful tales of Boot Hill, and information on the buffalo, elk and longhorn cattle moseying along the trails. The ice-skating rink (ice skates available) is free with paid admission. Must be seven or older for the horseback rides but there's a petting zoo in the stable for little buckaroos. Open (weather permitting) winter weekends, or during the week by reservation. Sleigh and wagon rides: Adults $7, children $4. Horseback rides: $18. 668-2121.

Adirondack Museum, Rte. 30, Blue Mountain Lake, is a natural for youngsters. The lakeside museum explores the history of the Adirondacks from its early pioneer days to its development as a resort in the 20th century. Some of the sights that will fascinate young and old alike are an ornate railroad car, a tiny hermit's hut, and canoes and other watercraft. Children can build (and sail) their own toy boat in the Boatbuilder's Shop; visit with makers of packbaskets and rustic furniture; go rowing in a traditional Adirondack wooden skiff; climb aboard the Porter engine; and (Weds-Thurs.) meet with "Teddy Roosevelt." Lake View café and museum shop with toys and historical games. Open daily Memorial Day-Oct 15, 9:30am-5: 30pm. Adults $10, seniors $9, military ID, students and youths (7-17) $5, children under 7 are free. 352-7311. www.adkmuseum.org

Berkshire Museum, 39 South St. (Rte. 7), Pittsfield, Mass., has a stegosaurus out front – a 26-foot-long, 10-foot-high model named Wally. Inside, families can find out about real stegos at the "Dino Dig," an interactive excavation display that is just one of the museum's gazillions of imaginative exhibits and learning programs. One recent example is the "Microbes: Invisible Invaders, Amazing Allies" exhibit, with a "Microbial Bake-Off" by local chefs. There are loads of activities specifically for pre-schoolers, such as "Greet the Greeks," with a Grecian-statue art project. In addition, children can get their hands wet in the "Touch Tank," one of the aquarium's 26 tanks of fish, reptiles and plants from around the globe. Or they can attend costumed world-culture and dance performances, observe the 3D Floor Show, join in monthly scavenger hunts, and display their handiwork in the Refrigerator Art gallery. And then visit the wacky Vend-O-Mart for a snack. The museum has equally imaginative "Weird Science" classes for adults. $10 Open Mon-Sat. 10am-5pm, Sun. noon-5pm. Adults $8, students/seniors $6, youths (3-18) $5, children under 3 are free. Free for all ages on birthdays. (413) 443-7171. www.berkshiremuseum.org

Berkshire Scenic Railway Museum, Willow Creek Rd., Lenox, MA., is the restored 1903 Lenox station that once greeted frequent trains to and from New York City. Inside can be found antique rail equipment, model railroads, and local-history displays. The museum also offers a "short shuttle" train ride, and festive events for children during summer (call for a schedule), and holiday events including a train-hopping Halloween witch (Oct. 28-29) and Santa Claus (Dec. 16-17). Child-oriented gift shop. Open weekends and holidays. Memorial Day-Oct. Adults $2.50, seniors $2, children under 14 $1. (413) 637-2210

BTF Plays!, Main Street, Stockbridge, presents theater productions for young audiences in the 122-seat Unicorn Theater. A division of the Berkshire Theater Festival, these plays for children are very inventive – a zany, modern-musical version of *The Odyssey* being one example. Ticket prices are moderate. (413) 298-5536.

Annual Frog Jump, Parade Ground Village (Rte. 9 and Dunning St.), Malta, is held every August for frog trainers 12-and-under who want to compete in an old-fashioned frog jump competition. The event is strictly BYOF (Bring Your Own Frog), and coordinators advise participants to get to know their frogs and practice motivational techniques in advance. Spectators are encouraged to dress in froggy fashion, and to assist in rounding up runaways. The jump is non-discriminatory (toads allowed), and also features rides, face painting, a petting zoo, pony rides, and magicians and other live entertainment. All proceeds benefit the Round Lake Youth Baseball commission. 399-5517.

Kaleidoworld, Catskill Corners, Mt. Tremper (Rte. 28, just outside Woodstock), is both a crafts shop and a children's fantasyland of light and color. It boasts the world's largest kaleidoscope, along with three magical "optic attractions," including a giant starship that uses imagery from the Hubble Telescope for a tour of the universe. The gallery exhibits the electronic arts of light sculptors, and there's a 60-foot-high Hall of Mirrors and a Crystal Palace. And lots of kaleidoscopes, telescopes and other colorful creations for visitors to peer into, ride on, and interact with. The Kaleidostore displays and sells custom-made kaleidoscopes, from simple and inexpensive to fine-art creations. Open daily 10am-7pm. Closed Tues., Oct. 13-July 3. Adults $10, seniors and children $9 (not recommended for toddlers). Discounts for families and groups. Catskill Corners is located in the heart of the Catskill Mountains in a converted barn and contains several unusual, child-oriented shops. (914) 688-5300. www.catskillcorners.com

Mac-Haydn Theatre Inc., 1925 Rte. 203, Chatham, produces plays "in the round" in a rustic, hillside theater. Low-priced musical adaptations of popular children's stories are performed for youths of all ages on weekend mornings in July and August. 392-9292.

Walter Elwood Museum, 300 Guy Park Rd., Amsterdam, is one of only two public-school-operated museums in the state. Planned 50 years ago by Walter Elwood to be child-oriented, the museum features colorful exhibits on life in the Mohawk Valley, with a focus on local history, Native American culture, and nature and animals. History rooms with costumed mannequins bring the past to life for even the youngest visitors, while the art gallery upstairs displays artworks by school children in addition to a collection of regional art. The gift shop offers Native American, Eskimo, and early-Americana arts and crafts. Open Sept-June, Mon-Fri., 8:30am-4pm; July-Aug., Mon-Thurs., 8:30am-3:30pm, Fri. 8:30am-1pm. Closed holidays. Free. 843-5151.

Inventive birthday parties are offered by all the above museums, and many hold themed slumber parties as well. The State Museum coordinates overnight group camp-ins (60-100 youngsters and adults), including sleepovers in the Iroquois Longhouse.

Photography by: Gary Gold

TRANSPORTATION

For almost 400 years Albany has been a port of entry, and the hub of a region that was settled for its transportation opportunities. Site of the country's first railroad and earliest municipal airport (on ground chosen by Charles Lindbergh), the Capital Region has always been an easy place to get to and from. Today, modern superhighways such as the Thomas E. Dewey Thruway and the Adirondack Northway provide a corridor connecting the entire Northeast. As of 2002, the attractive and efficient Rensselaer Rail Station makes traveling by train even easier, while major redevelopment of the Albany Airport has made national and international travel more convenient than ever.

Major road names and route numbers are listed at the end of the chapter.

AIRPORTS

Albany International Airport
737 Albany-Shaker Rd., Albany (off the Northway at Exit 4, follow signs), 242-2200.

AIA evolved from the first municipal airport in the United States to an impressive yet visitor-friendly travel complex. The major air center for the Capital Region, northeastern New York, and western New England, the airport is located within easy access to all major inter-state highways. The 1,000-acre complex, which contains a wide range of facilities and services, is currently engaged in a $232 million upgrade to maintain safety and to meet the needs of air travelers well into the 21st century. The airport information booth is located on the first level between the ticket area and the baggage-claim area.

Parking is available in a variety of locations and prices. The adjacent, short-term lot allows 30 minutes of free parking for pick-ups and drop-offs. An economy remote lot provides long-term parking and includes a free shuttle. A covered glass walkway connects the ground lots to the terminal.

Transportation can be found at the taxi stand just outside the first-floor baggage claim area. The CDTA Shuttlefly Bus services the airport several times an hour between 6am and 11pm. Rental-car counters can be found in the baggage claim area. Many local hotels provide transportation to and from the terminal; direct phones are located at the reservation center in the baggage claim area.

Amenities include well-designed food and beverage concessions including the Landslide Café (second level); a range of services from banking to shoe shines; convenience shops and Departure, a unique retail concession featuring hand-crafted gifts, artworks, jewelry, and books from 60 regional cultural institutions (top of elevator, second level near parking bridge).

AIA Gallery is located on the third level. This well-regarded art space is open 7am-7pm daily and features three major exhibits a year. In addition to the gallery, exhibit cases and large-scale artworks can be viewed throughout the terminal. www.albanyairport.com

Airline Information 518-242-2477
Air Canada 888-247-2262
American Airlines 800-433-7300
American Eagle 800-433-7300
Continental Express 800-525-0280
Continental Connection 800-525-0280
Delta 800-221-1212
Northwest 800-225-2525
Southwest 800-435-9792
United Airlines 800-241-6522
United Express 800-428-4322
US Airways 800-428-4322

BUSES

Capital Region Buses

Capital District Transportation Authority, 482-8822

CDTA was created in 1970 by the New York Legislature "to transport customers safely and reliably at reasonable cost." A fleet of 231 vehicles serves the four-county area with 44 regular routes, in addition to rural routes in outlying communities. Schedules are available at hundreds of outlets, including shopping malls, libraries, visitor centers, news stands, and state offices. Many buses are low-floor, lift-equipped; people with disabilities pay half fare. Free Park & Ride lots are located throughout the transit area with connecting buses providing express service during peak hours. Fare: $1-$1.35. Exact change required. Discounted Swiper cards are available. www.cdta.org

Albany Free Shuttle Bus runs a loop around downtown Albany destinations (Empire State Plaza, Capital Hill, Broadway). The shuttle can be boarded every 15 minutes at downtown CDTA bus stops during early morning and late afternoon, and every 40 minutes mid-day. For a route schedule, call 482-8822.

Upstate Transit, 584-5252
Weekday commuter service from Saratoga Springs to downtown Albany with stops including Clifton Park and Ballston Spa. Upstate's 52-passenger, deluxe motorcoaches are clean, very comfortable, and staffed by courteous drivers. The fare includes a free transfer to CDTA buses. $3-$5. www.upstatetours.com

Long-Distance Buses

The following bus lines can be boarded at the Albany Bus Terminal, 34 Hamilton St. (at Liberty St., off Broadway), Albany, 434-8095.

Adirondack Trailways, 800-225-6815
This family-owned company has been in the motorcoach business since 1926. Daily service to northern cities and towns including Glens Falls, Lake George, Chesterton, Lake Placid, Saranac Lake, Malone and Potsdam, plus Montreal and Toronto. Daily direct service from Albany to New York City. Narrated tours on weekends; some routes have free bike storage.

Bonanza, 1-888-751-8800
Daily service to New York City, Connecticut, Rhode Island, and Massachusetts, including the Berkshires, Boston, and Cape Cod. www.bonanzabus.com

Greyhound Lines, 800-231-2222
Greyhound is the largest provider of inter-city bus transportation in the country and serves more than 2,600 destinations. Daily express service to New York City, Boston, Washington D.C., and Philadelphia. Daily service to Amsterdam, Utica, Syracuse, Rochester, and Buffalo. www.greyhoundlines.com

Peter Pan, 800-343-9999
Daily service throughout the Northeast, from New Hampshire to Washington D.C., including Connecticut, New Jersey, and an extensive number of stops throughout Massachusetts.

Vermont Transit (Greyhound counter), 800-451-3292
Daily service to Vermont including Bennington, Arlington, Manchester, Rutland, Middlebury, and Burlington, plus connections to New Hampshire, New England, and Canada. Bicycles and skis must be boxed, baggage fee up to $15. www.vermonttransit.com

Charter Buses

Hart Tours Inc.
1 Becker Terrace, Delmar, 439-6095
Motorcoach charters and group tours along the Eastern Seaboard, also package trips to Las Vegas, New Orleans, Orlando.

Premiere Limousine Service
456 North Pearl St., Albany, 1-800-515-6123
Long-distance touring services including stretch limos and 21-passenger VIP motorcoaches with sofa seating, VCRs, and galleys. www.premierelimo.com

Upstate Transit Tours
Geyser Rd., Ballston Spa, 584-5252
Charters nationwide, special-occasion transportation, executive motorcoaches featuring all amenities (galleys, VCRs). Inexpensive, well-planned group day trips (New York City, Atlantic City, Boston). www.upstatetours.com

Wade Tours and Travel Agency
797 Burdeck Ave., Rotterdam, 355-4500
This family-owned business has 75 years' experience in motorcoach charters. It also offers scenic one-day excursions such as Berkshires foliage tours, "Hudson Valley Castles," Connecticut River steam train and riverboat tours, West Point and Culinary Institute of America trips, "Great Camps of the Adirondacks," music and art tours, casino jaunts, and NYC shopping trips, plus national- and world-travel packages. www.wadetours.com

Yankee Trails
3 Avenue Ext., Rensselaer, 286-2400
Wide range of motorcoach charter services and group tours including one-day excursions to sporting events, entertainment events, casinos, fairs, and scenic attractions of the Northeast, plus weeklong excursions to popular destinations across the country. www.yankeetrails.com

CAR SERVICES

Albany Parking Authority provides information on city and public parking garages and parking lots. Downtown Albany has 900 metered parking spaces, which are free on weekends and after 6pm weekdays. 465-2143.

Commuter Register Website (www.commuter-register.org/) allows people to advertise for free for a carpool, or to form a carpool with others. For carpool information in Albany, call 458-2164.

Premiere Limousine Service
456 North Pearl St., Albany, 1-800-515-6123.
Chauffeur-driven transportation services 24-hours daily, including limos, double-stretch limos, sedans and vans; from simple pick-ups (Albany Airport, SPAC, Pepsi Arena, rail stations) to all-day outings. Group packages, plus corporate clientele and special-occasion services. www.premierelimo.com

Thruway road conditions are available by calling 1-800-THRUWAY (847-8929). www.thruway.state.ny.us

TRAINS

Amtrak is the sole provider of inter-city passenger train service in the U.S., traveling to over 500 destinations in 46 states. The Capital Region is one of the few areas that still enjoys passenger train service in all four directions, and many of these routes travel through the most scenic terrain in the Northeast. Amtrak's average on-time performance is higher than the average on-time performance of passenger airlines. Children ride half price every day. 1-800-USA-RAIL. www.northeast.amtrak.com

The following Capital Region rail stations are serviced by CDTA buses.

Rensselaer Rail Station
555 East St., Rensselaer, 462-5763
A key stop in the busy Northeast corridor, the Rensselaer Station is the 13th busiest in the nation. Opened in fall of 2002, this striking, $53.1 million, 72,000-square-foot facility was designed by a Schenectady architect in the neo-classical style, with colorful, terrazzo floors, cathedral ceilings with skylights, and a copper dome and other motifs from the great age of rail travel. The facility contains a post office, a café and a news stand; an art gallery is planned for the mezzanine. There's also a three-level parking garage ($5 per day) and covered walkways and platforms with views of the trains. Seven Schenectady-built turboliners provide high-speed service between the Rensselaer Station and Penn Station in New York City. www.cdta.org

Schenectady Rail Station
332 Erie Blvd., 346-8651

Saratoga Springs Rail Station
West Ave. & Station Lane, 587-8354
The station is currently undergoing a $6 million renovation that will integrate the 1950s brick building with the city's historic architecture, increase capacity, and improve service to and from the Saratoga-Adirondack region.

SPECIAL NEEDS SERVICES

CDTA STAR (Special Transit Available by Request), 482-2022 (TDD: 482-9024)
Specialized STAR buses provide demand-based transportation to residents with
disabilities. Curb-to-curb para-transit service is available for shopping, socializing,
appointments, or work, by one-day advance reservation to certified riders. A STAR
card is obtained through a physician's or other referrals. CDTA requests that
reservations be made 48 hours in advance. Call for schedules and information on
certification. $2-$2.75.

Center for the Disabled Transportation Service
700 South Pearl St., Albany, 436-7575
Handicapped-accessible vans and buses transport disabled and elderly individuals
to medical appointments, shopping, and social outings within the Capital Region.
Small fee.

Albany

Senior Citizen Transportation Service
25 Delaware Ave., Albany, 434-4219
Provides transportation for any resident age 60 and older to medical appointments,
area senior-citizen centers, shopping, banking, and other needed places.
Transportation for the handicapped is also available. Small fee suggested, 24-hours
notice required.

Troy

Rensselaer County Department for the Aging, 270-2734
Provides transportation for senior citizens to area senior-citizen centers, to social
services and medical appointments, and for shopping. Appointments may be
made daily between 8:30am and noon on a first-come, first-served basis. Small
donation suggested.

Schenectady

Red Cross of Northeastern New York BUS, 374-9180
Provides free transportation for Schenectady County residents age 60 and over
who are unable to find any other means of transportation. Elderly residents are
driven to medical appointments, grocery shopping, hair appointments and other
life needs, and to social activities. The BUS service, which utilizes a variety of
vans, is 95-percent volunteer staffed and welcomes qualified volunteer drivers.

Saratoga

Senior Transport, 884-4110
Provides free transportation to Saratoga County residents age 60 and over, including medical appointments in and out of the county. Riders must be able to access the vehicle; reservations are taken 24 hours in advance. The Saratoga County Office for the Aging oversees a variety of other transportation services for the elderly and handicapped. 482-2022. www.co.saratoga.ny.us

TAXIS

Taxis can be hailed from street corners, at the railroad station, at the airport, and at bus terminals. A full listing of city and suburban taxis is found in the yellow pages of the telephone directory. Area cabs are non-metered and operate on a fee schedule determined by zones.

*Amtrak's Northeast Timetable booklet, CDTA bus schedules, and parking-information pamphlets can be found at the four urban visitor centers (see pgs., 1, 14, 21, 27).

ROAD NAMES AND NUMBERS

The interchange of names and numbers of routes can be confusing for newcomers. The following is a list of alternate names for the same roads.

Adirondack Northway 1-87
Albany to Binghamton, exit 25a on Thruway 1-88
Albany to Boston (toll) 1-90
Central Ave. in Albany, to State St. in Schenectady . . . . Rte. 5
Delaware Ave. to Loudonville Rd. . . . . Rte. 9
East-West Arterial joining the Northway,
    Exit 24 of the NYS Thruway and the MA. Turnpike I-90
Latham Circle East to Troy . . . . Rte. 2
Latham Circle West to Schenectady . . . . Rte. 7
Albany to Buffalo on Thruway I-90
Albany to New York City on Thruway I-87
Riverfront Arterial . . . . Rte. 787
Slingerlands By-pass . . . . Rte. 85
Troy-Schenectady Rd. . . . . Rte. 7
Madison Ave. – Western Ave. (downtown Albany to Guilderland) . . . . Rte. 20

Parker Inn, Schenectady

Photography by: Steve Lakatos

LODGING

From inexpensive motor inns to grand hotels, the Capital Region is chockablock with welcoming accommodations. Many of these lodgings utilize the area's historic architecture, and almost all of the larger facilities offer high-tech business services and convention capabilities. Private baths and air conditioning are standard for the below entries unless otherwise noted, and almost all offer group discounts and corporate packages. Please call ahead to confirm rates and other details (such as service charges). Hotels with exceptional dining rooms are cross-referenced to Restaurants and Eateries. For additional information on recommendations, see "Tourism" (pg. 329) in Information and Resources.

At the end of the chapter is a section on unique fine-dining inns and resort hotels not far from the Capital Region. Although located in scenic areas, these establishments are worthy destinations in themselves.

DISTINCTIVE HOTELS

Century House Inn
Rte. 9, Latham, 785-0931
This family-owned hotel is a longtime local favorite, with 64 deluxe rooms, luxury suites, and long-term apartments. The hotel has an inn-like ambience, and offers a fitness center, outdoor pool, tennis courts, conference and meeting accommodations, and a half-mile backyard nature trail. A country-buffet breakfast is served from the adjacent Century House Restaurant (see Restaurants, pg. 70). Rates $115-$175. www.thecenturyhouse.com

Crowne Plaza
State St. and Lodge St., Albany, 462-6611 (800-2CROWNE)
Owned by the international Six Continents Hotels chain (which also owns Holiday Inn), the Albany Crowne Plaza is a 15-story hotel with a contemporary ambience and 384 spacious rooms with all amenities, including cable TV. The hotel features a full complement of business services, in addition to the 10,000-square-foot Ten Eyck Ballroom. The Crowne is located just minutes from the Empire State Plaza Convention Center, and a short walk from the Pepsi Arena and many other downtown attractions. The hotel includes a casual restaurant and an Irish-style pub. Rates: $119-$169 www.crowneplaza.com

Desmond Hotel

660 Albany-Shaker Rd. (I-87 Exit 4), 869-8100 (800-448-3500)
Located less than a mile from the Albany Airport, the Desmond is minutes away
from major interstates north, south, east and west. A luxury-class hotel, it has
324 spacious rooms and suites, handsome colonial décor (oriental carpets to
18th-century replica furnishings), and a charming indoor courtyard with trees
and brick walkways. The hotel also contains a ballroom, heated indoor pools, a
gym, and two restaurants: the fine-dining Scrimshaw (see Restaurants, pg. 73),
and the casual Simpson's. Convention facilities include a variety of fully equipped
meeting rooms, private boardrooms, and an amphitheater. Rates: $135 (off-season
double room) to $230 (peak-season deluxe suite). http//desmondny.com

Gideon Putnam Hotel

24 Gideon Putnam Rd., Saratoga Springs, 584-3000
A Saratoga tradition since the 1930s, this Georgian-Revival hotel offers 120 rooms
including porch and parlor suites, all tastefully decorated to reflect the Georgian
era. Set amid the lofty pines of the Saratoga Spa Park (see Recreation and Sports,
pg. 153) this year-round recreational resort becomes a hive of glamorous activity
every August during racing season. The hotel serves a legendary Sunday
brunch, in addition to the fine dining available in the elegant Georgian Room
(see Restaurants, pg. 79). The lobby contains a high-quality gift shop. Early
reservations are required for August. Off-season rates: $99-$204. Track-season
rates: $170-$530. www.gideonputnam.com

Glen Sanders Mansion Inn

1 Glen Ave., Scotia, 374-7262
One of America's oldest country manors, this 1663 mansion is located along the
north bank of the Mohawk River, where it remained a family home for 303 years
(after it was sold, the original furnishings, silver, and artwork were acquired by
Colonial Williamsburg). In 1988 the house was converted to an inn and restaurant,
and expanded in 1995 with a landscaped addition. The inn's riverfront ballroom,
gourmet restaurant, private dining room, intimate lounge, and banquet facilities
are located in the mansion. The addition offers 20 rooms with a colonial ambience
and modern amenities, plus two patio suites with private balconies or French
doors. All rooms include the latest in business services and a bountiful buffet
breakfast. Rates: $139-$295. www.glensandersmansion.com

Longfellows Inn

500 Union Ave., Saratoga Springs, 587-0108
This striking inn was created out of a 1915 dairy barn, with sleek, Shaker-style
décor and an indoor courtyard with a pond and waterfall. It offers 18 luxury
rooms (cable TV, baths with Jacuzzis) in double, queen, and king sizes, plus
"king lofts" and "loft suites" with separate sitting areas and skylights. The inn

has several beautiful meeting rooms accommodating 15 to 200 people, including a chalet-style loft reception hall, and all with A/V-computer equipment and teleconferencing capability. The inn also has a fine-dining restaurant (see Restaurants, pg. 79). Rates: $95-$294. www.longfellows.com

Mallozzi's Belvedere Hotel
1926 Curry Rd., Schenectady, 630-4020
Opened in 2002, this four-star boutique hotel offers 29 "designer-inspired" rooms with every amenity (including VCRs and free video library), plus two luxury suites with Jacuzzis, sofa beds, stereo systems, and refrigerators. Deluxe breakfast buffet included. The hotel is home to Mallozzi's Restaurant & Bar. Rates: $80-$150.

Parker Inn
434 State St., Schenectady, 688-1001
In October of 2002, the 1906 Parker Building opened as the Parker Inn, a first-class hotel located in historic downtown Schenectady. Once the tallest building in the city, the restored, eight-story Parker offers 23 rooms and six suites with every amenity (cable TV, continental breakfast), plus a presidential suite with Jacuzzi. Two meeting rooms with high-tech video-conferencing capability are available, in addition to a business center. The first floor contains a stylish lobby, cocktail lounge, and wine-and-coffee bar. The Parker is adjacent to one of the region's finest entertainment venues, Proctor's Theatre, and the inn's lobby and lounge can be accessed through Proctor's arcade. Rates: $75-$225. www.parkerinn.com

BED & BREAKFASTS AND SMALL INNS

Angel's Café/B&B, LLC
96 Madison Ave., Albany, 426-4104
Adaptive reuse of Federal Style town house attributed to Philip Hooker, which was the residence of Governor Yates. Three rooms with a roof top deck. Breakfast is included. Brunch is open to the public and is served from 10:30am-5:00pm on Saturday and Sunday. Rates: $115-$225. www.angelsbedandbreakfast.com

Apple Tree Bed & Breakfast
49 West High St., Ballston Spa, 885-1113
This Second-Empire townhouse is located in Ballston Spa's historic district, close to the Kayderosseras River (and just a couple of miles from Saratoga Springs and SPAC). The inn offers five Victorian-style rooms, one with whirlpool bath and private entrance, and all with TV/VCR, individual climate control, and continental breakfast, plus afternoon tea (evening dessert and coffee during racing season). Guests are welcome to enjoy the beautifully nostalgic parlor, library, and dining room, along with the porches and gardens. Off-season rates: $95-$125. Track-season rates: $175-$200.

Batcheller Mansion Inn
20 Circular St., Saratoga Springs, 584-7012 (800-616-7012)
Built in 1873, this landmark Gilded Age mansion of Moorish minarets, paneled wainscoting and elaborate woodwork is truly a step back in time to a more gracious era. Opened as an inn in 1994, it offers nine suites and rooms, each with uniquely sumptuous décor and modern amenities including TV and mini-fridge. The palatial "Diamond Jim Brady" suite has a pool table, divans, and a fireplace. Guests may also enjoy the library, dining room, side porches, and the opulent main room with its velvet sofas, Venetian crystal chandelier, oil paintings, and grand piano. Off-season rates: $120-$235. Peak-season rates: $260-$395. www.batchellermansioninn.com

English Garden Bed & Breakfast
205 Union St., Schenectady, 372-4390
The Ellice Sanders Home is a 1775 Federal house recently converted to an intimate B&B featuring – you guessed it – an English garden. It also has three Victorian-style rooms with modem hook-ups and crystal chandeliers. Complimentary breakfast is included. Guests are welcome in the original "tea room," which features a Dutch-hearth fireplace, and on the charming verandah overlooking the garden. The upstairs "party room" with garden views is available for business luncheons and conferences, and can be converted to a large guestroom. Discounts for weekday business travelers are available. Located in the historic Stockade District, the inn is a short walk from the Van Dyck restaurant and jazz club. Rates: $115-$135. www.theenglishgardenbandb.com

Gregory House Country Inn & Restaurant
Rte. 43, Averill Park, 674-3774
This atmospheric, 1830 homestead is marked by its original handcrafted iron gate, welcoming guests to 12 cottage-style rooms. A three-star inn, it features a large, attractive common room with big-screen TV, an outdoor pool, and personalized hospitality. La Perla, the inn's fine-dining restaurant (see Restaurants, pg. 79), includes a cozy pub. Located 15 minutes from downtown Albany and Troy. Rates: $100- $125. www.gregoryhouse.com

Kings-Ransom Farm Bed & Breakfast
178 King's Rd., Schuylerville, 695-6876
Country hospitality and tranquil surroundings add to the charm of this bucolic B&B, located on a family-owned dairy farm (feel free to ask for a farm tour). The farmhouse has three spacious, upstairs rooms, each with its own country décor, along with an outdoor pool, screened porch with views of the Green Mountains, and country roads and woodlands for strolling. A full breakfast is included. The inn is 12 minutes from Saratoga Springs and the Saratoga Battlefield. Rates: $125. Track season rates: $165-$195.

Mansion Hill Inn

115 Philip St., Albany, 465-2038 (888-299-0455)
Established in 1984, Mansion Hill was the first B&B in downtown Albany. This Victorian-style inn (within three buildings) offers eight rooms with individual climate control, queen-size beds, and a full breakfast from the four-star Mansion Hill Restaurant (see Restaurants, pg. 80). A local favorite, the inn is also a popular way station for celebrities performing at nearby Capital Repertory Theatre. Mansion Hill is conveniently located close to the Empire State Plaza and the Pepsi Arena. Rate: $175. www.mansionhill.com

Morgan State House

393 State St., Albany, 427-6063 (888-427-6063)
Located on "mansion row" in historic downtown Albany, across the street from scenic Washington Park, this converted 19th-century townhouse is operated in the tradition of a fine European hotel. There's an elegant, mahogany-paneled lobby and a charming garden patio in addition to nine rooms (some with park views) furnished with antiques and the Morgan's signature feather beds. Amenities and a continental breakfast; business services and a private conference room for small meetings are available. A local award winner, the State House does not have a sign out front, to preserve the privacy of guests. Rates: $135-$260.

Washington State House is located three doors west of the Morgan State House. A nine-story, 1920s building, the Washington is ideal for extended stays, offering studio condominiums and corporate suites, each with a mix of antiques and traditional furnishings, plus wired work areas and dining areas with kitchens or kitchenettes. Rates: $135-$150.

Pine Haven Bed & Breakfast

531 Western Ave., Albany, 482-1574
This lovely urban B&B retains the ambience of the Victorian home it once was. In addition to its charming reading/relaxing areas, cozy dining room, and furnished front porch, the inn offers rooms with old-fashioned brass beds and modern conveniences including TV. Pine Haven is just a few minutes drive from St. Rose College, St. Peter's Hospital, and downtown Albany, and a short walk from a children's theatre. Low monthly rates available. Rates: $59-$89. www.pinehavenbedandbreakfast.com

Olde Judge Mansion

3300 Sixth Ave., Troy, 274-5698
"Troy's best-kept secret," this majestic, 1890s mansion was restored as an inn in 1994, and offers four rooms (single, double and queen size) as well as privacy and personal attention. Guests enjoy kitchen privileges, laundry facilities, a game room (smoking), and secured off-street parking. The inn is located just minutes from Russell Sage College, RPI, Emma Willard School, and the city's historic attractions. Rates: $45-$60.

Saratoga Inn
434 Church St., Saratoga Springs, 584-0920
This converted 1860 farmhouse is situated on five acres among pine trees and flower gardens. The inn is decorated with oak and maple antiques, and has five charming rooms (king, queen and double twin); three upstairs, and two with fireplaces. The very affordable rates include a full Irish breakfast. Off-season rates: $75-$95. Peak-season rates: $95-$165. www.saratogabandb.com

Six Sisters Bed & Breakfast
149 Union St., Saratoga Springs, 583-1173.
Yes, the innkeeper really does have six sisters, who helped create the unique style of this 1880s Victorian inn and its four beautifully decorated rooms. Graced by oak floors, oriental carpets, antique furnishings, and touches of yesteryear, such as the wide verandah with rocking chairs and views of flower-laden Union Avenue, Six Sisters has been recognized for its ambience by several national magazines. Amenities include private balcony and/or whirlpool bath, and a home cooked, family-style breakfast. Spa packages available Nov-April. Off-season rates: $75-$150. Track-season rates: $260-$335. www.sixsistersbandb.com

Westchester House
102 Lincoln Ave., Saratoga Springs, 587-7613
This enchanting, Eastlake-style Victorian house is nestled in a residential neighborhood of tree-lined streets and flower gardens. Each room features its own fanciful decor, and guests are welcome to enjoy the library, parlors, dining room, wraparound porch, and garden walkways. Business amenities include data ports and voice mail in every room. Off-season rates: $105-$185. Track season rates: $225-$325. www.westchesterhousebandb.com

MOTELS & MODERN INNS

Albany County

Quality Inn
5 Watervliet Rd. (just off Everett Rd.), Albany, 438-8431
Conveniently located adjacent to all major interstates, the inn has 216 rooms, indoor and outdoor pools, a banquet/conference facility for 12 to 300 people, a health club, and a restaurant. Rates: $89-$95

Clarion Inn & Suites
611 Troy-Schenectady Rd., Latham, 785-5891
Located just off the Northway (Exit 6) and three miles from the Albany Airport, this brightly modern facility has 136 rooms with mini-fridges and microwaves, plus business-class rooms, suites, and deluxe suites with Jacuzzis. It offers business services and a conference center, an exercise facility, outdoor pool, and banquet space. A Bennigan's Grill &Tavern is located on the premises. Complimentary breakfast, and kids stay free. Rates: $59-$109.

Cocca's Inn
831 Rte. 9, Latham, 785-6626 (888-4-COCCAS)
This family-owned motel is comparable to national chain motels but with lower rates. Its 66 units range from simple rooms to long-term efficiencies to luxurious executive suites with Jacuzzis and data ports. This Cocca's (there are four) offers a moderately priced all-you-can-eat buffet at lunch and dinner. The inn is located across from the Latham Circle Mall and Latham Farms, and five minutes from Albany Airport. Rates: $60-$150. www.coccas.com

Hilton Garden Inn
800 Albany-Shaker Rd., Colonie, 464-6666
This business hotel offers "focused service" for its 155 rooms, which include mini-fridges, microwaves, and workstations. The inn has an indoor pool and whirlpool, meeting facilities, and is located on a wooded landscape across from Albany Airport. Rates: $89-$159.

Holiday Inn-Turf on Wolf
205 Wolf Rd., Albany, 458-7250 (800-465-4329), TDD: 800-238-5544
This conveniently located, family-owned Holiday Inn offers six floors with 309 high-quality rooms, and is especially conscientious about access for the disabled. The Inn includes a business center, gym, indoor and outdoor pools, and the Turf House Grille and lounge. Rates: $100-$150.

Marriott Courtyard Albany
189 Wolf Rd., Albany, 482-8800
Conveniently located off I-87, this full-service Marriott is one mile from Albany Airport, five miles from downtown Albany, and close to four major shopping centers. Renovated in 1998, it is tastefully decorated with eight floors and 359 rooms (VIP rooms available); indoor and outdoor pools, a health club, a 24-hour business center, meeting rooms, and a restaurant. Rates: $148-$184.

Residence Inn by Marriott
Rte. 7, Latham, 783-0600
Residence Inns are designed for extended stays, with over 100 suites with separate working, living, and sleeping areas, plus fully equipped kitchens and work stations. The size selection ranges from two-floor, two-bedroom penthouses to studio suites. All amenities, including breakfast daily. Rates: $124-$174.
www.mariotthotels.com

Ramada Inn-Downtown
300 Broadway, Albany, 434-4111
Located across from the SUNYA Plaza, and close to the Pepsi Arena and the Corning Riverfront Preserve. Rates: $79-$89. www.ramada.com/ny

Ramada Inn-Limited
1630 Central Ave., Albany, 456-0222
Corporate guests a specialty, 101 large rooms, Jacuzzis available. Rates: $79-$99.
www.ramada.com/ny

Stone Ends Motel
Rte. 9W, Glenmont, 449-5181
Newly remodeled with 40 standard rooms, Jacuzzis available. Rates: $50-$65.

Rensselaer County

Best Western Rensselaer Inn
Sixth Ave. and Fulton St., Troy, 274-3210
This longtime downtown inn offers 152 rooms, including deluxe king-size rooms with complimentary full breakfast. The inn has an outdoor pool, and a restaurant, Union Station, serving inventive American fare. Rates: $79-$99.

Fairfield Inn
124 Troy Rd. (Rte. 4), East Greenbush, 477-7984 (800-477-7984)
This Fairfield (the chain is a subsidiary of Marriott) has four floors and 105 standard and king-size rooms, plus an outdoor pool. Amenities include work desk and data ports, cable TV, and breakfast. Rates: $107-$119.

Schenectady County

Holiday Inn-Holidom
100 Nott Terrace, Schenectady, 393-4141
A "showcase" inn of 184 elegantly appointed rooms with all amenities, plus executive suites with wet bars, conference tables, continental breakfast, and use of a private lounge with complimentary hors d'oeuvres. The Holidom has recreational facilities and banquet space, and is located two blocks from NYNEX Training Center, and a half-mile from the GE Main Plant. Basic rate: $105.
www.holiday-inn.com/hotels/schdt

Ramada Inn-Schenectady
450 Nott St., Schenectady, 370-7151
Renovated in 2000, with 170 rooms, two deluxe business-class floors, a business center, health club, indoor pool, and Jacuzzi. Rates: $84-$99.
www.ramada.com/ny

Stardust Motor Inn
2700 Curry Rd., Schenectady, 355-8000
This extended-stay motel just might be "the best deal in town." The 50 rooms include 25-inch TVs with cable and VCR, message service, and computer jacks. Extra-large rooms for families available. Fax and copiers on the premises. The Stardust is located 15 minutes from Union College, General Electric, and downtown Schenectady. Rates: $60-$80.

Saratoga County

Holiday Inn-Saratoga
232 Broadway, Saratoga Springs, 584-4550
This award-winning Holiday Inn offers four floors with 168 rooms and suites with all amenities. Business services include secretarial service, and the banquet facility has an 800-person capacity. The inn has a 24-hour gym and indoor and outdoor pools. Located adjacent to historic Congress Park. Off-season rate: $140. Track season rate: $260.

Saratoga Motel
440 Church St., Saratoga Springs, 584-0920
Located on five acres on the northeast side of the city, this rustic motel enjoys a reputation for clean, comfortable, and very affordable accommodations since the 1950s. Knotty pine walls give a country feel to the nine rooms and two efficiencies, which include cable TV and mini-fridges. The efficiencies have kitchenettes and eating nooks. Off-season rates: $55-$75. Peak season rates: $120-$135.
www.saratogabandb.com

Not Far Away

Aubergine
Rte. 22 (intersection of Rte. 23), Hillsdale, 325-3412
The 1783 Dutch-Colonial hostelry that houses this four-star restaurant has a long history of culinary excellence and fine lodgings. Built by a Revolutionary War veteran, the inn hosted political dinners and dances; more recently, Aubergine has been recognized as a destination restaurant by several magazines. The menu specializes in elegant, French-inspired country cuisine, and features wild game, local ingredients, sumptuous desserts, and a superior wine cellar. Four intimate dining rooms are located on the first floor, along with a tavern with a copper bar. Upstairs are four lovely rooms (queen and double twin). Breakfast is available for $10. Dinner is served Weds-Sun., reservations required. The inn is conveniently located close to Lenox and Stockbridge. Rates: $95-$120. www.hillsdaleny.com

Equinox
Rte. 7A, Manchester Village, Vt., 802-362-4700
The Marsh Tavern dates to 1769; today, it is part of the Equinox resort hotel, which encompasses several beautifully preserved historic buildings providing 183 rooms, business suites, and townhouse accommodations. All the rooms have cable TV and data ports, and the townhouses include fireplaces, kitchens, porches, and gorgeous mountain views. Guests can play on the championship Gleneagles Golf Course (designed by Walter Travis), use the fitness spa, experience the thrill of flying a bird of prey at the British School of Falconry, master off-road driving techniques at the Land Rover Driving School, and enjoy fine dining at the elegant Colonnade or the casually atmospheric Marsh Tavern. In 2002, the Equinox was designated a "Connoisseur's Choice" by Connoisseur magazine. Rates: $225-$900. www.equinoxresort.com

Horned Dorset Inn
Main St., Rte. 8, Leonardsville, 315-855-7898
Located in a small farming town on the west side of the Unadilla Valley, this gracious Victorian inn consists of the 1860s Wheeler House and the elegant Horned Dorset restaurant next door. Furnished with antiques, the inn offers two guestrooms and two suites with Victorian sitting rooms and queen-size beds. Amenities include room-delivered breakfast by appointment and personalized service. The Horned Dorset restaurant is regarded as one of the finest in upstate New York; the menu changes daily and features fresh American ingredients prepared in the French classical tradition. The property is situated on 300 acres of fields, wooded hills, apple orchards, waterfalls, and hiking/skiing trails. Leonardsville is located four miles south of Rte. 20, and 30 minutes from Cooperstown, the Glimmerglass Opera, Hyde Hall, and Bouckville's antique district. Rates: $125 for rooms, $150 for suites. www.horneddorset.com

Mohonk Mountain House

1000 Mountain Rest Rd., New Paltz, (914) 255-1000
A National Historic Landmark, this fantastical 1869 "castle" of turrets and porches is situated on Lake Mohonk along the scenic Shawangunk Ridge, not far from downtown New Paltz. One of the last great 19th-century mountain resorts left in America, Mohonk includes thousands of acres of unspoiled forest and winding trails. Operated by descendents of the original proprietors, the resort offers 257 rooms in three styles: Tower, with working fireplaces and balconies; Victorian, with four-poster beds; and cozy Traditional. All the rooms feature an evocative mix of furnishings and settings, and include three meals daily from the hotel's three restaurants.

Activities range from horseback riding to golf to ice skating, in addition to interesting programs on gardening (the original gardens are beautifully maintained), cooking, painting, music, dance, bird watching, and more. The resort also has a massage center, a greenhouse, a barn museum, and an observation point. Six mountaintop cottages are available in season (advance reservations required). Children stay free. The grounds and restaurants are open to the public on a fee basis. Rates: $200-$670. www.mohonk.com

Lake Placid Lodge

Whiteface Inn Rd., Lake Placid, (877) 523-2700
Built in 1864 "in the shadow of Whiteface Mountain," the Lodge is a traditional Adirondack lodge of arching cedar branches, diamond-paned windows, and rustic furnishings. This romantic forest getaway, which includes an atmospheric common room and pub, has been listed as one of "the World's Best Places to Stay" by *Condé Nast Traveler*. Rooms feature deep-soaking (two person) tubs, queen- and king-size featherbeds, twig decks with breathtaking views of the lake or woods, and a full breakfast and afternoon tea. In addition to the lodge and lakeside building are several timber cabins, located a short (covered) walk from the lodge and distinguished by stone fireplaces, sitting rooms, and huge picture windows. A barge cruise of the lake is offered daily.

The Lodge is a recipient of *Wine Spectator's* Award of Excellence and is nationally renowned for its restaurant and wine cellar. The dining room (which is open to the public) is in the style of an Adirondack great camp suitable for a robber baron, and features New-American cuisine distinguished by local ingredients such as wild game. In addition to wining and dining, guests can hike the mountain (guides-for-hire are available); swim and fish in the lake; enjoy the lodge's canoes and mountain bikes; and play golf and tennis at the nearby Whiteface Club. Rates for lodge rooms and suites: $350-$725. Rates for cabins: $550-$950. www.lakeplacidlodge.com

Sagamore

110 Sagamore Rd., Bolton Landing, 644-9400 (800-358-3585)
This luxurious, year-round resort is located on a private island in Lake George.
The Main Hotel is a restored 1882 building offering 100 rooms with the ambience
and elegant service of a bygone era. Rustic lodges house another 240 rooms,
including 120 suites with wood-burning fireplaces and terraces. The Hermitage
Executive Retreat consists of ten bi-level suites with private meeting rooms.
The resort offers a European-style spa, a fitness center, a marina, and almost
every recreational facility imaginable, from indoor racquetball courts to a famed,
18-hole championship golf course designed by Donald Ross. Young vacationers
can enroll in the Teepee Club for child-style adventures. The Sagamore has six
dining establishments, including the four-diamond Trillium, which features
contemporary American cuisine and an award-winning wine cellar.
Rates: $145-$660. www.thesagamore.com

Sedgwick Inn

Rte. 22, Berlin, 658-2334
Situated in the beautiful Taconic Valley on the New York side of the Berkshires,
this 1791 colonial inn is a place of casual, old-world comfort. The Main House
provides five antique-filled guestrooms and a two-room suite, in addition
to a fireplace parlor and a glass-enclosed porch with garden views. The inn's
brookside annex has six colonial-style rooms with greater privacy. Rates include
a hearty breakfast, served on the porch (weather permitting). The Sedgwick
restaurant is renowned for its imaginative cuisine; the inn also offers a fitness
facility housed in an 1834 neo-classical building that once served as a Civil War
recruitment station. Surrounded by 12 wooded acres for strolling, the Sedgwick
is conveniently located close to Tanglewood and other Berkshire attractions.
www.sedgwickinn.com

The Inn at Shelburne Farms

1611 Harbor Rd., Shelburne, Vt., (802) 985-8498

This 1899 Queen Anne mansion on the shores of Lake Champlain was built by Dr. William Seward and Lila Vanderbilt Webb as part of a massive estate and "model" farm. It was maintained by the family as a private residence until 1976; the family's bedrooms are among the 24 guestrooms, many of which retain their original furnishings and wallpaper designs. Rooms have views of either the lake or Lila's English gardens. Two small cottages are also available. The inn's elegant, Federal-style restaurant serves contemporary cuisine prepared from regional ingredients.

The remaining 1,400 acres of Shelburne Farm have been preserved as a non-profit educational and conservationist center and include meadows, woodland, working farmland with dairy herds, and a cheese-making facility. Farm tours and walking tours are held daily. The inn and farm, both National Historic Landmarks, are located seven miles from Burlington. Open mid-May to mid-Oct. (the inn does not have AC or central heat). Rates: $95-$365. www.shelburnefarms.org

Photography by: Gary Gold

NOT FAR AWAY

The greater Capital Region is an area defined by spectacular natural beauty, from the vast blue expanse of Lake George to the breathtaking Catskill, Greene and Adirondack Mountains. This diversely scenic geography – which inspired the timeless paintings of the Hudson River School as well as the rustic furniture known as Adirondack – is also chock-full of charming towns and picturesque inns, prestigious art galleries and museums, and exceptional performance venues – not to mention a famed abundance of antique shops. This area is also one of the finest regions in the country for architectural sightseeing, most famously for the great estates of the Gilded Age and their lavishly romantic gardens. These grandly proportioned "cottages" evoke an elegant way of life not likely to be seen again, as well as illustrate the finest in 19th-century design and décor.

Listed below are some of the most interesting destinations to be found at a distance of less than two hours from downtown Albany. The chapter is divided into six sections: North (pg. 241), South (pg. 246), West (pg. 254), East (pg. 261) of the Capital Region, the Berkshires, (pg. 263), and the mid-Hudson Valley (pg. 273). All area codes are 518, except where noted.

NORTH OF THE CAPITAL REGION

Cambridge
New Skete Monasteries, 343 Ash Grove, Cambridge, is the home of a religious order of the Orthodox Church of America. The three monasteries of monks, nuns, and companions support their life of prayer by practicing various arts and making the fruits of their labors available to the public. The monks breed and train German Shepherds, and the nuns are famed for their cheesecakes and fruitcakes, which are sold in the gift shop. The shop also sells the order's exquisite icon art, smoked meats, and handcrafted dog beds, in addition to liturgical-music tapes and translations. The monasteries are situated on a quiet, beautiful mountaintop, and offer hospitality to visitors and pilgrims. Open Tues-Sat., 9am-4pm. Closed holidays. 677-3928. www.newskete.com

Shushan Covered Bridge Museum (Rte. 61), Shushan, is a museum of local history with two exhibit rooms: one is in the 1858, 164-foot covered bridge, which crosses the Battenkill; the other is in an 1852 one-room schoolhouse. Open Memorial Day to Columbus Day, Weds-Sun., 1pm-4pm. Free. 854-7220.

Glens Falls

Glens Falls is located at the foothills of the Adirondacks and was originally called "The Corners." The area was settled by Quakers from Dutchess County in the late 1700s, and started out as a few log homes along the road to Fort Edward. Sawmills built by patriarch Abraham Wing evolved into a timber trade, which became a booming lumber industry during the 19th century. This appealing and enterprising small city is still centered on wood pulp, although international paper companies have replaced the sawmills and log jams of yesteryear.

Chapman Historical Museum, 348 Glen St., is dedicated to the history of Glens Falls and Queensbury and their connection to the Adirondacks. It consists of the DeLong House, a furnished, late-1800s Victorian home built by hardware merchant Zopher DeLong; and a restored carriage barn with changing exhibits and research archives. The museum also features photographs by 19th-century Adirondacks artisan Seneca Ray Stoddard. Stoddard prints are available in the gift shop. Open Tues.-Sat., 10am-5pm; house tours at 10:30am and 4pm. Adults $2, seniors/youths $1, children under 12 are free. 793-2826. www.chapmanmuseum.org

Hyde Collection Art Museum, 161 Warren St., is an extraordinary place: both a rarified residence filled with exquisite antiques and decorative objects (the Hydes were prominent Adirondack industrialists), and a world-class art gallery spanning 300 BC to the 20th century. The museum was founded by continental collector Charlotte Pruyn Hyde from the greater Glens Falls area in 1952. Louis and Charlotte's original collection of European Old Masters, Impressionists, and American masterpieces are displayed in the Hydes' Florentine-style villa, complete with a sunlit courtyard and sculpture garden. Uniquely, the Hyde combines the intimacy of a history house with the sophistication of a modern museum complex. Superlative changing and traveling exhibits are displayed in four additional galleries, and performances and activities are offered in the Education Wing, which also houses a museum shop. Open Tues.-Sat., 10am-5pm (Thurs. until 7pm); Sun., noon-5pm. Guided tours 1pm-4pm. Closed holidays. Free. 792-1761. www.hydeartmuseum.org

Queensbury Hotel, 88 Ridge St., was built in the mid-1920s by the Glens Falls business community, and is considered the regal symbol of the city's industrious past. The large ballroom – which once hosted big band stars such as Benny Goodman and Guy Lombardo – retains its original grandeur, as does the lobby with its marble fireplace, grand piano, and wall-size oil portrait of nearby Cooper's Cave (used to illustrate a 1920s edition of Last of the Mohicans). Visitors are welcome in these rooms, which have hosted many legendary personalities, including Louis Armstrong, Robert Kennedy, and Bob Dylan. The Queensbury now sees more corporate executives than living legends, and offers 125 guestrooms with all amenities. 792-1121.

Lake George

Lake George, Rte. 9, is a spectacular natural lake, 32 miles long and justly famed as "the Queen of Lakes." It's especially paradisiacal for sailboating, and the public beach allows for beautiful views of its blue expanse and the Adirondacks on the horizon. Lake George Village is a hubbub of summer entertainment and nightlife; during the day its bustling streets can be navigated by trolley. This popular resort also has a long and dramatic history as a military crossroads. www.visitlakegeorge.com

Fort William Henry, 48 Canada St., Lake George Village, is a reconstruction of the British fort made famous by James Fenimore Cooper's *Last of the Mohicans*. Built on the original foundation, the fort displays artifacts and exhibits from its archeology digs, and has an original cannon salvaged from the lake in the 1950s. Tour guides dressed in period garb narrate the desperate 1757 battle of the French and Indian War and the infamous massacre that followed, but the fort's most popular attractions are the authentic flint musket firings, cannon demonstrations, and grenadier bomb-toss. Be sure to take a walk along the battlement for its panoramic views of the lake. Located above the tourist strip, the fort provides teenagers with a colorful alternative to the village's video arcades, while little ones can get a start on history with the "Indian and Soldier" storytelling hour (held three times a day). Open daily May 3-Oct.15, 9am-5pm (later in July and Aug.). Adults $10, seniors $9, children $7.50. 668-5471.

Great Escape Fun Park & Splashwater Kingdom, 1172 Rte. 9, is a two-in-one amusement complex where the hours fly by like a ride on the whirligig. Garden walkways connect 140 acres of themed "towns" with 125 attractions geared to thrill seekers of all ages. Daredevil or rail clinger, there's a ride for every member of the family: The rampaging Steamin' Demon, perhaps? Or the heart-stopping Rotor, which pins you to the wall while the floor spins away? The Comet, which climbs nearly 100 feet skyward, is ranked in the top ten of roller coasters worldwide. Milder types can try the twirling gondola or scenic train rides. Rent a locker and stash your swim gear for when the day gets hotter – the water park has five pools, play fountains, waterslides, and waterfalls. A variety of shows include the new Grand Illusion magic show, and a dozen food concessions cater to every taste. Open daily Memorial Day-Labor Day, 11am-6pm (later in July and Aug.) Adults $33, youths (under 48") $17, seniors $20. 792-3500.

Lake George Steamboat Company, Steel Pier Beach Rd., Lake George Village, was founded in 1817, shortly after the introduction of steam-powered boats to the lake. The company offers a variety of cruises, from narrated historical outings to evening extravaganzas with dining, dancing and live bands. Lac Du Saint Sacrement is the biggest and most modern of the lake's cruise ships, built to accommodate large groups and first-class dining and entertainment. It offers luncheon and dinner cruises. Minne-Ha-Ha is an authentic paddlewheeler built in the village in 1969. Its one-hour narrated lakeshore cruises, with a steam-powered calliope playing merrily from the top deck, are a beloved tradition. It also offers moonlight cruises with riverboat jazz and dancing. Mohican was built in 1907 as a steel-hulled incarnation of an earlier boat. It offers the only complete tour of the lake, a narrated excursion into Paradise Bay. Open May-Oct. Prices are moderate, from around $6 to $34. 668-5777. www.lakegeorgesteamboat.com

Magic Forest, Rte. 9, Lake George (one mile south of Lake George Village) boasts the world's largest Uncle Sam (36-feet tall), as well as 25 themed rides, a Ferris Wheel, a live-animal exhibit, and three shows daily – the most popular being Rex the Diving Horse. Open daily June 23-Labor Day (weekends starting in mid-May), 9:30am-6pm. Adults $15, children $13. 668-2448.

Marcella Sembrich Opera Museum, 4800 Lakeshore Drive (Rte. 9N), Bolton Landing, is a nostalgic reminder of the resort's golden age. Housed in the pink-stucco summer studio used by Sembrich (1858-1935), a famed Metropolitan Opera soprano, the museum features memorabilia of Sembrich's career and mementos of other opera stars, including a 1905 grand piano used by Paderewski. The house is appointed with period furnishings and curios, and visitors can walk along 1,000 feet of scenic lakeside paths. Open daily June 15-Sept.15, 10am-12:30pm and 2pm-5:30pm. Free. 644-9839.

Sumptuous Settings, 4590 Lakeshore Dr., Bolton Landing, is located in a "French chateau" stocked with antiques in every category: fabrics (including Victorian and French trims and laces), crystal, silver, china, chandeliers, linens, and vintage collectibles. Personal service provided by the owners, who live onsite. 644-3145.

Adirondack Mountains

Adirondack Park is six-million acres of deep wilderness ranging over nearly a third of New York State. It encompasses thousands of lakes and ponds, 30,000 miles of rivers, and 46 high peaks. The snow starts early and stays well into spring, providing ideal conditions for almost every winter sport. Summer offers white-water rafting, camping, horseback riding, and delicate wildflowers. In the hiking season of autumn, the foliage turns to jewel tones. And year-round, the lofty pines, majestic views, and fresh mountain air serve as a tonic to the spirit.

Adirondack Bed & Breakfast Collection, Elizabethtown, provides information on picturesque inns in the Adirondack and Champlain region. Call for a brochure, or visit online. (888) 222-9789. www.adirondackinns.com

Adirondack Museum, Rte. 30, Blue Mountain Lake, is located in the scenic heart of Adirondack Park. Described as "the Smithsonian of the Adirondacks," the museum travels through two centuries of history, from early pioneer life to the region's 20th century development for recreation and commercial gain. Large-scale displays recreate that transition; from a peddler's wagon to a stagecoach, a hermit's hut to a grand hotel. Exhibits focus on logging, boating, road and rail transportation, mining, and rustic furniture. The museum also features an exceptional collection of paintings, photography, and folk art. Outdoor recreation is available (see Parents and Children, pg. 215). Visitor center, lake view café, and museum shop. Open daily Memorial Day-Oct 15, 9:30am-5:30pm. Adults $10, seniors $9, military/students/youths (7-17) $5, children under 7 are free. 352-7311. www.adkmuseum.org

Fort Ticonderoga, Fort Rd. (one mile east of downtown Ticonderoga), is an adventure in military history. The 1755 stone fortress is situated on a hill at the "choke-point" of Lake George and Lake Champlain, providing breathtaking views as well as a vivid recreation of soldiering at this strategic bastion. A barracks museum illustrates the 18th-century history of the region, in addition to the fort's role in the Seven Years' War and the American Revolution. Daily artillery demonstrations, musketry drills, and a fife-and-drum corps (weather permitting), as well as three Grand Encampments staged by hundreds of re-enactors (June-Sept.), and a Native Harvest Moon Festival (Oct.), bring the fort to colorful life. The grounds include the Carillon Battlefield, Mount Defiance, and the recently restored King's Garden (June-Sept.). Loghouse restaurant and souvenir shop. Open early-May to late-Oct., 9am-5pm (until 6pm July-Aug.) Adults $12, seniors/students $10, youths $6. Admission is free for children under 7 and local residents. 585-2821. www.fort-ticonderoga.org

Friends Lake Inn, 963 Friends Lake Rd., Chestertown, is a former 19th-century boarding house with 17 rooms and 32 km of groomed cross-country ski and snowshoe trails. It's also located just minutes from Gore and West Mountain ski centers. And if a day in the great outdoors leaves you feeling like an icicle, the inn features roaring fires and a sauna. The restaurant is famed for its creative American cuisine and expansive wine cellar. Rates from $275, including candlelight dinner and country breakfast. 494-4751. www.friendslake.com

Gore Mountain Ski Center, Peaceful Valley Rd., North Creek (see Recreation and Sports, pg. 181).

SOUTH OF THE CAPITAL REGION

West of the Hudson River

East Durham

Irish American Heritage Museum, 2267 Rte.145, is an educational institution established in 1992 to preserve and interpret the history of the Irish in America. The 1860 farmhouse – meticulously restored and converted to a state-of-the-art gallery space – contains the "The Great Hunger" display, focusing on Ireland's potato famine of the mid-1900s, in addition to scholarly yet popular changing exhibits that travel the country. Open June-Sept., Thurs-Sun., noon-4pm. Adults $3, seniors/youths $2, families (of any size) $9. 634-7497. www.irishamericanhermuseum.org

Coxsackie

Bronck Museum, Pieter Bronck Rd. (Rte. 9), is an early Dutch farmstead containing colonial buildings, cemeteries, and fields. The 1663 Stone House is the oldest dwelling in upstate New York, built by Pieter Bronck to establish a claim on his enormous settlement (in the 1650s, Pieter ran a tavern on Pearl Street in Albany). The steeply gabled Brick House was built in 1738 by his grandson, Leendert. Each of the three barns is architecturally noteworthy, signifying changes in farming techniques over the centuries. The farmstead is a National Historic Landmark, occupied by eight generations of Broncks for 276 years. The family's silver, glass and china are on display, along with original furnishings, regional-history exhibits, and an important collection of paintings, including a 1710 portrait by Nehemiah Partridge and a rare Dutch scriptural painting. The visitor center, research library, and museum shop are housed in the farm's agricultural outbuildings. Open Memorial Day-Oct.15, Tues-Sat., 10am-4pm; Sun. 1pm-5pm. Adults $4, seniors $3.50, youths (6-16) $2, children under five are free. 731-6490.

Combo tickets are available for the Bronck Museum and Thomas Cole's Cedar Grove (see below entry).

Four-Mile Point Preserve, Four-Mile Point Rd. (Rte. 385), is a 7.6-acre riverfront park created in 1992. Once slated for development, the park offers a picturesque shoreline, a tranquil inland pond, a 60-foot ridge with dramatic vistas, a wetland-wildlife viewing platform, bird watching, and canoe and kayak access to the Hudson River. Picnic areas and parking. Open 9am-dusk daily. Free. www.scenichudson.com

Catskill

Catskill Game Farm, Rte. 32, has been family owned for almost 80 years, and is a popular childhood tradition for the entire region. Established for the conservation of endangered animals, the farm contains spacious habitats and gardens for the animals to live and breed in. More recent are the amusement-park attractions, but wildlife is still very much in evidence, including prairie dogs, camels, giraffes, wallabies, a pygmy hippo, and a reptile house. Favorites for children are the baby-animal nursery; the feeding area where deer, goats, emus and llamas roam; the elephant ride; and a rather spectacular playground. Admission covers all activities except the mechanical rides. Animal shows are held daily Memorial Day-Labor Day. Indoor and outdoor food concessions, plus picnic tables for bring-your-own lunches. Open daily April 27-Oct 31, 9am-5pm (until 6pm in summer). Adults $16, children (4-11) $12, seniors $14. Season pass for adults $28, for children $20. 678-9595. www.catskillgamefarm.com

Thomas Cole's Cedar Grove, 218 Spring St., Catskill, is an 1815 Federal-style brick building with extraordinary significance for the art of the United States. It was here in 1825 that a young Englishman, Thomas Cole, established a tradition of native American landscape painting that came to be known as the Hudson River School of Art, and it was here that he gave art lessons to Frederick Church (see "Olana," pg. 254) The house was recently restored – reclaiming Cole's beloved views of the northern Catskills, which are identified by a marker on the porch – and contains exhibits relating to the first and second generations of Hudson River School artists, as well as Cole sketches, small paintings, and memorabilia. The house is furnished with period and family possessions: Of particular interest is the artist's painted sketch box. Look for the renovation of Cole's original studio in the near future. Open for guided tours mid-May-Oct., Fri-Sat., 10am-4pm; Sun., 1pm-5pm. (Tours are approx. 30 min.) Adults $4, seniors $3.50, youths (6-16) $2. 943-7465.

Saugerties

Located at the foot of the Catskill Mountains and by the shores of the Hudson River, Saugerties developed after the building of the Erie Canal. This attractive river town retains much of its 19th-century architecture, as well as several pre-Revolution stone houses sitting on hills and surrounded by huge old trees. The historic, eight-block downtown is fertile ground for antique hunting and book collecting.

Cafe Tamayo, 89 Partition St., Saugerties, this gourmet bistro serves dinner Weds-Sat., and Sunday brunch. (845) 246-9371.

Hope Farm Press, 252 Main St., was established in 1959 by a retired NYC librarian with an interest in regional history. The press now has the largest selection of New York State titles anywhere – over 3,000 new and used. Along with biographies and travelogues, you'll find books on Native American culture, steamboats, trains, nature, geology, genealogy, tourism, and military history. Open Mon-Sat., 10am-6pm. (845) 246-3522. www.hopefarmpress.com

Kiersted House, 119 Main St., was built in 1727 as the home of the first doctor in Saugerties, Dr. Christopher Kiersted. This architecturally exceptional stone house was recently acquired by the Saugerties Historical Society, which is exploring its history and significance to share with the public. Open May-Dec., Sat-Sun. Call for hours and information on special events. Free. (845) 246-9529.

Krause's Homemade Candy, 41 Partition St., homemade candy by the same family that owns the much-loved candy store in Albany. Chocolate, fudge, and peanut-brittle are made fresh every day, in addition to a wide selection of other candies. Open daily. (845) 246-8377.

New World Home Cooking Cafe, Rte. 212 (3.5 miles from downtown Woodstock), has been described as a "Woodstock yardsale version of Le Cirque." This colorful café serves healthy, assertively flavorful world cuisine made from regional and organic foodstuffs, and is famed for its Cajun pepper shrimp and Jamaican jerk chicken – as well as for its chef-owner, Ric Orlando, of Ric's Kitchen cooking show. The wine list complements the menu with bold, fruity selections with "pizzazz." Live music, open daily. (845) 246-0900.

Saugerties Lighthouse Conservancy, Lighthouse Rd. (off Mynderse St.) is a fully restored, 1868 lighthouse with a small museum displaying artifacts of the lighthouse and the history of the heyday of the area's waterfront. It can be reached by ferry or by trail through the lighthouse nature preserve. Overnight accommodations in two upstairs guestrooms are available. Open Memorial Day-Oct., Sat-Sun. and holidays, 2pm-5pm or by appointment. Adults $3, children $1. (845) 247-0656.

Opus 40 & Quarryman's Museum, 7480 Fite Rd., is a highly unusual environmental-sculpture garden made out of bluestone from a local quarry. It was built over a lifetime by one man, Bard College professor and stone sculptor Harvey Fite, who picked up some masonry tips while restoring Mayan ruins in Honduras in the 1930s. Ramps through the six-acre artwork lead to dramatic platforms, benches, fountains, and ornamental spaces enhanced by small contemporary pieces. There are plantings and beautiful vistas everywhere, and the overall impression is a powerful one. Open Memorial Day-Columbus Day, Fri-Sun. and holiday Mondays, noon-5pm. The museum is located on the second floor of Fite's workshop. Adults $6, students/seniors $5, children over five $3. Call to confirm hours. (845) 246-3400.

Sauer Farm, 640 Kings Highway, sells raw milk and organic eggs. In season, the fruit stand offers raspberries, pears, apples, melons, sweet corn, and more. Open daily 10am-8pm; fruit stand July-Oct. (845) 246-2725.

Woodstock

Woodstock is best known for an event that happened elsewhere: the 1969 Woodstock music festival, which was held 50 miles away in Bethel. What this wooded little village does have is a 100-year-old summer arts colony – and a resident population of musicians, dancers, writers, sculptors, painters, and craftspeople. Not surprisingly, the downtown is a treasure trove of unique craft shops and art galleries. www.woodstockonline.org

Woodstock Artists Association, 28 Tinker St., provides information on exhibits throughout the area. Established in 1920 to display and collect the artworks of area artists, the WAA functions as a meeting place, art museum, and local gallery. Open Thurs-Mon., noon-5pm. (845) 679-2940. www.woodstockart.org

Byrdcliffe Arts Colony is the summer arts retreat built in 1902 by English visionary Ralph Radcliffe Whitehead as a Ruskinian Arts and Crafts community. Situated on a 300-acre wooded campus, Byrdcliffe was the genesis of the town's development as a renowned center for contemporary art. It has nurtured the work of hundreds of artists, including Charlotte Perkins Gilman, Harry Hopkins, Isadora Duncan, Thomas Mann, and Wallace Stevens. Now supervised by the Woodstock Guild, the colony continues its mission of providing a quiet, stimulating place for artisans to work during summer. Byrdcliffe Theater presents avant-garde theatrical performances during the season. Visitors are welcome to tour the site, and maps and information are available through the Woodstock Guild, located at the Kleinert/James Art Center.

Kleinert/James Art Center, 34 Tinker St., hosts performing, visual, and literary artists, and offers year-round classes in stone carving and jewelry making. The Fleur de Lis gallery exhibits and sells local artwork. The center also houses the Woodstock Guild. Open year-round, call for hours. (845) 679-2079. www.woodstockguild.org.

Maverick Concerts, Maverick Rd. (one mile from junction of Rte. 28), is an offshoot of Brydcliffe and has been presenting world-renowned chamber music ensembles in its woodland hall since 1916. Concerts are held late June to early Sept., Sat. at 8pm and Sun. at 3pm. Seating is first-come, first-served. Free children's concerts are held Sat. at 11am. (845) 679-8217. www.maverickconcerts.org

Woodstock Inn On the Millstream, 38 Tannery Brook Rd., has lovely grounds with gardens and a cascading millstream. An easy walk to town, its 18 rooms and efficiency units have motel privacy with B&B ambience, as well as AC and cable TV. Rates from $99, breakfast included. (845) 679-8211 or (800) 697-8211.

Mount Tremper

Marketplace at Catskill Corners, 5340 Rte. 28, has seven unusual country shops in the renovated 1841 Risely Barn. Gourmet foods and a soda fountain, science and nature toys, rustic furniture and decorative housewares, and stuffed animals and kaleidoscopes can all be found in this scenic marketplace. Many of the goods are child-oriented, especially in the fantabulous Kaleidoworld (see Parents and Children, pg. 217). Open daily 10am-7pm. (888) 303-3936. www.catskillcorners.com

Catamount Café, Resort at Catskill Corners, Rte. 28, is located in a lodge in the Catskill Forest Preserve. It offers "farmhouse cuisine" from the Catskills, including fresh fish and game, and gourmet grilled items. Dinner daily, Sunday brunch. (914) 688-7900.

East of the Hudson River

Kinderhook

Kinderhook is the oldest village in Columbia County. Once a colonial agricultural community, it retains the peaceful ambience of an 1800s farming village, and the streets are lined with buildings that once hosted General Burgoyne, Benedict Arnold, and other personages from the Revolutionary past. Martin Van Buren, the son of a tavern keeper who became the eighth president of the United States, was born here in 1782.

Carolina House, Rte. 9 (half-mile from Kinderhook Square), is a converted log cabin with an appealingly rustic ambience, serving a Southern-style menu specializing in fried chicken, ribs, corn chowder, blackened beef, and seafood. Dinner: Weds-Mon. 758-1669.

James Vanderpoel House, 16 Broad St. (Rte. 9), is a circa-1820 Federal-style brick house reflecting the elegant lifestyle of a prosperous village lawyer. The house is noted for its graceful staircase and fine cabinetry, and features early 19th-century furniture and decorative arts, and exhibits on local history. Open Memorial Day to Labor Day, Thurs-Sat., 11am-5pm; Sun 1-5. Adults $3, seniors/youths $2, children under 12 are free. 758-9265.

Kinderhook Antique Center, Rte. 9H, offers ten dealers specializing in 18th- and 19th-century American furniture, textiles, and rare books. Open daily year-round. 758-7939.

Luykas Van Alen House, Rte. 9H, is a 1737 Dutch farmhouse built by Van Alen, a farmer and merchant. The interior features 18th-century furnishings and decorative arts. The site offers an evocative view of early farming life, and the exterior was filmed as a setting for Martin Scorsese's *The Age of Innocence*. On the grounds is the Ichabod Crane Schoolhouse, a one-room school typical of the era. Washington Irving's gangly Ichabod was based on the school's first teacher, Jesse Merwin. Open Memorial Day-Labor Day, Thurs-Sat., 11am-5pm; Sun. 1pm-5pm. Adults $3, seniors/youths $2, children under 12 are free. 758-9265.

Martin Van Buren's Lindenwald, 1013 Old Post Rd., was the home of President Martin Van Buren after his return from the White House in 1839. The Federal-style brick mansion was built in 1797 by Judge Peter Van Ness, and expensively redesigned to reflect Van Buren's Victorian taste by renowned architect Richard Upjohn. This National Historic Site has been restored to its appearance during the president's occupation (1841-1862) and features period furnishings and many architectural details of note, including the Romanesque entranceway. Of particular interest are the beautifully illustrated wallpaper panels, imported from France by Van Buren and meticulously conserved in the 1980s. Van Buren is buried with his wife and family in Kinderhook Reformed Cemetery (Albany Ave.), which dates to 1817. Every Dec. 5, the day Van Buren was born, a ceremony is held there in his honor. Open for guided tours Memorial Day-Oct., 9am-4:30pm; open weekends through Dec. 6. Adults $2, youths under 17 are free. 758-9689.

North Point Cultural Arts Center, Rte. 9 (just outside the village) is located in a restored 1920s dancehall. It hosts a variety of musical events, as well as plays and literary readings. There are two performance spaces: The 150-seat concert hall and a more intimate coffeehouse. The center is home to Stage Works, an Equity company that presents classic and contemporary theater. 758-9234.

Chatham

Mac-Haydn Theater (Rte. 203), presents lively renditions of popular Broadway musicals from late May to early September. Plays are produced "in the round" in a rustic, hillside theater just outside of Chatham. Low-priced musical adaptations of popular children's stories are performed for children of all ages on weekend mornings in July and August. 392-9292.

Old Chatham Sheepherding Company, Shaker Museum Rd., produces and sells award-winning, handcrafted sheep's-milk cheese and yogurt. Made by traditional European methods, the company's signature artisan cheeses (Hudson Valley Camembert, Ewe's Blue) receive rave reviews from distinguished chefs and food critics. Visitors are welcome at the farm, where more than 1,000 East Frisian crossbred sheep graze on 600 acres of rolling pasture. Products are available through the office, Mon-Fri., 9am-5pm. (888) SHEEP60. www.blacksheepcheese.com

Shaker Museum and Library, 88 Shaker Museum Rd., Old Chatham, interprets and conserves Shaker material culture. Housed in a restored barn and outbuilding, the museum is renowned for its unparalleled collections of 1700s and 1800s Shaker artistry, featuring oval boxes, baskets, furniture, textiles, seed packets, machines, and other masterpieces of craftsmanship, which are displayed in changing exhibits. Gift shop and picnic area. Special events are held year-round. (The museum is planning to move to the Great Stone Barn of the North Family in Mt. Lebanon by 2005.) Open May 25-Oct. 27, 10am-5pm. Closed Tues. (research library open year-round, $25 per hour). Adults $8, seniors $6, youths (6-17) $4, children under 5 are free. 794-9100.

Hudson

Hudson was originally settled in the late 1700s by whaling families from Nantucket and New England seeking fishing waters away from British war ships. The city's decline in the mid-1900s worked to its advantage, preserving the land and sparing its early-1800s architecture and "gangway alleys." Over the last decade, Hudson has become the Northeast mecca for fine-antique shopping; the five-block downtown is filled with over 70 antique shops and crafts stores, as well as numerous art galleries.

Walking-tour pamphlets of the historic downtown can be found at the Hudson Chamber of Commerce, 729 Warren St., 828-4417. A photo-filled shopping brochure is available from the Hudson Antiques Dealers Association at 822-9397. For information on auctions, contact the Stair Galleries at 851-2544.

American Museum of Fire Fighting, 117 Harry Howard Ave., features displays of fire-fighting equipment from 1731 to 1900, including an 1850 hand-carved fireman statue from Coney Island, and a magnificently ornate 1846 hand engine. But the tour-de-force here is the fantastic collection of vintage fire-fighting vehicles from the horse-drawn, steam-powered, and early motor-truck eras. The extensive memorabilia collection ranges from helmets and uniforms to primitive water buckets. Dedicated to the history of firefighters everywhere, this huge museum is a wonderful place for the whole family. Open daily 9am-4:30pm (closed major holidays). Free. 828-7695. hudson.hvnet.com

Carrie Haddad Gallery, 622 Warren St., exhibits contemporary paintings, drawings, and photographs by Hudson Valley artists. Open Thurs-Mon., 11am-5pm. 828-1915.

Earth Foods, 523 Warren St., is one of the busiest eateries in town. This bright and friendly café features organic, made-from-scratch foods with many vegetarian and vegan offerings, in addition to excellent soups and breads, and ethnic dishes. Homemade desserts include a variety of cheesecakes. The expresso bar uses organic coffee beans; the café also serves wine, beer, and fresh juices. Breakfast and lunch daily. 822-1396.

Hudson City Bed and Breakfast, 326 Allen St., is a postcard-pretty Second Empire house built in the 19th century by a railroad tycoon. The inn is located a short walk from Warren Street. 822-8044. www.hudsoncitybnb.com

Hudson Opera House, 327 Warren St., was constructed in 1855 as Hudson's first City Hall; the auditorium upstairs was used as a theater. The building was saved from demolition in the 1990s by a grass-roots effort that transformed this historic structure – the fourth oldest surviving theater in America – into a non-profit performance space presenting concerts and drama and dance performances, as well as readings, lectures, art exhibitions, and community events. Open Mon-Sat., noon-4:30. 822-1438.

Pleshakov Music Center, 544 Warren St., was established by renowned concert pianists Elena Winter and Vladimir Pleshakov, who were trained in the classical European tradition. The couple performs as a duo, solo, and with acclaimed guests and ensembles. The center possesses three antique pianos from the 1700s and 1800s, which can be heard in monthly concerts. One of the pianos is a Tischner from a Russian palace of Czar Nicholas Romanov I – the only one in the world in private ownership. 671-7171. www.pleshakov.com

Red Dot, 321 Warren St., is a Euro-style bistro with great food, including terrific burgers and fancy frites. Serving dinner Mon-Sun., brunch on Sun. 828-3657.

Time and Space Limited, 434 Columbia St., is a multi-media cultural center located in a restored bakery. TSL presents socially aware theatrical performances and regional art exhibits, and screenings of independent and documentary films. 822-8448.

Olana State Historic Site, Rte. 9G (one mile south of the Rip Van Winkle Bridge), will fascinate anyone interested in American painting, architecture, landscape design – or the spectacular scenery of the Hudson River and Catskill Mountains. A fantastical Moorish "castle," Olana was built between 1870 and 1890 by Frederick Edwin Church, a landscape painter of the Hudson River School. Church, who extended the teachings of Thomas Cole (see above entry) to the vistas of the Americas, was internationally acclaimed for such breathtaking works as *Heart of the Andes*. Using the architecture of the house and grounds as a "canvas," Olana is one of the artist's greatest masterpieces, designed in collaboration with Calvert Vaux but reflecting Church's eclectic interests and aesthetic. The exotic structure features unique décor (including Church paintings and treasures from his travels abroad), and is especially interesting for its use of color. The windows open on many of the "most beautiful and wondrous views" immortalized by the artist, while the various carriage trails each reveal a different vista.

Open daily by guided tour June-mid-Oct., Wed-Sun., 10am-6pm. Open April-May and late Oct., 10am-5pm. Closed major holidays. Adults $3, seniors $2, children (5-12) $1. Tours are approx. 50 min. The last tour starts an hour before closing, and it's advisable to arrive early since the day's tickets sell out quickly. Reservations (two weeks notice) are recommended for those traveling from a distance. 828-0135. www.friendsofclermont.org

WEST OF THE CAPITAL REGION

Esperance

Landis Arboretum, Lape Rd. (adjacent to Schenectady County), is an exhibition landscape of 100 acres holding over 2,000 species of plants, many of them exotic trees, bushes and flowers from far-off lands (requiring devoted attention). In 2001, it was designated an old-growth forest headquarters, in recognition of the ancient trees that still exist on the hill above including the 400-year-old "Great Oak." Another popular sight for drawing and photographing is the twisted and gnarly "Contorted Beech" from Europe. The arboretum's mission is to foster an appreciation of trees and other plants and their importance in the environment, and visitors are welcome to tour the grounds – which provide stunning views of the Schoharie valley – or attend one the many gardening classes and workshops.

Informative, scenic activities include the Big Tree Trip, Owl Prowl, and Herpetology Hike. The Landis library of botanical specimens can be viewed by appointment. Plant sales of unusual and well-grown specimens are held annually in spring and fall. Open dawn to dusk. Free (donations welcome). 875-6935.

Johnstown
Johnson Hall State Historic Site, Hall Ave., contains the 1763 mansion of Sir William Johnson, a pivotal figure in colonial history. A Georgian-style mansion of wood built to look like stone, this National Historic Landmark was the center of a diplomatic estate designed to encourage settlement and promote trade with the Indians. A mill, blacksmith shop, Indian store, and other related buildings were added toward that aim. The museum displays artifacts of Sir William and his tumultuous era, as well as memorabilia on his wife, Molly Brant, a Mohawk Indian who was one of the founders of the Anglican Church in America. Visitors are welcome to wander through the grounds and gardens. Open May-Nov., Adults $3, seniors $2, children $1. Guided tours available. 762-8712.

Canajoharie
Canajoharie Library and Art Gallery, 2 Erie Blvd., is one of the finest small art galleries in the country, built in 1925 by local resident Bartlett Arkell, the founder of Beach Nut Foods. The permanent collection of over 350 important paintings and sculptures – including 21 oils and watercolors by Winslow Homer – offers an exceptional perspective on the major movements of American artistry, from colonial art to the Hudson River School to the Ashcan School. Open Mon-Fri., 10am-4:45pm (until 8:30pm on Thurs.), Sat. 10am-1:30pm. Free. 673-2314.

Van Alstyne Homestead Society, Moyer St., is one of the earliest museums in the country, organized in 1889 and housed in the 1740s fortified homestead of Martin Van Alstyne. The original south parlor has been restored and furnished to reflect life as the Van Alstynes might have lived it at a time when Canajoharie was a dangerous wilderness. The museum also features two centuries of domestic and military artifacts; a display of turn-of-the-century regional watercolors by Rufus Grider; and a 1920s history room dedicated to a former occupant, the Fort Rensselaer gentlemen's club (one club member was Bartlett Arkell). Guided tours by appt. Free. 673-3317.

Wintergreen Park is located 1.5 miles from the village and contains the spectacular Canajoharie Gorge, a fossil-encrusted geologic wonder. Woodland trails, barbecue pit, picnic tables, snack bar and facilities. Open Memorial Day-Labor Day. Free. 673-5508.

Fonda

This Mohawk Valley town encompasses the 1740 settlement of the Fonda family, Dutch ancestors of the actors Henry, Peter, and Jane Fonda. But the original settlers were Mohawk Indians who arrived more than 500 years ago, and in some ways, history has come full circle: In 1993, a traditional Mohawk community was established on the old Fonda property.

Mohawk Indian Bed and Breakfast, Rte. 5, is operated by a traditional community of Mohawk families on the site of the last Mohawk village in the country (1700-1776). The inn's four rooms have private baths and include breakfast. Annual powwows are held on the grounds, which are close to the river. The Kanatsiohareke gift shop sells Mohawk crafts, apparel, goods, and books. Open daily, 9am-5pm. 673-5092.

Mohawk-Caughnawaga Indian Museum, Rte. 5, focuses on the ancient culture and history of Native Americans in the Mohawk Valley. Located in a 1800s farmhouse near the excavation site of a 17th-century Indian village, the museum contain artifacts from the archeological dig, which is staked out for viewing. Nature trails and picnic areas.

National Shrine of Blessed Kateri Tekakwitha is a rustic chapel within the museum. In 1676, in a chapel on this peaceful wooded spot, Kateri chose to be baptized a Catholic, despite the violent persecution of her Mohawk-Algonquin relatives. "The Lily of the Mohawks," as she was known, was beatified in 1980. Devotional-crafts shop. 853-3646. Open daily, May to Oct., 10am-4pm. Donation suggested. 853-3646.

Howes Cave

Howe Caverns, Rte. 7 (1-88 west to Exit 22), was formed millions of years ago by an underground river, and subsequently made accessible to the public by the modern elevator. Starting 156 feet below the surface, the 80-minute guided tour follows brick walkways that wind through prehistoric "temples" to a quarter-mile boat ride around an underground lake. The tour is illuminated by hidden lighting designed to enhance the beauty of the massive limestone formations. Special lantern tours (by reservation) recreate the experience of the caverns' discovery in 1922, throwing mysterious shadows on the grotto walls. You might want to bring a jacket – the caverns are a crisp 52 degrees year-round. Open daily 9am-6pm; July-Sept., 8am-8pm. Adults $14, youths (7-12) $7, children under 7 are free. 296-8990. www.howecaverns.com

Iroquois Indian Museum, Caverns Rd. (intersection of Rtes. 7 and 145), is housed in an inventively longhouse-style building, and honors the art, history, archeology, crafts, and cultural survival of the Iroquois. The 45-acre grounds include two 1800s longhouses, an extensive children's museum, an outdoor amphitheater, and a nature park for the study of plants and animals from an Iroquois perspective. During summer, the museum holds crafts classes and social-dance performances. Open Tues-Sat., 10am-5pm, Sun. noon-5pm. Open one hour later Memorial Day-Labor Day. Closed Jan-March. Adults $7, seniors/students $5.50, youths (5-12) $4, children under 5 are free. 296-8949. www.iroquoismuseum.org

Sharon Springs

Sharon Springs (at crossroads of Rtes. 10 and 20) is a 19th-century mineral-springs resort that was eclipsed in popularity by Saratoga Springs (and its racetrack) around the turn of the century. By 1970, the village's Victorian-style Main Street was an abandoned ruin. Recently, a grassroots renewal has resulted in a charming way station for visitors to Cooperstown, the Glimmerglass Opera, and the Mohawk Valley. Restored to their former glory are grand hotels, Greek-Revival water temples, summer mansions, and a 1910 gazebo – walking the village streets, which are well marked with informative plaques, is truly a step back in time. In addition to its unique shops, the village has a public swimming pool and pond. A free, six-week summer concert series is held in Chalybeate Park. 284-3015. www.sharonsprings.com

American Hotel, Main St., is located in the historic heart of Sharon Springs. The stately, 1847 white-clapboard hotel offers nine Victorian-style rooms with private baths, and one suite. The excellent restaurant and pub are open to the public. Rates from $120. 284-2105. www.americanhotelny.com

Imperial Sulphur Spa-Baths, 248 Main St., is a historic public bathhouse that still offers invigorating sulphur baths. Assorted spa-package prices available. The five public springs surrounding the baths flow freely with mineral water. Open July- Aug. 284-2285.

Roseboro Hotel, Main St., was once the grande dame of the village (look for the cast-iron fountain out front) and is gradually reclaiming that distinction. Constructed from three hotels that were joined in 1900, the Roseboro's recent and ongoing restoration includes a 90-seat restaurant – with Roman-style chandeliers and oak floors – offering a New-American menu, live entertainment, and dining on the hotel's atmospheric porches. The 1850s Howland House wing is filling with lovely shops (five so far). And in the foreseeable future, the Roseboro will again have hotel rooms for occupancy. Closed in winter. 284-2020. www.roseboro.com

Sharon Historical Museum, Main St., contains Victoriana room exhibits and displays of local artifacts and historical photos of the village. The grounds include an 1860 one-room schoolhouse and a privy. Open July-Aug., 2pm-4pm, or by appointment. Free. 284-2350.

Sharon Springs Emporium, Main St., offers arts and crafts, antiques and household items, and art-objects and paintings – all under one roof. 284-3205.

Cooperstown

The birthplace of baseball is generally believed to be Cooperstown, where folklore has it that one afternoon in 1839, Abner Doubleday invented the game that quickly became America's pastime. Maybe it was the beer that inspired him: hops farming was the region's primary industry. The downtown is a good place for shopping for collectibles, vintage items, and baseball memorabilia. Scenic Lake Otsego is the "glimmerglass" of James Fenimore Cooper's Leather-Stocking Tales. Natty Bumppo's cave is marked by a roadside plaque on the east side of the lake.

Parking is limited in summer, but old-fashioned trolleys provide transportation through the village and to major attractions. Two- and three-way ticket packages are available for the Farmer's Museum, the Fenimore Art Museum, and the National Baseball Hall of Fame and Museum. (888) 547-1450.

Blue Mingo Grill, 2-1/2 miles north of Cooperstown on Rte. 80. Located at Sam Smith's Boatyard, the cuisine is international and innovative. Lunch and Dinner, Mid-May to Labor Day, closed Wednesdays in May and June. (607) 547-7496.

Farmer's Museum, Lake Rd. (Rte. 80), is a rural, 19th-century living-history village that provides an ideal outing for the whole family. The Main Barn – a grand stone building that was once part of a dairy farm – has exhibits pertaining to early farming life. In the Manufactory, wallpaper is made by hand on the only press of its kind. In the village (a grouping of authentic buildings), a blacksmith forges metal on his anvil, meals are cooked over an open hearth, horse carts trot by, cows are milked, and hops are dried on poles. Teams of oxen work the fields, and up the hill in the Seneca Longhouse are exhibits of Native American culture. Among the sights are heritage-breed animals, 1800s-style gardens, and the infamous "Cardiff Giant." The cycle of the seasons is represented by special events such as maple sugaring, sheep shearing, an autumn harvest festival, and a candlelight holiday evening with St. Nick. Open April-Nov, Tues-Sun., 10am-4pm. Open daily June-Sept., 10am-5pm. Adults $9, youths (7-12) $4, children under 7 are free. (888) 547-1450. www.farmersmuseum.org

Fenimore Art Museum, Lake Rd. (Rte. 80), is housed in a 1930 mansion built on the site of James Fenimore Cooper's home overlooking Otsego Lake (the original manor burned down in 1853, two years after Cooper died there). The museum features American fine art, folk art, and contemporary photography; as well as memorabilia, furnishings and paintings relating to the Coopers of Cooperstown. A wing devoted to the museum's acclaimed collection of North American Indian art opened in 1995, along with a state-of-the-art gallery for national traveling exhibits. Museum shop, café, and terrace gardens. Ganosote is the museum's reproduction of an 18th-century Iroquois bark house and hunting and fishing camp, set on the shores of Lake Otsego. In season, costumed interpreters demonstrate the traditional skills of the Indians of central New York.

Open April-Dec., Tues-Sun., 10am-4pm. Open daily June-Sept., 10am-5pm. Closed major holidays. Adults $9, youths $4. (888) 547-1450. www.fenimoreartmuseum.org

Glimmerglass Opera, Rte. 80 (two miles south of Rte. 20), is an internationally acclaimed summer festival attracting audiences from around the globe (see Arts, and Venues, pg. 52) The opera's 900-seat Alice Busch Opera Theater is located on 43 acres along the shore of Otsego Lake, and visitors are welcome to enjoy the beautiful grounds. Tours of the theater offer a behind-the-scenes view of how the opera works, from costuming to set design. A trolley runs from the Otesaga Hotel to the theater during the season. (607) 547-2255. www.glimmerglass.org.

Hyde Hall, Mill Rd., is a singularly important building, both architecturally and socially. The 50-room, classical-style country mansion was built 1817-19 by George Hyde Clarke, descendent of a wealthy British-colonial family. It was designed by esteemed Albany architect Phillip Hooker, with limestone walls 190-feet high and soaring, neo-Palladian rooms surrounding an open, stone-paved courtyard. The hall remained in the Clarke family until 1963, and has an interesting genealogy as well as original furnishings. It is currently undergoing an extensive restoration, offering visitors the opportunity to view the restoration-in-progress of a "showcase" residence. The hilltop site was chosen by Clarke from his vast landholdings, a portion of which became Glimmerglass State Park. On the remaining grounds is the unique "Tin Top" gatehouse, and a carriage barn which houses a visitor center.

In addition to its scenic views of Lake Otsego, the hall offers two major pops concerts and a chamber-music series every summer. Open for tours Thurs.-Tues., mid-May-Oct. Open daily July-Aug. Adults $7, seniors $6, youths $4. (607) 547-5098. www.hydehall.org

National Baseball Hall of Fame and Museum, 25 Main St., is the definitive repository of the game's artifacts and treasures, and a symbol of one of the highest honors to be awarded to an athlete. Established in 1939, this "field of dreams" celebrates the game and its place in American culture with all the legends, memorabilia and magic a fan could hope for. The new "Underground Movement" exhibit gives visitors a glimpse into the storied history of New York's subway series. Open daily 9am-5pm, open later May-Sept., and weekends. Closed major holidays. Adults $9.50, seniors $8, youths (7-12) $4. (888) 425-5633. www.baseballhalloffame.org

Otesaga Hotel, Lake St., is a historic Grand Hotel with a famous golf course, the Leatherstocking. This distinguished neo-Georgian resort has 136 rooms and suites offering every amenity, including breakfast and dinner. The hotel verandah and golf course overlook Lake Otsego. Peak-season rates from $285. (607) 547-9931. www.otesaga.com

Smithy-Pioneer Gallery, 55 Pioneer St., is housed in one of the region's oldest buildings, a 1786 blacksmith shop with original forge, anvils and tools. Smithing workshops are available. The gallery displays changing exhibits of regional art, and there's a sculpture garden out back. Open June-Sept., Tues-Sat., 10am-5pm; Sun. 1pm-5pm. Free. (607) 547-8671.

EAST OF THE CAPITAL REGION

Bennington, Vermont

Bennington is an especially scenic New England town, located at the foothills of the Green Mountain National Forest. The drive itself is splendid: Rte. 7 comes to a rise at the border between New York and Vermont, and all the beauty of this rural area is on display. Although the region is postcard pretty throughout the year, it's especially scenic in autumn when the foliage turns to brilliant colors. Bennington is also famed for its hand-made pottery – a major industry since 1793, when the town's first kiln was built by a Revolutionary War veteran. Bennington can easily be traversed by foot or bicycle on its many trails.

Apple Barn and Country Bake Shop, Rte. 7, sells apples, fresh-pressed cider, and the state's largest selection of Vermont-made products: maple syrup and candy, cheese, fudge, honey, hard cider and wine. Pick your own berries in season, and don't forget to visit the "pumpkin-eating dinosaur." Open April-Nov. (802) 447-7780. www.theapplebarn.com

Bennington Battle Monument, 15 Monument Circle, was completed in 1891 to commemorate the Battle of Bennington. During the Revolutionary War, the colonial militia under General John Stark, with the aid of the Green Mountain Boys, defeated the British troops of General Burgoyne – a prelude to Burgoyne's surrender at Saratoga. The 304-foot-high obelisk marks the site of the arsenal that was successfully defended. At the base is a visitors center with a display illustrating the battle, and information on climbing the monument. An elevator goes to the upper lookout, which has a view of three states. Open daily April-Oct., 9am-5pm. (802) 447-0550.

Bennington Chamber of Commerce, 100 Veterans Memorial Dr., serves as a visitor center, offering maps, brochures, information on special events, and self-guide tour pamphlets. Open Mon-Fri., 8:30am-4:30pm; open weekends mid-May-mid-Oct., 9am-4pm. (802) 447-3311.

Bennington Center for the Arts, Rte. 9 at Gypsy Lane, is surrounded by 13 megalithic standing stones, making the approach as evocative as the galleries inside. The center focuses on Art of the West, wildlife art, Native American arts and crafts, "wind sculptures," American watercolors, and images of New England. Open May-Oct., Tues-Sun., 11am-5pm. Donation suggested. (802) 442-7158.

    Oldcastle Theatre Company, Bennington Center for the Arts, has been a professional troupe for 30 years, and presents musicals, mysteries, comedies, and youth theater, June-Oct. (802) 447-0564. www.oldcastle.org

Bennington Museum, Main St., is renowned as the finest regional history-and-art museum in New England. Founded in 1928 and located in an imposing stone church, the museum focuses on southern Vermont and the adjoining areas of New York. It features early-American furniture, glass, paintings, sculpture, Bennington pottery, a significant collection of Hudson River School paintings, and the largest public collection of paintings by Grandma Moses, the beloved American folk artist. The little schoolhouse attended by Moses and members of her family now houses memorabilia and exhibits on her life and achievements. Open daily Nov-May, 9am-5pm; June-Oct., 9am-6pm. Adults $6, seniors/students $5, children under 12 are free. (802) 447-1571.

Blue Benn Diner, Rte. 7, is one of Vermont's famously old-fashioned diners, and has been operating out of an original dining car since the 1940s. Non-traditional items as well as classic diner fare. Open daily. (802) 442-5140.

Camelot Village Craft Center, Rte. 9, features the products of over 250 regional artisans in the form of hand-made pottery, hand-milled soap, gifts, home décor items, dip-your-own candles, and more – all housed in a huge, historic barn. Open daily 9:30am-5:30pm. (802) 447-0228.

Covered Bridges are a popular attraction in southern Vermont, and Bennington has three Town lattice-style bridges within a mile or two from downtown. A self-guide tour pamphlet is available at the Bennington Chamber of Commerce.

Lively's Livery, 193 Crossover Rd., offers horse-drawn wagon tours throughout the area, including one of the three covered bridges, during which the clip-clop of horse hooves adds to the recreation a time when the bridges were a necessity. Also available are children's red-wagon rides and elegant carriage service – the livery is known for its rare American Cream draft horses. Adults $25, children sitting on laps are free. (802) 447-7612.

Monument Avenue is the heart of Old Bennington, lined with clapboard colonial homes, beautiful old trees, and several historic structures – including the Village Lion Fountain, once a water trough for horses. A self-guide walking tour is available at the Bennington Chamber of Commerce. (802) 447-3311.

Old First Church, Monument Ave., was built in 1805 on the site of Vermont's first meeting house, and is known as "Vermont's Colonial Shrine," in honor of the state's earliest history, much of which occurred on this spot. The evocative church still serves an active congregation, and visitors are welcome from April to October. (802) 447-1223.

    Old Burying Ground, behind Old First Church, is the final resting place for the founders of the town as well as soldiers from the American Revolution and poet Robert Frost and his family. Many of the tomb markers are Puritan style.

Park-McCullough House, corner of Park St. and West St., is a Victorian mansion completed in 1865 for entrepreneur Trenor Park and his wife, Laura Hall. Their daughter Eliza entertained President Benjamin Harrison in the house, which is a classic example of Second Empire-style. The 35-room interior is distinguished by walnut paneling, Italian-marble mantels, parquet floors, and bronze chandeliers. Park's descendents lived in the house until 1965, leaving it in nearly original condition, along with the family's Chinese porcelains and fine furnishings. The lovely lawns and gardens are complemented by a charming playhouse, and the carriage barn holds a collection of carriages, horse-drawn buggies and sleighs, and fire-fighting equipment. In late October, the house presents a variety of "Haunted Mansion" activities for kids and adults, including a "Moonlight Madness" tour. Open daily 10am-4pm, May-Oct. 21. Adults $6, seniors $5, youths (12-7) $4, children under 12 are free. (802) 442-5441. www.park-mccullough.org

Potter's Yard, 324 County St., has been in existence for over 50 years. Bennington Potters, the country's largest art-production pottery, is located in a converted gristmill. In addition to a vast array of pottery, it sells unique kitchenware and woolens, and is renowned as the finest discount-outlet store in the region. Free factory tours and demonstrations are held weekdays at 10:30am and 1:30pm. Open Mon-Sat. 11:30am-5pm, Sun. 10:30am-5pm. (802) 447-7922.

THE BERKSHIRES

The Berkshires are the highlands of Massachusetts – a gorgeously scenic region of rising mounts, waterfalls, and quiet woodlands. Settled in the early 1800s, its bucolic New England charm made it the summer locale for both artists and affluent vacationers. In the 19th century, it developed a reputation for "arts and letters" due to the works of residents Herman Melville, Nathaniel Hawthorne, and Edith Wharton. Many of its grand mansions, built as summer "cottages" more than a century ago, have been converted into arts venues or luxurious inns. Writers, composers, choreographers, and performing artists flock to the area during summer, making the area a national destination for cultural events. More recently, the Berkshires have become a year-round recreational resort, with activities from horseback riding to ballooning. (800) 237-5747. www.berkshires.org

Williamstown
Williamstown, the home of Williams College, looks like the setting for a Hollywood movie: A quaint New England town with splendid trees, wide streets, and impressive old houses. Appropriately enough, Hollywood celebrities are often spotted here in the summer, when they come to hit the boards and sharpen their theatrical skills.

Clark Art Institute, 225 South St., is a superlative museum of the fine arts, established in 1955 by Robert Sterling Clark, heir to the Singer sewing machine fortune, and his French-born wife, Francine. Their extraordinary personal collection formed the basis of the institute's world-class painting collection of French Impressionists (Monet, Degas, and more than 30 Renoirs), American classics (Homer, Remington), European Masters (Goya, Fragonard, Turner), and Northern and Italian Renaissance masterpieces (Perugino, Ghirlandaio). The intimate galleries also display exquisite decorative arts (including English and American silver), sculpture by salon masters, and changing exhibits of prints, drawings, pastels, watercolors, and photography. The extensive multi-media resource center, which holds more than 200,000 volumes, is open to the public. The institute's two striking buildings are situated on scenic meadowland perfect for a picnic lunch. Museum shop and restaurant. Open Tues-Sun., 10am-5pm; open daily July and Aug. Closed major holidays. Adults $10 (free Nov-May), youths under 18 are free. (413) 458-9545. wwwclarkart.edu

Suchele Bakers, 37 Spring St., bake from scratch with all-natural ingredients. Choose from wholesome breads, muffins and scones, or go for something more luscious, such as pies, cakes, and tarts. Open Mon-Sat., 7am-5pm; Sun. 8am-2pm. (413) 458-2251.

Williams College Museum of Art, Main St., is an exceptional college art museum, housing 11,000 works that span the history of art. The 14 galleries emphasize modern art, American art from the 1700s to the present, and non-Western art. Along with other changing exhibits is Artworks, a series of one-person shows of contemporary art and site-specific installations. The museum is distinguished architecturally by the neoclassical rotunda of the original structure, an 1846 brick octagon designed for the college's first library. Museum shop. Open Tues-Sat., 10am-5pm; Sun. and Mon. holidays, 1pm-5pm. Closed major holidays. Free. Tour guides are available by appt. (413) 597-2429. www.williams.edu/WCMA

Williamstown Theater Festival, Rte. 2, is regarded as the finest regional summer theater in the Northeast, an evaluation based on its artistic values, impressive coalitions of talent, and sheer verve. From mid-June to late August, the festival presents over 200 performances of classic and new plays, which frequently go on to bigger venues, including Broadway. Nestled in the Berkshire hills, the festival has three stages: the 520-seat Adams Memorial Theatre, or main stage; the 98-seat Nikos, for new plays in development and one-person plays; and a free outdoor theater. Past participants include luminaries from stage and screen, from Blythe Danner to her daughter, Gwyneth Paltrow. Schedules are released in early April. Box office: (413) 597-3400. www.wtfestival.org

North Adams

This tiny but disproportionately interesting area is known as "The Town of Steeples and Peaks" in homage to its many historic churches and scenic vistas. Nearby Mount Greylock, the state's highest summit, is the site of festive sports events year-round.

Appalachian Bean Café, 67 Main St., is within walking distance to MASS MoCA and Heritage State Park. A local favorite, it serves breakfast and lunch daily. (413) 663-7543.

Delftree Farm, 234 Union St., grows gourmet shittake mushrooms – in an old mill building, where biotechnology reproduces ancient Japanese cultivation techniques. Delftree is an acclaimed supplier to fine restaurants (including Le Cirque and the Four Seasons) and also sells these certified-organic delicacies retail and by mail order. Visitors are welcome to view the "farm," pick-up free recipes, and purchase freshly harvested shittake. (413) 664-4907.

MASS MoCA, 87 Marshall St., is the largest center for contemporary visual and performing arts in the United States. An "open laboratory" for the development and presentation of post-modern art forms, it encourages visitors to experience all stages of art making. Nineteen dramatically spatial galleries are housed in six of the 27 buildings of a vast old factory, where 19th-century industrial architecture intriguingly reflects on the futuristic visions within. The center features a far-ranging collection of exhibits, site-specific commissions, sound-art installations, and multimedia theatrical performances; dance and music concerts; and digital media, animation and film presentations. The focus is on the work of artists charting new territory, as well as works that are rarely exhibited because of physical demands such as scale and technological complexity.

Opened in 1999 and still evolving, the center describes itself as "a supercollider for arts and technology." Another way to describe this endlessly interesting site is "you've never seen anything like it." The 200-year history of the factory, and its fascinating transformation into MASS MoCA, is described in a brochure, "From Mill to Museum," and by short wall texts in the galleries. A gift shop, café and ice-cream parlor are located in the lobby. Open daily June-Oct., 11am-5pm (until 7pm on Fri.); Nov-May, Tues-Sat., 10am-4pm. Summer/fall admission: Adults $8, youths (6-16) $3. Winter/spring admission: Adults $7, seniors $4, youths $2. Children under 6 are free year-round. (413) 662-2111. www.massmoca.org

Natural Bridge State Park, just north of downtown, is a small park with a wondrous natural marble arch 500 million years in the making. The rushing waters of a 500-foot-long gorge can be viewed from the walkway above.

Porches Inn, 231 River St. was constructed in 2001 and followed the cutting-edge example of MASS MoCA by transforming six dilapidated Victorian rowhouses into a sophisticated and boldly colorful inn. *Condé Nast Travel Guide* lists Porches on its "2002 Hot List" of hotels worldwide for the "wit and ingenuity" of its design, and "state-of-the-art" bathrooms. The 50 rooms and suites (eight with private porches) feature a retro-industrial ambience that pays homage to new-millenium art as well as the buildings' history as mill-worker housing. The inn has a heated outdoor pool and year-round hot tub, and a verandah with rocking chairs that looks across the way to MASS MoCA's exhibition building. Summer rates from $160. (413) 738-5500. www.porches.com

Pittsfield

Berkshire Museum, 39 South St., founded in 1903, is a small museum packed to the gills with interesting exhibits – including a 26-tank aquarium – on three floors. The museum focuses on art, history, and the natural world. Natural Science comprises the largest collection, with the Dinosaurs and Paleontology Gallery usually stealing the show with its interactive "Dino Dig" (see Parents and Children, pg. 216). The art collection is distinguished by ancient art from around the world, as well as European art from the 14th- to 19th-centuries. Open year round, Mon-Sat. 10am-5pm, Sun. noon-5pm. Adults $8, students/ seniors $6, youths (3-18) $5. Free for all ages on birthdays. (413) 443-7171. www.berkshiremuseum.org

Hancock Shaker Village, intersection of Rtes. 20 and 41, is an outdoor history museum and authentic working farm, established in 1960 by one of the last acts of a Shaker community dating to 1783. The 1,200-acre site contains 20 original buildings, livestock, and herb and vegetable gardens – preserving and interpreting three centuries of Shaker life and work. The village holds the largest (and one of the finest) collections of Shaker furniture, artifacts and inspirational art, exhibited in 95 room settings. Of particular interest in this amazing restoration are the 1826 round stone barn, the gambrel-roof meetinghouse, the historic-breeds animals, and the demonstrations of Shaker farming techniques and crafts making. Events include antique shows, barn dances, harvest dinners, and crafts classes. Museum shop and café. Open daily May-Oct, 9:30am-5: 30pm for self-guided tours; Nov-April, 10am-3pm for guided tours. Adults $15, youths under 18 are free. (413) 443-0188. www.hancockshakervillage.org

Herman Melville's Arrowhead, 780 Holmes Rd., was the home of the great American writer during his most prolific years (1850-63), and where he wrote *Moby-Dick* and *The Piazza Tales* (the original copy of the tale "I and My Chimney" is on view). The 1780 farmhouse, which remained in Melville's family until 1927, has been beautifully refurbished to approximate its appearance during his ownership. The grounds include the barn where he spent many hours with Nathaniel Hawthorne discussing their writings, and a nature trail with views of Mt. Greylock, a major inspiration for Melville. Museum shop. Open daily late May-Oct., 9:30am-5pm; guided tours on the hour. Open Nov-May by appointment. $5 adults, $3 students, children under 5 are free. (413) 442-1793. www.mobydick.org

Herman Melville Memorial Room, 1 Wendell Ave., is housed in the Berkshire Athenaeum, and contains a collection of books, pictures, letters, and memorabilia relating to the author and his life in Pittsfield. (Melville's grandfather, Thomas Melville, was a founder of Pittsfield.) Open Mon-Thurs., 9am-9pm; Fri-Sat., 10am-5pm. Free. (413) 499-9486.

Lenox

Located in the beautiful Berkshire countryside, Lenox was a prosperous farming and mill town that was suddenly "discovered" in the mid-1800s by the rich and powerful of Boston and New York City. The subsequent building boom of extraordinary – and extraordinarily large – mansions earned the town the nickname of "the Inland Newport." After a post-war decline, a new era began in the 1930s, when music lovers began sponsoring symphonic performances during summertime. In 1937, the Boston Symphony Orchestra played its first summer concerts at the Tanglewood estate between Lenox and Stockbridge. (413) 637-3646. www.lenox.org

Blantyre, Rte. 20 (just outside of Lenox), is an award-winning country inn, formerly a 1902 residence modeled on a feudal Scottish manor with towers and turrets. Famed for its exceptional French cuisine, extensive wine cellar, and Gilded-Age ambiance, the 23-room inn is rated as one of the best in the country. The 100-acre grounds have ample recreational facilities, including a croquet lawn. (413) 637-3556.

Candlelight Inn, 53 Walker St., offers the atmosphere and hospitality of a classic New England inn. The eight charming guestrooms have private baths and AC, and include a continental breakfast. The public is welcome at the Candlelight Restaurant, which has four dining rooms and an American-continental menu that changes seasonally. Rates from $70. (413) 637-1555.

Frelinghuysen Morris House & Studio, 92 Hawthorne St. (adjacent to Tanglewood), is a highly unusual estate, designed as a showcase for modern art, architecture, history and lifestyles – the house was home to pioneering Cubist artists Suzy Frelinghuysen and George L.K. Morris, a couple at the forefront of 1930s American abstract art. Throughout the strikingly modernist house – designed by Stockbridge architect John Butler Swann and preserved as it was in its 1940s heyday – are works by Picasso, Braque, Leger and Gris, as well as wall murals and sculptures. The beautiful grounds contain a renowned woodland sculpture by Gaston Lachaise. Open July 4-Labor Day, Thurs.-Sun., 10am-3pm. Call for hours Sept.-Oct. Adults $8, youths $3. (413) 637-0166. www.frelinghuysen.org

Inspired Planet Gallery, 36 Pittsfield Rd. (Rte. 7), exhibits and sells fascinating artworks from the remote corners of the world. In 1999, composer Tan Dan created "an ethereal sound that came out of nowhere" during his performance of "Red Forecast" at Tanglewood. The "ethereal sound" was made by Buddhist singing bowls borrowed from Inspired Planet. Gallery objects range from ritual wands from Africa and the Himalayas to traveling Buddhist altarpieces and Tibetan medicine charts to paintings from Thailand and Peru. Located on a farm, Inspired Planet also has a barn full of folk-art animals, and sales rooms of jewelry, exotic-travel photos, unusual housewares, and sacred figurines from little-known cultures. Open daily April-Dec., call for hours. (413) 637-2836. www.inspiredplanet.com

The Mount, Rte. 7, was the summer home of the American writer Edith Wharton (1862-1937), Pulitzer Prize-winner for *The Age of Innocence*. The creation of the classical-style mansion in 1902 provided Wharton with the opportunity to demonstrate her influential ideas on architecture, landscape gardening, and interior design. As critics have proclaimed, Wharton's magnificent "country house" was the exemplar of the newly dawned American Renaissance. The Mount is currently in the final stage of a monumental restoration transforming the unique mansion (and its gardens) into a tribute to Wharton's life and writings, and a center for recognizing the achievements of women.

Edith Wharton Restoration presents an interesting summer lecture series at Seven Hills Inn (see below entry). Gift shop. Open by guided tour May 26-Oct. 31, 9am-5pm (last tour at 4pm). Adults $7.50, students and youths (13-18) $5, children (6-12) $3, children under 6 are free. (413) 637-1899. www.edithwharton.org

Shakespeare & Company, 70 Kemble St., is one of the largest and most critically revered Shakespeare festivals in the country, producing the plays of Shakespeare as well as dynamic adaptations of Edith Wharton, Henry James, and other Berkshire writers. In 2001, the company left its longtime home at the Mount for a new residence a block away, in Lenox Center. The $5 million, 63-acre complex houses three performance spaces: The two-level, 466-seat Founder's Theatre; the charming, 99-seat Spring Lawn Theatre, located in the salon of a historic mansion; and an outdoor stage in Rose Meadow. Look for an authentic recreation of Shakespeare's 1587 Rose Playhouse in the near future. The festival runs May-Oct. $10-$50. The box office is open 10am-2pm, or until curtain time. (413) 637-3353. www.shakespeare.org

Seven Hills Inn, 40 Plunkett St., is a converted baronial mansion that once belonged to Boston socialites. The enchanting guestrooms include 15 Manor House rooms decorated with period antiques (some have working fireplaces and/or jet tubs), and 37 Terrace House rooms furnished in elegant country décor. All rooms have AC and cable TV. Presentations from the Mount (see above entry) are held in the inn's elegant convention suites. Summer rates from $115. (413) 637-0067. www.sevenhillsinn.com

Tanglewood, West St. (Rte. 183), is the summer home of the Boston Symphony Orchestra (see Arts and Venues, pg. 51), located on the majestic grounds of a historic estate donated to the symphony in the 1940s. The verdant site contains the Music Shed amphitheater, the more intimate Ozawa Hall, the Tanglewood café (frequented by musical stars), and an excellent music-and-gift shop. In addition to the BSO, summer at Tanglewood offers concerts by guest orchestras such as the Israel Philharmonic Orchestra, three shows by the Boston Pops, and the Boston Early Music Festival. Also on the star-studded bill are chamber ensembles and legendary pop singers, as well as a Fourth-of-July family festival and a weekend jazz festival in early September. Box office: (617) 266-1492 or 266-1200. www.bso.org

Ventfort Hall Museum of the Gilded Age, 104 Walker St., was once considered the most beautiful residence in Lenox. And it will be again: concerned citizens saved the abandoned building from demolition in the mid-1990s, and it is currently undergoing a meticulous, 10-year restoration. The Elizabethan Revival mansion with Flemish-Baroque elements was completed in 1893 for Sarah Spencer Morgan, sister of financier J.P. Morgan. Even by the opulent standards of the Gilded Age, this red-brick-and-brownstone structure was dressed to impress, with rare, Cuban-mahogany panels, ornately carved plaster moldings, a 90-foot verandah, and 17 fireplaces. An example of the ingenuity of the restoration is how the warped mahogany ceiling panels have been milled into smaller panels for wainscoting.

The exterior, and the magnificent great hall and staircase, provided the setting for the orphanage in the 1999 Oscar-winning film *The Cider House Rules*. A behind-the-scenes photographic exhibit of the filming is on display, along with changing exhibits of Ventfort's glittering past, and the history and significance of the Gilded Age in Lenox. The principal rooms were restored and opened to the public in summer 2001, and visitors can view the ongoing restoration in the remaining rooms. The museum also offers interesting lectures and social events on a regular basis. Open daily May-Nov., limited hours in winter. Call for guided-tour schedules and/or event schedules. Discounted group tours are available by appt. year-round. Adults $8, children (12-and-under) $4. (413) 637-3206. www.gildedage.org

Stockbridge

Originally a settlement for missionary work with the Housatonic Indians, Stockbridge developed into a peaceful valley town in the early 1700s, protected from the ravages of Indian warfare by the natives' respect for progressive missionary John Sergeant. The town's most famous resident, however, is Norman Rockwell, and its evocative Main Street has changed very little from its depiction in his famous painting, Stockbridge Main Street at Christmas.

An American Craftsman, 36 Main St., displays an exceptional collection of craft art, including serious glass works, fine jewelry, and one-of-a-kind art boxes. Open daily 11am-7pm; winter 11am-5pm. (413) 298-0175.

Berkshire Botanical Garden, Rtes. 102 and183, is a living museum of over 2,500 plants, as well as a relaxing oasis of seasonal color and fragrance. The 15-acre center features intricately designed landscapes, historic herb gardens, vibrant annual and perennial beds, colorful vegetable demonstration plots, flowering crab apples, a Manet-like pond garden, and a children's garden. There are also specialty greenhouses, a primrose walk, and hundreds of varieties of roses, lilies and daffodils. A blackboard announces the day's flowers in bloom. Founded in 1934, the center offers educational programs on the art and enjoyment of growing things, and year-round horticultural events, including the Berkshires' oldest and largest community festival, held the first weekend in Oct.; and the acclaimed "Sculpture in the Garden" exhibit every July. Garden gift shop. Open daily May-Oct., 10am-5pm. Adults $7, seniors/students $5, children are free. (413) 298-3926. www.berkshirebotanical.org

Berkshire Theatre Festival, East Main St., presents professional productions of traditional plays from May through October. The third oldest theater festival in the country, BTF is renowned for attracting famous actors to its floorboards, from Ethan Hawke to Hal Holbrooke. The historic Playhouse (a converted 1888 casino designed by Stanford White) is augmented by the more adventurous Unicorn Theater in an adjacent building, and BTF Plays!, the festival's youth theatre (see Parents and Children, pg. 216). Box office: (413) 298-5576 or (413) 298-5536. www.berkshiretheatre.org

Chesterwood Estate & Museum, off Rte. 183, south of Rte. 102, was once the home and summer studio of Daniel Chester French, sculptor of the Lincoln Memorial and the Concord Minuteman. On display in the authentically furnished, 1897 farmhouse is the plaster cast French used as a model for the seated Lincoln. There's also a plaster Poe and a bronze Emerson. Contemporary sculpture is exhibited in the Barn Gallery. Museum shop. Open daily May-Oct., 10am-5pm. Adults $8.50, youths (13-18) $5, children $3. The Living History Tour and Dramatic Tour require reservations. (413) 298-3579. www.chesterwood.net

Federal House Inn, 1560 Pleasant St., South Lee, is a stately, 1824 house framed by old copper-beech trees and tall pines. The inn offers seven light and airy rooms furnished with antiques and queen-size, four-poster beds. The inn's historic ambience includes a wood-burning fireplace, and a complimentary hearty breakfast is served in the elegant dining room. Federal House is located across from the Housatonic River at the base of Beartown State Forest, one mile from Stockbridge. Off-season rates: $100-$175. Summer rates: $145-$245. (800) 243-1824. www.federalhouseinn.com

Mission House Museum & Gardens, 19 Main St., was built in 1739 by Stockbridge's first missionary, John Sergeant (whose brother-in-law founded Williams College). The house was rescued in 1927 by Mabel Choate, who lived in Naumkeag across the street. Choate moved Sergeant's post-and-beam house to its present location; the restoration was supervised by Fletcher Steele and reflects the Colonial Revival movement of the early 20th century. The house is also notable for its Connecticut River Valley doorway, and contains original furniture and artifacts as well as furnishings from the same era belonging to Choate's ancestors. Open daily Memorial Day-Columbus Day, 10am-5pm. Adults $5, youths (6-12) $3. (413) 298-3239. www.thetrustees.org

Naumkeag House & Gardens, Prospect Hill Rd., is the gabled mansion designed in 1885 by Stanford White for Joseph Hodges Choate, ambassador to England and an attorney for Vanderbilts and Morgans. The 28 rooms contain the Choate family's outstanding collection of Chinese porcelain, antique furniture, and elegant rugs and tapestries. The library has Morris chairs and Sargent charcoals. The strikingly scenic gardens include a shimmering stand of birch trees with an unusual footbridge, and a Chinese garden and temple designed by Mabel Choate and Fletcher Steele. Open daily May 27-Columbus Day, 10am-5pm. Adults $9, youths (6-12) $3. (413) 298-3239.

Norman Rockwell Museum, Rte. 183, has the world's largest collection of original art by America's most loved illustrator, a Stockbridge resident for the last 25 years of his life. The displays of paintings, drawings, and sketches – which change yearly – include Stockbridge Main Street at Christmas, The Four Freedoms, and other important large-scale works. Adjacent to the museum is Rockwell's studio, which houses a studio-related collection and personal items. The gift shop specializes in books and prints. Open daily May-Oct.,10am-5pm; winter weekdays 10am-4pm (except for the studio). Closed major holidays. Adults $10, 18-and-under free with paid adult. 413-298-4100. www.nrm.org

Red Lion Inn, 30 Main St., has served travelers since 1773 when it was a tavern stagecoach stop on the dusty road from Boston to Albany. It's one of the grandest – and last – of the 18th-century inns in continuous use. The authentic colonial ambience (pewter and Staffordshire appointments, antique furnishings, roaring winter fires) take visitors back to a more gracious era, yet the 109 romantic-country rooms (including suites) feature every modern amenity, and windows look out on the bustle of Main Street. The formal dining room features continental cuisine with regional ingredients; the Lion's Den pub serves a light menu with entertainment; Widow Bingham's Tavern serves traditional fare; and in warm weather food and cocktails are served in the flowering courtyard. Summer rates from $105. (413) 298-5545. www.redlioninn.com

Williams and Sons Country Store, Main St., offers nostalgia in the form of kitchen utensils, glassware, Americana and folk prints, toys, cards, cookbooks, imported jams and teas, and best of all, penny candy. Open daily 10am-5pm. (413) 298-3016.

THE MID-HUDSON VALLEY

The rapid expansion of the railroads in the mid-1800s made the Hudson Valley more accessible to New York's wealthy elite, who built lavish summer homes here to escape the city's heat and to enjoy the area's scenic views of the Catskill Mountains across the river. These historic residences offer an opportunity to explore the arts, culture and private lives of people who shaped America's destiny.

Germantown

Clermont State Historic Site, 1 Clermont Ave., is in many ways the ultimate history house. Preserved to its circa-1920 appearance, the 1686 estate was home to the Livingstons, the politically and socially prominent descendents of Scots-born Robert Livingston and Alida Schuyler Van Rensselaer. The first house was built in 1728, and was lived in by Robert R. Livingston, a drafter of the Declaration of Independence who was instrumental in the Louisiana Purchase and Fulton's invention of the steamboat. The rambling, 490-acre site is intimately entwined with the history of early America, right down to the dock that held the Clermont, the first steamboat. The centerpiece of this endlessly interesting site is the 1780s manor house, built on the foundation of the original home (which was burned by the British) by Margaret Beekman Livingston, whose first guests were General Washington and his wife, Martha. The Georgian manor was subsequently enlarged several times.

The manor's architecture, its grounds and gardens, and the 12,000-object collection all reflect the ownership and influence of seven generations of Livingstons from 1728 to 1962. Highlights of the heirloom collection are a 1794 Gilbert Stuart portrait of Chancellor Livingston; a Louis XVI clock celebrating the Paris balloon flight of his two sons; and a Launnier mirror. The grounds are graced by ancient oaks, English rose gardens, and an 1830s lilac walk. Several historic outbuildings are accompanied by colonial ruins, and the carriage barn houses a visitor center. Hikers and bicyclists are welcome on the carriage trails. The site holds historical events from April-Dec., including a 4th-of-July battle reenactment. Open by guided tour April-Oct., Tues-Sun. and Mon. holidays, 11am-4pm. Weekends only Nov-Dec. Adults $3, seniors $2, children $1. The grounds and the visitor center are open year-round, 8:30am-dusk. Free. 537-4240.

Annandale-On-Hudson

Montgomery Place, Rte. 9G (three miles north of the Kingston-Rhinebeck bridge), is one of the most meticulously preserved of all the great estates in America. A National Historic Landmark, the federal-style house of stuccoed fieldstone was built in 1804 by Janet Livingston Montgomery in honor of her late husband, General Richard Montgomery, an early Revolutionary War hero. It was later remodeled by architect A. J. Davis, who added balustrades and designed the Swiss cottage; the romantic landscapes were influenced by the great Andrew Jackson Downing. The house sits on 430 riverside acres, and offers many things to do outside of touring the palatial interior. Visitors are welcome to relax on the gracious north porch, stroll through the gardens and pre-war greenhouse, take in the stunning views of the Catskill Mountains, pick apples or raspberries in season, and walk along the woodland trail to the Sawkill falls. Montgomery Place is also host to the Hudson Valley Wine & Food Festival every June. Museum and garden shop. Open April-Oct., Weds-Mon., 10am-5pm (last tour at 4pm). Open weekends Nov-Dec. Adults $7, youths $4, grounds only $4. (845) 758-5461. www.hudsonvalley.org

Red Hook

Poets' Walk Romantic Landscape Park, 103 River Rd., is a 120-acre riverfront oasis where Washington Irving (and Livingstons and Astors) once strolled. Graveled and mown paths wind through sunlit fields, thick forests, and rolling hills. Designed in 1849 by landscape architect Hans Jacob Ehlers to celebrate the connection between nature and poetry, the walks are divided into distinct "rooms," each with its own ambience. The park is surrounded by 800 acres of conserved land, buffering it from the outside world. There are no facilities, so bring a snack, enjoy the rustic benches and stunning views, and read a poem. Or write one. Open dawn to dusk. Free. (845) 473-4440.

Ralph Pitcher & Sons, 41 Pitcher Rd., are producers of hybrid anemones, a.k.a. the "Lilies of the Field" in the Bible. In 1936, Ralph Pitcher obtained seeds from Jerusalem via Holland; these beautiful flowers are now grown by the third generation of Pitchers. The greenhouse also offers specialty-cut flowers at wholesale prices. (845) 876-3974.

Rhinebeck

Rhinebeck is one of the few villages remaining in the Hudson Valley. The evocative village center is a hive of leisurely activity in pleasant weather, and contains a wide variety of shops and unusual boutiques, including the Beekman Arms Antique Market (behind the Beekman Arms Hotel on Rte. 9, 914-876-3477), and the Rhinebeck Antique Center (7 West Market St., 914-876-8168). The Upscale Farmer's Market in the village parking lot (East Market St.) runs from June to October, Sundays 10am-2pm. After a shopping spree, parents and children can take a dip in Crystal Lake, or an outing at the Lion's Club Mini-Park, both of which are walking distance from the village. For more information, contact the Chamber of Commerce information booth at 19 Mill St., (845) 876-4778.

Beekman Arms, Rte. 9, is America's oldest continuously operated hotel. Built in 1766, its colonial ambience is well preserved, and the guestrooms above its famous tavern are still in use. Most of the 63 full-service rooms, however, are in additional buildings, old and new, behind the original hotel. Rates from $105. (845) 876-7077. www.beekmanarms.com

Delamater House is a block north, and part of the same complex. Built in 1844 by A. J. Davis, the architect for Lyndhurst in Tarrytown, the white-clapboard house is one of the few examples of early American Gothic still in existence. It has seven guestrooms. Rates from $99. (845) 876-7080.

Mills Mansion, Old Post Rd., Staatsburg (midway between Rhinebeck and Hyde Park), is an elegant example of the great estates built by American financial leaders during the Gilded Age. In 1895, financier Ogden Mills and his wife, Ruth Livingston Mills, hired the prestigious architectural firm of McKim, Mead and White to transform Mrs. Mills' childhood home into a lavish, beaux-arts mansion with 65 elaborately decorated rooms. The building retained many of its original features, however (including Livingston family portraits), and the combination of European grandeur with a reverence for family heritage makes the mansion a quintessentially American Renaissance estate.

Situated on 192 acres within Mills-Norris State Park, the mansion's "backyard" has graduated hills with unimpeded river views, providing a popular site for winter tobogganing. The grounds are open year-round, dawn to dusk. Call ahead to confirm hours for the mansion, which is currently undergoing a long-term renovation. Open April-Oct., Weds-Sat., 10am-5pm; Sun. noon-5pm. Special hours in Dec. Adults $3, seniors $2, children $1. (845) 889-8321.

Wilderstein, 330 Morton Rd. (Rte. 85, off Rte. 9), is a 40-acre, mid-1800s homestead with a fairy-tale-style residence at its center. Originally an Italianate villa built by Thomas Suckley, a real-estate tycoon descended from the area's pioneering Livingston and Beekman families, the mansion was expanded into an ornate Queen Anne mansion by his son, who added a multi-gabled third floor with a dramatic, circular tower. The homestead's varied terrain was lavishly landscaped by Calvert Vaux in the American-Romantic style, and includes a turreted carriage house, a Shingle-style gatehouse, and a Colonial-Revival potting shed. The interiors, containing ancestral objets d'art, furnishings, paintings, and photographs, offer a travelogue through the design and decorative arts of the 19th century.

This important Hudson Valley estate, which has an intriguing history intimately linked to nearby Top Cottage (see below entry), was donated to Wilderstein Preservation by Margaret Suckley, who was born in the house in 1891 and lived there until her death 100 years later. The Vaux carriage trails and nature paths are open dawn to dusk. Open May-Oct., Thurs-Sun., noon-4pm, and for special events year-round. Admission $7. Youths 12-and-under are free. Gift shop. (845) 876-4818. www.wilderstein.org

Hyde Park

Originally a fishing village – and the site of the country's first caviar factory – this picturesque river town was named after Sir Edward Hyde in the early 1800s; in 1895, Hyde Park was referred to by the New York Times as "the little colony of aristocrats up the river." The National Historic Sites listed below are maintained by the National Park Service. Informative brochures are available for each site. (845) 229-9115.

Home of Franklin D. Roosevelt, 4079 Old Post Rd., is a family home as well as a national monument to President Franklin Roosevelt, who lived here most of his life. Once called Springwood, the circa-1800 farmhouse was purchased by Franklin's father in 1867 and enlarged several times; the fieldstone wings and terrace were added by Franklin and his mother (the original Victorian clapboard is still visible in the back). Maintained as it was in 1945 during the President's final stay, the house is filled with furnishings, family mementos, and other reminders of its occupants. The wooded, 290-acre site includes a carriage house and icehouse, and the rose-garden gravesite of Franklin and Eleanor. Visitor center with bookstore.

    Franklin D. Roosevelt Library and Museum is on the same site. The museum, which F.D.R. helped to establish, contains artifacts ranging from his boyhood pony cart to his White House desk and famous Ford, as well as changing exhibits and a World War ll display. The library holds official papers from his terms as governor and president, and his personal collection of naval prints and models. It's also the only presidential library with a section honoring a First Lady: The Eleanor Roosevelt Gallery, added in 1971, documents her groundbreaking work as a diplomat and humanitarian. Museum shop. Open daily by guided tour, 9am-5pm. Adults $10 (includes home, museum and library), youths under 17 are free. (845) 229-9115.

Hyde Park Trail, Rte. 9, is an 8.5-mile system of hiking trails connecting several parks and historic sites within the town. The five-part trail, which passes through forest areas planted by FDR, is marked by green-and-white signs with a tulip-tree emblem: the tulip tree (or yellow poplar) was his favorite. One of the trails runs conveniently from the Franklin D. Roosevelt home to Val-Kill. Deer and other wildlife are plentiful, and a brochure with map is available. (845) 229-8086.

Top Cottage, Potter's Bend Rd., the hilltop retreat built by Franklin D. Roosevelt, was restored and opened to the public in 2001. For more than two years in the late 1930s, while grappling with the Depression and Fascist aggression, Roosevelt helped design and supervise the construction of this Dutch-style stone cottage overlooking his ancestral estate on the Hudson (the stones came from old walls in his fields). It is believed to be the first residence designed by and for a disabled person. This is where F.D.R. served hot dogs to the Queen of England, and where he spent time with his "closest companion," Margaret Suckley. The contents of the house were dispersed, and it will remain unfurnished. Visitors to the Roosevelt home and library can take a park shuttle bus to the cottage. Open daily May-Oct., 9am-5pm. Adults $5, youths under 17 are free. (845) 229-9115.

Val-Kill Cottage, St. Andrews Rd., was Eleanor Roosevelt's personal retreat from 1927 to 1946. Programs focus on her political activism, personal challenges, home life, and international diplomacy – the house was visited by John F. Kennedy and Nikita Krushchev, among other world leaders. The two-story fieldstone building was initially a factory started by Eleanor and three associates to provide jobs for youths during the Depression – today, Val-Kill furniture, pewter and weavings are prized by collectors. This is the only National Historic Site dedicated to a First Lady. Visitors are welcome to wander the grounds, which include a rose garden, pond, stone cottage, and the trail that Eleanor used to visit Top Cottage. Open by guided tour May-Oct., Thurs-Mon., 9am-5pm. Adults $5, youths under 17 are free. (845) 229-9115.

Vanderbilt Mansion, Albany Post Rd., is the incomparably elegant beaux-arts mansion built by industrialist Frederick William Vanderbilt, the most successful of the sons of "Commodore" Cornelius Vanderbilt. Designed by McKim, Mead and White, and decorated with the best $100 million could buy, the 50-room house looks almost exactly as it did when the Vanderbilts used it for gala balls and lavish dinners. The Romantic Landscape grounds, which provide gorgeous views, are as famed as the mansion, and include formal rose gardens and several interesting outbuildings. Picnicking spots can be found by the riverside. The guesthouse serves as a visitor center and bookstore. Open daily 9am-5pm. The grounds are open 8am-dusk. Adults $8, youths under 17 are free. (845) 229-9115.

Millbrook

Innisfree Gardens, Tyrrel Rd., Millbrook, is a man-made natural wonder designed and built by Walter Beck over a period of 22 years (1930-1952). Beck "created" the landscape, moving rocks, streams and waterfalls around a 40-acre lake; constructing terraces, slopes and walls; and decorating the space with plants and vines. Inspired by a 1,000-year-old Chinese model, the artist improved on nature with drama but not artifice. Open May-Oct. Adults and youths $3. (845) 677-8000.

Trevor Zoo, Millbrook School Rd. (Rte. 44, east of Millbrook Village), is a unique zoological experience accommodating 120 exotic and indigenous species. The focus is on wildlife conservation, with an emphasis on endangered-species protection and habitat preservation. Sanctuaries within the six-acre facility include "Australia," "Asia," and "The Tropics." Among the species on view are ring-tailed lemurs, wallabies, arctic fox, Sika deer, white-napped cranes, and red pandas. The zoo's educational mission extends to all visitors, who hopefully will gain a greater understanding of wildlife and the environment. Open daily 8am-5pm, including holidays. Adults $4, children $3 ($2 off-season) Call ahead for discounted group rates. (845) 677-3704. www.trevorzoo.org

Vineyards thrive along the Hudson Valley, which is America's oldest wine region. Benefiting from the river's warming effect on the air, wine has been made here continuously for over 300 years, since French Huguenots first settled in New Paltz in 1677. The region pioneered the French-American grape varieties Seyval Blanc and Baco Noir, and is also known for more delicate European grapes such as Chardonnay.

The scenic wineries listed below welcome the public for tours and wine tastings. It's advisable to call in advance, especially off-season.

Dutchess Wine Trail begins at Alison Wines and Vineyard, just north of Red Hook (off Rte. 9), continues to Millbrook Vineyards (considered one of the finest New York vintners) and concludes at the especially scenic Clinton Vineyards. The wineries are within 30 min. of each other (between the Taconic State Parkway and Rte. 22), and along the way you'll pass orchards, woodlands, trout streams and lakes, and a fabled mansion or two. The trail is not well marked, but a brochure with maps and directions is available. (845) 373-9021. www.dutchesswinetrail.com

Alison Wines and Vineyard, Pitcher Lane, Red Hook, produces fine white and red wines. Open daily April-Oct., Nov-Dec., Sat-Sun. (845) 758-1234.

Cascade Mountain Winery and Restaurant, 835 Cascade Mountain Rd., Amenia, is a third-generation, family-farm winery that offers tours and tastings year-round. Among the specialties are Chardonnay, Cabernet Sauvignon, and Seyval Blanc. The restaurant pairs the wines with local produce. Open spring-summer-fall, 10am-5pm. (845) 373-9021. www.cascademt.com

Clinton Vineyards and Winery, Schultzville Rd., Clinton Corners, features award-winning white wines, champagne, and pure-fruit dessert wines. Be sure and visit the driftwood sculpture of a horse in the beautiful fields; in the wine shop, look for the "Menage a Trois" gift box of three dessert wines noted by the *New York Times*. Vintner luncheons by group reservation. Open Fri-Sun., 11am-5pm, year-round, or by group appointment. (845) 266-5372.

Millbrook Vineyards and Winery, 26 Wing Rd., Millbrook, is set amid 30 picturesque acres. It offers tours and tastings of its critically acclaimed European varietals, including Pinot Noir, Cabernet Franc, and an especially popular Chardonnay. Vineyard Grille in season. Open daily noon-5pm, year-round. (845) 677-8383.

Russell Sage College, Troy

Photography by: Gary Gold

EDUCATION

The Capital Region's numerous institutions of higher learning have achieved national rankings for educational value, research grant investments, academic quality, and alumni achievement. They also provide a massive graduate recruitment pool, and contribute to local cultural life and athletic events. In addition, the area's elementary and secondary schools offer a wide selection of excellence. Yearly tuition figures are approximate and subject to change. Financial assistance is available for almost all of the below entries.

ELEMENTARY AND SECONDARY SCHOOLS

Public Schools

The counties of the Capital Region all have comprehensive educational systems grades K-12. They work together to provide competitive intramural athletic leagues and to share resources. Information regarding public schools and their programs and services is available through the individual school districts. For more information: 462-7100.

Magnet schools within the Albany school district include:

Thomas O'Brien School of Science and Technology, Lincoln Park, offers full-day pre-K through grade 6. O'Brien is partnered with the nearby State Museum. 462-7262.

Albany School of Humanities, 108 Whitehall Rd., offers full-day K through grade 6 and offers dance, art, Spanish, and other cultural courses. 462-7258.

Philip Livingston Magnet Academy, 315 Northern Blvd., is a middle school with a 1,100-seat auditorium and dance and drama studios. Livingston is located adjacent to Tivoli Lakes Park. 462-7154.

Applications for these schools may be obtained from the city school-district offices. Students are accepted by lottery, with an emphasis on racial balance. www.albany.k12.ny.us

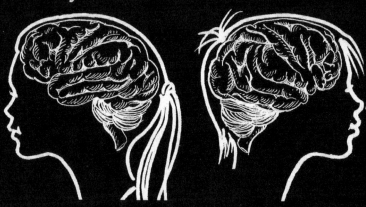

Parochial and Diocesan Schools

The Roman Catholic Diocese operates an extensive system of primary schools in the Capital Region (32 in Albany alone). Most are affiliated with and partly financed by local parishes; students pay a fee based on ability to contribute and/or the number of children per family enrolled at the school. The diocese also operates four high schools: Bishop Maginn High School in Albany, Catholic Central High School in Troy, Notre Dame-Bishop Gibbons in Schenectady, and Saratoga Central Catholic High School in Saratoga Springs. No student is denied entrance to any of the schools on the basis of religion or financial status. 453-6666. www.rcdaschools.org

Private and Independent Schools

In addition to local public schools, area residents may choose from a variety of educational institutions with differing objectives and diverse approaches. Because the nature of education is dependent on individual values, the descriptions below are limited to the input offered by administrators of the schools and catalogue copy. All schools in this section accept students regardless of race or creed.

Academy of the Holy Names, 1065-1075 New Scotland Ave., Albany, is a private Catholic day school for girls founded in 1884. Two buildings on a 64-acre suburban campus contain an elementary school (pre-K to grade 8), and a college-preparatory upper school (grades 9 to 12). Sponsored by the Sisters of the Holy Names, the academy is dedicated to preparing students to become moral, intellectual, spiritual, and cultural leaders, while providing a same-sex environment that fosters self-confidence and the pursuit of excellence. Average number of students is 530. Tuition: $6,500-$7,600. 438-6553, 489-2559. www.community.timesunion.com/holynames/

Albany Academy, 135 Academy Rd., Albany, is an independent school for boys pre-K to grade 12. Established in 1813 (with many prominent Albanians among its graduates), the academy remains dedicated to helping each boy reach his full potential – academically, athletically, artistically, and socially. Small classes allow teachers to prepare students for positions of leadership and achievement. The school takes pride in its impressive record of college placement with the nation's most prestigious institutions. Begun in the 1870s, the Cadet Battalion teaches discipline through activities based on a military model. The academy is also committed to athletic excellence and offers an array of exceptional sports facilities, including an indoor hockey rink and swimming pool, and 15 acres of playing fields. Cross enrollment with Albany Academy for Girls is available for grades 9 to 12, in addition to a post-graduate grade 13. The preschool is coed. Average number of students is 425. Tuition: $10,000-$17,000. 465-1461. www.albany-academy.org

*Ten Things
You Should
Know About
Doane Stuart...*

1. Doane Stuart is the Region's only nursery through grade 12, coeducational independent school.

2. We take pride in 100% college admission to many of the most select colleges and universities in the country.

3. We enjoy the Region's only formal, chartered partnership with our area's largest research university, The University at Albany.

4. Our average class size is 14 students.

5. Doane Stuart boasts average SAT scores more than 200 points above the national average and more than 100 points above the independent school average.

6. We have a student to faculty ratio of 7:1.

7. We share partnerships that extend from the Albany Institute of History and Art and Albany College of Pharmacy to Lagan College in Belfast, Northern Ireland.

8. Doane Stuart is an interfaith community and our nation's only successfully merged Catholic/Protestant school.

9. We are located on an 80-acre campus with magnificent playing fields, nature trails and pool.

10. Our students contribute over 5,000 hours of community service annually.

**For more information, please contact the
Admission Office at (518) 465-5222**

www.doanestuart.org

COEDUCATION • PARTNERSHIP • LEADERSHIP

Albany Academy for Girls, 140 Academy Rd., Albany, was founded in 1814 as one of the first schools to be devoted exclusively to the education of young women. This independent, college-preparatory school for girls pre-K to grade 12 features challenging programs in athletics and the arts, and a curriculum that spans classical studies to cutting-edge technology. It also offers the best of two worlds: the advantages of a single-sex environment that encourages girls to excel, as well as the opportunity for cross enrollment in high school with neighboring Albany Academy. French is taught from second grade on, and the Odyssey Project, the academy's computer-skills initiative, has received national attention. Average number of students 350. Tuition: $10,000 to $15,000. 463-2201. albanyacademyforgirls.org

Brown School, 150 Corlaer Rd., Schenectady, is an independent school offering small classes and an individualized approach to education from (three-day) pre-K to grade 8. Founded in 1893, the school's mission remains unchanged: to inspire students to love learning while striving for academic excellence. The curriculum emphasizes language arts and foreign languages, as well as history, mathematics, and science. The school's heterogeneous population provides the opportunity to instill respect for individual differences whether cultural, social, economic, or other. Average number of students is 340. Tuition: $4,800 to $7,050. 370-0366.

Christian Brothers Academy, 12 Airline Dr., Albany, is a Catholic private military high school for boys grades 6 through 12, located on a 126-acre campus. Founded in 1859 by the De La Salle Christian Brothers, the school is dedicated to instilling Christian values while providing a solid academic program, and to developing the talent and leadership ability of each student. The JROTC program is accredited as an Honor Unit with Distinction, and CBA's nine varsity athletic programs are highly regarded, as is the school's regimental band. Average number of students is 380. Tuition: $7,200 to $7,700. 452-9809. www.cbaalbany.org

Doane-Stuart School, Rte. 9W, Albany, is a 150-year old, coeducational, interfaith independent school, the nation's only successfully merged Catholic/Protestant school. A premier college preparatory school, Doane Stuart focuses on serious study, social responsibility, and a strong foundation of faith from Nursery to Grade 12. The school's 80-acre campus includes: classroom buildings, Gothic-revival chapel, Buddhist temple, playing fields and courts. It enjoys a chartered partnership with the University at Albany and also partners with the Albany College of Pharmacy, the Albany Institute, and Lagan College in Belfast, Northern Ireland. Average number of students: 280. Tuition: $9,675-$14,825. 465-5222. www.doanestuart.org

Emma Willard School, 285 Pawling Ave., Troy, was founded in 1814 by education pioneer Emma Hart Willard and is among the first institutions for the higher education of women in America, and academic excellence is a renowned tradition. The school serves boarding and day students for grades 9 to 12, and for the post-graduate year. The college preparatory program is complemented by independent study in the community, a visual and performing arts program, leadership training, and competitive interscholastic athletics. The historic, 137-acre campus features Tudor-Gothic architecture (see Points of Interest, pg. 19). Average number of students is 300. Tuition: $19,250 (day students) to $31,200 (boarding). 274-4440. www.emma.troy.ny.us

Free School, 8 Elm St., Albany, established in 1969, is the oldest alternative free school in the region. It serves pre-K through grade 8. The ratio of teachers to students provides a closely-knit educational atmosphere, and the school's emphasis is on developing a sense of self and the ability to meet challenges. Tuition is on a sliding scale. 434-3072.

Hebrew Academy of the Capital District, 54 Sand Creek Rd., Albany, is a coed school offering grades K to 8. The academy was founded to provide close study of Judaic and secular studies for young people, and preparation to pursue both at more advanced levels. The orientation of the small classes is to approach all subjects with an awareness of their meaning in the context of Jewish traditions. Average number of students is 180. Tuition: $6,400-$7,700. 482-0464.

LaSalle Institute, 174 Williams Rd., Troy, is a Catholic college-preparatory school for boys grades 6 to 12, conducted by the Christian Brothers. LaSalle has an accredited Junior ROTC program for grades 9 to 12. College credit courses are available through an arrangement with neighboring Hudson Valley Community College. Average number of students is 600. Tuition $6,700 to $7,400. 283-2500.

Loudonville Christian School, 374 Loudon Rd., Loudonville, was founded in 1960 to help Christian parents provide a thorough education committed to high scholastic standards and an evangelical world view. From pre-K to grade 12, biblical truth is integrated into all subjects. In addition to academic and extra-curricular programs, students are involved in daily prayer, bible classes, and weekly chapel services. The high school offers accelerated programs in math, science, Spanish, and German. Average number of students is 330. Tuition: $2,900-$5,450. 434-6051.

St. Gregory's School For Boys, 121 Old Niskayuna Rd., Loudonville, was founded in 1962 to offer accelerated courses for boys grades 1 to 8, with the aim of preparing students for advance entry into the most competitive secondary schools in the country. A challenging program promotes strong work habits and study skills, as well as Christian principles and academic excellence. French is taught from pre-K on, computer science from the first grade, and Latin in grades 7 and 8. The preschool and kindergarten programs are coed. Average number of students is 200. Tuition: $6,600 to $9,000. 785-6621. www.saintgregorysschool.org

Saratoga Independent School, 8 Division St., Saratoga, is a private elementary school for grades K to 6. SIS was founded to empower each student to become a confident learner who is capable of critical thinking, problem solving, and teamwork. Average number of students is 50. Tuition: $6,500. 583-0841. www.siskids.org

Susan Odell Taylor School, 116 Pinewoods Ave., Troy, was founded in 1998 by Susan Odell Taylor, a former teacher with the venerated children's-school program at Emma Willard. The school offers pre-K to grade 6 in small, multi-age classrooms, with enriched programs in music, art and language. The emphasis is on individualized, hands-on learning that respects and addresses each child's strengths and challenges. Average number of students is 50. Tuition: $6,800-$7,200. 274-4994. www.taylorschool.org

Waldorf School of Saratoga Springs, 62-66 York Ave., Saratoga Springs, offers a comprehensive education based on the work of Rudolf Steiner, addressing all the needs of a child while promoting unity between home, school, and community. Spring Hill serves grades 1 to 12 in three buildings: the "Children's Garden," an elementary school, and a high school located at 122 Regent St. Average number of students is 250. Tuition: $1,700-$8,350. 584-7682. www.waldorf.saratoga.ny.us.

Woodland Hill Montessori School, 100 Montessori Place, North Greenbush, was established in 1965 and is one of the oldest Montessori schools in the country. In 2002, the school moved from its original site in Rensselaer to a spacious, $3 million hilltop campus. This flourishing institution is known for its challenging educational program and supportive environment for children ages 3 to 14. Based on the century-old Montessori method of nurturing a child's natural love of learning, the curriculum emphasizes individual and cooperative skills in math, science, social studies, music, dance, and physical education. Average number of students is 160. Tuition: $6,600-$7,000. 283-5400. www.woodlandhill.org

COLLEGES AND UNIVERSITIES

State University of New York is both the youngest and the most comprehensive public-university system in the United States. SUNY was created in 1948, although some individual campuses date to the early 1800s. In its first half-century, SUNY became a diversified yet integrated system offering a full range of quality academic programs. Graduation from SUNY two-year colleges guarantees admission to SUNY senior colleges.

Two-Year Colleges

Adirondack Community College, 640 Bay Rd., Queensbury, is a two-year state college offering certificate and degree programs in liberal arts and sciences, computer technology, business services, protective services, and health professions. Average number of students is 600. Tuition: $2,500 (out-of-state residents: $4,950). 743-2200.

Hudson Valley Community College, Vandenburgh Ave., Troy, is a full-service, two-year state college and the second largest institution of higher learning in the region. It offers more than 50 degree and certificate programs through its four schools: Business, Engineering & Industrial Technologies, Health Sciences, and Liberal Arts & Sciences. It also has the only dental-hygiene program in the greater Capital Region. HVCC's Workforce Development Institute coordinates customized training with area businesses and government agencies, while the academic programs are designed to promote compatibility and transferability to four-year colleges. The campus includes an all-purpose sports center with a fieldhouse and an ice rink. Average number of students is 10,000. Tuition: $2,350 (out-of-state residents: $6,135) 629-4822. www.hvcc.edu

Maria College, 700 New Scotland Ave., Albany, is a coed, private, two-year college sponsored by the Sisters of Mercy. Classes are kept small to insure the personal quality that is Maria's hallmark. Fields of study include business, liberal arts, early-childhood education, and allied health. The nursing program utilizes nearby St. Peter's hospital, and a state-of-the-art facility was established for the Computer Information Systems degree. Maria offers two options in addition to the traditional daily schedule: an evening degree and the Weekend College, which makes it possible to earn an associate degree in a two-year time frame. Average number of students is 900. Tuition: $6,600. 438-3111. www.mariacollege.edu

Sage College of Albany, 140 New Scotland Ave., established in 1957 as a coed junior college, merged with Russell Sage Evening Division in 2001 to become a four-year college (see below entry). SCA now offers "Design Your Own Degree" associates programs. Tuition: $13,750. 244-2000. www.sage.edu

Schenectady County Community College, 78 Washington Ave., Schenectady, is a two-year state college offering 35 career and transfer programs, as well as one-year certificate programs. SCCC also serves business and industry through customized training programs, and non-credit offerings in vocational and avocational areas. The college is one of the few two-year colleges in the nation to hold the prestigious National Schools of Music accreditation, and is also known for its culinary-arts programs. The new Gateway building offers advanced technological resources. Average number of students is 4,000. Tuition: $2,500 (out-of-state residents: $4,800). 381-1366. www.sunysccc.edu

Four-Year Colleges and Universities

Albany College of Pharmacy, 106 New Scotland Ave., Albany (see Professional Schools, pg. 294).

College of St. Rose, 432 Western Ave., Albany, is a coed, private liberal-arts college that takes pride in the personal quality of its educational programs even while undergoing a large-scale expansion. CSR offers 41 undergraduate degrees and 28 Master's degrees, and is especially esteemed for its programs in special education, communication disorders, psychology, and art and music education. New programs include Sports Management and Information Technology. In 2002, the college completed its $15 million, state-of-the-art Lally School of Education, a regional force in teacher-training preparation. In addition, the Adult Weekend Advantage program, held every other weekend, has a range of courses including business, computer science, education, and English. The college also has a day-student Adult Continuing Education Division. Average number of students is 4,500. Tuition: $15,250. 454-5111. www.strose.edu

Sage Colleges, Troy and Albany, are described as "Three colleges, two cities... a world of opportunity."

Russell Sage College for Women, 45 Ferry St., Troy, was founded in 1916 (see Points of Interest, pg. 18) for the revolutionary purpose of preparing women to participate fully in society. Russell Sage today is a comprehensive, residential undergraduate college with a focus on the liberal arts and sciences, in addition to professional programs in health sciences, education, and the performing arts. The historic campus is conveniently located in the heart of downtown Troy. Average number of students is 850. Tuition: $19,200 (boarding: $21,800-$25,570). 244-2000. www.sage.edu

Sage College of Albany, 140 New Scotland Ave., was established in 1957 as a coed junior college. In 2001, it merged with the Russell Sage Evening Division to become an innovative college of applied sciences with an emphasis on new and emerging professions in arts and design, communications, business, legal studies, education, and information technologies. Dominating the campus is the Opalka Gallery, a high-tech art gallery constructed in 2002 to complement the school's new fine-arts building and BFA-degree program. SCA also offers "Design Your Own Degree" associates programs, and the Center for Extended Learning specializing in bachelor-degree completion for working adults. Average number of students is 800. Tuition: $13,750. 244-2000. www.sage.edu

Sage Graduate School, Troy and Albany campuses, is a coed graduate college offering advanced study in professional fields with an emphasis on health science, education, psychology, and administration; and a focus on applied research. Tuition: $440 per credit. 244-2000. www.sage.edu

Siena College, 515 Loudon Rd., Loudonville, is an independent, residential, coed Catholic liberal-arts college under the auspices of the Franciscan Order. Founded in 1937 as a small men's school, Siena now offers 25 majors through three schools: the School of Liberal Arts, the School of Business, and the School of Science. In addition, the college has affiliations with Albany Medical College, New York University, and other colleges. Siena is known for its top-notch athletics programs, with 19 NCAA Division 1 sports programs. The men's basketball team – the Saints – makes its home at the Pepsi Arena and is a popular contributor to the region's sporting events. In 1999, the school constructed the state-of-the-art Standish Library. Average number of students is 2800. Tuition: $17,600. 783-2307. www.siena.edu

Skidmore College, 815 North Broadway, Saratoga Springs, is an independent, residential, coed liberal-arts college committed to providing a superior education in the humanities, sciences, and social sciences, in addition to career preparation in fields such as business, social work, fine arts and the performing arts. Skidmore is a closely-knit community with a student-faculty ratio of 11 to 1. Founded in 1903 as an "industry club" for young women, the college became coed in 1971, shortly after leaving its downtown buildings for a new, wooded campus. Its University Without Walls is one of the earliest non-traditional degree programs in the country. The college is also known for the excellence of its athletic programs, including lacrosse, golf, and a prestigious equestrian program (the riding center is adjacent to the campus). In addition, the Tang Teaching Museum and Art Gallery (see Arts and Venues, pg. 63) provides opportunities for interdisciplinary arts studies. Average number of students is 2,200. Tuition (including room and board): $33,900. 580-5000. www.skidmore.edu

Rensselaer Polytechnic Institute, 110 8 St., Troy, is an independent, top-tier technological research university with global recognition. Sustained by a historic, 175-year tradition of excellence in education, the school experienced rapid growth over the last decade, and is currently engaged in an ambitious, $135 million campus improvement effort. RPI has five departments: the Schools of Architecture,

Engineering, Humanities, and Science, and the prestigious Lally School of Management and Technology. In addition, doctoral degrees are granted in philosophy and engineering. The arts program includes the state-of-the-art iEAR Studios for electronic art and music. The RPI campus is situated above the city on a park-like campus that blends postmodern style with 19th-century charm (see Points of Interest, pg. 20). Average number of students is 6,000. Tuition: $27,700. 276-6000. www.rpi.edu

Union College, Union St., Schenectady, describes itself as an "independent, primarily undergraduate, residential college for men and women of high academic promise and strong personal motivation." Established in 1795, Union was the first college chartered by the Regents of the State of New York, and is believed to have the oldest campus in the United States (see Points of Interest, pg. 26) This venerable institution, which became coed in 1970, enjoys a long-standing reputation of academic excellence and student and alumni loyalty. The liberal-arts curriculum encompasses over a 1,000 courses in the humanities, sciences, and engineering. Average number of students is 2,000. Tuition: $27,300. 388-6000. www.union.edu

University at Albany, 1400 Washington Ave., Albany, is the largest educational institution in the greater Capital Region, offering advanced professional, doctoral and research missions in 70 major fields as well as 76 master's and 38 doctoral degrees. Admission is highly competitive: the university's graduation rate is 15 points higher than the national average. UAlbany has been rated in the top 25 of the nation's "Best Buys" in higher education by *Money* magazine, and is consistently rated in the top ten for many of its individual programs. Programs ranked among the nation's best include Criminal Justice, Education, Information Technology, Management Information, Public Finance and Budget, Public Administration and Policy, Clinical Psychology, and Sociology. Average number of students is 17,000. Tuition: $3,400 to $5,100 (out-of-state residents: $8,300 to $8,420). 442-3300. www.albany.edu

UAlbany is the product of 150 years of dynamic change, and is composed of three campuses. The Downtown Campus (between Washington and Western Avenues) is the oldest in the state university system, with roots dating to 1844 (the school's emblematic history can be found at the UAlbany web site). The East Campus is a technology complex (see Information and Resources, pg. 329). The geometric Uptown Campus was designed in 1964 by noted architect Edward Durrell Stone. A rectangular "academic podium" of 13 buildings, all connected by a continuous roof and lower-level corridor, are complemented by a 23-story tower at each quadrangle. In the center of the complex is a reflecting pool, fountain, and carillon tower. Visitors are welcome to roam the grounds and enjoy the university's art museum (see Arts and Venues, pg. 64).

Professional Schools

University Heights, New Scotland Ave., Albany, is the name of the landscaped area that connects Albany Law School, Albany College of Pharmacy, and Albany Medical College. All three colleges are part of Union University, along with Union College and the Dudley Observatory in Schenectady. This extended campus includes a 119-unit complex of student apartments; a multitude of student-oriented businesses and services are within walking distance. www.uniteddevcorp.com

Albany College of Pharmacy, 106 New Scotland Ave., Albany, has provided students with a pre-eminent education in the field of pharmacy for over 120 years. Today, ACP's rigorous degree programs lead to the Bachelor of Science in Pharmaceutical Science; the Doctor of Pharmacy, Pharm. D.; and the Non-Traditional Doctor of Pharmacy. ACP also offers an accelerated program in conjunction with Union College toward a Master of Science-Clinical Leadership in Health Management, and a certificate program in Cytotechnology. The college is dedicated to preparing students for licensure; for careers in research laboratories, government agencies, retail and hospital pharmacies; to enter other areas of science and business, or for entry to graduate school in dentistry or medicine. Average number of students is 650. Tuition: $16,100. 445-7200. www.acp.edu.

Albany Law School, 80 New Scotland Ave., Albany, is one of the oldest law schools in the United States, and has occupied its stately, Tudor-Gothic main building since 1929. More recently, the campus was augmented by a 45,000-square-foot building to house new programs such as the award-winning Clinical Legal Studies Program. The school's proximity to the state capital offers opportunities for meaningful internships in the courts, the government, and public- interest organizations, as well as valuable experience in private law offices. Degrees offered include J.D., M.S. in Legal Studies; J.D./M.B.A.; J.D. M.P.A.; J.D./M.S.W.; J.D. M.R.P., as well as a three-year program leading to the J.D. degree. In addition, Albany Law cooperates with several Capital Region colleges to grant six-year joint degrees. Average number of students is 700. Tuition: $26,100. 445-2311. www.als.edu

Albany Medical College, 47 New Scotland Ave., Albany, was founded in 1839 and is one of the oldest private medical colleges in the nation. Today, AMC continues to pursue excellence in the education of health-care personnel, in research in the basic and clinical medical sciences, and in services to the community, as well as preparing undergrads to pursue any area of medicine. The college is administratively linked to the Albany Medical Center, providing a wide range of clinical experiences through affiliations with numerous area hospitals. In addition, AMC's proximity to the NYS Department of Health affords ample opportunities for the interchange of scientific information, instruction, and collaboration on research projects. Tuition: $30,000. 262-3125. www.amc.edu

Rockefeller School of Public Affairs and Policy, 135 Western Ave. (Milne Hall), Albany, is a UAlbany graduate institution founded in 1960 "to ensure better government," and to focus on issues of politics, policy, and management. It has two departments: the School of Political Science, which offers a full range of subject areas; and the School of Public Administration, which is ranked in the top five percent of all PA programs. Located just a few blocks from the State Capitol Building, the school's proximity to one of the foremost centers of government has helped it to become nationally recognized. Tuition: $4,800. 442-5244. www.albany.edu/rockefeller

BUSINESS SCHOOLS

Bryant & Stratton Business Institute, 1259 Central Ave., Albany, was founded in 1854 and is still owned and operated by descendants of the Bryant and Stratton families. The motto "Turn potential into power" encompasses the school's strengths in information technology, business, accounting, paralegal, and more. Day and evening classes available. Average number of students is 350. Tuition: $296. per credit hour. 437-1802. www.bryantstratton.com

Mildred Elley, 800 Loudon Rd. (Latham Circle Mall), Latham, was founded over 80 years ago to provide job training to women; more recently, it has evolved into a coed business school known for its efficient and convenient degree and certificate programs. The college's high-demand career fields include business management, paralegal studies, medical assistant, travel & tourism, office technologies, and information technology. New students are accepted at the start of each 8-week module. Tuition: $11,160 (certificates) to $18,600 (degrees). 786-0855. www.mildred-elley.com

HOSPITAL-BASED NURSING SCHOOLS

Ellis Hospital School of Nursing, 1101 Nott St., Schenectady, is a non-profit, private institution founded in 1903. The school offers associate's degrees in nursing, with an emphasis on specialty areas such as intensive-care nursing. The curriculum consists of 42 credits in nursing and 30 college credits, spanning four semesters and one summer session. Average number of students is 70. Tuition (for 21-month course): $8,700. 243-4471. www.xap.com

Memorial Hospital School of Nursing, 600 Northern Blvd., Albany, offers RN degrees and is affiliated with Northeast Health, allowing students to participate in clinical and observational experiences in a variety of health-care settings. Graduates can pursue a BSN degree at Russell Sage College. Tuition: $285 per credit hour (includes lab fee). 471-3260. www.NortheastHealth.com

Samaritan Hospital School of Nursing, 2215 Burdett Ave., Troy, offers RN and LPN degrees, and is affiliated with Northeast Health, allowing students to participate in clinical and observational experiences in a variety of health-care settings. Graduates of the RN program can pursue a BSN degree at Russell Sage College. Tuition: $285 per credit (includes lab fee). 271-3285. www.NortheastHealth.com

CONTINUING EDUCATION

A number of local institutions provide college education and degree programs for adults, shaping their curriculums to be available and manageable for those in adult circumstances. In addition, continuing education is an important component in the offerings of many undergraduate and professional institutions in the area, some of which offer programs designed to help graduates keep their skills and information up-to-date, or to develop a new field of interest.

Empire State College, 845 Central Ave., Albany, is a leader in nontraditional higher education, serving adult students who choose to study in an independent, flexible manner. ESC is known for its high level of student satisfaction, and offers a wide variety of individually designed programs, including five master's degree programs. Degree credits incorporate life and work learning, and include one-to-one tutorials and guidance from mentors. ESC has locations across the region, and "distance learning" is provided both online and in print. Tuition: $137 per credit. 485-5964. www.esc.edu

Excelsior College (formerly Regents College), 7 Columbia Circle, Albany, was established in 1970 to make education available and flexible for adult students. It offers 30 associates and bachelors degrees. Students are supported every step of the way, working with advisors to complete courses in business, liberal arts, nursing, and technology, and to earn credits through a variety of methods, including traditional college courses, proficiency examinations, special assessment, military education, and evaluation of business and industrial training. The college also offers two master's-level programs, in nursing and liberal studies. Excelsior is the oldest and largest college in the country devoted exclusively to adult learners. Military personnel receive free exams and special fees. Tuition: for information on the fee schedule, call 888-647-2388. 464-8500. www.excelsior.edu

AMC/Excelsior College Project Learn, Albany Medical Center, 201 New Scotland Ave., Albany, is a collaborative venture in nursing education between Albany Medical Center and Excelsior College. It assists working, self-directed employees to obtain specialized degrees, expand their career potential, and enhance the quality of health care in the community. Project Learn offers degree information, student advisement, program planning, study group facilitation, learning resources guidance, financial-aid information, and on-campus courses. 262-4067.

OTHER EDUCATIONAL VENTURES

Knowledge Network, 19 Aviation Rd., Albany, is the largest continuing education program in the region. Established in 1981, the company publishes a monthly catalogue with more than 100 courses in the areas of computer training, cooking, business, photography, mind & body, writing, sports, creative arts, and foreign languages. Knowledge Network has a practical approach: recruit talented practitioners and make their services accessible at reasonable times, places, and cost. Courses range from single-evening sessions to six-week semesters. Tuition: $39 to $150. 438-5669. www.knowledgenetwork.org

Empire State Youth Orchestra, 432 State St., Schenectady, was founded in 1979 to provide high-quality training for talented school-age musicians from the Capital Region. The orchestra plays regularly scheduled concerts at various venues in the area, as well as Tanglewood and Carnegie Hall. ESYO encompasses two full orchestras, six companion ensembles, the Youth Orchestra for training younger musicians, and a string-training program for inner-city children. This orchestra has influenced the lives of thousands of youngsters in hundreds of positive ways. Auditions are held yearly. More information is available through ESYO, 432 State St., Suite 217, and through Proctor's Theatre, 382-7581.

New York State Summer School of the Arts, State Education Dept., Albany, offers exciting and challenging summer-training programs to New York State students grades 8 to 12. Students work with internationally acclaimed artists and artistic companies at eight component schools – Ballet, Choral Studies, Dance, Jazz Studies, Media Arts, Orchestral Studies, Theater, and Visual Arts. The Ballet, Dance, Jazz and Orchestral Studies programs are held in Saratoga Springs. About 600 talented young artists are chosen by audition each year, and many go on to distinguished careers in the arts – as did Capital Region native and Grammy-nominated jazz musician Stephon Harris. NYSSSA is supported by the Office of the Governor and funded by the New York State Legislature. Applications are available through the Education Dept., or at the NYSSSA Web site. Tuition: $900-$1,350. 474-8773. www.emsc.nysed.gov/nysssa/

Cultural Education Center, Albany: New York State Museum, New York State Library, New York State Archives
Courtesy New York State Museum

LIBRARIES

The public libraries of the Capital Region are more than repositories of books and papers: They're a cultural force in the community and a gathering place for groups of varied interests. All the below libraries offer a wide range of services including free lectures and readings, local history and genealogy resources, inter-library loan, videos and audio books, and activities for youngsters. And all have a knowledgeable and helpful staff. Library cards for temporary residents are available.

PUBLIC LIBRARIES

Albany Main Library, 161 Washington Ave., is a comprehensive learning center, with for-use computers, for-loan art works, a large children's reading room, and the Albany Room (second floor), a research room for local, regional, and state history. Also on the second floor is the Albany Center Galleries. A café is on the main floor. Free computer training is offered Tuesdays 9:30am-11:30am (registration required). Live at the Library presents acoustic-music performances. Open Mon-Thurs. 9am-9pm; Fri. 9am-6pm; Sat. 9am-5pm; Sun. 1pm-5pm. 427-4300. www.albanypubliclibrary.org

Albany Branch Libraries (call for hours):

Delaware, 485 Delaware Ave. 463-0254
Howe Branch, Schuyler and Broad St. 472-9485
New Scotland, 369 New Scotland Ave. 482-6661
Pine Hills, 517 Western Ave. 482-7911

Troy Main Library, 100 Second St., is housed in a beautiful historic building (see Points of Interest, pg. 18) with stained-glass windows and marble sculpture. The library hosts a free Business Breakfast Series on the second Wednesday of the month in fall and spring, at 7:45 am. It also offers free computer classes (registration required), and "computer tutors" on Mondays, 6pm-8pm (also available at the Lansingburgh branch on Fridays 10am-1pm). Open Mon-Tues. 9am-9pm; Weds-Fri. 9am-5pm; Sat.10am-5pm (until 1pm in summer). 274-7071. www.uhls.org

Troy Branch Libraries (call for hours):

Lansingburgh, 114th St. and 4th Ave. 235-5310
Sycaway, Hoosick St. and Lee Ave. 274-1822

Schenectady Library, 99 Clinton St. (across from City Hall), has 20 for-use computers, and a very active children's room with a play area for toddlers. It houses the Small Business Information Center and hosts literacy volunteers. Open Mon-Thurs., 9am-9pm; Fri-Sat. 9am-5pm; Sun. 1pm-5pm. 388-4500. www.scpl.org

Schenectady Branch Libraries (call for hours):

Duane Branch, 1331 State St. 386-2242
Glenville, 20 Glenridge Rd. 386-2243
Hamilton Hill, 700 Cray St. 386-2244
Mont Pleasant, 1026 Crane St. 386-2245
Niskayuna, 2400 Nott St. East. 386-2249
Rotterdam, 1100 North Westcott Rd. 356-3440
Quaker Street, Bull St. & Rte. 7 895-2719
Scotia Branch, 14 Mohawk Ave. 382-3506
Woodlawn, 2 Sanford St. 382-3508

Saratoga Springs Public Library, Saratoga Springs, is part of the Southern Adirondack Library System. In 1995, it moved to a spacious building in Saratoga's historic downtown. The second floor houses the Saratoga Room, a research facility for the city's colorful history that contains books, photos, prints, and archival materials. The Activity Room hosts storytelling for toddlers. Book Bag, the library's popular used-book shop, also sells new works by local authors. Open Mon-Thurs., 9am-9pm; Fri. 9am-6pm; Sat. 9am-5pm; Sun. 11am-5pm. 584-7860. www.library.saratoga.ny.us.

The public libraries of the Capital Region invite residents and regular visitors to be Friends of the Library by making a small donation each year. Members receive a monthly calendar of events and notices of special programs. Many local libraries could not exist without Friends support.

SPECIALIZED LIBRARIES

Albany Institute of History and Art Library (formerly the McKinney Library), 125 Washington Ave., Albany, is a non-circulating repository of more than one million primary-source items related to the history of the Capital Region, and including photographs, manuscripts, architectural drawings, maps, broadsides, and ephemera – in addition to a collection of 1600s-1800s bibles from prominent Albany families. These materials augment the museum's collections of fine arts, decorative arts, and historical artifacts. Per-day fee is the $5 museum admission. Open by appointment only. 463-4478. www.albanyinstitute.org

New York State Archives, Cultural Education Center (*third floor), Madison Ave., Albany, shares a research room with the State Library. But this fascinating resource is not itself a library: it's a repository for learning with a mission to preserve community heritage, improve citizen access to records, and enrich educational and historical research. The archives hold 100 million original and unpublished documents, some of them over 350 years old, including photos, maps, film scripts, military-service records, adoption records, Native American records, and genealogical information. Materials must be viewed on site; calling in advance is recommended to best facilitate staff services. A workshop catalogue is available. Open Mon-Fri., 9am-5pm. Closed state holidays. Free. 474-8955. www.sara.nysed.gov

New York State Library, Cultural Education Center (*third floor), Madison Ave., Albany, is a research library serving the government and citizenship of New York state. Established in 1818, it is the nation's largest state library, and a leader in the use of technology to provide information services, with over 1,000 databases and electronic references. The collection of 20-million items includes rare books and manuscripts, and ranges from major holdings in state and federal documents to law, medicine, social sciences, art, American literature, and business. Materials are available for use within the building. Direct borrowing privileges are granted to permanent state employees, and resident attorneys and physicians. All other patrons may borrow material through inter-library loan. The Talking Book and Braile Library provides recorded books and magazines, and the equipment to play them, to the visually impaired. Open Mon-Fri., 9am-5pm. Closed state holidays. Free. 474-5355. www.nysl.nysed.gov

In 2003, after completion of a $7.5 million renovation, the State Library and Archives will move to the 11th floor.

ACADEMIC LIBRARIES

All of the colleges in the Capital District have libraries designed primarily to serve the needs of students and faculty but most are open to the general public as well. Some research privileges are restricted to students; visitors not affiliated with a college can inquire at the reference desk for services.

University at Albany libraries are the largest and most comprehensive in the region, and are ranked among the top 100 libraries in the country. In addition to the University Library are three specialized libraries that are also open to the public. Hours may change during college vacations so it's advisable to call ahead. http://library.albany.edu/

Thomas E. Dewey Graduate Library, Hawley Building, 135 Western Ave. (downtown campus), contains 130,000 volumes. Topical strengths include public administration, public policy, federal and state case and statutory law, social welfare policy, service and practice, criminology, and the criminal justice system. The library has traditional print resources and an array of electronic resources. Reference inquiries may be made in person at the reference desk, or over the phone. Individual consultations with subject specialists can be scheduled. 442-3693.

Hawley Hall was built in 1909 as part of the original state college, and is worth a visit for the 23 oil-painted panels by Tiffany Studios muralist William Van Ingen. These evocative scenes of early Albany and New York State history were created under the WPA and were recently restored. The hall is also adorned with early 20th-century stained-glass windows.]

M. E. Grenander Department of Special Collections and Archives, New Library Building (third floor), 1400 Washington Ave., is a repository for manuscripts, archives, original materials, and rare books – including 1700s European and American books and 1600s Hebrew and Judaic books. Among its rarified holdings are an Old Albany-related collection, a German-Intellectual Émigré collection, a Historical Children's Literature collection, and the University Archives, which date to 1844 and UAlbany's roots in the State Normal School. Exhibits from the special collections are mounted on a regular basis. 437-3935

Science Library, New Library Building, 1400 Washington Ave., is the largest library in the building, occupying three complete floors and housing 600,000 volumes. It includes collections for the departments of Atmospheric Sciences, Biological Sciences, Chemistry, Computer Science, Geology, Physics, and Mathematics and Statistics. Access to the full complement of networked resources is available from computer workstations. General reference resources can be found at the reference desk. Individual consultations with subject specialists can be scheduled. 437-3948.

Scribner Library at Skidmore College, 815 North Broadway, Saratoga Springs, has a general circulating collection of more than 300,000 books with strengths in literature, history, art, political science, and economics; as well as an extensive library of non-fiction videos, and holdings in federal and state government documents, maps and resources. The Special Collections and Archives includes a rare-book collection of contemporary American and European writers; a visual resources collection of almost 50,000 digital and analog images relating to art, dance, film and theater; and the Edna St. Vincent Millay collection. Exhibits from the special collections are mounted on a regular basis. 580-5000. www.skidmore.edu

The colleges of Union University have specialized collections available to the public on a non-circulating basis.

Albany College of Pharmacy Library
O'Brien Building, 106 New Scotland Ave.
Open Mon-Thurs. 8am-11pm. 445-7217.

Schaffer Law Library at the Albany Law School
80 New Scotland Ave.
Open Mon-Fri. 9am-5pm. 445-2340.

Schaffer Library of Health Sciences of Albany Medical College
47 New Scotland Ave.
Open Mon-Fri. 8am-5pm. 262-5530.

Albany Medical Center Hospital   *Photography by: Gary Gold*

HEALTH CARE

One of the greatest assets of the Capital Region is its exceptional roster
of sophisticated health care facilities, including three of the country's top 100
hospitals and one nationally renowned medical complex. It would not be
possible to describe all of the myriad health services the area has to offer; the
below entries cover major hospitals and clinics, and some special services.

Regional Poison Center 1-800-336-6997

EMERGENCY DEPARTMENTS

Albany

Albany Medical Center, 41 New Scotland Ave., Albany 262-3131
Albany Memorial Hospital, 600 Northern Blvd., Albany. 471-3111
St. Peter's Hospital, 315 South Manning Blvd., Albany 482-0125

Troy

St. Mary's Hospital, 1300 Massachusetts Ave., Troy 268-5697
Samaritan Hospital, 2215 Burdett Ave., Troy 271-3424

Schenectady

Ellis Hospital, 1101 Nott St., Schenectady. 243-4121
St. Clare's Hospital, 600 McClellan St., Schenectady 382-2222

Saratoga

Saratoga Hospital, 221 Church St., Saratoga Springs 583-8313

Albany Medical Center Health Sciences Complex encompasses a vast array
of specialized health-care services and clinics located throughout Albany County,
and is therefore listed ahead of the alphabetical sections of hospitals and
special-care services.

Albany Medical Center
41 New Scotland Ave., Albany, 262-3125
The AMC health-sciences complex is ranked among the highest quality medical facilities in the nation. The center integrates the many programs of Albany Medical Center Hospital (see below entry) with Albany Medical Center College – founded in 1839 as one of the country's first private medical schools. AMC has undergone a far-reaching expansion over the last few years; services now range from a unique pediatric intensive-care unit to the region's first heart-transplantation program. Serving 25 counties in northeastern New York and western New England, the center has earned numerous awards and accolades for its technological advances, delivery of clinical care, and education and research efforts. Recent state-of-the-art additions include the Department of Neurology, and the Institute for Vascular Health & Disease. AMC is also equipped with a heliopad: Look atop the 8-story patient tower and you're likely to see a rescue helicopter either landing or readying for take off. www.amc.edu

HOSPITALS

Albany

Albany Medical Center Hospital
43 New Scotland Ave., Albany, 262-3125
AMCH is a major academic medical institution and tertiary-care hospital equipped to treat the most seriously ill and injured patients. The hospital provides the most technologically advanced forms of clinical treatment and research. Components of the hospital include New York State's designated Regional Trauma Center, Perinatal Care Center, and AIDS Treatment Center, as well as a birth center, and kidney, bone-marrow, and pancreas transplantation programs. The Emergency Care Center is currently nearing completion of a $10.6 million expansion. One of the top 100 hospitals in the country, AMCH is renowned for its ability to combine innovative technology with patient-oriented care. Free cancer screenings and other screenings (vascular, colorectal) are held on a regular basis. www.amc.edu

Albany Memorial Hospital
600 Northern Blvd., Albany, 471-3221
Established in 1868, AMH is a 165-bed community hospital now at the forefront of acute care and ambulatory surgery. In addition to its highly regarded intensive care units, the hospital's services include the Heart Program, specializing in outpatient treatment of congestive heart failure; the Hand Rehabilitation Center for hand, arm, and neck disorders; and the Diabetes Treatment Center. AMH is also known for its kidney-stone treatment, and wound, ostomy, and skin care program.

Children's Hospital
41 New Scotland Ave. (Building A), Albany, 262-5588
A component of Albany Medical Center, this is the only hospital in the greater
Capital Region devoted exclusively to the treatment of youngsters. The 125-bed
facility brings together the full array of pediatric, medical, and surgical specialties –
including 80 full-time physicians trained in 34 subspecialties – essential to caring
for critically ill children. Services range from healthy-child programs to open-heart
surgery and stem-cell and bone-marrow transplants, as well as accommodations
for family members to stay overnight. The hospital is affiliated with five specialty
pediatric clinics located in Albany County.

Child's Geriatric Organization
25 Hackett Blvd., Albany, 292-1300
Founded in 1972, Child's Nursing Home was originally affiliated with the
adjacent Child's Hospital, which is now a part of Albany Medical Center. Child's
today combines the services of a hospital and a nursing home into a non-profit
geriatric facility consisting of a rehabilitative hospital, a long-term home-health
program, and a licensed home-health care agency serving 18 counties.
www.childsgeriatric.org

St. Peter's Hospital
315 South Manning Blvd., Albany, 525-1550
Founded in 1869 by the Sisters of Mercy, St. Peter's today is a technologically
advanced medical complex ranked among the top 100 cardiac hospitals in the
country, and the first in New York State. St. Peter's also provides an integrated
continuum of care from birth center to hospice. The hospital's many components
include the state-of-the-art Breast Center, sophisticated emergency services,
two long-term nursing-care facilities, and St. Peter's Addiction Recovery Center.
Called SPARC, the center is a medically supervised, 40-bed facility offering
inpatient detoxification and rehabilitation, multi-disciplinary treatment, and
individualized patient support. SPARC is located in Guilderland (458-8888).
www.stpetershealthcare.org

Stratton VA Medical Center Hospital
113 Holland Ave., Albany, 626-5000
Opened in 1951, Stratton VA is the only veteran's hospital in the region, providing
comprehensive inpatient care and a full range of outpatient services to military
veterans within a 100-mile radius. Acute- and intermediate-care beds for 90 patients
are augmented by the primary-care program, which extends to 12 community
clinics. A recognized cancer center, "the VA" also specializes in cardiac rehabilitation,
nuclear medicine, post-traumatic stress disorder, compensated work therapy,
geriatric services, and hospice care, as well as diagnostic laboratory medicine.
A helpful veterans' service center is located on the first floor.

Troy

St. Mary's Hospital
1300 Massachusetts Ave., Troy, 268-5000
St. Mary's originated in the 1840s, when the Daughters of Charity provided assistance to fever-stricken immigrants. In 1995, the hospital merged with the equally venerable Leonard Hospital, creating one of the finest community facilities in the area. In 2000, St. Mary's was ranked as one of the top 100 hospitals in the country for its new intensive-care unit, located in the specially designed DePaul wing. In addition to a comprehensive surgical center, other specialty centers include cardiac, oncology, diabetes, and alcohol detox and rehabilitation. The new wing also includes a pediatric unit and an 8-room childbirth center. St. Mary's is the anchor location for Seton Health, an integrated outpatient network providing more than 20 health-care facilities throughout the Capital Region. www.setonhealth.org

Samaritan Hospital
2215 Burdett Ave., Troy, 271-3300
Samaritan opened in 1898 in the Troy Orphan's Asylum, and moved a few years later to its present location at the corner of Burdett and Peoples Avenues. A community hospital with a 238-bed capability, Samaritan provides a full range of services, including emergency, diabetes, wound/skin, cardiology/stroke, behavioral health, and maternity and women's-health services. It also contains a sleep lab. Samaritan, Albany Memorial Hospital, and Eddy Cohoes Rehabilitation are components of Northeast Health, a non-profit network that operates several primary-care clinics in the Capital Region. www.nehealth.org

Schenectady

Bellevue Women's Hospital
2210 Troy Rd., Niskayuna, 346-9400
Founded in 1931, Bellevue is the only women's health facility in the Northeast providing medical, surgical, and obstetrical services to women of all ages. The 40-bed, non-profit hospital is augmented by several specialized centers of advanced care, including the BreastCare Center, with services ranging from mammography to reconstructive breast surgery; a high-tech neonatal center with neonatalists on staff 24 hours a day; and ten state-of-the-art family birthing suites. Other services include colorectal screening, osteoporosis screening and prevention, and alternative-medicine practices such as acupressure, shiatsu, and biofeedback. The hospital is also home to a sophisticated fertility clinic, the Capital Region Genetics & IVF Center (see below entry). Bellevue has received national recognition and rates extremely high in customer-satisfaction surveys. (the web site contains an easy-to-use health information resource.) www.bellevuewoman.com

Ellis Hospital
1101 Nott St., Schenectady, 243-4000
Founded over 100 years ago, Ellis today is a non-profit, 368-bed teaching hospital, equipped with an unusually wide scope of services for a community facility. Ellis is known for its treatment of the most critically ill patients. The hospital includes a highly regarded heart center for cardiac surgery, a neurological unit, and a women's health center, and offers oncology treatment, sports medicine, and geriatric services. Adjacent to the hospital is Ellis' residential, 82-bed skilled-nursing facility, which specializes in complex cases.

St. Clare's Hospital
600 McClellan St., Schenectady, 382-2000
Established in 1949, St. Clare's is a multi-purpose, 200-bed hospital. In addition to general medical care, it specializes in physical therapy, cardiac and pulmonary rehabilitation, wound care, and sleep disorders. The hospital also includes a birthing center and a new surgical facility. www.stclares.com

Sunnyview Rehabilitation Hospital
1270 Belmont Ave., Schenectady, 382-4500
Founded in 1928, Sunnyview is one of the largest and most comprehensive rehabilitation facilities in the Northeast, serving both children and adults in 22 counties and beyond. The caring, committed staff includes subspecialized physicians, rheumatologists, physiatrists, and doctoral-level psychologists and specialty nurses. A state-of-the-art facility, Sunnyview has been recognized by *US News and World Report* as one of the nation's top 50 hospitals for rheumatology. In addition to the treatment of rheumatoid arthritis, osteoarthritis, osteoporosis, lupus, and degenerative joint diseases, the hospital also specializes in rehab programs for brain/trauma, pulmonary/cardiac, spinal-cord injuries, and sports injuries. Sunnyview is equipped for all stages of rehabilitation, from acute care to re-entry into the community, and is also known for its hand therapy, treatment of swallowing/nutrition disorders, and orthopedics. Adjunct therapies such as water therapy, chair yoga, and driver training assist in the attainment of maximum function. Sunnyview offers extensive outpatient services, and is located adjacent to Ellis Hospital, which provides emergency support.

Saratoga
Four Winds Hospital
30 Crescent Ave., Saratoga Springs, 584-3600
This private, home-like facility provides high-quality inpatient, outpatient, and intermediate mental-health treatment to children, adolescents, and adults. Located on 26-landscaped acres, FWH contains an 88-bed facility and three cottage settings. It utilizes a multidisciplinary approach that involves a range of professionals from psychiatrists to expressive-art teachers. The hospital specializes in providing safe and caring treatment of youngsters, in addition to individualized programs for substance abuse, eating disorders, and trauma/abuse issues. www.fourwindshospital.com

Saratoga Hospital
211 Church St., Saratoga Springs, 587-3222
Founded in 1891 as a 20-bed community hospital by a group of local women, SH gradually expanded into today's 243-bed facility with 160 staff physicians, an intensive-care unit, and the capability to treat almost every medical condition. In addition to programs for 30 specialties, this non-profit hospital contains a women's-health center, the state-of-the-art Same Day Surgery Center, and the Hearing Shop, which offers medically integrated audiology services. The hospital's outpatient care is augmented by Wilton Medical Arts, home to some of the most advanced diagnostic equipment in the region (580-2273).

SPECIAL CARE SERVICES

Capital District Psychiatric Center
75 New Scotland Ave., Albany, 447-9611
CDPC is a state-run facility providing inpatient treatment and rehabilitation
to patients with serious and persistent mental-illness diagnoses. Outpatient
services for children, adolescents, and adults include an adolescent crisis
residence, two adult community residences, and three adolescent day-treatment
programs. CDPC is located adjacent to the Albany Medical Center and serves
a nine-county area.

Capital Region Genetics & IVF Center
2210 Troy Rd., Niskayuna, 346-9400
Located at Bellevue Women's Hospital, this sophisticated fertility clinic has a
30-percent success rate – considerably higher than the national average. Services
include infertility diagnoses, in-vitro fertilization, intracytoplasmic sperm injection,
cryopreservation, intrauterine insemination, a donor egg program, and a support
group. The center is affiliated with the internationally respected Genetics and
IFV Institute in Fairfax, VA.

Center for the Disabled
314 Manning Blvd., Albany, 489-8336
Founded in 1942 as a small nursery school for children with cerebral palsy,
CFTD has grown into a non-profit regional provider for 300 different disability
diagnoses. In addition to educational, vocational, and residential programs, the
center provides a full array of progressive medical services for disabled people
of all ages. Specialized primary-care programs include pediatrics, family care,
internal medicine, dentistry, and women's health, plus auxiliary services ranging
from audiology to optometry. New in 2002 is the Multiple Sclerosis Care Center;
other new opportunities include aquatic therapy, and specialized neurological
care (including epilepsy care) in affiliation with Albany Medical Center. On-call,
24-hour emergency service is available. www.centercares.org
    St. Margaret's Center for Children, 27 Hackett Blvd., Albany, 591-3300.
Founded in 1883 as part of the Episcopal Diocese of Albany, St. Margaret's is
a skilled nursing facility providing expert clinical care to individuals with very
severe disabilities. The center is the only long-term care facility in the state
devoted exclusively to medically fragile infants, children, and young adults.
The center's Daylight Adult Day Care is an innovative health program for
people 21 and older with various chronic conditions and disabilities. Daylight
offers a unique opportunity for clients to participate in social, medical, and
therapy programs in the company of their peers.

Eddy Cohoes Rehabilitation Center
421 West Columbia St., Cohoes, 238-4069
Established in 1989, "the Eddy" is the only physical rehab center in the state
devoted exclusively to caring for adults 55 years-of-age and older who have
experienced bone fractures, arthritis, strokes, amputations, and other serious
impairments. The 94-bed main facility provides two levels of care previously not
available to the senior population: an acute-care rehab program for those who
may benefit from short-term, intensive treatment; and a skilled-nursing rehab
program for those whose other health conditions require a less intensive treatment
approach. Services include physical and occupational therapy, speech/language,
medical treatment, and recreational therapy. Additional services to help individuals
regain independent functioning and maximize quality of life include driver
assessment and community re-entry skills. Outpatient medical treatment,
rehabilitation, and social day services are available.

Marjorie Doyle Rockwell Center, located on the Eddy Cohoes campus, is a
high-quality residential facility devoted exclusively to individuals with Alzheimer's
disease and other dementias (238-4150).

Ronald McDonald House of Albany
139 South Lake Ave., Albany, 438-2655
Ronald McDonald Charities is a nationwide network of houses customized and
staffed to serve as a home-away-from-home for families of seriously ill children
who are being treated at area medical centers. The Albany House is located in
two connected Victorian houses close to Albany Medical Center, and contains
16 guest rooms, living areas, a play room, a train room, and kitchens. The House
provides a place for ill children to play, while offering comfort, support, and
respite to their families. Serving over 500 families a year from 35 counties, the
staff is augmented by many volunteers. Suggested donation is $10 per night.
www.rmhofalbany.org

Planned Parenthood, Inc.
1-800-230-PLAN
A national non-profit organization, Planned Parenthood provides professional
medical examinations and counseling, medically supervised contraception,
infertility services, abortion referrals, pregnancy tests, STD and HIV testing,
rape-crisis intervention, biopsies, prenatal care, family-planning services, and
education on sexual responsibility. The organization maintains seven clinics
in the four-county region, call for locations.

Visiting Nurse Associations of Albany/Rensselaer, Schenectady, and Saratoga Counties

35 Colvin Ave., Albany... 489-2681
108 Erie Blvd., Schenectady 382-7932
634 Plank Rd., Clifton Park 371-0890

Since 1919, the VNA has helped patients in need of home nursing skills. Today, these skills encompass a full range of services, managed by a nurse or therapist under the physician's orders. Patients not only receive individualized care, available 24-hours daily, but also the education and assistance necessary to help meet the challenges of an illness or injury. Whether the prognosis is for a full recovery, the condition chronic, or the illness terminal, the VNA will be there. The association is partly funded by donations.

Caring Connection is a VNA affiliate offering additional services to customize patient care. Qualified visiting professionals range from speech therapists to nutritionists (584-3702).

INFORMATION & RESOURCES

The capital city, Albany, is a comfortably sized city of around 100,000 people, conveniently located 143 miles north of New York City, 165 miles west of Boston, and 220 miles south of Montreal. Albany is the center of the Capital Region, a metropolitan community of approximately 875,000 people, composed of Albany, Rensselaer, and Schenectady Counties. In recent years, however, it has come to include Saratoga County – and is often designated as the Capital-Saratoga Region. Within the four counties, you can move in a short amount of time from historic downtowns to rural farmland to pristine wilderness – a wondrous geography that encompasses a rare pitch-pine barrens and estuaries with bald eagles.

Although definitions of "the Greater Capital Region" vary, for general purposes it's agreed that the area is comprised of seven counties (Albany, Columbia, Rensselaer, Saratoga, Schenectady, Washington, and Schoharie) and seven cities (Albany, Troy, Watervliet, Cohoes, Schenectady, Rensselaer, and Saratoga Springs). For travel and tourism purposes, the designation of "greater" also includes southern Vermont and western Massachusetts. Both areas are less than an hour's drive away.

This chapter has two parts. The first part is on the media: whether a daily newspaper or the telephone directory, the media is the most immediate source of information. The second part describes the resources most likely to be of value to new residents, including some of the many organizations that benefit or help to maintain the region's unique and enjoyable characteristics.

Visitors may want to start with "Tourism" at the end of the chapter (pg. 329).

THE MEDIA

Newspapers
Daily Gazette, 2345 Maxon Rd., Schenectady, has been a family-owned local newspaper for over a century. It covers the Capital Region with a focus on Schenectady County. 374-4141. www.dailygazette.com

Metroland, 4 Central Ave., Albany, 4th floor, is an alternative news-and-arts weekly covering the greater Capital Region. Published by its editor-in-chief, a local resident, this free paper comes out every Thursday, and contains comprehensive calendar listings of the week's events. Metroland can be found at numerous retail and restaurant outlets, and in the lobby of 4 Central Ave. 463-2500. www.metroland.net

The Record, 501 Broadway, Troy, is published by the Journal Register Company and covers Rensselaer County. The Thursday edition contains Stepping Out, an arts and leisure supplement. The Record has been serving the Troy community for over 100 years. 272-1200.

The Saratogian, 20 Lake Ave., Saratoga Springs, is published by the Journal Register Company and covers Saratoga County. 584-4242. www.saratogian.com

Community News, Clifton Corporate Park, is a weekly paper by the same publisher. It covers news and events concerning southern Saratoga County. 371-7108.

Times Union, Box 15000, Albany, is published by Capital Newspapers, a subsidiary of the Hearst corporation. It covers the greater Capital Region, with specialized geographic editions available. The Thursday edition includes Preview, a weekly arts and entertainment supplement; and Automotive Weekly, a digest on automotive matters. Extensive real estate and classified sections are published daily. With a circulation of over 100,000, "the T.U." is the largest newspaper in the area. 454-5694. www.timesunion.com

Regional Magazines

Adirondack Life is an interesting magazine with magnificent photography. Published bi-monthly, it covers the natural resources, arts and crafts, recreation, history, and conservation of the Adirondack Mountains region. Subscriptions are $21.95 per year. 1-800-877-5530. www.adirondacklife.com

The Conservationist is an engaging and informative family magazine published bimonthly by the New York State Department of Environmental Conservation. It covers topical issues related to wildlife, waterways, fishing, hiking, hunting, recreation, and children's nature studies. Subscriptions are $12 per year. 402-8047. www.dec.state.ny.us

Hudson Valley, 40 Garden St., Poughkeepsie, is a lively, informative, and beautifully photographed magazine published for over 30 years by a local family. It covers the culture, lifestyle, recreation, environment, history, arts, people, and events of the Hudson River Valley from Yonkers to Troy. Subscriptions are $14.95 per year. (800) 783-4903. www.hudsonvalleymagazine.com

Special Interest Publications

The Business Review, 2 Computer Drive West, Albany, provides news and information (most of it exclusive) about businesses and the business community in northeastern New York. It also supplies classifieds and "fresh business leads." Subscription includes the paper's annual prospecting tool, *The Book of Lists*. Subscriptions are $80 per year. 437-9855. www.bizjournals.com

The Evangelist, 46 North Main St., Albany, is published by the Albany Roman Catholic Diocese, and covers the greater Capital Region. It carries local and national news regarding the Catholic Church, in addition to features, columns, scripture, and a community calendar. 453-6688.

The Jewish World, 1104 Central Ave., Albany, is published by a local owner. It comes out every Thursday and covers news and features of interest to the Jewish community of the greater Capital Region. "The World" is available at some newsstands. Subscriptions are $23 per year, $26 for residents outside of Albany County. 459-8455.

New York Archives is a quarterly magazine published by the Archives Partnership Trust. It features articles utilizing the New York State Archives by authors, scholars, and journalists, and includes practical tips on preserving family documents and "finding those elusive ancestors." The evocative cover art is distinguished by historic photographs from the Archive collection. Subscriptions are available through membership in the Trust, $35 per year. 473-7091. www.nyarchives.org

Want Ad Digest, 870 Hoosick Rd., Troy, is a weekly classified-ad handbook covering upstate New York, Vermont, and western Massachusetts. In operation since 1962, it can be found at most retail magazine racks. Subscriptions are $182 per year, half-year rates are available. 279-1181.

Public Radio

WAMC-Northeast Public Radio (90.3 FM), Albany, is a non-profit, listener-supported station, and the second largest producer of public-radio programming in the country. It airs a wide variety of programming throughout the greater Capital Region, including local and national news shows and several live-broadcast music shows, such as the Boston Symphony (weekends, July-Aug.), and regularly scheduled local performances. Other music shows range from Afropop (Sun., 8pm) to jazz (Sun., midnight). Two of the station's most popular programs are "Capital Connection," a provocative forum on New York State government (Fri., 8:30pm), and "Hudson River Sampler," a folk-music show (Sat., 8pm-10pm). Listeners can attend live tapings at the WAMC Performing Arts Studio (see Arts and Venues, pg. 48). 465-5233. www.wamc.org

WMHT (89.1 FM), Schenectady, is a member-supported station broadcasting news and music programs throughout the greater Capital Region. A sampling of the weekly schedule includes BBC Global News at 6pm, "A Singer's Notebook," "The American Sound," "Brave New Music," "The Grand Piano," and the very popular "No Ticket Required," which airs excerpts from regional concert performances. 356-1700. www.wmht.org

WMHT-Rise is a 24-hour radio information service for the blind and print disabled. It transmits on a subcarrier of the main WMHT-FM signal through a specially-tuned receiver, giving listeners access to readings of local and national periodicals, books, and special programming. Receivers are loaned free of charge to eligible applicants. 357-1700. www.wmht.org

Television

Five local stations are available to all Capital Region residences:

Channel 6, WRGB, an affiliate of CBS.
Channel 10, WTEN, an affiliate of ABC.
Channel 13, WNYT, an affiliate of NBC.
Channel 17, WMHT, an affiliate of PBS.
Channel 23, WXXA, an affiliate of FOX.

WMHT Education Telecommunications (Channel 17), Schenectady, broadcasts a variety of quality local programming, including weeknight shows on organic cooking, health advice, state politics, and area happenings and attractions. The station's educational series and award-winning local documentaries are highly recommended. 357-1700. www.wmht.org

Maps

Chambers of Commerce (see pg. 321) provide free maps of their cities and counties.

Hudson River Waterfront Map is a waterproof, easy-to-read map of the river from New York harbor to the federal dam in Troy. It marks the locations of marinas, boat-launch sites, riverside towns, historic attractions, waterfront restaurants, and public campgrounds. The waterfront map is available for free from the New York State Division of Tourism. (800) 232-4782.

Jimapco, 2095 Rte. 9, Round Lake, creates and publishes a large assortment of city, county, and regional maps, including a state atlas, road maps, and recreational maps for hiking, fishing, camping, and boating. Owned and operated by a local family, the company's geography includes most of New York, Vermont, Massachusetts, and New Hampshire. Jimapco maps are known far and wide for their accuracy and ease of usage. The Jimapco store, at the same address, also sells hundreds of national and international maps, plus globes, compasses, mapping accessories, books, and interactive CD-Rom maps. In addition to the store, these maps are available at numerous retail outlets (including Stewart's Shops), and can be ordered online. 899-5091. www.jimapco.com

Mapquest is the first consumer-focused, interactive mapping site on the web, providing reliable maps and driving directions for millions of locations. Customers simply enter an address to easily access location markers, find places of interest, and customize road-trip plans. Many of the web sites in this guide contain Mapquest maps, which can be accessed through an array of mobile devices, including Internet-ready cell phones, wireless modems, and PDAs. www.mapquest.com

Web Sites

Capital District Regional Planning Commission provides detailed information on the region's municipalities, demographics, employment, education, taxes, and elected officials. www.cdrpc.org

New York State Citizens Guide provides online access to state services, answers to state-related questions, and information on state licenses, taxes, recreation, and tourism. www.nysegov.com

INFORMATION 411
Weather and Time 782-1111

RESOURCES

Business Development

Center for Economic Growth, 63 State St., Albany, is a private, non-profit, business-supported organization dedicated to developing and promoting regional efforts to attract high-tech talent and companies, and to providing innovative services to bolster local businesses. CEG assists local manufacturing and technology companies with effective strategies for increasing productivity, and by providing cost-effective solutions. The CEG web site posts business news and events, job openings, press releases, and links to area businesses and services. 465-8975. www.ceg.org

Downtown Albany Business Improvement District, 522 Broadway, is a non-profit, private-public partnership whose mission is to restore, promote, and maintain the viability of downtown Albany, and to improve the quality of life for all those who live, work and visit the capital city. The BID's activities range from improvements to the infrastructure to providing grants to merchants for exterior improvements. 465-2143.

Downtown Schenectady Improvement Corp., 433 State St., is a city-county development group helping to spearhead the city's downtown revitalization. The group promotes business expansions and renovations, works to attract investment and new ventures, and initiates public projects for beautification and maintenance, such as road and sidewalk improvements. 377-9430.

Hudson River Economics Group, 270 River St., Troy, serves small businesses and municipalities by offering economic, marketing, and management consulting services, in addition to financial forecasting, research and analysis. 272-1853.

Lark Street Neighborhood District Management Association, 245 Lark St., Albany, works to improve the business climate, arts and culture, and structural aesthetics of this historic neighborhood, which is home to over 60 restaurants, shops, services, and galleries. The Business Improvement District supervises the street's many happenings, such as Lark Fest and Holiday Lights on Lark. It also publishes a quarterly newsletter and maintains an informative web site with a calendar of events. 434-3861. www.larkstreet.org

Saratoga Convention & Tourism Bureau, 10 Railroad Place, provides information on seasonal events, group-tour and convention planning, food and beverage services, and business services. The bureau maintains the Saratoga Springs Convention Center and publishes a meeting-planners guide. 584-1531. www.discoversaratoga.org

Chambers of Commerce

The region's chambers of commerce operate a variety of programs to facilitate the participation of their members within the community; to develop the leadership skills of local executives and merchants; and to enhance connections between business and education organizations. Chamber personnel work in cooperation with regional economic development resources and advocate for their areas with state and local government. Chamber memberships confer benefits in advertising and promotion, networking, and inclusion in special programs.

Albany-Colonie Regional Chamber of Commerce
107 Washington Ave., Albany, 431-1400
1 Computer Drive South, Colonie, 458-9851
www.ac-chamber.org

Cohoes Chamber of Commerce
169 Mohawk Ave., Cohoes, 237-1766
www.cohoeschamber.com

Rensselaer County Regional Chamber of Commerce
31 Second St., Troy, 274-7020
www.rensccochamber.com

Saratoga County Chamber of Commerce
28 Clinton St., Saratoga Springs, 584-3255
www.saratoga.org

Schenectady County Chamber of Commerce
306 State St., Schenectady, 372-5656
www.schenectadychamber.org

Employment

The Region's Top Ten Private-Sector Employers in order of size:

General Electric Co.
Albany Medical Center
Golub Corp. (Price Chopper)
Northeast Health
Mercycare Corp.
KAPL Inc. (Naval research and development)
KeyCorp.
Hannaford Bros.
Stewart's Ice Cream Co. Inc.
Niagara Mohawk Power Corp.

Environmental Protection

Environmental Clearing House of Schenectady, 2858 Aqueduct Rd.,
Niskayuna, is a member-supported, volunteer organization providing outdoor
education and information about environmental issues. ECOS offers numerous
activities designed to raise awareness of environmental topics, including nature
classes, wildflower and fall-foliage walks, weekend ski trips and field trips,
and an annual Mohawk River clean-up. It publishes a monthly newsletter with
a calendar of events, as well as a catalogue of books, including the excellent
Natural Areas series of regional outdoor guidebooks. 370-4125.

Nature Conservancy Eastern New York Chapter, 200 Broadway (3rd floor), Troy, was chartered in 1954. It manages dozens of nature preserves throughout eastern New York, conserving a magnificent variety of ecosystems and species, as well as working with businesses, communities, and people to balance growth and protection. Unique regional habitats under the eastern chapter's stewardship include the Albany Pine Bush, the Barberville Falls in Poestenkill, Wilton Wildlife Preserve & Park, the Mill Creek Marsh in Stuyvesant, and the Christman Sanctuary in Schenectady County. For information, directions, or a copy of the chapter's preserve guide, call 272-0195.

Save the Pine Bush is a volunteer, non-profit organization dedicated to saving the Albany Pine Bush, a globally rare, pitch-pine and scrub-oak barrens located near Crossgates Mall between Albany and Guilderland. The group battles development by forcing the government to follow environmental-preservation law. Founded in 1978, SPB has been pivotal in the conservation of this unique and beautiful ecosystem (see Recreation and Sports, pg. 158), which is home to many endangered species, including the famous Karner Blue Butterfly. The group sponsors seasonal nature hikes, and dinners with guest speakers. For more information or to make a donation, contact the Social Justice Center, 33 Central Ave., Albany, 434-4037. www.albanypinebush.org

Scenic Hudson Inc., founded in 1963, is a nonprofit environmental organization and separately incorporated land trust dedicated to protecting and enhancing the scenic, natural, historic, agricultural, and recreational treasures of the Hudson River and its valley. The group's victorious battle to save Storm King Mountain from a Con Edison proposal to build one of the world's largest hydroelectric plants is credited with launching the grass-roots environmental movement. To date, Scenic Hudson has protected 17,700 acres of land in nine counties, and created or enhanced 28 parks and preserves for public enjoyment, including the viewscapes of Olana (see Not Far Away pg. 254). (845) 473-4440. www.scenichudson.org

Sierra Club Hudson-Mohawk Group is the local arm of the largest and strongest grass-roots conservation organization in the country. The Hudson Mohawk Group has more than 2500 members from the greater Capital Region, and as with the parent club, the group's purpose is to explore, enjoy, and protect the area's natural resources. Membership offers information from the national level, enjoyable programs on environmental topics, popular group outings, participation in advocacy efforts, and subscriptions to the award-winning national publication, *Sierra*, the state chapter's *Sierra Atlantic* newspaper, and the Hudson-Mohawk Group newsletter. 393-7100.

Historic Preservation

Central Park Rose Garden Restoration Committee, 40 Puritan Dr., Schenectady, is a grass-roots group that plants, protects, expands, and conserves the park's beautiful rose gardens. 355-5798.

Historic Albany Foundation, 89 Lexington Ave., Albany, is a non-profit organization founded by residents in 1974 to promote and advocate for the appreciation and preservation of architecture in the Albany area. HAF programs include technical assistance and free preservation workshops. The Parts Warehouse supplies architectural salvage parts from doorknobs to doorways. HAF maintains an inventory of vacant historic buildings and is involved in the stabilization of historic structures such as Arbor Hill's magnificent St. Joseph's Church. 465-0876. www.historic-albany.org

Hudson-Mohawk Industrial Gateway, foot of Polk St., Troy, is a non-profit educational corporation located in the Burden Iron Works Museum. The Gateway advocates for the preservation and promotion of the 19th-century industrial heritage and architecture of the communities at the confluence of the Hudson and Mohawk Rivers. It provides consulting on industrial history and preservation issues, in addition to conducting interpretive guided tours, day trips, and river cruises highlighting the area's age of enterprise. Some of the more popular tours feature Meneely bells, Tiffany windows, and Oakwood Cemetery. 254-5267. www.troyvisitorcenter.org

Preservation League of New York State, 44 Central Ave., Albany, is dedicated to preserving the state's irreplaceable heritage of historic buildings, districts, and landscapes. Founded in 1974, the non-profit league provides technical and legal expertise, produces informative publications, serves as a resource center for organizations and individuals, raises community awareness of the economic and aesthetic benefits of historic structures, and represents the cause of historic preservation in the halls of government. 462-5658. www.preserveny.org

Saratoga Springs Preservation Foundation, 117 Grand Ave., Saratoga Springs, preserves and protects the historic heritage of the city by maintaining and enhancing its architecture, culture, and landscapes while providing education and promoting community involvement. The non-profit foundation was established in 1977; today, Saratoga Springs has six National Historic Districts and over 1,000 historic structures, including the Saratoga Race Track (see Points of Interest, pg. 31). The city has been nationally recognized for its preservationist endeavors and historical ambience. The foundation sponsors walking tours and social events throughout the year. 587-5030. www.saratogapreservation.org

Washington Park Conservancy was formed in 1985 by a group of local citizens to restore, protect, and promote this beautiful and historic Albany park (see Points of Interest, pg. 13). The group's primary task is the implementation of a comprehensive master plan to assure the park's future for generations to come; it also raises funds for improvements and plantings. For information, write to Washington Park Conservancy, P.O. Box 1145, Albany, 12201.

Pets

Animal Protective Foundation of Schenectady, Inc., 53 Maple Ave., Scotia, was established in 1931 for the purpose of eliminating pet overpopulation and animal suffering, and to enhance human-animal relations through education. The foundation operates a state-of-the-art facility equipped to provide maximum care to animals in need, along with a quality adoption center and "the Pet Mobile," a veterinary clinic-on-wheels. Among the shelter's services are extensive pre-adoption care, tattoo and microchip owner IDs, and dog-obedience classes. The foundation creates engaging public outreach programs such as the summertime "Pet Professor" program for kids, and the annual Fireplug 500 Walk for Animals (see Seasonal, pg. 198). 374-3944. www.animalprotective.org

Mohawk & Hudson River Humane Society, 1 Oakland Ave., Menands, has as its motto: "Saving every living creature since 1887." The society takes in stray, abandoned, and injured animals from Albany, Rensselaer, Schenectady, and Columbia Counties. It provides healthy dogs and cats for adoption; adoptees are spayed or neutered, wormed, and vaccinated. The society works with animal rescue groups, and has a peace officer to handle animal cruelty cases. The shelter also offers weekly dog-obedience classes, a grooming center, periodic rabies clinics ($5), and a canine memorial and burial site. Open Mon-Sat., 10am-4:30pm. 434-8128. www.capital.net

Pet Smart is a socially responsible, national pet-store chain. The three area stores offer adoption clinics, animal-wellness clinics, and grooming centers. A percentage of the proceeds are donated to local animal-welfare groups.

161 Washington Ave. Ext., Albany 452-5683
609 Troy Schenectady Rd., Latham 785-4621
3033 Rte. 50, Saratoga 580-9374

Whiskers Animal Benevolent League, Albany, is a small, volunteer-run, no-kill animal shelter dealing primarily with stray, abused, and abandoned felines. The league provides assistance with spaying and neutering, a pet-friendly landlord list, and socialized, healthy animals for adoption. The web site (updated daily) has postings for lost and found animals and pictures of adoptables. 448-9565. www.albany.net

Senior Citizen

Albany County Department for the Aging. 447-7177
Rensselaer County Department for the Aging 270-2730
Schenectady County Department for the Aging. 382-8481
Saratoga County Office for the Aging. 884-4100

Lake George Factory Outlets (see Shopping, pg. 99) has Senior Day every Tuesday, offering additional savings to shoppers age 65 and over.

Golden Parks Program provides for residents age 62 and older (with a New York State driver's or non-driver's license) to obtain free vehicle access to all state parks and arboretums, and fee reductions at state historic sites and state-operated swimming, golf, boating and tennis facilities. 474-0456, 486-1899 (TDD). www.nysparks.state.ny

Seniors Connect @ the Library, Albany Public Library, 161 Washington Ave., provides free computer classes to senior citizens. Class size is limited to 12; reservations required. 427-4303.

Senior Sundays at Corning Riverfront Preserve, Maiden Lane, Albany, offer a leisurely summer afternoon with picnic food, live entertainment, and river breezes. These social gatherings attract an average of 400 people on scheduled Sundays during July and August. For more information, call 465-3325.

TECHNOLOGY

Albany Nano Tech, 251 Fuller Rd., Albany, is a fully integrated resource for research and development, prototyping, pilot manufacturing, and education that manages a strategic portfolio of state-of-the-art laboratories, supercomputers and shared-user facilities, in addition to an array of research centers. Established in 1993 and operated under the University at Albany, ANT now works with over 100 companies worldwide, accelerating the commercialization of technologies by offering a one-stop-shop for technology development assistance. 437-8686. www.albanynanotech.org

CESTM (Center for Environmental Sciences and Technology Management), 251 Fuller Rd., Albany, is a comprehensive research facility that supports a high-tech business incubator specializing in start-up companies in the high-tech field. CESTM operates under the University at Albany. 437-8686. www.albanynanotech.org

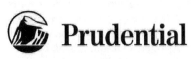

Rensselaer Technology Park, 385 Jordan Rd., North Greenbush, is a university-related park for technology ventures seeking a unique environment focused on the interface between industry and education. Park companies can access the physical and human resources of Rensselaer Polytechnic Institute; in turn, faculty and students can use the park's facilities as a "living laboratory." The scenic "RPI Tech Park" encompasses 1,250 acres and 2,300 employees. 283-7102. www.rpi.edu.org

Science & Technology Law Center, 385 Jordan Rd., North Greenbush, was established by Albany Law School in 1998 as a resource in regard to the legal issues critical to forming and retaining high-tech industries in New York State, while working to establish the area as a center of excellence for technology-related legal research and expertise. The center specializes in university-industry partnerships and offers discounted legal services and advice to emerging technology companies. 283-8890. www.als.edu

Tech Valley Software Alliance was initiated to respond to the needs of the growing software industry in the Capital Region – which now includes more than 250 technology companies and more than $300 million in sales and revenues. Local software companies, in partnership with the Center for Economic Growth and area colleges and universities, have made it their mission to grow the software industry to $1 billion in sales by the year 2004. The alliance is steered by a committee comprised of the region's leading software executives. 465-8974. www.ceg.org

University at Albany East Campus, East Greenbush, located in the former Sterling Winthrop complex, brings together modern office space and high-tech labs in a setting that maximizes the region's research and development strengths. The campus' mixed-purpose buildings provide an interactive environment for uniting UAlbany's education, scientific, and economic development capabilities with those of industry and other research institutions. 402-0283. www.albany.edu

TOURISM

Albany Visitor's Guide is available by calling or stopping in at the Albany Heritage Area Visitors Center, 25 Quackenbush Square. The center also supplies the annual *New York State Travel Guide*. Fall foliage reports and winter ski conditions can be accessed at the web site. 434-0405. www.albany.org

Albany City Trolley operates out of Quackenbush Square, and offers three different narrated tours; the Downtown Tour, the Historic Homes Tour, and the Historic Cathedrals Tour (see Points of Interest, pg. 12, 13). Adults $10, seniors $9, children 14 and under $5. 434-0405. www.albany.org

American Country Collection, 1353 Union St., Schenectady, is a reservation service for bed & breakfast homes and country inns. ACC represents almost 100 lodgings in the cities of Albany, Troy, Schenectady, and Saratoga Springs, as well as in the mid- and lower-Hudson Valley, Vermont, and western Massachusetts. Most of the inns are unique structures located near lakes or ponds, or by museums, historic sites, or scenic farms. Guests can book rooms knowing that all accommodations are personally inspected by director Carol Matos, whose visits ensure the recommended B&Bs are clean, comfortable, and providing the utmost in service and hospitality. For information or reservations, call 370-4948 or (800) 810-4948. wwwbandbreservations.com

New York State Canal Corporation supervises the recreational development of the state's 524-mile canal system while preserving the historic and natural environment of its trails and adjacent communities. The best known of the state's four canals is the 125-foot-wide Erie Canal, which cuts a scenic path through the Capital Region. Originally a major commercial waterway that contributed to the area's rise to prominence in the mid 1800s, the Erie today is a major tourist destination for boaters and anglers. The canal towpath, once trod by barge mules, is now maintained for the enjoyment of hikers, bikers, and skiers. The Canal Corp. supplies information on vacations and excursions, trail use, tolls, lockside parks and historic sites, and the lifts-and-locks system (which operates 7am-10pm daily, May-Nov.). The web site posts a regularly updated "Notice to Mariners." 436-2700 or 800-4-CANAL-4. www.canal.state.ny.us

New York State Heritage Area System

This state-local partnership preserves and develops areas of historic and cultural significance for New York State. There are four heritage areas in the Capital Region: Albany, Hudson-Mohawk (Troy, Cohoes, Green Island, Waterford and Watervliet), Schenectady, and Saratoga. Described individually in Points of Interest, the Heritage Area Centers provide information, brochures, maps, and tour pamphlets. Staffed by knowledgeable and helpful personnel, these centers are recommended not just for sightseers, but also for residents who want to learn more about the area they live in.

Albany Heritage Area Visitor Center, 25 Quackenbush Sq. 434-1405
Cohoes Riverspark Visitor Center, 58 Remsen St. 237-7999
Saratoga Springs UCP Visitor Center, Drink Hall, 297 Broadway 587-3241
Schenectady Heritage Area Visitor Center, Nott Terrace Heights 382-8667
Schuyler's Canal Park Visitor Center, Fort Hardy Park, Schuylerville 695-4195
Troy Riverspark Visitor Center, 251 River St. 270-8667
Waterford Canal Visitor Center, Tugboat Alley 233-9123

Saratoga Circuit Tours, 417 Broadway, Saratoga Springs, offers a variety of guided tours covering Saratoga Springs and the surrounding area. Tours include a two-hour history tour, a ghost tour featuring many of the haunted buildings described in the popular book *Saratoga County Ghosts*, an architecture tour, and a Greenridge Cemetery Genealogy Tour. Open daily 9am to 6pm. Year-round, groups only. $100 per group. 587-3656.

Sloop Clearwater   *Photography by: Chris Bowser*

HISTORY AND HERITAGE

"You are here" is a common designation on travel brochures and maps. But why you are here usually can't be found in a tour pamphlet. For visitors and residents of the Capital Region however, the answer is easy: You are here because of beaver-skin hats.

In 1600s Europe, the desire for fur-trimmed clothing had outstripped the supply. The rage for beaver coats, capes, muffs and, most especially, hats, fueled the fur trade in the New World. Albany began as a roughshod outpost of the Dutch East India Company, the firm that enriched the Netherlands through its adventurous pursuit of global trade routes. Albany, then called the Beverwyck, "the place of the beaver" in Dutch, is just about the only colonial city that was founded purely for profit.

And exceedingly profitable it turned out to be. Not long after its discovery, the outpost was the hub of the fur trade in North America, exporting tens of thousands of animal skins to the furthest reaches of Europe. But if beaver-skin hats hadn't been so fashionable, the Dutch might not have bothered with building the fort that would eventually become the capital city of New York State.

The first known inhabitants of the upper-Hudson region were Paleo-Indians, Ice-Age nomads who hunted mastodons and mammoths with stone-tipped spears. Three hundred years before the arrival of Europeans, the area was populated by Woodland Indians, hunters who had developed agriculture and lived in villages. The eastern side of the Hudson valley was occupied by the Algonkian-speaking Muhheakunuk – or as the Dutch called them, "Mahicans." Albany was their primordial Fire Place, where tribes would gather for trade and ceremonial events. To the north and west were their deadly enemies, the Iroquois, a powerful confederation of five nations: Mohawks, Senecas, Onondagas, Oneidas and Cayugas.

In September of 1609, the Mahicans stared in astonishment at a ship with sails making its way up the river. It was the Half Moon, a small schooner commanded by Hendrick Hudson, an English mariner under the commission of the Dutch East India Company. According to an account by one of the ship's crew, "The people of the Countries came flocking aboard, and brought us beaver skinnes and otter skinnes, which we bought for Beades, Knives and Hatchets." But the intrepid Hudson wasn't looking for animal skinnes. He was navigating the river in search of a northwest passage to the Far East. After four days of exploration, he took possession of the country in the name of the Lord States-General of Holland, and then sailed back to Europe in disappointment. His favorable report of the area's opportunities did not go unnoticed, however, which is why the river bears his name.

In 1613, the Dutch sent another expedition, establishing Fort Nassau at the foot of the Normanskill a few miles below Albany. A primitive structure with only two cannons, the fort served as a headquarters for Dutch fur traders. The ships that sailed the river were owned by private trade companies, and Dutch skippers often became embroiled in disputes with the crews of English ships poaching on their territory. As a result, the Netherlands chartered the Dutch West India Company to protect its interests, and invested the company with almost absolute authority over "the New Netherlands." It later opened a main office in New Amsterdam (New York City).

The region's first settlement was founded in 1624 when 18 families of Walloons-French-speaking Protestant refugees – arrived in Albany under the patronage of Dutch West India. They settled in the area that is now Madison Avenue and Broadway, and the company built a small, crude fort out of logs for their protection. There was a makeshift moat but no stockade at Fort Orange, and threats from the Indians, inflamed by the impolitic behavior of traders down river, kept the settlement small.

Self-interest drew the Dutch, and later the English, into a symbiotic relationship with the Indians, keeping tensions in check. The fur trade brought trader and hunter together socially, and the Indians quickly became accustomed to the Europeans' cloth, kettles, rum, and guns – a firearm could be had for six beaver pelts. The tolerant Dutch, unlike the French in Canada, made little effort to convert the Indians to their religion, further reducing the potential for antagonism. The Iroquois, more than most Eastern natives, resisted all pressure to forsake their aboriginal beliefs.

With the arrival of the English in increasing numbers, the Dutch government needed to strengthen its claim on the area. In 1629, to encourage immigration by people who would develop the land by farming, the Netherlands established a patroon system that gave authority over large tracts of land to anyone who could settle 50 adults on the land within 50 years. That was how Kilaen Van Rensselaer, a diamond merchant from Amsterdam, acquired 800,000 acres on both sides of the river (encompassing most of today's Rensselaer, Albany, and

Columbia counties). The settlers who came under Van Rensselaer's patronage – basically as indentured servants, for the patroon had feudal power over the land – were not just his fellow Dutchmen. They were Swedes, Norwegians, Danes, Irish, Scots, and Germans. The patroonship was called Rensselaer's Wyck.

The three cities that evolved from the patroonship – Albany, Troy and Schenectady – came about because of the rivers. The waters of the Hudson and the Mohawk provided settlers with a means of transportation to the interior. The soil was rich and the rivers teemed with shad, bass and perch, but not everyone could survive in the harsh frontier environment. After the first brutal winter, many newcomers sailed back to New Amsterdam. Those that stayed, and those that came after, quite naturally wanted to improve their hardscrabble lot through the booming fur trade, so they clustered their wooden homes around Fort Orange.

The village that sprawled haphazardly around the fort was a contentious, violent place, where pigs rooted through garbage on the streets and tavern brawls were a frequent sight. Beyond the fort was a dangerous wilderness inhabited by wolves, warring Mahicans and Mohawks, and rogue pioneers. As was typical in American settlements of the 17th century, most of the people in New Netherlands came because they hoped to improve their social and economic position – or to escape from legal troubles. Between a handful of law officials and the wilderness rabble were the burghers: merchants, tavern keepers, and craftsmen, along with a few slaves from Africa and the West Indies.

Clashes of interest soon erupted between the patroonship, which wanted to clear the land for grain and timber; and Dutch West India, which wanted to keep the forests intact for hunting. Pieter Stuyvesant, the company's director-general in America, was summoned from New Amsterdam to impose order. He declared the land around Fort Orange for the distance of a cannon shot (about 3,000 feet) to be "the Beverwyck," and banned patroon settlers from the area. In 1652, after years of belligerence from both sides, the Beverwyck become a separate entity from Rensselaerswyck.

Van Rensselaer, once a farmer himself, never set foot in his vast landshare, which was the only successful privately owned colony in America. He died in 1646, leaving the estate in the hands of his son and establishing a unique American dynasty that would last well into the 19th century. Long before that, however, the area's beaver population was hunted into extinction and farming began in earnest.

The patroon's able steward and cousin, Arendt Van Curler, was a brave and diplomatic man highly regarded for his influence with the Indians, which he gained by treating them fairly. In 1661 Van Curler, with the approval of Gov. Stuyvesant, purchased from the Mohawks a large tract of fertile land known as "the Great Flats," about 20 miles west of Albany. He settled it with 14 families who were eager to get away from the domination of the patroon and find arable land of their own. The settlers built a small village beside the confluence of the Mohawk River and the Binne Kill, which became known as Schenectady. The name was derived from the Iroquois description of the area: Schau-naugh-ta-da, which signified "across the pine plains." To define their land and defend themselves against their enemies – the French in Canada – the settlers erected a stockade around the village. More than 300 years later, the area is still called the Stockade.

The early Dutch settlers often crossed the Hudson a few miles north of Albany at a spot called Ferry's Hook. In 1659, a Dutch mill owner named Jean Barentz Wemp obtained a tract of land near the crossing where the Hudson and Mohawk flowed together. He had to pay off the Indians as well as Van Rensselaer, and then died shortly after. But by the 1700s, Ferry's Hook was a hamlet of small farms, all trading with Fort Orange. Most of the land came into the possession of the Van der Haydens, a farming family who operated the ferry. This prospering agricultural community would eventually became Troy, a development that was driven by the water power of its many creeks, or "kills."

In 1664, the English peacefully seized New Netherlands from the Dutch, by way of four warships and very generous terms of surrender. The Beverwyck was renamed Albany, after the Duke of York and Albany. The region didn't become distinctively English until much later, however, retaining its Dutch language and governing system throughout the 1600s. The Anglican (Episcopal) Church was not organized until the 1700s; it's likely that the English Church was slow in getting established because many of the arriving English officials intermarried with Dutch families and thus became communicants of the Dutch Church. The landscape would continue to be distinguished by Dutch characteristics, such as steep gabled roofs, for a century to come. Remnants of the Dutch language still linger in place-names like Claverack, Voorheesville, Guilderland, Kinderhook, and Watervliet.

In 1668, Gov. Thomas Dongan, a British colonel who was also a Gaelic-speaking son of an Irish baronet, was petitioned by local leaders to expand Albany's borders. Forcing a claims release from the patroon in Rensselaerswyck, Dongan signed a charter making Albany a city. The charter was boldly progressive for its time, and did not win Dongan many fans in Parliament. Pieter Schuyler, a young wilderness fighter, was appointed as the first mayor. Schuyler won the loyalty of the Iroquois against the French, fortified the city's defenses, and turned the Albany militia into the first adequate fighting unit in the state. Albany is still governed under its original charter, and an oil portrait of Schuyler hangs in the mayor's office to this day.

War, more than anything else, brought change to the three settlements. The first outbreak of the struggle for European control of the New World occurred in Schenectady, a rapidly growing township of farmers. While the war over the succession to the throne of England raged in Europe, English and French colonists raided each other's territories, introducing the settlers to the horrors of border warfare. In the dead of winter of 1690, a battalion of French Canadians and their Indian allies attacked the Stockade, slaughtering 63 of the inhabitants, carrying off 27 captives to Canada, and burning the village to the ground.

The survivors – most of them had escaped to Fort Orange – planned to abandon the settlement, but several Mohawk Indians, led by one named "Lawrence," persuaded them to stay. With the help of the Mohawks and their neighbors in Albany, the settlers rebuilt a larger village on the same land. The area prospered. Trading and the need to transport goods from Albany to the western hinterlands and back were the cornerstones of Schenectady's economy. Transport was improved after a short canal was built under Schuyler's directorship. A century later, the railroads would turn Schenectady into "the Gateway to the West."

Located at the crossroads of rivers and mountain ranges, the region was also an ideal place for the strategic movement of troops – making it a more dangerous place for settlers. A military road followed an ancient Indian warpath from Albany north to Saratoga, linking the settlements. During the years of the four French and Indian wars (1689-1763), which pitted the British and Iroquois against the French and Algonquins, the upper-Hudson Valley served as a corridor for the transport of military supplies and troops. Albany became the northernmost defensive outpost against the French in Canada.

Throughout the 1600s and for most of the 1700s, Albany held a position of importance out of proportion to its modest size. During the 75 years of the French and Indian Wars, the Albany of Dutchmen, Englishmen, Indians, Irish, and Germans was destined to struggle through battles and internal rivalries to mature at last as a real city. Uniting against a common enemy – the French – gave the motley colonials a sense of camaraderie that transcended their national origins. They became Americans.

The Plan of the Union, the predecessor of the Declaration of Independence, was drafted in Albany by Benjamin Franklin and others in 1754. The city's position was pivotal to the struggle for freedom: The British held New York City, the Americans held West Point. The conflict crippled vital shipping activity. The British knew that if they could capture Albany, they could easily seize West Point by a simultaneous attack from north and south, and could then control all movement from Canada to New York Harbor. But that never happened.

Toward the end of winter in 1777, the colonial militia under Gen. Philip Schuyler and the British army of Gen. John Burgoyne began the maneuvers that led to the famous battles in the fields and wilderness between Saratoga village (present-day Schuylerville) and Stillwater. American troops advanced from the Mohawk Valley to protect the route to Albany while Burgoyne headed south from Canada. By the time the two armies finally met in combat, Schuyler had been relieved of his command for losing Fort Ticonderoga to the British. He was replaced by Gen. Horatio Gates, who marched north from the Waterford-Cohoes area. Yet it was Schuyler's preparations that slowed Burgoyne's advance from Lake Champlain to Albany and provided enough time for Gen. George Washington (a seasoned veteran from the final French and Indian War) to strengthen the Northern Army.

Victory was needed for more than tactical reasons – a successful battle against the British would earn the new nation credibility with France. In September and again in October of 1777, the British campaign was defeated. Suffering heavy losses, Burgoyne surrendered at Stillwater. The British abandoned all hope of capturing Albany. France sent supplies, troops, and warships. And the world's attention was drawn to the fledgling United States. The battles of Saratoga are justly famed as "the turning point of the American Revolution."

Oddly enough, it was during these years of military and political turmoil that a group of people came whose ways were of peace and community. In 1774, Ann Lee and a handful of her followers fled persecution in England to establish a utopian society in the New World. This tiny, evangelical-Christian sect called themselves the Believers, but were known as the Shakers, on account of how they would shake and tremble while in a state of religious fervor. The Shakers settled in a swampy part of Watervliet (present-day Colonie) in 1776, and gradually founded other societies in the Northeast.

Agriculturists and craftsmen, they left a distinctive mark on the region. Shakers practiced celibacy, open confession, communal ownership, equality of the sexes, and the consecration of their labors. This divine labor resulted in remarkably fine furniture, tools, and handicrafts. The sect gained large numbers of converts from 1790 to 1850, but dwindled precipitously around the turn of the century. The last eldress of the Watervliet community died in 1938; the few Shakers left moved to Mount Lebanon and Hancock, Mass. Today, Shaker goods are highly valued by collectors and museums, and the Colonie gravesite of Mother Ann attracts visitors from far and wide.

In 1765, after the last of the French and Indians wars, Schenectady was chartered as a borough. Troy was chartered as a village in 1791. And In 1797, the state legislature officially declared Albany as the state capital of New York. (Albany was chosen over New York City because it was safer from attack by sea.) Toward the close of the century, the region entered a new era. Northern travel was safe, the population was swelled by arrivals from New England, and the early saw mills gave way to more advanced industrial facilities – all factors contributing to a 19th-century boom in construction and commerce.

As with the earlier communities of Albany, Troy and Schenectady, the settling of Saratoga also pertained to water: the carbonated waters of its mineral springs, whose medicinal benefits had been discovered by the Iroquois. After the Revolution, Saratoga quickly evolved from a combat zone to a primitive resort. This far-sighted transformation was accomplished most famously by Gideon Putnam, a lumberman who settled near High Rock Spring in 1795, purchasing the land around Congress Spring shortly after. In 1802, he built the ambitious, three-story Putnam's Tavern and Boarding House. One of the resort's earliest promoters was the battle-weary Gen. Washington, a legendarily hard campaigner whose aches and pains were relieved by the mineral springs. Other veteran soldiers soon followed, including Gen. Schuyler, who brought his aristocratic wife, Catherine Van Rensselaer.

In 1710 there had been an influx of Palatine Germans fleeing the war-ravaged Rhineland, but it wasn't until after the Revolution that immigration reached substantial numbers. Freedom from persecution, the prospect of land, and escape from famine brought waves of Europeans throughout the 1800s – by mid-century, Albany was one-quarter Irish. Immigrant labor was welcome, for the era of the region's great construction projects was at hand. Foremost among them was the Erie Canal. Running 363 miles through an untamed wilderness marked by hilly terrain and turbulent streams, it was one of the longest and most ingenious locked canals ever built. Accommodating a water-level difference of 568 feet between its two terminals at Albany and Buffalo, the canal's opening in 1825 was the culmination of astounding feats of engineering and physical labor. The canal cut travel time between Lake Erie and the Hudson River from almost a month to about a week. It wasn't long before local wholesalers reported a 400-percent increase in business.

In Cohoes, the 1839 construction of a dam across the Mohawk River above the Cohoes Falls contributed to the area's tremendous water power. Textile mills were built beside the falls, and factories and mill houses were erected along the roads leading to it. In Waterford, the opening of the Champlain Canal, and the construction of smaller "power canals" such as the King's Canal, created another boom town for manufacture. Factories were built along the canals, as were knitting mills, flour mills, saw mills, dye works, paper companies, and machine and twine factories. With an abundance of lumber moving through the area from the Adirondacks, papermaking plants prospered. And so did the brewing industry: The high quality of the water flowing into the area made it an ideal location for beer making. The American Industrial Revolution had begun.

Troy's advantageous location, precisely at the head of navigation on the Hudson and by the side of the Wynantskill and the Poestenkill, propelled the city to a leading position in industrial productivity and innovation. A river also fueled Schenectady's economic growth. Situated by the Mohawk River and the Erie Canal, the area was a prime site for manufacture. Albany, the northern terminus of the deepwater Hudson River channel, became a bustling transshipment point between ocean-going vessels and canal boats heading to the west. North Albany was the largest lumber market in the East, and a crucial link in the shipment of white pine from the vast forests of the Adirondacks. Water power also facilitated local factories in turning out a wide array of products, the most famous being those derived from the iron and textile industries.

In 1828, Ebenezer Brown, a retired minister who owned a small notions shop, began to market detachable collars. These labor-saving collars were the invention of a Troy housewife, and were made by local women in their homes. With the subsequent invention of the sewing machine, this "piecework" grew into a major industry that moved from the home into the factory. At the peak of "the collar and cuffs trade," more than twenty collar manufacturers flourished in Troy, most notably the mighty Cluett, Peabody & Co. The collars were a fashion staple for almost a century, and Troy produced 90 percent of them. Around the same time, four bell-casting companies made West Troy the most important bell-making center in America. Among them was the Meneely Bell Company, esteemed world-wide for the rich and musical tones of Andrew Meneely's bells and chimes. Most famously, the company cast the 1876 replacement bell for the cracked Liberty Bell in Philadelphia. The Meneely "Centennial Bell" still resides in the belfry of Independence Hall.

Henry Burden, a Scottish-born engineer who headed the Burden Iron Works, invented a world-famous horseshoe-making machine capable of producing one horseshoe per second, eventually reaching a capacity of 51 million horseshoes in one year (and putting local smithies out of business). His horseshoe production was so vital to the Union Cavalry during the Civil War that it was believed the Confederacy sent spies to Troy to try and steal his industrial secrets and sabotage his factories. Metal plates for the Civil War ship The Monitor were also made in local mills. At the time of the 1840 census, Troy was the fourth-wealthiest community per capita in the United States.

The same years witnessed the birth of other major industries. Under the management of Erastus Corning, the Albany Iron Works became one of the largest industrial establishments in the country. The visionary Corning was also instrumental in the creation of the first railroad, which ran from Albany to Schenectady. A rail line from Albany to Troy, and one from Schenectady to Utica, quickly followed, further developing the economic opportunities of the three cities. Corning was a key player in the consolidation of these regional rail lines into the legendary New York-Central Railroad, facilitating commerce between the Capital Region and New York City. Increased contact with New York City helped to foster Albany's maturation as the capital city.

By 1851, the Schenectady Locomotive Works, later to become the American Locomotive Company (ALCO), was building train engines for railroads all over the world. Rail transport inspired Thomas Edison to relocate his machine works to Schenectady, where he conducted research into electrical lighting systems and streetcar motors. The General Electric Company was formed in 1892 when Edison's company merged with several other electrical firms. Employment opportunities attracted droves of workers, and new housing developments turned the outlying areas of the city into bustling neighborhoods almost overnight. Between 1880 and 1910, the population tripled, and Schenectady was known far and wide as "the City that Lights and Hauls the World." This thriving center of science and industry was also affiliated with the invention of radio, modern refrigeration, and the fuel cell.

Further north, "society" was journeying in great numbers from all over the east coast to partake in Saratoga's healthful mineral waters and gracious ambience. After the Civil War, when the advent of the railroad made traveling less arduous, a new class of rich Americans – including Cornelius Vanderbilt and Jay Gould – also made the rural village their summer destination. Leisurely pastimes such as the morning stroll to the springs and boating on the lake accelerated into exciting, even risque pursuits such as horse racing, casino gambling, and dancing the hop. "The Queen of Spas" attracted a colorful clientele – financier "Diamond Jim" Brady and his mistress, opera star Lillian Russell, among them. The summertime exploits of the rich and infamous were eagerly chronicled by newspapers around the country.

Caught up in this change, Saratoga started taking on a more fanciful, extravagant appearance, proclaimed by opulent buildings decorated in the latest High-Victorian fashion. The village became known for the extravagant size of its luxury hotels, many of them sporting block-long piazzas for patrons to see and be seen upon. The springs supported subsidiary industries such as barrel-making and bottling plants for selling the water, and carbonic-gas companies.

The entire region experienced an unprecedented economic expansion. The tremendous wealth of the cities was poured into colleges, churches, and great works of public architecture designed by the most eminent architects. Between 1867 and 1899, the astounding State Capitol Building was constructed atop State Street. Like the patroons of old, the new industrial tycoons were eager to demonstrate their affluence, most visibly with urban mansions furnished with exquisite porcelains, portraits and furniture. Growth in industry created opportunities for local craftsmen to fill a range of household needs, from ornamental iron railings to fabulously ornate yet fuel-efficient cast-iron stoves.

The rise of high finance in Albany led to the construction of magnificent bank buildings all along State Street, giving the old avenue the nickname of "Banker's Row." In 1921, Cluett, Peabody & Co. in Troy introduced the Arrow shirt. The popularity of the attached-collar shirt was considerably boosted by "Sanforization," a process to limit shrinkage developed by Sanford Cluett. Schenectady's explosive growth continued through the first half of the 20th century as its factories were used in the production of heavy military equipment and trains for transport. In nearby Watervliet, the arsenal founded for the War of 1812 worked day and night to turn out modern artillery and anti-aircraft guns for the two world wars.

Between the wars, the region jumped with cultural and entertainment attractions. In May of 1930, Proctor's Theater in Schenectady was the site of the first public demonstration of an astonishing new technology: Television. An orchestra was led by the blurry image of a conductor, transmitted to Proctor's from the General Electric laboratories over a mile away. In 1930s Saratoga, President Franklin D. Roosevelt and a local developer preserved some of the spa's park-like grounds, and constructed bathhouses, a hall of springs, a summer theater, and the elegant Gideon Putnam Hotel. The area would eventually become Saratoga Spa State Park. The Troy Music Hall, opened in 1875, hosted Paderewski and Rachmaninoff early in the century, and after "the great war," the proscenium was graced by Vladimir Horowitz, Arthur Rubenstein, and virtually every other musical legend of the era. A thriving vaudeville theater, the floorboards of the Cohoes Music Hall were illuminated by Buffalo Bill Cody, Harry Houdini, the divine Sarah Bernhardt, and George M. Cohan; and later, Count Basie and Glen Miller. Schenectady's wondrously ornate Proctor's Theater hosted Harry Houdini, Louis Armstrong, and Duke Ellington. In Albany, 20 movie houses flourished, with the rococco Palace Theater boasting the most lavish décor.

By the 1940s, however, the gilded age was long over. Albany, Troy and Schenectady experienced a prolonged reversal of fortune that began in the 1920s when Prohibition left thousands of brewery workers without a job. With the advent of inexpensive, fuel-driven factory equipment the region's industrial base declined disastrously. Persistent labor troubles drove factories to the South where labor was cheaper, while other industries moved west to be closer to the materials they had been transporting to the area for processing. When highways replaced water transport, all three cities lost their competitive advantage. Another element in the decline was the monopolistic attitude of industrial magnates, who concentrated commercial power in the hands of a few, keeping new industry out of the region.

In Saratoga, the decline started when Prohibition and anti-gambling pressure put a damper on the city's high-rolling nightlife. By the 1940s, the popularity of local spring water had been eclipsed by nationally marketed soda-fountain beverages. Casino gambling was finally abolished in 1951, by which time the New York State Thruway had opened up vacation destinations at greater distances. Increased mobility led to a diminished clientele for the colossal hotels. In Albany, the dominance of the automobile eradicated the great railroad yards.

Businesses failed. Jobs became scarce. Investment capital evaporated. The tax base shrank as professionals left the cities for the suburbs, spurred by racial tensions and the proliferation of suburban schools subsidized by the state. In Albany, which was cushioned economically by the growth in state government, urban flight was compounded by urban blight. The interstate separated the city's downtown from its waterfront. Drastic urban renewal programs throughout the region demolished important urban landmarks, illustrious hotels, and century-old brownstones. Hundreds of small rowhouses were replaced by high-rise housing projects. In Troy and Schenectady, construction projects designed to compete with suburban malls failed miserably. The old neighborhoods deteriorated, majestic theaters went dark and fell into disrepair, prestigious department stores either closed or moved to suburban malls, and crime rates began to rise.

Recessions in the early and late 1990s hit the region particularly hard. By 1996, Troy was on the brink of bankruptcy. But as the last few years have shown, time has altered but not eradicated the region's innovative developments, and recovery is well underway. In many respects, the region's glorious past is part of its salvation. Schools and universities founded centuries ago draw students and faculty from all over the world. The area's three national-caliber academic research facilities – Rensselaer Polytechnic Institute, the University at Albany, and Albany Medical College – all date to the early 1800s. Established by the last patroon in the 1820s, RPI today is a global leader in technology research, education, and innovation. One example is MapInfo, founded by four RPI students in 1986 and currently the world leader in desktop mapping software. The region's other significant technology research and development resources include the General Electric Global Research Center in Schenectady. Upgraded in 2002, this state-of-the-art facility conducts research into biotechnology, nanotechnology, photonics, and advanced propulsion.

"Tech Valley," as the region is increasingly coming to be called, is home to hundreds of cutting-edge technology companies and services. Established in 1993 by UAlbany, Albany Nano Tech works with over 100 technology companies worldwide, and has an estimated worth of over $500 million. Corporate research is also carried out by local firms, including Albany Molecular Research, Plug Power, Mechanical Technology Inc., and Intermagnetics General. Government-funded research is conducted at the Knolls Atomic Power Laboratory, the Kenneth Kesselring Site, and Benet Laboratory, where high technology is applied to advanced weapons systems. Benet is located at the Watervliet Arsenal – a munitions factory founded for the War of 1812 that is now one of the most sophisticated heavy-machinery facilities in the nation.

The area is also realizing the benefits of a high-quality labor force, produced by 18 institutions of higher learning and boasting a higher general level of educational achievement and Ph D's than the national average. The area's prestigious arts centers and performance venues attract visitors and support the artists who contribute to the region's aesthetic quality of life. This growing subculture of artists, along with historic preservationists and "new urbanists," are infusing the downtowns with a new and creative vitality. Visionary public-private partnerships and a closer working relationship with the state have also reaped benefits.

In its fourth century and still surrounded by natural beauty, the Capital Region is also a rapidly growing heritage-tourism destination, a place where visitors can enjoy an abundance of museums, landmark architecture, and nationally – significant historical sites in an unhurried atmosphere. Discovered a decade before Plymouth Rock, Albany is the oldest continuously occupied capital in America. Troy's Gilded-Age downtown has been called "a living museum" on the nation's industrial history. Schenectady contains one of the most intact colonial-era historic districts in the country. And every August, celebrities, society, and locals converge at the 19th-century Saratoga Racetrack. In 2002, this venerable sporting venue set an all-time-high attendance record.

Also in 2002, the Hudson River Way was built to reconnect Albany's historic downtown to its ancient waterfront. Nearby, in a pond a stone's throw from the site of old Fort Orange, a colony of beavers is thriving for the first time in 300 years. Fortunately for them, beaver-skin hats are out of fashion.

Washington Park, Albany   *Photography by: Gary Gold*

SUGGESTED READINGS

Many of the entries in the preceding chapters contain a great deal of history, architectural significance, or have interesting stories attached to them. For further exploration of the greater Capital Region, the following books are recommended.

NON-FICTION

Albany Architecture: A Guide to the City
Edited by Diana S. Waite. Mount Ida Press Ltd., 1993.
A definitive survey of the historic architecture of the capital city, comprehensively supported with photographs. Includes walking-tour routes and an excellent introduction to early Albany history.

Albany: Capital City on the Hudson
By John J. McEneny. American Historical Press, 1998.
Contains an excellent chronology, insightful essays on the city's 19th- and 20th-century political and social history, and historical photographs.

Albany Institute of History and Art: 200 Years of Collecting
Edited by Tammis Kane Groft and Mary Alice Mackay.
Albany Institute of History and Art, 1999. A comprehensive overview of the AIHA's decorative-arts collections from the 1600s to the present, with photo essays on 130 regional objects featuring stunning color plates of furniture, portraits, sculpture, ceramics, costumes, Albany-made silver, and Hudson Valley School oil paintings.

An Albany Girlhood: Huybertie Pruyn Hamlin
Edited by Alice P. Kenney. Washington Park Press Ltd., 1990.
Lively autobiographical sketches of upper-class life on Elk Street, 1873-1898, by a member of Albany's eminent Pruyn family.

Capitol Story
By C.R. Roseberry. State of New York, 1964.
Clearly written, generously illustrated history of the magnificent State Capitol Building.

Digging Up History
By Gerald Bradfield. French and Indian War Society, 2001
The pivotal and tragic history of Fort William Henry, told through archeological evidence, eyewitness accounts, and anecdotal recollections from Bradfield, the fort's curator. Provides an exciting overview of the Lake George area from prehistoric Indian habitation to the 1980s.

Down from Troy: A Doctor Comes of Age
Richard Selzer M.D. William Morrow and Co., 1992.
Having grown up in Troy during the depression, the author describes the richness and diversity of life in Troy during the 1930s and 40s.

Enclave of Elegance: The General Electric Realty Plot
By Bruce Maston. Schenectady Museum, 1984.
Handsomely illustrated overview of the evolution of a unique neighborhood, with commentary on architectural details.

Flashback: A Fresh Look at Albany's Past
By C.R. Roseberry, edited by Susanne Dumbleton. Washington Park Press Ltd., 1986.
Essays on seminal events and figures of national prominence in the region.

George S. Bolster's Saratoga Springs
By Carola Beverly Mastrianni and Michael Noonan. Donning Co., 1999.
Photo essays on Saratoga Springs with 300 prints from the historic George S. Bolster Collection.

The Governor Nelson A. Rockefeller Empire State Plaza Art Collection and Plaza Memorials
By Denis Anderson and Glen Lowry, with Michael Fredrickson, photographer. Rizzoli, 2002.
Lavish photographs and expert essays on "the most ambitious public art project ever conceived," the 100 modernist masterpieces assembled at the plaza. Includes an in-depth account of the politics surrounding the formation of the collection, and six photo gatefolds.

Hudson Mohawk Gateway: An Illustrated History
Thomas Phelan & P. Thomas Carrol. American Historical Press, 2001.
Highly interesting, handsomely illustrated overview of Rensselaer County's industrial and architectural heritage. Includes essays by guest experts.

Illustrated Treasury of the American Locomotive Company
By O. M. Kerr and H. Stafford Bryant. W.W. Norton, 1990.
Photographic album of Schenectady-made ALCO trains-steam, diesel, and electric – prefaced by a short history of the company. "The foremost photo collection of North American trains to be found...a must for railroad fans."

Landmarks of Rensselaer County, New York
By George Baker Anderson. D. Mason and Company, 1987.
Detailed narrative of the county's early history, towns and leading citizens.

The Making of Ironweed
Claudio Edinger, photographer. Penguin, 1988.
Photographic chronicle of the filming of the William Kennedy novel in Albany, Troy, and surrounding communities. Introduction by Kennedy.

The Marble House in Second Street:
Biography of a Townhouse and its Occupants, 1825-2000
John G. Waite Associates. Rensselaer County Historical Society, 2000.
Detailed architectural analysis of Troy's innovative Hart-Cluett mansion, with interesting opening essays on the Harts and Cluetts, two of Troy's most industrious families.

The Markers Speak: An Informal History of the Schenectady Area
By John Birch. Schenectady County Historical Society, 1962.
History of Schenectady told through the historic markers in the Stockade area.

Murder at Cherry Hill
By Louis C. Jones. Historic Cherry Hill, 1982.
Gripping true tale of love, intrigue, and murder at the historic house on South Pearl Street, told through first-person accounts.

O Albany! Improbable City of Political Wizards, Fearless Ethnics, Spectacular Aristocrats, Splendid Nobodies, and Underrated Scoundrels
By William Kennedy, Viking Press and Washington Park Press Ltd., 1983.
This vibrant "urban tapestry" focuses on all the people suggested in its title.

Old Albany, Volumes I-V
Edited by Morris Gerber. Portofino Publishing, 1985
Valuable collections of photographs and reprints of newspaper articles and columns, including many superb historic photographs by Stephen Schreiber.

Ornamental Ironwork:
Two Centuries of Craftsmanship in Albany and Troy, New York
by Diana S. Waite, Mount Ida Press, 1990.
Handsomely illustrated, expert analysis of the area's superlative interior and exterior decorative ironwork.

The People's Choice: A History of Albany County in Art and Architecture
By Allison Bennett. Purple Mountain Press, reprinted 1992
Illustrated, well-regarded history of Albany County from 1630 to 1900.

The President as Architect: Franklin D. Roosevelt's Top Cottage
By John G. Waite Associates. Mount Ida Press, 2001
The illustrated story of the design and construction of F.D.R.'s "stone house," one of three buildings designed by an American president and believed to be the first residence designed by a disabled person for use by a disabled occupant. Compiled by the Albany architectural firm that helped to restore the cottage. Forward by Geoffrey C. Ward, editor of *Closest Companion*.

Refusing Ignorance:
The Struggle to Educate Black Children in Albany, New York,
1816-1873. By Marian I. Hughes. Mount Ida Press, 1998
With prodigious research and dedication, the award-winning educator Marian Hughes uncovers the stirring story of how courageous black teachers in the capital city fought to build a foundation of knowledge for their children during the segregated 19th century.

Remembrance of Patria:
Dutch Arts and Culture in Colonial America 1609-1776
By Roderic H. Blackburn and Ruth Piwonka,
Albany Institute of History and Art, 1988.
Richly illustrated analysis of Dutch culture and art before the Revolution.

A Resourceful People: A Pictorial History of Rensselaer County, New York
Rensselaer County Historical Society, 1987.
Photos from RCHS's incomparable collection, accompanied by informative text.

Saratoga County Ghosts
By David J. Pitkin. Aurora, 1998
A local bestseller drawn from anecdotal and first-person ghost sightings in Saratoga.

Saratoga Lost: Images of Victorian America
By Robert Joki. Black Dome, 1998
Evocative essays on the history of Saratoga Springs, with a focus on the lost grandeur of the Aristocratic and Victorian eras. Illustrated with hundreds of rare photographs of vanished architectural legends such as the Grand Union Hotel and the Congress Spring Arcade.

Saratoga Springs: A Season of Elegance
By William Strode, Thomasson-Grant Inc., 1986
Gorgeous photographs of Saratoga at its most glamorous, by a two-time Pulitzer Prize-winning photojournalist. Includes rare photos of the interior of Yaddo, celebrations in private homes, and up-close depictions of Thoroughbreds in action.

Saratoga: Queen of Spas
By Grace Maguire Swanner, M.D. North Country Books, 1988.
Early history of Saratoga Springs and mineral springs in general, with an emphasis on the spa's health benefits. Illustrated with historical photos and engravings.

Saving Union Station: An Inside Look at Historic Preservation
By Thomas Finnegan, Washington Park Press Ltd., 1988.
Beautifully illustrated chronicle of the rescue and restoration of Albany's landmark Union Station in the 1980s.

Schenectady's Golden Era (Between 1880 and 1930)
By Larry Hart. Old Dorp Books, 1974.
A thorough history of Schenectady by a *Schenectady Gazette* columnist and historian for Schenectady County. Includes an appended chronology of historic events in the area.

Seventeenth Century Albany: A Dutch Profile
Charlotte Wilcoxen, Albany Institute of History and Art, 1981.
Scholarly essays on life in the city's first century.

Troy: A History of the Collar City
By Don Rittner. Arcadia, 2002
Thorough, readable account of the development of Troy, from prehistory to the 20th century. Includes 100 historical photographs.

BIOGRAPHY

Closest Companion:
The Unknown Story of the Intimate Friendship Between
Franklin Roosevelt and Margaret Suckley
Edited by Geoffrey C. Ward. Houghton Mifflin, 1995.
The little-known story of Roosevelt's romantic friendship with his younger distant cousin, begun in 1922 and lasting until the president's death in 1945.

The Imperial Rockefeller
By Joseph Persico. Simon & Schuster, 1982
Insightful look at Nelson A. Rockefeller, the patrician governor who built the Empire State Plaza.

The Jameses: A Family Narrative
By R.W.B. Lewis. Farrar Straus Giroux, 1991.
An acclaimed biography that includes an opening chapter on the James family in Albany.

Mayor Corning: Albany Icon, Albany Enigma
By Paul Grondahl, Washington Park Press Ltd., 1997.
In-depth examination of the life, times, and political clout of the Albany mayor, who had the longest mayoral run in U.S. history. Includes treatment of Corning's influential forebears.

FICTION

A number of gifted novelists and biographers have published acclaimed books set in the greater Capital Region. Their stories have contributed significantly to the region's sense of itself, as well as enhancing the area's stature across the country.

Billy Phelan's Greatest Game
By William Kennedy. Viking Press, 1978.
Raucous depiction of the dazzling and dangerous world of politics and nightlife in 1938 downtown Albany.

Dexterity
By Douglas Bauer. Simon and Schuster, 1989.
Portrayal of a young woman's search for herself in the years after her first child is born, set in a small town in northern Columbia County.

The Flaming Corsage
By William Kennedy. Viking Press, 1996
Atmospheric story of wealth, class and love in Albany, circa 1884-1912.

Fire Along the Sky
By Robert Moss. St. Martin's Press, 1991.
First book of a trilogy set in the region during the colonial period, and centered on the fascinating war hero and Indian Affairs diplomat, Sir William Johnson.

The Ink Truck
By William Kennedy. Viking Press, 1969.
Engrossing fictionalized account of a newspaper strike in 1960s Albany.

Ironweed
By William Kennedy. Viking Press, 1983.
Francis Phelan's return to Albany to seek forgiveness for having abandoned his family, set on Halloween, 1938. Winner of the National Book Critic Circle's Award and the Pulitzer Prize, 1983.

Legs
By William Kennedy. Viking Press, 1982
Fictional portrait of the legendary underworld figure (and real-life Albanian) Legs Diamond, who with his showgirl mistress blazed a gaudy trail across the tabloid pages of the 1920s and 1930s. "Pure literary excitement."

Mohawk
Richard Russo. Random House, 1986.
The first novel by Gloversville native Russo (*Nobody's Fool, Empire Falls*) focuses on several hard-luck characters living lives of extreme and extremely funny longing in a Mohawk Valley town. An "awesome depiction of the physical and emotional presence of the Mohawk itself."

Quinn's Book
By William Kennedy. Viking Press, 1988.
The acclaimed coming-of-age story of Billy Quinn, in search of himself in 1850s Albany.

Risk Pool
By Richard Russo. Random House, 1988.
A "wonderfully funny and perceptive" 30-year saga of a boy growing up in a small Mohawk Valley tannery town, and his relationship with his hell-raising father.

Roscoe
By William Kennedy, Viking Press, 2002
The seventh novel in Kennedy's Albany cycle follows a quick-witted lawyer-politician through the first half of the 20th century. "A comic vision of the dark side of politics."

Saratoga Trunk
By Edna Ferber. Doubleday, 1941
Incisive social portrait of love and money in the mid-1800s, culminating at the glamorous resort of Saratoga Springs.

Through the Darkest Hour
By Larry Hart. Old Dorp Books, 1990.
Fictional portrayal of a Union College man's adventures during the Civil War, written by a Schenectady County historian.

Very Old Bones
By William Kennedy. Viking Press, 1992.
The Phelan family saga – begun in Billy Phelan's Greatest Game and Ironweed – continues into 1950s Albany.

INDEX

Notes

Notes